HOW
TO WATCH
TELEVISION

User's Guides to Popular Culture

Founding Editors: Ethan Thompson and Jason Mittell

Bringing together dozens of tightly focused original essays from today's leading scholars on popular culture, User's Guides offer accessible, engaging cultural criticism across a host of media, past and present. Designed to engender classroom discussion by placing popular culture in broader social and cultural contexts, User's Guides demonstrate how to meaningfully engage what we consume the most.

How to Watch Television
Edited by Ethan Thompson and Jason Mittell

How to Play Video Games
Edited by Matthew Thomas Payne and Nina B. Huntemann

HOW TO WATCH TELEVISION

SECOND EDITION

EDITED BY

ETHAN THOMPSON
AND JASON MITTELL

NEW YORK UNIVERSITY PRESS

NEW YORK

NEW YORK UNIVERSITY PRESS
New York
www.nyupress.org

References to Internet websites (URLs) were accurate at the time of writing. Neither the author nor New York University Press is responsible for URLs that may have expired or changed since the manuscript was prepared.

Library of Congress Cataloging-in-Publication Data
Names: Thompson, Ethan, editor. | Mittell, Jason, editor.
Title: How to watch television / edited by Ethan Thompson and Jason Mittell.
Description: Second edition. | New York : New York University Press, 2020. | Series: How to | "This revised edition includes 22 new essays that expand the scope of the book in a number of ways. All of the new entries come from authors who were not in the first edition (except new chapters from the two editors) . . . . The 18 essays that remain from the first edition were some of the most successful pieces according to faculty and students who used the book, and cover many programs that still remain well-known years later. It was difficult removing the other essays from the original, as they all added important perspectives on a range of programs; thankfully, NYU Press has made all of these first edition essays available on their website so that readers can still access them"— Preface to the second edition. | Includes bibliographical references and index.
Identifiers: LCCN 2019029653 | ISBN 9781479890637 (cloth) | ISBN 9781479898817 (paperback) | ISBN 9781479837441 (ebook) | ISBN 9781479890668 (ebook)
Subjects: LCSH: Television programs—United States. | Television programs—Social aspects—United States. | Television programs—Political aspects—United States.
Classification: LCC PN1992.3.U5 H79 2020 | DDC 791.45/70973—dc23
LC record available at https://lccn.loc.gov/2019029653

New York University Press books are printed on acid-free paper, and their binding materials are chosen for strength and durability. We strive to use environmentally responsible suppliers and materials to the greatest extent possible in publishing our books.

Manufactured in the United States of America

10 9 8 7 6 5 4 3 2 1

Also available as an ebook

Contents

Part III. TV Politics: Democracy, Nation, and the Public Interest

Part IV. TV Industry: Industrial Practices and Structures

Part V. TV Practices: Medium, Technology, and Everyday Life

Preface to the Second Edition

The first edition of this book emerged from an idea that Ethan Thompson pitched to Jason Mittell back in 2011. Thompson wrote that there is "a real need for essays that model for undergraduates how scholarly television criticism and intellectual inquiry works by focusing on a particular program in accessible language, applying existing scholarship, and suggesting a way of looking at it—without necessarily trying to break new ground in television studies." In academia, this was a fairly radical idea: publishing original scholarship whose primary audience was not other scholars but rather undergraduate students and other educated readers interested in learning more about media. The first edition of the book realized this idea through the support and editorial guidance of NYU Press, publishing forty essays, each analyzing an individual television program through accessible language and focused argumentation.

Nearly a decade later, this approach is still unusual within academia, even though "public scholarship" has become more acceptable as an approach. But we were gratified by the reception of the book from a wide range of readers, especially students who seemed excited to use the essays as models for their own critical writing and analysis. We were excited that colleagues in the related field of videogame studies were inspired to create a spinoff of sorts, publishing *How to Play Videogames* in 2019. And we were inspired to continue this approach by editing a second edition of the book, which we've been calling *How to Watch MORE Television*.

This revised edition includes twenty-two new essays that expand the scope of the book in a number of ways. All of the new entries come from authors who were not in the first edition (except new essays from the two editors), mostly inviting scholars early in their academic careers to the book. We sought out essays that explored ideas and topics that were missing from the first edition, including intersectionality, disability studies, and interpretive communities. We targeted analyses of programs that were more global in origin, and more broadly representing various genres and industrial formations. The result is a more diverse, inclusive, and wide-ranging assortment of essays that we believe will speak to today's students better than the first edition.

The eighteen essays that remain from the first edition were some of the most successful pieces according to faculty and students who used the book, and cover many programs that still remain well known years later. It was difficult removing the other essays from the original, as they all added important perspectives on a range of programs; thankfully, NYU Press has made all of these first edition essays available on their website so that readers can still access them. We thank the authors of all of these essays for their contributions to the original book and hope that readers continue to reference these online-only essays:

- *Auto-Tune the News*: Remix Video (David Gurney)
- *The Cosby Show*: Representing Race (Christine Acham)
- *The Dick Van Dyke Show*: Queer Meanings (Quinn Miller)
- *Entertainment Tonight*: Tabloid News (Anne Helen Petersen)
- *Eva Luna*: Latino/a Audiences (Hector Amaya)
- *Family Guy*: Undermining Satire (Nick Marx)
- *Homicide*: Realism (Bambi L. Haggins)
- *It's Fun to Eat*: Forgotten Television (Dana Polan)
- *Jersey Shore*: Ironic Viewing (Susan J. Douglas)
- *Life on Mars*: Transnational Adaptation (Christine Becker)
- *M*A*S*H*: Socially Relevant Comedy (Noel Murray)
- *Monday Night Football*: Brand Identity (Victoria E. Johnson)
- *NYPD Blue*: Content Regulation (Jennifer Holt)
- *Onion News Network*: Flow (Ethan Thompson)
- *Phineas & Ferb*: Children's Television (Jason Mittell)
- *The Prisoner*: Cult TV Remakes (Matt Hills)
- *Samurai Champloo*: Transnational Viewing (Jiwon Ahn)
- *Star Trek*: Serialized Ideology (Roberta Pearson)
- *30 Days*: Social Engagement (Geoffrey Baym and Colby Gottert)
- *Tim & Eric's Awesome Show, Great Job!* Metacomedy (Jeffrey Sconce)
- *The Twilight Zone*: Landmark Television (Derek Kompare)
- *The Wonder Years*: Televised Nostalgia (Daniel Marcus)

Even though the full collection of essays from both editions spans a wide range of topics, national traditions, genres, and theoretical concepts, the book is not meant to be comprehensive. The essays here are organized alphabetically within five broad topical areas—there is no implied sequence to read them, as they all offer insights into the broad and expanding realm of television, with more programs and outlets than ever before. No book could even attempt to represent the full scope of the medium. Discerning readers should look for the gaps in coverage and questions left unanswered—and we challenge you to write your own essays that explore and explain something new about the endless possibilities of how to watch television.

—*Jason Mittell and Ethan Thompson, May 2019*

Introduction

An Owner's Manual for Television

ETHAN THOMPSON AND JASON MITTELL

Imagine that you just purchased a brand new television, and inside the box, along with the remote, the Styrofoam packaging, and various cables, was this book: *How to Watch Television*. Would you bother to open the cellophane wrapper and read it? Sure, you might scan through the "quick start" guide for help with the connections, and the new remote control may take some getting used to, but who needs instructions for how to *watch* what's on screen? Do-it-yourself manuals abound for virtually every topic, but TV content is overwhelmingly regarded as self-explanatory, as most people assume that we all just know how to watch television. We disagree. Thus, this is your owner's manual for how to watch TV.

First, a word of warning: this particular manual is not designed to tell you what to watch or not watch. Nor does it speak with a singular voice or seek to produce a consensus about what is "good" and what is "bad" on all those channels. In other words, the forty writers who contribute critical essays don't all agree on how to watch television. Despite the hundreds of years of cumulative TV-watching and dozens of advanced degrees among them, you can rest assured that, in many cases, they would disagree vehemently about the merits of one TV show versus another. This collection draws upon the insight of so many different people because there are so many different ways to watch TV and so much TV to watch. To be sure, the writers of many of these essays might "like" or "dislike" the programs they write about—sometimes passionately so. But we are all concerned more with thinking critically about television than with proclaiming its artistic or moral merits (or lack thereof). This book collects a variety of essays and presents them as different ways of watching, methods for *looking at* or *making sense of* television, not just issuing broad value judgments. This is what good criticism does—it applies a model of thinking to a text in order to expand our understanding and experience of it. In our book, those "texts," a term scholars use to refer to any cultural work, regardless of its medium, are specific television programs. Too often, people assume that the goal of criticism is to judge a creative work as either "good" or "bad" and provide some rudimentary explanation why. Let us call this the "thumbs up/down" model of criticism. This model is useful if one is skimming television listings for something to pass the time, but not so useful if one wishes to think about and understand what's in those listings.

The "thumbs up/down" model reduces criticism to a simple physical gesture, possibly accented by a grunt. In contrast, we want to open up a text to different readings, broaden our experience of a text and the pleasures it may produce, and offer a new way to think about that text. Criticism should expand a text, rather than reduce it, and it is seldom concerned with simplistic good or bad judgments. In fact, most of the contributors to this volume would feel uncomfortable if they were forced to issue such a judgment on the programs they write about with a "thumbs up" or "thumbs down" icon next to the title of each essay. While most of the authors do provide some judgment of the relative worth of the program they analyze, those evaluations are always more complicated than a simple up or down verdict. One of the ironies of media criticism is that the individual who is probably more responsible than anyone else for the popularity of the "thumbs up/down" model is Roger Ebert, one of America's most thoughtful, articulate film critics from the 1960s until his death in 2013. Yet it was a succession of television shows starring Ebert and fellow critic Gene Siskel—first *Sneak Previews* (PBS, 1975–1982), then *At the Movies* (syndicated, 1982–1986) and *Siskel & Ebert* (syndicated, 1986–1999)—that popularized "thumbs up/down" criticism. How can we reconcile the fact that Ebert, an insightful critic and compelling writer, could also have helped reduce criticism to the simplest of physical gestures?

The answer, of course, is that Ebert didn't do it; a television program did, and television criticism can help us to understand why. If we examine the structure of these programs, we can see the usefulness of the "thumbs up/down" gimmick. Film, television, theater, and book reviews all have a long history in popular newspapers, magazines, and broadcasting, following the common model of making a value judgment and providing the reasons for that judgment. Sometimes the judgment is a vague endorsement of the work owing to particular qualities, while other times it is quantified—"3 out of 5 stars," for example. But in all those cases there are typically clear rationales, with the "stars" or "thumbs" providing a quick reference and reason to read further. There were movie critics on TV before *Sneak Previews*, but this program's innovative structure featured two critics discussing a number of films, with one critic introducing a clip and launching a conversation or debate about the film's merits. The "thumbs" metric provided a jumping off point for discussion, and guaranteed that the two had something concrete to agree or disagree about with a reliable and consistent structure for each review. At the end of each episode, the hosts recapped their judgments on each film, giving viewers a shorthand reminder to consider the next time they themselves were "at the movies." While "thumbs up/down" might be a reductive form of media criticism, it made for entertaining and sometimes useful TV, creating film criticism uniquely suited for the television medium. By looking at the various Siskel & Ebert TV shows and thinking about how "thumbs up/down" might have "fit" with the television medium, we can understand that program and appreciate it beyond whatever effect it might have had on narrowing the public's expectations about what media criticism does.

It is notable that while there have been television shows focused on film criticism and book criticism (like C-SPAN's *Book TV*), there has never been a TV program focused on television criticism. In fact, television criticism has an unusual history within popular media—traditionally, television reviews were published in newspapers upon the debut of a show if at all, rather than dealing with an ongoing series as episodes aired. Magazines like *The New Yorker* or *Newsweek* might run pieces analyzing an ongoing series, but not with any comprehensive structure or commitment to covering a series as it unfolds over time. The rise of online criticism in the twenty-first century has drastically changed the terrain of television criticism, as sites like *The A.V. Club* and *HitFix*, as well as the online versions of print magazines like *Time* and *Hollywood Reporter*, feature regular coverage of many series, reviewing weekly episodes of new shows and returning to classic television series with critical coverage to inspire rewatching them. Noel Murray's series "A Very Special Episode" at *The A.V. Club* is an example of such "classic television" criticism, featuring this tagline: "Sometimes a single TV episode can exemplify the spirit of its time and the properties that make television a unique medium." This book shares that critical outlook, and an expanded version of Murray's essay on "The Interview," a *M*A*S*H* episode, was included in its first edition.

Despite the rise in robust television criticism in popular online sites, academics have been less involved in such discussions of the medium. While the histories of academic fields like literary studies, film studies, art history, and music include many critical analyses of specific works, television studies as a field features far less criticism of specific programs. In part this is due to the series nature of most television, as the boundaries of a "text" are much more fluid when discussing a program that might extend across months, years, or even decades. Additionally, television studies emerged as an academic field in the 1980s and 1990s under the rubric of Anglo-American cultural studies, an approach that emphasizes contexts over texts, and thus much of television scholarship is focused on understanding the industrial, regulatory, and reception contexts of the medium more than critical analyses of specific programs. Books examining a particular program do exist, but critical works in television studies more typically focus on a format or genre (reality TV), a decade (the 1960s), or a methodology or area of study (industry studies). There are exceptions to this, of course; online academic journals like *FlowTV* often feature short critical essays on particular TV series. But we believe that there is a crucial role for television scholars to use our expertise about the medium's history, aesthetics, structures, and cultural importance to provide critical analyses of specific programs. Additionally, we want to see scholars writing for audiences broader than just other scholars, so we have commissioned shorter essays than typically found in an academic journal or book, and asked that they be written accessibly for students and a general readership.

While there is no single method employed by the dozens of authors found in this volume, most essays can be described as examples of *textual analysis*. The shared approach assumes that there is something to be discovered by carefully examining a cultural work, or "text"—in the case of this book's topic, that means watching a television program closely. In some cases, the text might be a single episode or two; in others, the essay looks more broadly at a particular series, or multiple programs connected by a key thread. But in each case, the author uses a "close watching" of a program to make a broader argument about television and its relation to other cultural forces, ranging from representations of particular identities to economic conditions of production and distribution. The goal of such textual analysis is to connect the program to its broader contexts, and make an argument about the text's cultural significance, thus providing a model for how you can watch television with a critical eye—and write your own works of television criticism.

A piece of television criticism, like the ones modeled in the rest of this book, can have a wide range of goals. Certainly all the book's authors believe that watching television is an important and pervasive facet of modern culture, and that taking time to analyze programming is a vital critical act. Some authors are more invested in understanding television as a specific medium, with industrial and regulatory systems that shape its programming, and its own unique formal system of visual and aural communication that forge TV's modes of storytelling and representation across a number of genres. Others regard television more as a window to broader social issues, whether by establishing norms of identity categories like gender or race or by framing political agendas and perspectives. These are not opposing perspectives, as television critics can think about the interplay between the medium itself and its broader context—indeed, every essay in this book hopes to shine a light on something about television itself as well as something broader within our culture, as we believe that knowing how to watch TV is a crucial skill for anyone living in our media-saturated world.

Of course, for many people reading this book, the idea of "watching television" might seem like an anachronism or a fossil from the previous century—what with so many electronic gadgets and "new media" surrounding us these days, why single out television? Television can seem to be an object from another era, quaint in its simplicity and functions. Such a response is the product of a very limited notion of what "television" is, and indeed, if you do think of TV as just a piece of furniture around which the family gathers each night, then there is something potentially outdated about television. However, television is (and always has been) more than just furniture, and now in our era of convergence among different technologies and cultural forms, there is more TV than ever. New or emergent forms of television work alongside the residual or "old," and it's important to remember that the majority of viewers still do most of their watching on traditional television sets. If we define the word "television" literally down to its Latin roots, it is often translated as "remote seeing." By thinking about television not as furniture but as "remote seeing" (and hearing) of sounds and moving images from a distant time or place, we can recognize that so many of our new media interactions are new kinds of television that we integrate into our lives alongside the familiar and pleasurable uses of TV we've known for so long.

Rather than radically reconfiguring our uses of media culture, new technologies and media forms emerge and find a place among and alongside those forms that already exist; a medium might ebb and flow in popularity, but seldom disappears altogether. And one of the most important aspects of all forms of media engagement, whether watching on a television set or mobile phone, is that these forms of engagement become part of our everyday lives, adapting to our geographical, technological, and personal contexts. Moreover, while new technologies might enable some to claim that they do not watch television, we believe that people who say they don't watch TV are either lying or deluding themselves. TV is everywhere in our culture and on many different screens, as we often watch television programs on our computers, or play videogames on our televisions. People who say they don't watch TV are usually suggesting they don't watch *those* kinds of TV shows that they assume less sophisticated viewers watch uncritically. But even as it gets reconfigured in the digital era, television is still America's dominant mass medium, affecting nearly everyone.

A brief anecdote about the dual editors' own media consumption practices while writing this introduction point to the role of television and other technologies in contemporary life. One of the editors of this book (Ethan) began writing the first draft of this introduction while watching a professional football game live via satellite television at a ranch in rural south Texas. The other editor (Jason) was at that very time travelling by train with his family across Europe, where they were watching Looney Tunes cartoons on an iPad. Ethan was watching a program via the latest digital high-definition TV technology, but in a highly traditional way—live broadcast to a mass audience sharing the same act of "remote seeing." Certainly one of the great pleasures of watching televised sports, which remains one of the most popular and prevalent forms of television today, is the sense of communal participation in an event as it occurs, shared by viewers both within the same room and across the globe; this experience depends on liveness, even at the cost of watching commercials and boring bits that modern technologies like DVRs can easily bypass. As a fan, Ethan watches for the sense of participation in what is happening at the time—a case of old-fashioned remote seeing enabled by new technologies.

Jason's experience is quite different, but still falls under the general category of "watching TV." As his kids watched Looney Tunes on a European train, they embraced one of television's long-standing primary functions: allowing children to see things beyond their personal experiences. This literally was "remote seeing," as his kids were watching something from a distant time and place: Looney Tunes were created as animated shorts screened in American movie theaters from the 1930s to 1950s, but they thrived throughout the second half of the twentieth century as a staple of kids' TV, and more recently through numerous DVD releases. Shifting these classic cartoons to an iPad enables a mobile viewing experience that trades the imagined community of the television schedule for the convenience of on-demand, self-programmed media consumption. While technically there is no "television" involved in watching cinematic cartoons on a mobile digital device, we believe that the cultural practices and formal elements established via decades of television viewing carry over to these new technologies, making watching TV a more prevalent and diverse practice in the contemporary era of media convergence.

These brief descriptions of watching television foreground our diverse viewing contexts, which help make watching TV such a multifaceted cultural practice—we multitask, watch on a range of screens in unusual places, and experience television programming across timeframes spanning from live to decades-old, and spatial locations from rural Texas to European trains and beyond. The rest of the book focuses less on specific viewing practices, and more on how we can use our expertise as media scholars to understand the programming that we might encounter in such diverse contexts. This is the goal of any form of criticism: to provide insight into a text, not to proclaim a singular "correct" interpretation. Indeed, there is no such "correct" interpretation, any more than there is a "correct" way to watch a football game or cartoon.

The essays in this book cover a representative sampling of major approaches to television criticism, and they are quite different from one another in terms of the TV they analyze and their methods of analysis. However, they do share some basic assumptions that are worth highlighting:

1. TV is complicated. This can mean many different things. Sometimes the text itself is formulaic, yet its pleasures are complicated. Other times, the narrative of a TV program doesn't present a clear plot, yet attempting to puzzle out the story is a fundamental pleasure. Sometimes where a program comes from is complicated— the question of who created and is responsible for it can, for example, be less than straightforward. Or perhaps the meanings expressed by a show are complicated, presenting contradictions and diverse perspectives than can be interpreted. The bottom line is that television criticism seeks to understand and explain TV, no matter how simple or complex it might seem at first glance.

2. To understand TV, you need to watch TV. This might seem obvious, but there is a tradition of critics writing about television (usually to condemn it) without actually taking the time to watch much of it, or even to specify what TV texts they are criticizing. Judgments like these tend to be common amongst politicians, pundits, and anyone else looking to use television as a convenient "bad object" to make a point. Understanding TV requires more, though—and more than just watching TV, too. That is, some types of television require particular viewing practices to really understand them, such as the long-term viewing of serials and series, or the contextualized viewing of remakes or historically nostalgic programming.

3. Nobody watches the same TV. We watch a wide variety of programs, and even in those cases when we watch the same programs, we often watch them in vastly different contexts. Television is still a mass medium experienced by millions, but the specific experience of watching television is far from universal. While television in a previous generation was more shared, with events like the moon landing or the finale of *M*A*S*H* drawing the attention of a majority of Americans, even then our experiences of watching television were diverse, as viewers often think quite differently about the same texts.

4. Criticism is not the same as evaluation. You don't have to like (or dislike) a particular television program to think and write critically about it, and our goal is not to issue a thumb up or down. However, evaluative reactions to a text can be a useful way to get started thinking critically about television, as you attempt to figure out what you are reacting to (or against). Many of these essays foreground their authors' own evaluative reactions to programs that they love or hate (or even feel ambivalent about), but in every case, the critic finds his or her particular program interesting. Exploring what makes it so is a worthy goal for television criticism.

What follows in this book is a set of critical analyses that model how we might watch a particular television program that we find interesting. The programs represented are widely diverse and even eclectic, including undisputed classics, contemporary hits, and a few that you might not have heard of before. They cover a range of genres, from cooking shows to cartoons, sports to soap operas, and they span the medium's entire history. Even so, we do not claim to be comprehensive—there are countless other programs that might be the subject of such works of television criticism. We have focused primarily on American television, or in a few cases how non-American programming is seen in an American context, although given the pervasive reach of American television throughout the globe, we hope that international readers will find these critical works helpful as well. The authors are media scholars with a range of expertise, experiences, and backgrounds, offering a wide range of viewpoints that might highlight different ways of watching TV. Each essay starts with a brief overview of its content, and ends with some suggestions for further reading to delve deeper into the relevant topic and approach.

Each of these critical essays can be read on its own, in any order. We encourage readers to go straight to a particular program or approach that interests them. However, we have organized the book into five major areas to assist readers looking for essays that speak to particular issues or approaches, as well as instructors seeking to assign essays in relation to particular topics. Essays in the first section, "TV Form," consider aesthetics, analyzing visual and sound style, production techniques, and narrative structure, and showing how television style is crucial to understanding television content. The essays in "TV Representations" focus on television as a site of cultural representation of different groups and identities, including race, ethnicity, gender, and sexuality. Although many essays in the book are politically concerned, those in the "TV Politics" section look more explicitly at public affairs, government, and national and global boundaries in both fiction and factual programs. In "TV Industry," essays focus on economics, production, and regulation in historical and contemporary television culture. Those in "TV Practices" consider television in the context of everyday life, and the ways in which engagement with television texts carries across media and technologies. In the contemporary digital convergence era, it is increasingly important to think beyond a single television screen into a multiplication of media and devices.

Finally, while most owners' manuals get filed away and forgotten or thrown in the recycling bin unread, we hope this one will enjoy a more enduring presence. This book, the essays inside it, and the critical methods the authors employ, all seek to expand the ways you think about television. If the book itself doesn't earn a spot next to your remote control, we have no doubt that some essay inside it will form a lasting impression. Perhaps it will provoke you to think differently about a program you love (or hate), or it will make you a fan of a program you had never seen or even heard of before. Better yet, we hope *How to Watch Television* will prompt you to think critically and apply the methods you've read about in your own original way, while discussing or writing about a program of your own choosing. That is how this owners' manual can prove to be more permanent than others: as you flip through the channels, and especially when you stop to view a particular program, we hope that you cannot help but think critically about the television that you watch.

FURTHER READING

Butler, Jeremy G. *Television: Visual Storytelling and Screen Culture.* 5th ed. New York: Routledge, 2018.

Gray, Jonathan, and Amanda D. Lotz. *Television Studies.* 2nd ed. Boston: Polity, 2019.

Mittell, Jason. *Television and American Culture.* New York: Oxford University Press, 2010.

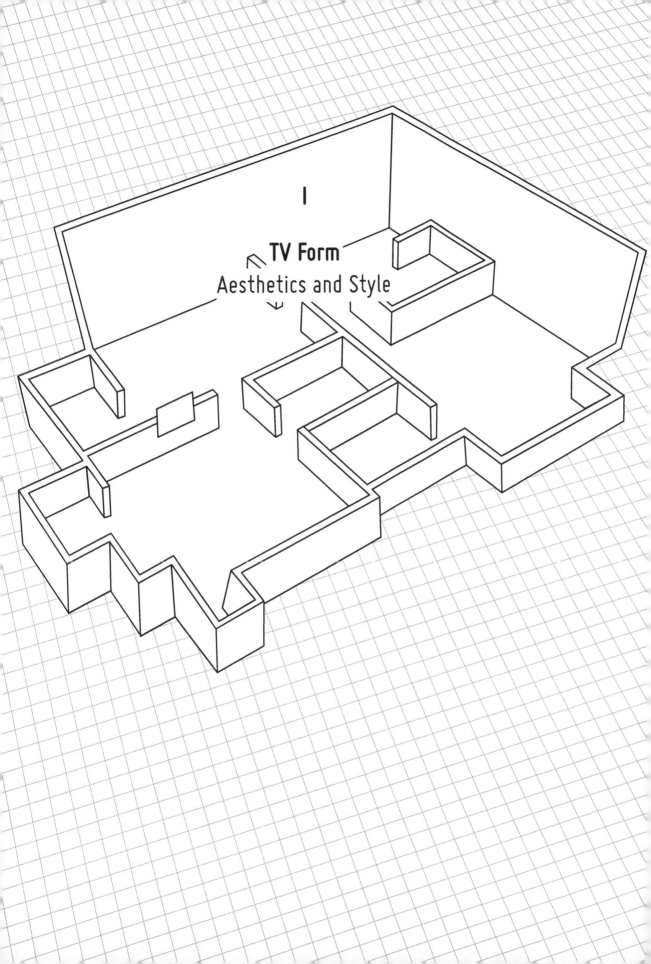

TV Form

Aesthetics and Style

1

Better Call Saul
The Prestige Spinoff

JASON MITTELL

Abstract: Few aspects of television more typify the American commercial medium than the spinoff, a new program that emerges out of a successful series to sustain its brand past the original's shelf life. However, contemporary television is marked by the rise of prestige drama, a mode of storytelling hailed as culturally legitimate and artistically groundbreaking that seems to refute the imitative logic of spinoffs. This essay analyzes spinoff *Better Call Saul's* pilot episode to understand how the series managed to do the seemingly impossible: re-create the popular, critical, and creative successes of *Breaking Bad* by straddling the line between prestigious originality and commercial copying.

In the late 1940s, when television was still in its infancy, the acerbic radio comedian Fred Allen offered a quip that captured a widespread skepticism toward the medium: "Imitation is the sincerest form of television."[1] Allen was highlighting how most critics perceived the emerging medium: a commercial industry driven to create derivative programming, rather than innovative, original works. Such dismissive attitudes are still widespread, as many people note how television programming is so frequently imitative of previous hits, derives from preexisting properties, or combines two successful works to create the illusion of something new. The spinoff is one prominent form of imitation driven by economic incentives, taking characters from one popular series and creating a new program around them.

However, contemporary American television has been marked by a shift in the medium's cultural legitimacy—more than ever before, television is regarded as a place where innovative storytelling can thrive, even eclipsing film and theater as the most lauded dramatic medium. Series like *The Sopranos*, *The Shield*, *The Wire*, and *Mad Men* all succeeded by being nonderivative innovative works, rather than commercially motivated imitations, suggesting that some television might be immune to the industrial drive to copy, clone, and monetize successes. Such programming, often labeled "prestige television," places a premium on originality, and few series in television history have been more lauded and acclaimed than *Breaking Bad*, AMC's drama about a chemistry teacher turned drug kingpin.

Breaking Bad ended in 2013 with a promise that its narrative universe was not yet over: AMC announced that they were developing a spinoff series, *Better Call Saul*, that would take place years before *Breaking Bad*'s narrative, focused primarily on secondary character Saul Goodman, played by Bob Odenkirk. This prequel pitted two television tendencies against each other: formulaic commercial cash grab meets artistically legitimized prestige television. How could one of television's most acclaimed originals jettison that originality to spawn a derivative spinoff? This essay explores the tensions between originality and imitation as embodied in the pilot episode of *Better Call Saul*, an example of the unusual format of a "prestige spinoff."

Spinoffs date back to television's prehistory in radio, when the popular comedy *Fibber McGee and Molly* yielded a new series in 1941, *The Great Gildersleeve*, about the secondary character Throckmorton P. Gildersleeve. As a prototypical spinoff, *Gildersleeve* built upon the original's popularity and tone, aiming to remain similar to *Fibber McGee*'s humor and style without simply being a copy. For decades, spinoffs have taken one or more secondary or guest characters from the original and placed them in the center of a new series in nearly every television genre: sitcoms (Robin Williams guest starred on *Happy Days* in 1978 to launch *Mork & Mindy*), Westerns (1958's *Bronco* from *Cheyenne*), science fiction (*Torchwood* launched in 2006 from the long-running *Doctor Who*), soap operas (*General Hospital* yielded *Port Charles*), medical dramas (*Grey's Anatomy* led to *Private Practice*), and even reality shows (*Here Comes Honey Boo Boo* came from *Toddlers & Tiaras*) and talk shows (*The Colbert Report* extended a character from *The Daily Show*). Many spinoffs emerge after the conclusion of the original, taking characters into new scenarios to extend the original's popularity—sometimes with great success, as with *Frasier*'s acclaimed eleven-season run matching the longevity of the original series *Cheers*, but often in short-lived misses, as with *AfterM*A*S*H* (from *M*A*S*H*) and *Joey* (from *Friends*). A spinoff universe can be vast and varied, as with the landmark sitcom *All in the Family*, which yielded spinoffs ranging from long-running successes (*The Jeffersons*), important groundbreaking series (*Maude*), and short-lived failures (*Gloria*), as well as "second-generation spinoffs" from its own spinoffs, such as *Good Times* and *Checking In*.

A common critical assumption is that spinoffs are more commercially motivated than artistically justified. Media scholar Todd Gitlin wrote the landmark account of the American television industry in the 1980s, diagnosing a pervasive tendency for the medium to privilege commerce over creativity: In labeling television programs as "self-imitating artifacts," he distinguished "between the normal imitativeness of art and the industrialized excess that is television's sincerest form of fawning on itself."[2] Gitlin claims that spinoffs take "self-imitation far beyond the limits of previous forms. . . . Most spinoffs are like wealthy heirs, living off capital accumulated by the forefathers."[3]

While few critics today are as dismissive of spinoffs as Gitlin was in the 1980s, skepticism remains commonplace. As *Breaking Bad* was wrapping up in 2013, news of a Saul Goodman spinoff was met with widespread skepticism. As TV critic June Thomas wrote, "I doubt the role is substantial enough to sustain a whole show," especially when compared to the quality of the original series.[4] Such doubts assumed *Saul*'s commercial motivations might tarnish *Breaking Bad*'s original creative heights—as Michael Arbeiter wrote, "We want our precious programs to stand independent of the executives' clutch. We wouldn't want ratings grabs to influence the plotlines of *Breaking Bad*, so we don't want them to influence the creation of an entire offshoot show."[5]

Much of this initial skepticism around *Better Call Saul* stemmed from the perceived quality of *Breaking Bad*, grounded in the context of how contemporary television storytelling differed from previous eras. While every era of television features a mixture of original, risk-taking programs with more formulaic, conventional, and derivative series, American television in the 2000s received increased cultural legitimacy, largely driven by the critical praise aimed at a number of innovative, narratively complex dramas, including popular series *The Sopranos*, *Lost*, and *The Shield*, as well as less commercially successful but acclaimed programs *The Wire*, *Boomtown*, and *Mad Men*. Such prestige dramas foreground shared norms and conventions of high-quality television, such as male antihero protagonists, dark themes, serialized narrative twists and innovations, bold visual style, and boundary-pushing depictions of violence, sexuality, and morality. Some series can fall squarely into this category, proclaiming their own seriousness and importance, while still being regarded as poorly done and derivative by critics, as with *Low Winter Sun* or *Ray Donovan*—such hyper-serious dark dramas even prompted their own parodies within other series, as with the fake *Darkness at Noon* appearing frequently on televisions within *The Good Wife*.

Concepts like "prestige" or "formulaic" are not inherent markers of quality; rather, they fit into larger constructions of taste and value embedded within broader cultural hierarchies such as gender, class, and education. Early television was viewed as a "lowbrow" medium compared to literature, theater, and film, largely because the domestic mass medium was seen as less elite and more the domain of women and children. As the category of prestige television rose in the twenty-first century, much of its cultural legitimacy was earned by distancing itself from traditional feminized genres such as melodramatic soap operas and embracing the cinematic and literary cachet of "serious drama" while employing established film writers, directors, and actors. A series like *True Detective* was hailed for its ambition through various markers of prestige, even though many critics questioned its overall quality, while *Jane the Virgin* was never treated as prestigious, despite being quite ambitious and high quality in its own ways—largely because it was building off soap opera traditions focused on the domestic lives of women. Even though a prestige drama *can* be great TV, we must not assume that *only* prestige series are high quality, nor that the sophisticated style of prestige is a guarantee of aesthetic success. Instead, we must remember that labels like "prestige," "quality," and "lowbrow" are all cultural constructions, used to reinforce hierarchies steeped in social power and identity.

Clearly there are inherent tensions within series that foreground their status as prestigious television, while embracing imitative impulses rather than developing their own innovations. This conflict becomes acute for spinoffs, as the form overtly embraces its debts toward another program rather than asserting uniqueness or originality. *Breaking Bad* is generally regarded as one of the pinnacles of prestige drama, charting an innovative approach toward antiheroes, embracing narrative and stylistic experimentation, and gaining both large audiences and critical acclaim. How can *Better Call Saul* follow in such prestigious footsteps while clearly embracing the imitative logic of spinoffs, straddling the line between derivative and original? To understand the cultural location of *Saul*, we can examine how it presents itself as both a continuation of *Breaking Bad* and an original innovative series on its own merits, analyzing the program's specific techniques that signal these dual identities. These codes of meaning-making address two sets of audiences (with clear overlaps): fans of *Breaking Bad* eager for more of the earlier series, and prestige viewers drawn to *Better Call Saul*'s sophisticated storytelling and style.

Appeals to these dual audiences were there from the start of *Saul*'s pilot episode "Uno." When it debuted on AMC on February 8, 2015, *Breaking Bad* had been off the air for fourteen months—long enough to establish distance from its spinoff but recent enough that fans were still invested in the series and remembered how the narrative ended for its various characters. Saul Goodman's ending was bleak: caught in Walter White's imploding criminal empire, he went underground and relocated under a new identity to Nebraska. As he told Walter in the penultimate episode, "From here on out, I'm Mr. Low Profile, just another douchebag with a job and three pairs of Dockers. If I'm lucky, a month from now, best-case scenario, I'm managing a Cinnabon in Omaha." *Better Call Saul*'s opening scene continues directly from the previous series, as it presents the character

FIGURE 1.1.
In the episode's teaser, we
see the title character in
hiding after *Breaking Bad*,
mournfully reliving his
previous glory.

under his new name, Gene Takavic, indeed managing a Cinnabon in Omaha.
However, the sequence is presented in a highly unusual style: a wordless montage
of black-and-white footage, with artful close-ups of pastry and Gene doing mundane tasks, over a 1939 recording of The Ink Spots singing "Address Unknown."
We see Gene fear that a burly customer might expose his secret identity, and follow Gene to his apartment, where he drinks whiskey and watches a videotape of
his television commercials for his old law practice, letting the repetition of the
catchphrase "Better Call Saul" sink in as he quietly weeps for his lost identity before the scene abruptly cuts off.

This six-minute pre-credit sequence embodies the dual impulses of the prestige spinoff. It highlights the familiar for dedicated *Breaking Bad* viewers—the
television commercials, the presence of actor Bob Odenkirk, and the narrative
continuity—in ways that highlight the spinoff as derivative. Even the portrayal
of the Cinnabon's mass-produced, factory-style mall food business evokes the
formulaic and standardized elements of commercial television and its pervasive
imitative logic. However, the tone and style of this sequence evoke the norms
of art cinema more than primetime television, with monochromatic images and
evocative shot compositions, the wordless portrayal of Gene's deep sadness and
fear, and the use of a fairly obscure piece of historical music as tonal counterpoint to the contemporary images. Nobody watching this episode without prior
knowledge would regard it as formulaic, derivative, or hyper-commercial, thus
establishing its legitimacy as prestige television within its opening moments.

The brief credit sequence for the series also contains these dual impulses toward distinction and imitation: every episode of *Better Call Saul* features a different set of images underlying the series title and names of creators Vince Gilligan
and Peter Gould. In the pilot, the image is of an inflatable Statue of Liberty, the
gaudy display outside Saul's office in *Breaking Bad*, but it is presented with bizarre
video effects that oversaturate the colors and glitch the figure; the titles themselves

are produced with bad special effects, evoking low-quality videotape production norms of the 1990s. The music is a fuzzy low-fi guitar riff that cuts off abruptly, suggesting a technical error. As Gilligan and Gould recounted, they wanted the credits to be "purposefully shitty," both to evoke the videotape aesthetic of Saul Goodman's commercials and to distinguish their credits from other prestige dramas, which "look very well-produced and beautiful and high-class."[6] Thus the credits directly contrast the arty aesthetics of the monochromatic opening sequence with a lowbrow cheap look, but the controlled design also distinguishes the series as part of the prestige tradition using ironically shitty style, straddling these cultural hierarchies within a compact twenty-second sequence.

The rest of the pilot lacks the aesthetic extremes of either the black-and-white opening or the gaudy, glitchy credits, but the episode certainly embraces the innovative stylistic flourishes and visual precision that typified *Breaking Bad*. "Uno" uses unpredictable close-ups, unusual angles, long takes, and impressionistic sound design to highlight its own aesthetic ambitions and distinguish *Saul* as part of the prestige drama tradition. Although "Uno" frames itself as a legal drama, with courtroom scenes and office politics inside a law firm, both the style and narrative structure highlight how *Saul* will avoid following genre conventions in keeping with the prestige drama mode.

Prestige dramas typically embrace narrative complexity, merging serialized storylines, episodic plots, and innovative techniques such as temporal play, twists, and reflexivity. *Better Call Saul* is notable as a prequel, a particularly challenging storytelling mode that precedes the original series chronology (aside from the opening teaser set after *Breaking Bad*). Since there are well-established "futures" for some of the characters, the series plays with how to creatively fill in the gaps in backstories. First and foremost, the series goes against its title by focusing on the main character before he adopted the pseudonym Saul Goodman, charting the legal career and personal life of Jimmy McGill, the character's real name as revealed on *Breaking Bad*. His transformation into Saul Goodman is much slower paced than viewers expected, as the character does not fully embrace the identity until the finale of season 4. For fans seeking Goodman's continued exploits bending the legal system to the point of criminality, the series fails to meet expectations. Instead, we get a protracted origin story, starting with Jimmy at a point of professional desperation, trying to make ends meet as a struggling lawyer with a shady past operating out of the backroom of a nail salon. The structure is the moral inverse of *Breaking Bad*: rather than watching a seemingly upright citizen transform into a vicious drug kingpin, we look backward at a corrupt lawyer's early career of trying to make good.

As the spinoff of one of the most successful and acclaimed prestige dramas, *Better Call Saul* builds on *Breaking Bad*'s narrative structure, especially through its integration of tightly plotted crime stories with slower-paced attention to character morality and relationships. The pilot episode incorporates both of these elements, with character drama flowing from Jimmy's challenging relationship with his brother Chuck, a successful lawyer sidelined by a confounding illness. As conveyed in the one scene between them, Jimmy clearly admires Chuck and tries to take care of him but also resents his older brother's arrogance and lack of empathy; Jimmy's love for Chuck is quickly established as the moral foundation for his actions, including an ongoing feud with Chuck's partner Howard. The final thirteen minutes of the episode present a caper plot, as Jimmy executes a con game to steal a client from Howard but violates Chuck's moral code in the process. This caper is reminiscent of *Breaking Bad*, which was notable for juxtaposing deep character drama with exciting set pieces that forced the characters to devise clever ways to escape perilous predicaments. Thus *Better Call Saul* adapts the narrative blueprint from its originating series by creating a variation on its approach to prestige drama, simultaneously embracing innovation and imitation.

Another important dimension of *Saul*'s storytelling is its pacing. Like *Breaking Bad*, the series swings between highly tense, fast-paced moments and glacially slow sequences with little dialogue or narrative information. The scene after the opening credits takes viewers to the narrative "present" of 2002, with a sequence of wordless shots of an Albuquerque courtroom waiting to begin its proceedings. This sequence runs for over a minute, generating viewer confusion and creating a restless mood counter to a pilot's need to convey narrative exposition efficiently. The action then cuts to an institutional bathroom, where we see close-ups of mundane objects over a male voice muttering to himself, seemingly a lawyer practicing his remarks as the bailiff comes to fetch him. The first dialogue occurs a full two minutes into this scene, as the character we'll come to know as Jimmy McGill enters the courtroom and delivers a brisk two-minute monologue, laying out his idealistic case defending his trio of adolescent clients facing unspecified charges. The scene then slows down again, as the prosecutor wordlessly ambles across the courtroom to set up a video monitor and play a videotape of the defendants committing their crime: breaking into a funeral parlor and gleefully recording themselves decapitating and having sex with the head of a corpse. In all, this six-minute scene offers almost no important information for the ongoing narrative but establishes a key tone for the series through its contrasting pacing: in a slow and quiet world, Jimmy is the driving force of energy and language, provoking humor and exciting contrasts. Additionally, this scene establishes the series as a legal drama (of sorts), but one that distinguishes itself from the genre via unconventional portrayals of courtroom dynamics, with a characteristic visual style, narrative pace, and edgy content.

FIGURE 1.2.

In the closing shot of *Better Call Saul*'s pilot episode, *Breaking Bad*'s Tuco Salamanca appears, offering an exciting callback for fans.

The pilot draws upon the imitative tradition primarily by evoking memories of *Breaking Bad*, reminding viewers of the Albuquerque setting, echoing themes of morality and character change, and reintroducing two familiar faces. Beyond the title character, we first get a glimpse of an old character at the fourteen-minute mark—Mike Ehrmantraut appears in an unpredictable locale, working as the parking lot attendant at the Albuquerque courthouse. This appearance provokes numerous questions for fans of the earlier series, as it seems far from what we'd learned of Mike's backstory as a police officer, and how we'd come to know him as an enforcer and investigator for a criminal drug enterprise. Although this is Mike's only scene in the episode, actor Jonathan Banks's name in the opening credits signals that the character will serve a major role in the ongoing series. The second character returning from *Breaking Bad* is more of a surprise, appearing only in the last moment of the pilot: Jimmy is held at gunpoint by Tuco Salamanca, a minor but memorable character from *Breaking Bad*'s early seasons. This reveal concluding the episode certainly triggers a wave of fan memories of Tuco and excitement to see his backstory before his death early in the original series, and feels like a direct continuation of the tone and genre of *Breaking Bad*'s crime story, rather than *Better Call Saul*'s originality as a character-driven legal drama.

Other moments in *Saul* evoke *Breaking Bad* through subtle parallels and continuities, primarily targeting hardcore fans who obsess over televisual details; such commitment to "forensic fandom" is a hallmark of narratively complex television. For instance, Jimmy meets clients at the diner Loyala's, an Albuquerque location that had appeared twice on *Breaking Bad*. The episode also provides parallels between Jimmy and Walter White, with actions echoing across the series—Jimmy's car windshield is fractured in an accident, evoking a repeating *Breaking Bad* trope where Walter's windshield was cracked three different times throughout the series. Similarly, Jimmy kicks and dents a chrome garbage can when leaving his brother's law firm, echoing Walter punching and denting a metallic paper towel dispenser. These minor parallels could be seen as formulaic rehashes from the original series, but they function more to convey character parallels and themes, entering the more prestigious realm of "allusion." Such intertextual references can be regarded as either lowbrow imitations or highbrow storytelling devices to subtly convey meanings—or both. *Saul* alludes to its own imitative history, as Jimmy quotes an iconic monologue from the 1970s film *Network*, an acclaimed critique of the television industry's lowbrow appeals and formulaic content: "You have meddled with the primal forces of nature!" By referencing *Network*, *Saul* winks to knowing viewers by acknowledging the commercial motivation of a spinoff, while also proclaiming its own cultural legitimacy through allusion to a celebrated film.

As of this writing, *Better Call Saul* has run for four seasons and established itself as one of television's most acclaimed dramas on its own terms, rather than just as a spinoff. It won a prestigious Peabody Award in 2017, one of only a handful of scripted spinoffs to accomplish that feat, along with *Frasier* and *Lou Grant*. Many critics and fans contend that it has eclipsed the original as their favorite series, suggesting that the shadow of imitation can be escaped. As co-creator Vince Gilligan recounts, the goal was just "to not be *AfterM*A*S*H*. That's about as high as we had set our sights: We wanted to not embarrass ourselves. We wanted our spinoff series to not take anything away from the original, to not leave a bad taste in the mouth of the fans of the original."[7] Beyond accomplishing this modest ambition, it is clear that *Better Call Saul* has created true originality through imitation, forging the unique hybrid of the prestige spinoff.

FURTHER READING

Mittell, Jason. *Complex TV: The Poetics of Contemporary Television Storytelling*. New York: New York University Press, 2015.

Newman, Michael Z., and Elana Levine. *Legitimating Television: Media Convergence and Cultural Status*. New York: Routledge, 2011.

Wanat, Matt, and Leonard Engel, eds. *Breaking Down* Breaking Bad*: Critical Perspectives*. Albuquerque: University of New Mexico Press, 2016.

NOTES

1. Quoted in Fred Allen, *"All the Sincerity in Hollywood . . .": Selections from the Writings of Radio's Legendary Comedian*, ed. Stuart Hample (Golden, CO: Fulcrum, 2001), 64.
2. Todd Gitlin, *Inside Prime Time* (original 1983; revised edition, Berkeley: University of California Press, 2000), 71.
3. Ibid., 69.
4. June Thomas, "Why the Saul Goodman Spin-off Is a Bad Idea," *Slate*, April 9, 2013, https://slate.com.

5. Michael Arbeiter, "'*Breaking Bad*' Saul Spin-off: Worst Idea or Best Idea?" Hollywood.com, April 9, 2013, www.hollywood.com.

6. Alan Sepinwall, "*Better Call Saul* Creators on the 'Purposely Sh—ty' Opening Title," *UProxx*, March 16, 2015, https://uproxx.com.

7. Quoted in Alan Sepinwall, "A Candid Conversation with Vince Gilligan on 'Better Call Saul,'" *Rolling Stone*, August 3, 2018, www.rollingstone.com.

2

Empire
Fashioning Blackness

RACQUEL GATES

Abstract: The popular television show *Empire* has attracted a huge following for its over-the-top storylines, memorable characters, catchy music, and distinctive fashions. In particular, Taraji P. Henson's character "Cookie" stands out, partly for her character's emotional complexity, as well as for her eye-catching fashions, which blend haute couture with signature markers of urban style. In this essay, Racquel Gates analyzes the ways that fashion on *Empire* conveys important information about race, class, and politics both on television and in American culture more broadly.

When the predominantly African American, primetime soap opera *Empire* premiered on FOX in 2015, the show immediately pulled viewers into its world of lush visuals, contemporary music, and dramatic storylines. An hour-long drama that focuses on the fictitious Lyon family and their music industry empire, *Empire* draws inspiration from the aesthetic and narrative conventions of predominantly white 1980s soap operas like *Dallas* and *Dynasty*, and the sensational plots and characters on contemporary African American cast reality television shows. Moreover, *Empire*'s representations of African American lives and experiences are connected to a much longer, complicated history of black representation on television and in film. These influences matter, as they establish *Empire* at the intersection of several related, yet uniquely distinct, cultural reference points, each of which carries its own code for referencing blackness and making blackness legible to viewers.

This essay focuses on one particular aspect of *Empire*: fashion. From the very first episode of the series, the fabulous and extravagant clothing worn by the characters on the show has captivated fans, journalists, and style bloggers.

In particular, the over-the-top fashions worn by the character Cookie—the family matriarch played by actress Taraji Henson—have inspired the most attention. Yet fashion is more than just adornment on *Empire*. Instead, the clothing and accessories that various characters wear provide important information about their personality traits, serving as a kind of narrative shorthand for viewers. Indeed, mise-en-scène in the form of costuming serves this purpose throughout television, as a way of conveying important information without sacrificing limited storytelling time. We might think of *King of Queens* character Doug's parcel carrier uniform, a constant reminder of the character's, and the show's, representation of a working-class identity. Likewise, Regine's wigs on *Living Single* served as a visual marker of the character's vanity. In addition to providing significant character information, the fashion on *Empire* connects the show to other black cultural reference points, such as Motown in the 1960s and 1990s hip-hop. Thus we can see how *Empire* uses fashion to convey information about blackness beyond the show's explicit references to race.

While it makes sense to analyze representations of race from a narrative perspective—focusing on how a media text frames blackness through its characters and stories—it cannot be the only way to examine these topics. Like all media texts, television is a collaborative process. We tend to focus on the most obvious contributors to a television show: the actors, directors, and writers. Yet the final product that makes it to the screen is also shaped by other creative talents who likewise contribute to the text: set designers, costume designers, music supervisors, and individual actors all bring their personal touches. Therefore, if we focus strictly on the *types* of images that a show presents as opposed to *how* the show visually articulates those images, then we risk missing out on the elements that make *Empire* unique and distinctive.

Therefore, by turning our attention away from narrative and toward some of the stylistic elements in *Empire*—in this case, fashion—we can reveal how the show codes blackness into its representations. This way of "encoding" blackness, to borrow from Stuart Hall, serves dual purposes. First, it functions to save valuable narrative time. As a melodrama, *Empire* often relies on appeals to the audience's emotions rather than detailed character development. The show needs to cover a lot of ground—love affairs, murder schemes, and secret children—and the twists and turns of the plotlines can easily dominate the story. While the series often addresses race quite explicitly, it prioritizes the interpersonal conflicts between the characters more, a hallmark of the melodramatic mode.

Second, this process of encoding serves to allow *Empire* to engage in more nuanced, culturally specific explorations of racial identity than its narrative format and targeted audiences allow. As I mentioned above, *Empire* does not avoid explicit portrayals of race and racism. Yet, as a show that deliberately courts both black and nonblack audiences, *Empire* must balance cultural specificity with universality. In other words, the show is very measured in the way that it presents blackness, in order to avoid making the show "too black" and therefore, presumably, unrelatable to nonblack viewers. Whether it is true that too much blackness in the show's diegesis would alienate nonblack viewers, it is very clear that those responsible for bringing the world of *Empire* to the small screen thoughtfully curate where and how blackness appears. For instance, the show makes visual connections between the fictional Empire dynasty and the real-life Motown Records via Lyon family patriarch Lucious's (Terrence Howard) hairstyle and clothing, subtly coding blackness into the "background" of the text while saving the "foreground" for more immediately relevant plot developments. This makes sense if we think about the fact that *Empire* airs on FOX, a network that has only recently begun to produce racially diverse programming, in spite of its early reputation as a home for black-cast (and black-produced) content.[1] As a program whose viability is largely predicated on its success with both black and white audiences, *Empire* must walk a fine line to provide viewers with content that is culturally specific as well as able to cross cultural lines.

On *Empire*, fashion is more than simple costuming: it provides information about the individual characters and connects them to broader aspects of black culture. A quick sketch of the main male characters demonstrates how the show accomplishes this. The first season of *Empire* focuses on the Lyon family's interpersonal conflicts and how they deal with external threats to their music empire. The three brothers of the Lyon family—Andre (Trai Byers), Hakeem (Bryshere Y. Gray), and Jamal (Jussie Smollett)—are radically different from one another, as conveyed through their styling. Andre, the CFO of the company, is the one son whose role is in the business side of the company, rather than the artistic side. He sports traditional business suits in dark colors and wears his hair in a conservative, closely cropped style. His thoroughly respectable attire signals his own respectability politics, the idea that members of a minority group make themselves less culturally specific and thus more acceptable to mainstream society.[2] Hakeem, the rap superstar of the family, dresses in hip-hop fashions and accessorizes with oversized jewelry consistent with rap "bling" culture. He also wears his hair in a high fade style with intricately shaved designs on the sides of his head, another emblem of hip-hop style and a throwback to 1990s black urban hairstyles. Finally, Jamal, the most musically gifted of the trio and a talented R&B singer, sports a hipster fashion aesthetic: slimmer-fitting clothes than Hakeem that combine a range of styles from urban to bohemian. His style conveys how Jamal does not fit neatly into existing categories of either fashion or personal identity, an important detail that reinforces his character's initial journey to reconcile his sexual identity with the private and public image that his CEO father, Lucious, wants him to present.

FIGURE 2.1. The styling of the three brothers of the Lyon family—Andre, Hakeem, and Jamal—conveys their deep character differences.

As the head of the Empire dynasty, Lucious Lyon's wardrobe and styling ground the show in black culture, past and present. In the pilot episode, Lucious wears his hair in a chemically straightened style, what we would call a "perm" or a "relaxer." The style is an anachronism, belonging more to the era of 1940s and 1950s black male fashion rather than 2015, when the show premiered and takes place. Producer Lee Daniels claims that Howard's coiffure was the actor's own choice, not the result of a discussion with Daniels or the vision of the show's creative team.[3] Melissa Forney, *Empire*'s lead hairstylist, confirms that Howard had initial creative control over his character's hair and wanted it to look "old school." As an "old school" hairstyle, Lucious's hair most readily calls to mind the "conk" hairstyle of R&B mogul Berry Gordy, founder of Motown Records, and one of the real-life figures on whom Howard's character is based.[4] Lucious's clothing during the first season furthers this connection: We see him in wide-collared shirts without ties, turtlenecks paired with blazers, vests, and silk scarfs draped around his neck. All of these sartorial choices visually connect him to a past era of black music production.

Although *Empire* takes place in current-day New York and centers on the worlds of hip-hop and R&B, Lucious's styling makes a visual connection to previous eras of black music making. Moreover, the style suggests the era before "black is beautiful" came into popularity and black men (and women) sported chemically straightened hair instead of their naturally curly and kinky textures. In this way, Lucious's hair in the pilot suggests that not only his hair but also perhaps his thinking is regressive. This fits neatly into a narrative about how his "old school" values do not allow him to accept that his son is gay.

Of all of the characters on *Empire*, however, it is Taraji Henson's Cookie that has truly captured the hearts of fans and on whom much of the discussion about fashion centers. Arguably the heart of the show, Cookie's character spans the most narrative and identity categories. When viewers first meet Cookie in season 1, scenes switch back and forth between flashbacks of Cookie in prison and

FIGURE 2.2.
Cookie's meticulously crafted
wardrobe has clear cultural
reference points and offers
narrative shorthand for her
character development.

present-day scenarios that show her trying to reclaim her place as the head of the record company. The show must find a way to capture all of the qualities that make Cookie who she is: tough, sexy, and business-savvy on the one hand, yet simultaneously warm, loving, and vulnerable on the other. In addition, the show must convey the time that Cookie has lost during her seventeen-year incarceration, a theme that informs much of her character. Because Cookie's character development alone could fill up an entire television show, the show uses her clothing as a kind of narrative shorthand.

How does *Empire* convey Cookie's class status and character traits? Her wardrobe is a meticulously curated assemblage of items that have clear cultural reference points. Stylist Rita McGhee selects Cookie's ensembles to suggest several things about Cookie's inner self and how she presents herself to the world. Her clothes, McGhee asserts, are Cookie's "armor" as she operates within a hostile environment.[5] In the first few episodes, Cookie often appears in animal prints to suggest several key aspects of her personality. She wears a leopard-print dress and matching coat in the pilot, a leopard-print dress with matching leopard-print hat and purse in the second episode, and a leopard-print skirt in the third. In the sixth episode of that season, she wears a leopard-print cat suit by luxury fashion designer Diane Von Furstenberg. Most obviously, the prints are a cheeky reference to her name: Cookie *Lyon*, and also suggest other qualities that we might associate with mothers in the animal kingdom: nurturing, yet ready to fiercely defend their offspring against any threat. The prints also suggest Cookie's "wildness" and inability to be "domesticated," in contrast to some of the other women characters, such as her romantic rival Anika. Cookie's animal prints are rivaled only by her equally impressive fur coats. The coats span a range of styles and colors from a short beige jacket to an over-the-top neon purple shrug. On an immediate level, the fur coats are a metaphor that suggests the vulnerable side of Cookie that she keeps hidden from the outside world. They are, according to McGhee, a "soft, warming, secure, luxe blanket."[6]

Cookie's clothes also convey important connections to black culture, past and present. This is particularly evident in the choice of furs that McGhee selects. Far from classic black minks, McGhee adorns Cookie in lavish designs that situate her in the contemporary hip-hop fashion aesthetic as embodied by performers like Lil' Kim, P. Diddy, Kanye West, Cam'ron, and others. At the same time, Cookie's furs visually reference the fashion of 1970s black culture, such as the opulent designs that Diana Ross sports in Berry Gordy's 1975 film *Mahogany* or the fierce jacket that the statuesque Tamara Dobson dons in *Cleopatra Jones* (Jack Starrett, 1977).[7] Yet the fur coats also reference the sartorial emblems of 1970s criminal underworld figures: pimps, drug dealers, and other hustlers. This is fitting given Cookie's backstory as a drug dealer.

Beyond narrative shorthand, Cookie's fashions also signify particular meanings about race and class. As Lee Daniels explains, "We're trendsetting—not just with music, but with costumes and hair design and ghetto fabulosity."[8] Daniels's use of the term "ghetto fabulosity" is especially important, as "ghetto fabulous" signifies a particular kind of classed blackness along with assumptions about taste. According to Urban Dictionary, to be "ghetto fabulous" indicates "the style of nouveau riche people who have grown up in ghetto or urban areas . . . the combination of bad taste, an urban aesthetic and desire to wear one's wealth. Basically, high priced but tacky clothing and accessories."[9] In many ways, the definition of "ghetto fabulous" accurately captures the dimensions of Cookie's character: She grew up in a poor, inner-city community and now finds herself with sudden wealth as she circulates in the upper-class world of the music industry. While I take issue with Urban Dictionary's definition of "ghetto fabulous" style as "tacky" (as "tacky" has very specific taste criteria that are based on white, middle-class norms), the second part of the definition does capture an essential idea about the relationship between Cookie's working-class background and the upper-class world in which she now circulates. Cookie has not grown up with wealth; she does not know the codes of upper-class style. Instead, she has imported the fashion aesthetics of her own black, inner-city environment into the contemporary world of *Empire*. Her look, therefore, is a "hood aesthetic" done in an expensive way. And her style is in line with the "bling" aesthetic of hip-hop culture, with its emphasis on flashy displays of wealth on the body.

The popularity of *Empire*'s fashions, spearheaded by Cookie's wardrobe, quickly led to a collaboration with luxury department store Saks Fifth Avenue for New York Fashion Week in September 2015. The store debuted its *Empire State of Mind* collection a week before *Empire*'s season 2 premiere: a series of luxe pieces inspired by the opulence of the show. The collection drew inspiration from *Empire*'s characters and traded on the overall "feel" of the show's black urbaneness and late-night soap opera glamor. While not the first clothing store to collaborate with a television show, the Saks/*Empire* collection is noteworthy because of the wide gulf between the demographic of the show and that of the department store.

The African American viewer that thrust *Empire* into its vaunted position no doubt bore little resemblance to the typical Saks customer. *NY Post* writer Robert Rorke noted the disconnect: "When Saks Fifth Avenue announced its partnership with Fox on a promotional deal to feature the fabulous loud fashions of their hit *Empire* at the department store, I wondered: Would Cookie Lyon, the fierce ex-con played so entertainingly by Taraji P. Henson, even shop there? Could she step off the elevator at the flagship store in Rockefeller Center, walk up to a salesperson and say, 'Get me a fake fur jacket, boo boo kitty, and I'd like it in grape'?"[10]

In fact, African Americans, regardless of socioeconomic level, have historically run into problems at high-end stores like Saks Fifth Avenue. In 2013, billionaire Oprah Winfrey asked to see a $38,000 designer handbag at a posh Zurich boutique, only to be rebuffed by a salesperson who told Winfrey that the bag was too expensive for her to afford.[11] The same year, African American teenager Trayon Christian was arrested in New York after purchasing a $350 belt from luxury department store Barneys, after the store claimed that he must have been using a fake debit card to make the purchase.[12]

These instances of "shopping while black" not only point to these stores' assumptions about black people's abilities to afford luxury goods but also suggest larger incongruities between blackness and its place in fashion. In a 2013 interview, for instance, rapper and mogul Kanye West described his irritation at the fashion industry rebuffing one of his ideas, only to see them eventually adopt it later: "Brought—brought the leather jogging pants 6 years ago to Fendi, and they said no. How many motherfuckers you done seen with a leather jogging pant?" West's anger not only stems from his frustration with not being taken seriously as a creative author of design but also is perhaps undergirded by the knowledge that the fashion industry has often co-opted elements of black, urban style (as well as that from other minority groups), while erasing their context and histories. For instance, in 2015 Givenchy designer Riccardo Tisci adorned his models with slicked-down "baby hair": the short, fluffy tendrils found along the hairline. The style, popular in black and brown urban communities for years, suddenly vaulted into the world of high fashion and celebrity, with a number of other white designers in various fashion weeks around the world following suit.[13] West's complaint treats the fashion industry as cultural appropriator, as an institution that has always capitalized on blackness while driving out black creative power.

The Saks/*Empire* venture, then, fits into a much larger, complicated relationship among fashion, black people, and blackness as marketable commodity. On the one hand, Saks deliberately approximates its own high-end version of "ghetto fabulous" fashion for delivery to its predominantly white, middle- to upper-class customer. Lee Daniels essentially validated this marketing strategy—trading on a flattened-out image of black identity and style in the form of "ghetto fabulousness"—when he relayed his own history with Saks at the fashion premiere: "When I was a kid, I used to boost—boosting is stealing. My sister and I, who Cookie is based on, used to go to Saks and we'd boost."[14] By relaying this story and attending the launch event, Daniels reinscribed a certain measure of black cultural authenticity into the discussion of style.[15] Yet at the same time, the entire marketing of the *Empire*/Saks collaboration, with pieces produced by high-end designers whose clothes would be financially inaccessible to many *Empire* viewers, erases the contributions of the real-life black people to this "ghetto fabulous" aesthetic.

The eye-catching fashions on *Empire* carry rich meaning about the characters, their lives, and their world. As a show that takes care to maintain a multicultural address, *Empire* uses fashion to draw connections to black culture outside of the show itself. In this way, the style functions as narrative shorthand that provides viewers with a host of information that the official storylines omit. At the same time, however, this shorthand also stands in for much more complicated and multilayered issues surrounding race, racism, class, and capitalism. As the show continues to grow in popularity and its style becomes ever more recognizable and profitable, it is important to remember that the attempts to celebrate and commodify *Empire*'s fashion aesthetic can also erase the contributions of the real-life people that inspired it. For all of these reasons, we should keep in mind that fashion on *Empire* is never simple window dressing but rather a dense and complicated site of the show's, and society's, cultural politics.

FURTHER READING

Click, Melissa A., and Sarah Smith-Frigerio. "One Tough Cookie: Exploring Black Women's Responses to *Empire*'s Cookie Lyon." *Communication, Culture and Critique* 12, no. 2 (March 2019): 287–304.

Higginbotham, Evelyn Brooks. *Righteous Discontent: The Women's Movement in the Black Baptist Church, 1880–1920*. Cambridge, MA: Harvard University Press, 1993.

Zook, Kristal Brent. *Color by FOX: The FOX Network and the Revolution in Black Television*. New York: Oxford University Press, 1999.

NOTES

I would like to acknowledge and thank Jéan-Claude Quintyne for his research help on a previous version of this essay.

1. The FOX network built its viewership in the early 1990s by targeting black audiences with a large slate of racially diverse programming yet largely abandoned this audience (and the

shows) after successfully winning white viewers. See Kristal Brent Zook, *Color by FOX: The FOX Network and the Revolution in Black Television* (New York: Oxford University Press, 1999).

2. Evelyn Brooks Higginbotham, *Righteous Discontent: The Women's Movement in the Black Baptist Church, 1880–1920* (Cambridge, MA: Harvard University Press, 1993).

3. "15 Epic Facts about *Empire*," E Online.com, www.eonline.com.

4. Notably, Lucious only wears this hairstyle in the pilot. By the time the series gets to its second episode (filmed well after the pilot), Lucious sports a short, cropped natural hairstyle.

5. Marjon Carlos, "Get That Cookie Look: Online Shopping with *Empire*'s Costume Designer," Fusion.net, last updated March 4, 2015, http://fusion.net.

6. Ibid.

7. McGhee borrowed most of Cookie's furs from her mother-in-law, Janet Bailey, ex-wife of legendary Earth, Wind, and Fire lead singer Philip Bailey, further highlighting furs as belonging to a past era of black glamor.

8. Megan Daley, "*Empire*: Cookie's Season 1 Fashion," Ew.com, last updated September 10, 2015, http://ew.com.

9. Urban Dictionary, s.v. "ghetto fabulous," www.urbandictionary.com.

10. Robert Rorke, "Would Cookie Lyon Really Shop at Saks?" *New York Post*, August 21, 2015, http://nypost.com.

11. Ethan Sacks, "Oprah Winfrey's Brush with Racism Sparks International Incident," *Daily News*, last updated August 9, 2013, www.nydailynews.com.

12. Kerry Burke, "Barneys Accused Me of Stealing Because I'm Black: Teen," *Daily News*, last updated October 24, 2013, www.nydailynews.com.

13. Caroline McGuire, "Is This the Style We'll All Be Wearing This Summer? 'Baby Hair' Becomes the Latest Beauty Trend to Hit Catwalks and Is Featured on Everyone from Katy Perry to Rihanna," *Daily Mail*, last updated March 16, 2015, www.dailymail.co.uk.

14. Ericka Goodman, "Lee Daniels Used to Shoplift from Saks," *The Cut*, September 13, 2015, www.thecut.com.

15. Interestingly, though Daniels and the entire *Empire* cast attended the Saks premier in New York, Taraji P. Henson was noticeably absent from the event. Whatever the reason, whether scheduling conflict or otherwise, the absence of "Cookie"—*Empire*'s fashion icon and the Saks line's muse—loomed large over the event. Devoid of her authenticating presence, the reality of the Saks Fifth Avenue collection became more apparent: a pastiche of the black aesthetics on *Empire* as filtered through the lens of established, recognizable, luxury fashion lines such as Jimmy Choo, Alexis Bittar, MCM, Helmut Lang, and Giuseppe Zanotti—brands that would already be familiar to the typical Saks customer.

3

House
Narrative Complexity

AMANDA D. LOTZ

Abstract: In her analysis of the medical/procedural program *House*, Amanda Lotz shows how a procedural program can exhibit narrative complexity and innovative techniques of character development. Lotz examines how a single episode draws upon a variety of atypical storytelling strategies to convey meaning and dramatize a central theme of the series: "everybody lies."

In the 2000s, some U.S. dramatic television entertained its audiences with increasingly complicated characters. Series such as FX's *The Shield*, *Rescue Me*, and *Sons of Anarchy* and AMC's *Mad Men* and *Breaking Bad* explored the complicated personal and professional lives of male characters and maximized the possibilities of television's storytelling attributes for character development. While several of these series can be properly described as character studies, other narrative forms also provided compelling examples for thinking about characterization, narrative strategies, and television storytelling. Series such as *CSI*, *Law & Order*, and the subject of this essay, *House, M.D.*, are organized episodically, so that they can be understood in individual installments, in stark contrast to the serialized character dramas on cable.[1] Yet even series that use limited serial components and instead structure their stories around solving some sort of legal or medical case within each episode can provide lead characters with the texture of depth and sophistication.

Episodically structured storytelling dominates the history of television, and this format has typically offered little narrative or character complexity; instead, characters are stuck in what Jeffrey Sconce describes as "a world of static exposition, repetitive second-act 'complications,' and artificial closure."[2] Such an assessment in some ways aptly characterizes the FOX medical drama *House, M.D.*

(hereafter *House*). The basic features of an episode of *House* vary little: an opening scene involving characters and settings outside those common to the show begins each episode. These scenes introduce viewers to the case of the week and often feature some sort of misdirection—for instance, it is not the overweight, middle-aged man complaining of chest pains who will become this week's case, but his apparently healthy wife who will inexplicably collapse. The series' opening credit sequence rolls, and we return from commercials to find Dr. Gregory House's diagnostic team beginning their evaluation of the opening's patient. The remaining minutes of the episode focus on the team's efforts to identify the patient's ailment in time to save him or her, embarking upon a series of misdiagnoses along the way. Various interpersonal complications are introduced and addressed throughout the case; typically, they are related to evolving romantic entanglements among the primary cast, although few of these complications are likely to be resolved in one episode. At some point near the end of the episode, House has a conversation—typically with his friend Wilson—about some other matter and becomes suddenly quiet, having just stumbled upon the possible diagnosis evading the team. The condition is caught in time and alleviated (although in some rare cases the team fails to find the diagnosis in time), and the "artificial closure" Sconce notes is achieved.

As a series that chronicles the efforts of a master team of diagnostic doctors to identify and treat the rarest of illnesses, *House* emphasizes the plot goal of diagnosis in each weekly episode. Where many other series attempt to balance serial and episodic plotlines through a serialized, overarching mystery (*Murder One, Burn Notice, Monk*), *House* solves its mystery each week; the exploits of its misanthropic, drug-addicted lead character are what propel serial action instead. The implicit central enigma of its cumulative narrative—or the eight-season total story of *House*—is whether the series' eponymous lead can ever be properly civilized. Can House exist without painkillers? Can he cultivate meaningful relationships? Can he be brilliant and happy?

Most series that are dominated by this logic of episodic storytelling emphasize plot action and consequently leave characters fairly static over time. Yet in recent decades, even some episodically structured series have indicated the possibility for complex character development, and as Roberta Pearson outlines, mundane plot action can serve this end. In her case study of *CSI*'s Gil Grissom, Pearson presents a six-part taxonomy of elements that construct the character: psychological traits/habitual behaviors; physical traits/appearance; speech patterns; interactions with other characters; environment (the places the character inhabits); and biography (character's backstory).[3] She uses this taxonomy to create a language for exploring the particularities of television characters, which, along with techniques of characterization—beyond the case study—have been a significantly under-explored area in the field. She notes that the rudimentary taxonomy works for characters in all moving image forms, but that specific media or narrative strategies may vary techniques. For example, the ongoing storytelling process in television series allows for much more character growth and change than in the limited storytelling period available to realist cinema.[4] Pearson's case is valuable for illustrating that even though many episodic series place little emphasis on character depth, this is a creative choice rather than an inherent feature of episodically structured shows.

To better understand attributes of episodic television storytelling and techniques of characterization, this essay analyzes a single episode of *House*, focusing on how narrative strategies convey meaning on multiple levels. The episode "Three Stories" conveys crucial character information in its basic plot, although the episode uses confounding techniques such as dream sequences, flashbacks, and imagined alternate realities—rarely clearly marked as such—to do so. The misdirection of these storytelling techniques reaffirms a central theme of the series: namely, that "everybody lies," which is House's personal outlook and dictates his particular approach to diagnostic medicine. Thus, this episode of *House* illustrates the complexity available to a series with a narrative structure that is generally rebuked for its reliance on formula and lack of nuance.

"Three Stories" is arguably the least routine episode of a series that normally maintains exceptional consistency. Although the selection of an aberrant case rarely offers sound footing for broader arguments, the unusualness of this episode underscores its significance and indicates the novelty of the series' approach to character development. Hence, it serves as the focus of this essay. The episode, the penultimate of the first season, finally explains the injury to House's leg, which has led to his chronic pain and perhaps his unhappiness—arguably his primary character traits. While this pain and unhappiness centrally define House, they are also what enable future serial storylines, such as his spirals through drug addiction, his efforts to get and remain clean, and his attempts to deal with human interaction and emotions without pharmaceutically induced numbness. House's struggles to alleviate his pain and his unhappiness—neither he nor the audience is ever fully aware whether these are separate conditions—are traced loosely in the cumulative narrative.

By the time "Three Stories" aired (twenty episodes into the first season) in May of 2005 and finally explained the origin of the lead character's primary character trait, *House* had established itself as a bona fide hit. The series benefited from airing during a post-*American Idol* timeslot, when the reality competition returned in January of 2005, but even this most enviable of lead-ins might not have been adequate to make such a contrary leading character so popular. Greg House remains the least conventionally heroic lead character to motivate a successful broadcast drama, although such flawed characters have been prevalent in recent years in the more niche-targeted storytelling space of original cable dramas. House's personal misanthropy functions as a guiding ideology of the series, which stems from his requirement that his team of diagnosticians work from the assumption that "everybody lies." House encourages his team to dismiss medical histories reported by patients and instead sleuth through their homes to uncover the truth or think of things patients may be unwilling to tell doctors.

"Three Stories" begins exceptionally, but not in a way that informs viewers just how significant the exception will become. It opens in the middle of a conversation between House and chief of medicine, Dr. Lisa Cuddy, in a way that violates the well-established pattern of opening episodes with a non-regular character experiencing a medical emergency. The conversation in Cuddy's office establishes that a fellow doctor is ill and that Cuddy needs House to replace him and lecture on diagnostic medicine to a class of medical students. House characteristically tries to refuse, but accepts a release from doing clinic hours—an activity he finds distasteful due to the mundane ailments he encounters—in exchange for agreeing to lecture. House leaves Cuddy's office and finds a woman named Stacy, who we learn is his ex-girlfriend, in need of his diagnostic skills for her husband. Despite its atypical inclusion of regular characters, this pre-credit sequence offers two obvious potential patients—the ill doctor whom House must replace and Mark, husband to Stacy—although the deviation from the usual location external to the hospital suggests a greater break with conventional form could be occurring as well. A viewer could reasonably presume the still-young series was varying its conventional start, but the opening of "Three Stories" offers the ultimate misdirection, as the episode eventually reveals that the conversation between House and Cuddy involves the case of the week.[5]

After the opening credits, House begins his lecture to the medical students. He poses that there are three patients with leg pain and asks the students to diagnose the cause, as he gradually builds the stories of the patients. Although the series rarely uses techniques such as dream sequences, flashbacks, or imagined alternate realities, this episode eschews the realist techniques that normally characterize *House* by portraying characters whose conditions and embodiments shift each time House retells their scenarios. The cases begin as that of a farmer, golfer, and volleyball player, but House rewrites their histories and attributes each time he elaborates on the cases to the students, making "reality" difficult to discern. The actor playing the farmer (a middle-aged man) also appears as the volleyball player at first as well—although House describes the volleyball player as a teen girl. The golfer is actress Carmen Electra as herself, yet Doctors Foreman, Chase, and Cameron are interjected into the cases in a manner suggesting the scenario is

FIGURE 3.1. In an atypical episode, *House* eschews realist techniques by portraying characters whose conditions and embodiments shift as House retells their scenarios. Here, actress Carmen Electra temporarily appears as an injured golfer.

real. Eventually three distinct actors embody the possible leg pain patients (none of whom are Electra) as House works through possible diagnoses, treatments, and consequences with the room of students.

Beyond the context of the lecture, this episode's inclusion of three different patients is uncommon, as the show usually features just one case. This unusual number of cases further confounds viewers' efforts to understand what is "really" going on, which isn't made clear until the episode is two-thirds complete. After multiple diagnoses and treatments of the farmer and volleyball player, House reveals the patient who began as a golfer, and is assumed to be a drug-seeker, has tea-colored urine. He offers a few additional indicators of the possible condition to the dumbfounded students when Dr. Cameron, a member of his diagnostic team, suggests "muscle death." House berates the students for not thinking of muscle death, while explaining that none of the man's doctors thought of it either, and that it took three days before the "patient" suggested it was muscle death. The episode then cycles back through vignettes in which the farmer and volleyball player are diagnosed and their doctors inform them that their legs may have to be amputated. When the episode turns back to the golfer/drug seeker/muscle death patient, Cuddy appears as the doctor. She delivers the news that amputation may be necessary. The scene transitions back to the lecture hall where House explains that an aneurism caused the muscle death, and a camera pan of the audience reveals all of House's team, Doctors Cameron, Foreman, and Chase, now seated in the back row, hanging on every detail. Foreman mutters, "God, you were right, it was House," and the scene cuts to House in bed as Cuddy's patient.

The remaining fourteen minutes of the episode shift to a more reliably realist style, although they do cut back and forth between flashbacks of House's treatment and his account of the tale to the class. In these scenes, the audience learns that Stacy was his girlfriend at the time of the aneurism, that House refused amputation—the better way to resolve the issue—and demanded a bypass to restore blood to the leg. But as Cuddy predicted, the pain was so great that he needed to be placed in a medical coma until the worst of it had passed. Stacy waited until House was in the coma and, as his legal health-care proxy, allowed further surgery to remove the dead tissue. House's ongoing chronic pain results from the extent of the muscle removed in this subsequent surgery and the delayed diagnosis.

Beyond the idiosyncrasies of this particular episode, *House*'s treatment of character development is uncommon in a number of respects. First, it is most curious that the series waits until nearly the end of its first season to explain the origin of House's chronic pain. A conventional way to compensate for building the series around such a disagreeable protagonist would be to add layers to the character, to explain the origin of his pain, and/or to give it a cause that would warrant and justify the subsequent suffering and attitude that results.[6] Consider how CBS's *The Mentalist* explained the steady agitation of its less-than-personable protagonist as a result of the murder of his wife and daughter. This backstory is explained multiple times in the pilot and reemerges constantly throughout the series so that new or occasional viewers thoroughly understand the personality traits of the character and see how the exceptional tragedy he experienced justifies his focused search for the killer.

Instead of following such conventional explication and reiteration, the first season of *House* offers little explanation for House's physical or psychic ailments until this episode. The unconventionality of this strategy of under-explanation is furthered by the degree to which future episodes of the series do not recall House's origin story to audience members who missed this particular episode. Such recapping is easily and unobtrusively performed in other series by recalling crucial background details when new cast members are added. For example, in this case a new doctor could be informed of why House needs a cane by another character. Each episode of *House* introduces a new patient and in most cases provides a moment where House's poor bedside manner could be explained as a result of his chronic pain, including some details of its origin. However, the series does not recall this episode, or the information imparted in it again until late in season seven. In the interim, an entirely new group of doctors have become

House's primary team, and the series never depicts them inquiring about House's pain or another character explaining the limp.

It is also notable that this crucial origin story is told in such a convoluted manner. Viewers do not realize they are being told House's story until they are deep into it, and even once Foreman makes clear the significance of the story, the preceding deviation from realist narrative and inconsistent blending of three different stories make it difficult to identify what parts of the previous narrative of the golfer/drug seeker were real. Moreover, why confuse the story by suggesting the patient could be a drug seeker? Viewers know House as a drug addict, but he would not have been before the injury. The significance of the episode's more complicated techniques becomes clear if one considers the narratives and narrative techniques not chosen: House could have directly explained the incident in telling another character why he and Stacy broke up; the classroom technique could have been retained with just one case; all three cases could have been used without the constant variation in situations. These "easier" ways of incorporating the same information suggests the choice of complex techniques was deliberate.

The episode provides an explanation for House's devotion to his guiding mantra that "everybody lies," a crucial component of his character's psychology, in two different ways. First, the audience and lecture hall of medical students see that diagnosticians must face unreliable information from patients through House's repeated and varied presentations of the patient's situations and ailments. Patients, even when not trying to confuse a diagnostician, change their stories and omit vital details in ways that require physicians to reconsider everything they thought they knew. The deviation from realist storytelling illustrates to the viewer how diagnosticians might also feel that they don't "know" anything. With the things thought to be certain and true proven false, the episode appears to allegorize House's view of the world and justification for his conviction that everybody lies. The episode also depicts House's betrayal by Stacy, providing insight into his general distrust of people outside of diagnostics. Stacy acts in what she believes is House's best interest once he is comatose and defies his expressed treatment desire. His insistence upon the medical possibility of maintaining the leg and his life appears irrational—at one point she asks if he'd cut off his leg to save her, which he acknowledges he'd do—but his faith in medicine proves wise. The suspicion with which House regards self-disclosures begins to make more sense in the context of this tale in which his closest confidant betrays his clearly expressed desires.

The writers of *House*, including, notably, series creator David Shore, who penned this episode, use unconventional techniques to provide more than the morsels of character development commonly offered in each episode, thus helping to compel the audience to take an ongoing interest in the series beyond the short-term gratification of seeing the case of the week solved and whether the doctors are able to save the patient. But despite this structural variation, the episode perpetuates the general beliefs and outlook of the series.

The question for the critical analyst, then, is what is the consequence of this unconventional treatment of character? Throughout most episodes and seasons, the origins of House's bizarre actions are commonly attributed to "House being House." This phrase, used most often by those who have a long relationship with House, such as Doctors Wilson and Cuddy, refers to House's monomaniacal and socially unacceptable behavior, often to suggest that abnormal behavior is consistent with what characters can expect from him. Some characters know his story, which is presented as a defining cause of his behavior. Yet knowing the origin of House's injury does not change how his team approaches him. Moreover, other characters who join later and never learn the truth do learn how to "treat" House nonetheless. To handle the situation of House—to deal with a friend and coworker who suffers constant pain—it makes no difference whether that pain originated from a rare infection, a stabbing wound, or an aneurism. The series' handling of House's truth thus affirms the series' principle that understanding a history doesn't help understand an illness—knowing why House has pain doesn't help in dealing with or helping him. "Three Stories" illustrates the need to look beyond plot structure in assessing the simplicity or complexity of narrative and character. Although the staid features of episodic structure might allow for repetitive act structure and enforced conclusions, this episode illustrates the creative possibilities in character development and series outlook that can still be incorporated.

FURTHER READING

DuBose, Mike S. "Morality, Complexity, Experts, and Systems of Authority in *House, M.D.*, or 'My Big Brain Is My Superpower.'" *Television and New Media* 11, no. 1 (2010): 20–36.

Mittell, Jason. *Complex TV: The Poetics of Contemporary Television Storytelling*. New York: New York University Press, 2015.

O'Sullivan, Sean. "Broken on Purpose: Poetry, Serial Television, and the Season." *Storyworlds: A Journal of Narrative Studies* 2 (2010): 59–77.

Pearson, Roberta. "Anatomising Gilbert Grissom: The Structure and Function of the Televisual Character." In *Reading CSI: Crime TV Under the Microscope*, edited by Michael Allen. London: Tauris, 2007.

NOTES

1. Episodic shows have an industrial advantage because their ability to be viewed out of order and haphazardly yields larger audiences and thus license fees in syndication.

2. Jeffrey Sconce, "What If? Charting Television's New Textual Boundaries," in *Television after TV: Essays on a Medium in Transition*, ed. Lynn Spigel and Jan Olsson (Durham, NC: Duke University Press, 2004), 97.

3. Roberta Pearson, "Anatomising Gilbert Grissom: The Structure and Function of the Televisual Character," in *Reading CSI: Crime TV Under the Microscope*, ed. Michael Allen (London: Tauris, 2007).

4. Ibid., 49.

5. Just as this essay was first completed, *House* aired episode 807, "Dead and Buried," in which it disregarded its usual opening structure for no apparent narrative reason.

6. For example, audience members could hardly shun House if his pain resulted from an injury suffered while saving a child or performing some other similarly heroic act.

4

Looking
Smartphone Aesthetics

HUNTER HARGRAVES

Abstract: Throughout the 2010s, a number of series branded as "quality" began to adopt a range of new aesthetic practices that simulate those of smartphone photography, manipulating color and saturation to produce something akin to the "Instagram effect" for television. Hunter Hargraves examines one such series, *Looking*, which focuses on a group of gay men living in San Francisco during the height of the city's Silicon Valley transformation, and questions how such aesthetic techniques speak to the series' ability to represent authentic queer life in San Francisco. Smartphone aesthetics, he contends, may curtail a series' potential to develop nuanced political critiques relating to the representation of cultural minorities, much like the social media platforms they attempt to emulate.

In the pilot episode of HBO's *Looking*, a dramatic comedy about three gay friends navigating professional and personal relationships in San Francisco, two of the leads try to make sense of how technology has helped—or hindered—gay urban dating. Patrick, a twenty-nine-year-old videogame developer, sits with his roommate Agustín, a thirty-one-year-old artist, in their kitchen. Patrick, introduced by the series as relationship-challenged, observes that "Instagram filters have ruined everything, and I can't tell if this guy is hot or not" before soliciting Agustín's opinion. Agustín chalks up Patrick's inability to notice the guy's lazy eye to his naivete before the two conclude that maybe a lazy eye can be "kinda hot." What is most striking about the scene, which otherwise documents a rather banal conversation between two close friends, is how composition and mise-en-scène coordinate with content. Illuminated by his laptop, Patrick sits at the table in focus with the background showcasing the soft green colors of plants and soft white

FIGURE 4.1.
The "look" of this shot from *Looking* mimics the photo filtering popularized by smartphone apps.

colors of natural light: in essence, mimicking the very process of photographic filtering made popular by smartphone apps such as Instagram, Hipstamatic, and Infinicam.

If Instagram filters have indeed "ruined everything," they also establish the dominant aesthetic of *Looking*, which was cancelled by HBO citing the second season's poor ratings, with the series' storylines more or less tied up in a 2016 film. Audiences, and some critics, found the narrative too ordinary and slow moving, and the series incited many debates within its representational demographic of urban gay men surrounding the authenticity of its plotlines about sex and relationships. Watching *Looking* as an urban gay male might elicit a number of affective reactions: nostalgia for sunny days in Dolores Park or for sweaty dance parties at the Stud; irritation toward characters who desire homonormative relationships; aesthetic satisfaction from the lush colors of Northern California; and anger at how privilege and money anchor the narrative. In this case, these affective poles of displeasure and pleasure represent the conflict that often appears between a text's politics and its aesthetics. But how might this ambivalence between politics and aesthetics reveal the impact of smartphone technology on contemporary television storytelling?

I highlight these tensions within *Looking* because the series interestingly stitches together its content with its form. It is set in a San Francisco that has undergone a number of cultural and economic shifts due to the explosive success of Silicon Valley tech corporations. Many blame affluent tech sector workers for driving up rents in the city and pushing poorer residents out of it. But technology is not only an ideological backdrop for *Looking* but also, as the aforementioned scene suggests, its dominant aesthetic: The series is shot to play with color, saturation, contrast, and brightness in order to "look" as if it was shot through an app such as Instagram on a smartphone. Without question, visual images have been transformed by the smartphone, through which selfies, filters, and tagging have been quickly incorporated into the photographic lexicon.

While most scholarship on the convergence between television and smartphones has focused on the spectator's increased individual agency over what, when, and where the individual watches, little analysis attends to the influence of smartphones—their aesthetic styles and behaviors—on the production and reception of television. This essay assesses the impact that these aesthetic considerations have on *Looking*'s ideological messages surrounding gay male sexuality. As a series, *Looking* plays with the boundary of form and content through its visually appealing style that limits a consideration of queer politics. Ultimately, smartphone aesthetics may be symptomatic of television's increased convergence with other media platforms, but they may also impose the limitations of those platforms onto the narrative, forcing audiences to balance aesthetic pleasures with the demands of representation.

Looking is one of many series whose aesthetics resonate with smartphone technology. Others we might include in this category include *Louie*, *Girls*, *Transparent*, *The Affair*, *Insecure*, and *Atlanta*. These series are (or were) all shot with a single camera and broadcast by cable, premium cable, and streaming services—markers of so-called quality television—while defying easy generic categorization. With the exception of *The Affair*, these series are dramatic comedies set in the present day that eschew conventions of the classic sitcom, aspiring instead toward both narrative and cinematographic realism. These series often employ retro color saturations, enhanced brightness, and overlapping textures in order to manipulate the televisual image. Notably, many of these series also place issues of identity at the core of their narratives, becoming controversial for their inability to represent fully the experiences of minoritarian groups (transgender people in the case of *Transparent*; millennial women in the case of *Girls*) with their particular characters and storylines. Many of these series (such as *Girls*, *Atlanta*, *Insecure*, and *Looking*) address these representational tensions by situating their characters as young professionals in the process of figuring out adulthood. Visual advertisements for these programs can signify this through the use of graphic design suggestive of smartphone aesthetics. *Looking*'s title card, for example, consists of its name in all caps outlined in bright shades of blue, as if made from neon tubing; promotional visuals for *Insecure* (HBO, 2016–present) displayed protagonist Issa Dee but altered with a misaligned RGB color separation. In both of these cases the condition of feeling insecure with one's self or "looking" for something to complete the self is crystallized through blurry visuals indicative of a hazy process of self-discovery.

While the manipulation of the visual image is now standard in the contemporary mediascape, these programs illustrate the emergence of a specific set of practices that produce what I call smartphone aesthetics. Commercial advertisers and cultural critics have noted the "Instagram effect," named after the most

FIGURES 4.2 AND 4.3.
The graphic design in
these promotional images
also is suggestive of smartphone aesthetics.

prominent social media smartphone app to feature handheld image manipulation.
Founded in 2010 by Kevin Systrom and Mike Krieger, the app quickly attracted
one million users in two months and was named by Apple as the "iPhone app of
the year" in 2011 before being acquired by social media titan Facebook in 2012
for roughly $1 billion. Instagram popularized the use of amateur manipulation
through the ability to change an image's brightness, contrast, warmth, saturation,
and sharpness, most easily through the use of preset filters such as Mayfair (described by Instagram as applying "a warm pink tone, subtle vignetting to brighten
the photograph center and a thin black border") or Willow ("a monochromatic
filter with subtle purple tones and a translucent white border").[1] Writing in *Wired*
magazine in 2011, Clive Thompson observed that the kind of composition offered
by Instagram filters gives "newbies a way to develop deeper visual literacy," since
users gain access to effects formerly attributed to chemical byproducts of material
film.[2] Along with other smartphone apps that allow users to manipulate certain
elements of the photographic image, Instagram can be seen thus as democratiz-
ing image-making, empowering users to assert control over the stylization of the
image, and thus how the subjects of the image are presented to the world.

　　Smartphone aesthetics are especially prominent in *Looking*'s first season,
which was shot by Reed Morano, the youngest member of the American Society

of Cinematographers (and as of 2015 one of only fourteen female active members of the professional organization). Morano has commented that she wanted to replicate within *Looking* a cinematic experience partially inspired by foreign independent films. "It's a look that was often associated with Fuji, but I feel like there's something interesting and anti-television about a kind of a faded blue, cooler tone," she noted in one interview. "You're feeling more green or cyan in the blacks, while I personally like keeping the highlights comparatively warm. Part of that look is some added contrast, and we'll be desaturating the image quite a bit—sort of an homage to the faded look of San Francisco. So I definitely think the show will have a unique look."[3] Specifically, Morano singles out the use of color as *Looking*'s aesthetic distinction, but this ambient finesse of the image aligns with the branding of HBO as "anti-television," as encapsulated, of course, in the notoriously value-laden tagline "It's not TV, it's HBO." In another interview, Morano ties the color schema of the series to executive producer Andrew Haigh's previous film, the 2011 SXSW darling *Weekend*: "The thing I kept coming back to was the color. Many TV shows occupy the same color space. What *Weekend* reminded me of, like a lot of work from the UK, was how it kind of had a cool, muted tone to it. I couldn't really put my finger on it, so I came up with my own version."[4] These cool, muted tones are especially present in the fifth episode ("Looking for the Future") when Patrick blows off work to spend time with budding crush Richie (Raúl Castillo), in which the two get stoned and explore Golden Gate Park, culminating in a shot just above the Sutro Baths and the Pacific Ocean that emphasizes lush blues and greens against a soft, beige-tinted sky.

This is a kind of televisuality that relies on its antithetical disavowal, common to series subject to what Dean DeFino has called the "HBO effect." *Looking* gives the impression that it could have been shot through a more advanced smartphone: It is shot digitally and, importantly, mostly handheld, without dollies or Steadicams. Rather than moving back and forth between medium shots or close-ups of faces—the camerawork indicative of multicamera sitcoms—*Looking* is predominantly shot on location with a single camera, using long shots and extreme long shots to establish San Francisco as an equal character, if not the main character, of the series. Instead of moving back and forth between medium close-ups of faces, the camera in dialogue scenes moves slower, creeping around the actors while emphasizing their surroundings: the shabby-chic apartment interiors familiar to any San Franciscan or the casual choreography of the city's neighborhoods. The series is peppered with "walk and talks," the conversational technique made famous by *The West Wing*. But whereas that series used movement to structure dialogue around speed, *Looking*'s characters move much more slowly, reflective of the laid-back California vibe its characters inhabit, or perhaps to invoke the ambulatory high of its frequently stoned characters.

What is interesting about Morano's description of how she shot the first season is her perhaps unintentional description of the visual practices of smartphone photography. In asserting that, as a professional cinematographer, she had leeway to "[come] up with her own version" of color composition, she also invokes the capacity to self-edit the image definitive of smartphone apps such as Instagram. Moreover, many of the filtering styles key to the Instagram effect mimic the style of traditional photographic technologies such as the daguerreotype, Kodachrome, or the Polaroid, a direct correlation to the "faded look of San Francisco" Morano aspires to with her camerawork.

The algorithms that drive this software are those of a control society, such that Instagram users create a distinctive, dividuated aesthetic underwritten by the same array of filtering options. According to Nadav Hochmann and Lev Manovich, the uniform appearances on Instagram photos create a sense of atemporality and shared aesthetics dependent upon the app's interface signature: An individual user's photos become unique through the same aesthetic filters used by all other Instagram users. Hochmann and Manovich's analysis of Instagram uses data visualization to conceptualize the practices unique to specific cities, or those cities' "visual signatures." "If Instagram's affordances indeed offer a new global style," they write, "its universality possesses distinctive characteristics in different social timespaces."[5] The idea of a regionally specific visual signature—warm highlights, a desaturated image—ties into the market logic of Silicon Valley, in which regionally networked publics emerge through social media, working in tandem with other data collection services to create targeted advertising profiles.

How one manipulates an image comes clearly across in *Looking*'s first episode, not only through Patrick's comment that "Instagram filters have ruined everything" but also when Patrick responds to his hunky (yet aging) friend Dom's (Murray Bartlett) question about his age by in turn asking "in daylight or candlelight?" The way in which light might be able to distort perception seems to structure the series' own narrative about queer self-exploration in a world oversaturated by technology: Instagram filters have ruined the ability to find a romantic partner, for example, because the normative standard by which the urban gay man finds sex, love, or some combination of the two is entirely mediated through digital spaces. The show's title, *Looking*, directly evokes this as well, with the word commonly used on smartphone apps such as Grindr and Scruff to indicate a user in search of casual sex.

Yet *Looking* also tenders another kind of digital malleability, one of San Francisco itself, which has struggled to broker its image as a bohemian mecca for cultural minorities with the rapid gentrification spurred by tech corporations. Critics of this gentrification frame the "techification" of San Francisco as a metaphorical urban death measured through extended temporalities of population displacement and lateral change, not unlike the process of slow death described in Lauren Berlant's formulation of cruel optimism. But while for many queer residents the struggle to survive exponential increases in the cost of living saturates urban life with a melancholic grittiness, *Looking*'s characters appear to be unaffected by San Francisco's status as the most expensive city in America in which to live. While some storylines peripherally mention these changes—Dom compares the present day to 1999 and the first dot-com bubble; Agustín notes that San Francisco has become overrun by "kimchi tacos"—none of its characters experience displacement in a diegetically significant way. The love-to-hate character of Agustín nearly approximates this in his unraveling development: At the beginning of the series Agustín moves in with his then boyfriend in Oakland, but following an ugly breakup, he moves back in with Patrick, embarking on drug-fueled binges that culminate in passing out on the street on more than one occasion. Yet Agustín's narrative drama is never truly economic but rather cultural in nature; though he doesn't pay rent, Patrick's tech salary can cover him, and as such Agustín's precarity functions to shore up his relationships with his friends and prospective crushes instead of rendering him homeless or, in what would be a more realistic scenario, prompting his exodus to more affordable locales outside of the Bay Area.

Indeed, this is perhaps a telling example of *Looking*'s politics as a whole: Being gay is only made legible through stable incomes propped up by Silicon Valley. This amounts to a filtering of sexuality through what Lisa Duggan has termed *homonormativity*: "a politics that does not contest dominant heteronormative assumptions and institutions . . . but upholds and sustains them while promising the possibility of a demobilized gay constituency and a privatized, depoliticized gay culture anchored in domesticity and consumption."[6] Assumptions such as monogamy and institutions such as marriage are rife within the series' construction of gay relationships; in the most climatic example of this, Patrick ultimately breaks up with his eventual boyfriend (and boss) Kevin (Russell Tovey) at the end of the second season after finding out that Kevin has a Grindr profile.

Such homonormativity, like its heterosexual counterpart, has two distinctive effects. First, it suggests a "post-gay" sensibility more interested in documenting queer subjects as ordinary rather than as invested in the political visibility congruent with identity politics. As Tim Teeman wrote for *The Daily Beast*, "*Looking* seems at special pains to be so nonpolitical, *so over* all the kind of nitty-gritty stuff that people do talk about and experience: marriage equality, homophobia, discrimination, the plight of gays abroad."[7] Such a review resonates with numerous descriptions of the series, including one from executive producer Haigh, as less about what it means to be gay and more about a group of men who happen to be gay. Second, its homonormativity removes the edge from the stereotypical depiction of San Francisco gay culture as salaciously hedonistic, rendering sexuality in rather stale terms. And indeed, most criticisms of *Looking* revolve around it being "boring," even from the series' defenders. This may be a part of a larger generic and aesthetic project of HBO, who programmed *Looking* with its widely discussed series *Girls* and the also short-lived *Togetherness* on Sunday nights: All, to varying extents, engage in citations of mumblecore cinema, focusing on the mundane problems of privileged, mostly white people often through improvised dialogue and the slow progression of plot. When applied to the concept of queer television, however, this produces an uncomfortable approach to the expectations many viewers have about the role of representation.

To claim that *Looking* is not representative of a coherently imagined gay community may be a common complaint, but it is not a necessarily deep critique. Rather, its productive value lies in how irritation and frustration become wielded as strategies for viewing: in forming the backbone of practices of antifandom, perhaps, or in asserting an affective texture to the politics of representation. Yet *Looking* presents this texture as aesthetically technological, illustrating how representation becomes literally filtered to beautify its characters in uniformly bland ways. In one *Out* magazine profile lauding the series, Christopher Glazek writes that "*Looking* does not rely on glittering wit, slick fashion, or edgy transcendence to power its storyline. It relies on the joy of recognition that sometimes accompanies viewing a well-calibrated reproduction of daily life."[8] The "well-calibrated reproduction of daily life," of course, is what attracts millions of users to apps such as Instagram, in which ordinary and ephemeral routines and rituals are captured, stylized, and presented to the general public. Instagram's interface does not privilege political discourse, as opposed to that of other social media apps such as Facebook, where one can engage in a heated political debate with estranged relatives, or Twitter, both the preferred platform of President Donald Trump and a tool erroneously credited with bringing democracy to many parts of the Middle East. The Instagram effect allows for brand stylization (of babies, vacations, food, or selfies) in narcissistically beautiful yet universally flattening ways. Perhaps it should then come as no surprise that a television series that evokes such a visual signature of San Francisco technoculture could not sustain itself against the demands of serial television, which require more attention to narrative storytelling and character development.

In his canonical essay "The Work of Art in the Age of Mechanical Reproduction," Walter Benjamin proffers the concerning idea that capitalism and fascism function through the aestheticization of politics. The discontents of different social groups, normally promoted through collective struggle, become neutered through mass reproduction and the loss of the art object's aura. For Benjamin, this is potentially liberating, as it allows for the formerly passive mass spectator to adopt a critical and rational stance.[9] *Looking*'s smartphone aesthetics certainly fits within such a schema, as the desire for accurate or realistic representation is an impossibility for *Looking*'s idealized post-gay audience. But *Looking* also surprisingly instructs to *look*, to shift televisual spectatorship away from its distracted reception (compounded in today's convergence culture with its attending devices) and to treat the program's lush aesthetics as background visual noise free from politics. In the very first scene of the series, Patrick attempts to cruise for sex in Buena Vista Park, a decidedly atechnological means for hooking up. Partially obscured by blurred leaves, Patrick and a bearded suitor begin to give each other a hand job, but Patrick cannot shut his mouth, asking the man if he "comes here a lot" as well as his name (violating virtually all cruising etiquette). The man, having had enough of Patrick literally seconds into the series, tells him to "stop talking" before an ill-timed phone call ends the encounter for good. What if, indeed, the audience were to take the anonymous man's cue, silencing the ordinary drama of urban gay men and refracting it into an indulgence in the purely visual? In encouraging the audience to always already be looking for something better, *Looking* outs itself perhaps not simply as anti-television, or as homonormative, but as an app running in the background, an imagescape that might be best viewed by hitting the mute button.

FURTHER READING

Chun, Wendy Hui Kyong. *Updating to Remain the Same: Habitual New Media*. Cambridge, MA: MIT Press, 2016.
Clare, Stephanie. "(Homo)normativity's Romance: Happiness and Indigestion in Andrew Haigh's *Weekend*." *Continuum: Journal of Media and Cultural Studies* 27, no. 6 (2013): 785–98.
Snickars, Pelle, and Patrick Vondarau, eds. *Moving Data: The iPhone and the Future of Media*. New York: Columbia University Press, 2012.

NOTES

1. See Instagram, "Instagram's Newest Filter: Willow," December 11, 2012, http://blog.instagram.com/post/37739409065/instagrams-newest-filter-willow-yesterdays; and "Instagram's Newest Filter: Mayfair," December 22, 2012, http://blog.instagram.com/post/38546919409/instagrams-newest-filter-mayfair-yesterdays.
2. Clive Thompson, "Clive Thompson on the Instagram Effect," *Wired* 20.01, December 27, 2011, www.wired.com.
3. American Society of Cinematographers, "Reed Morano Preps *Looking* in San Francisco," *Parallax View* (blog), August 28, 2013, www.theasc.com/site/blog/parallax-view/reed-morano-preps-looking-in-san-francisco.
4. Matthew Hammett Knott, "Heroines of Cinema: Reed Morano, the Next Big Thing in American Cinematography," *IndieWire*, November 28, 2013, www.indiewire.com.

5. Nadav Hochmann and Lev Manovich, "Zooming into an Instagram City: Reading the local through Social Media," *First Monday* 18, no. 7 (July 2013), https://firstmonday.org.

6. Lisa Duggan, *The Twilight of Equality: Neoliberalism, Cultural Politics, and the Attack on Democracy* (Boston: Beacon Press, 2003), 179.

7. Tim Teeman, "Yes, *Looking* Is Boring. It's the Drama Gays Deserve," *Daily Beast*, January 24, 2014, www.thedailybeast.com.

8. Christopher Glazek, "Modern Love," *Out*, January 14, 2014, www.out.com.

9. Walter Benjamin, "The Work of Art in the Age of Mechanical Reproduction," in *Illuminations*, trans. Harry Zohn (New York: Schocken, 1969), 217–52.

5

Mad Men
Visual Style

JEREMY G. BUTLER

Abstract: Through a detailed examination of how the visual look of *Mad Men* conveys the show's meanings and emotional affect, Jeremy G. Butler provides a model for how to perform a close analysis of television style for a landmark contemporary series.

Much has been written about the look of AMC's *Mad Men*—and not surprisingly, as the program has vividly evoked mid-century American life—the hairstyles and clothing, the offices and homes, and, of course, the chain-smoking and four-martini lunches of a particular, privileged segment of American society. However, *Mad Men* is more than a slavish reproduction of a bygone era. It sees that era through a contemporary filter that recognizes the despair and alienation that lay just beneath the surface. And it implicitly critiques the power structures of that time, which both casually and brutally subordinated working-class people, women, gays, and ethnic and racial minorities.

To understand how *Mad Men* accomplishes this critique, we need to look closely at its visual style. By "style," I don't mean just its fashion sense, although costume design is definitely a key stylistic component. Rather, I examine the program's style in terms of its mise-en-scène, or elements arranged in front of the camera, and its cinematography, or elements associated with the camera itself. Mise-en-scène covers set, lighting, and costume design, as well as the positioning of the actors on the set. Cinematography includes framing, camera angle, choice of film stock, and camera movement. In addition, it is also critical to attend to the program's editing design since editing determines what we see on the screen, for how long, and in what context. Together, then, mise-en-scène, cinematography, and editing are aspects of television style that showrunner Matthew Weiner, his crew, and his actors use to construct their twenty-first-century critique of 1960s American values.

To start an analysis of *Mad Men*'s mise-en-scène, we should look first at its set design, which serves the crucial function of establishing the program's time period. This is achieved both subtly—by the interior design of the rooms that characters inhabit—and not so subtly—by objects such as a March 1960 calendar that appears in close-up in the very first episode. Period authenticity is clearly important to showrunner Weiner, and the program contains remarkably few anachronistic objects, considering its relatively limited budget (when compared to feature films) and the grind of producing a weekly television program. However, period verisimilitude is not the only significant aspect of the set design. Equally important is the use of recurring sets to express the rigidity and repressiveness of early-1960s American society—as can be seen in the office of ad agency Sterling Cooper and the suburban home of Don and Betty Draper (both of which locales are replaced after season three).

The office set clearly reflects the power structure at the agency (figure 5.1). Secretaries are clustered together in a "pool," with their desks arrayed on an inflexible grid that mirrors the fluorescent lighting pattern above them. In this public space, they are at the mercy of the higher-ranking men of the office who make degrading, condescending comments about them, take their work for granted, and shamelessly ogle new hires, such as Peggy Olson in the first season. Except for the powerful and physically imposing office manager, Joan Harris, the women, including Peggy, have little control over their own space—unlike the men who move through it imperiously. The desk and lighting grids of the set design position them as if they were rats in an executive maze. Thus, the set design and the blocking of the actors' positions within it serve to dehumanize and contain the female characters.

The "mad men" are masters of their own spaces—afforded personal offices that physically separate them from the women. The higher up the corporate ladder, the more personalized these offices are, with agency head Bert Cooper's as the most distinctive. All who enter it are required, as per Asian custom, to remove their shoes, and then, once inside, they are confronted with Japanese erotic art and an abstract expressionist painting that is so mysterious and so massively expensive that employees sneak into Bert's office after-hours to stare at it in awe and incomprehension, while submissively holding their shoes in their hands.[1] Individual offices like Cooper's serve as spaces of authority, power, and privacy in contrast to the collective space of the secretarial pool.

Of course, Bert and the other men can move through the secretaries' space with impunity, as Pete Campbell does in figure 5.1. The social status and power attached to the private offices are made clear in Peggy's ascent from secretary to copywriter and full-fledged member of "Creative." Initially in the second season, she is forced to share space in what becomes the photocopy room, but eventually

FIGURE 5.1. The rigid power structure of the ad agency is visually manifested in the office spaces of *Mad Men*.

she gets her own office, and in the layout of the new Sterling Cooper Draper Pryce (SCDP) agency, she scores a prestigious one next to Don Draper's. However, the SCDP offices are not nearly as commodious as Sterling Cooper's. Contrasted with the wide-open space of Sterling Cooper's office, SCDP's diminished space visually echoes the diminished fortunes of the ad men as they struggle to start a new agency.

Mad Men's offices are not the only sets that repress and contain their characters. The homes and apartments of several characters serve important narrative functions as well. Central among these is the Draper home, the picture-perfect representation of affluent suburban existence, in which, however, the Draper family lives a less-than-perfect life. Indeed, with a disaffected daughter, a restless, adulterous mother, and a similarly adulterous father whose entire identity is also a fraudulent fabrication, the house is filled with melancholy and depression. In short, the idealized mise-en-scène of the Draper's home is frequently at odds with the despair of its inhabitants.

The pressures within their home finally result in divorce in the episode titled "The Grown-Ups," which was the next-to-last episode of season 3 and included events that coincided with President John F. Kennedy's assassination on November 22, 1963. The episode contains a breakfast scene with a set design that exemplifies *Mad Men*'s style of decor in that it could have been lifted from a 1950s sitcom or a *Good Housekeeping* article. Pine-paneled walls, avocado-green appliances, and an oh-so-modern (electric!) stovetop with a skillet of scrambled eggs are part of the mise-en-scène, as are 1963-appropriate props such as a glass milk bottle, a loaf of Pleasantville(!) white bread, and various knickknacks. Into this mise-en-scène are inserted the conventional suburban "housewife" in her housecoat, the conventional urban "businessman" in his suit, and a pair of conventional children in their pajamas. But the previous scene has been anything but conventional, as Betty angrily tells Don, "I want to scream at you, for ruining all of this [the suburban life and home]" (figure 5.2), and, saying that she doesn't love him anymore, demands a divorce. The next morning, as Don exits the house through the kitchen for what will be the last time, he and the children speak, but the "grown-ups" of the episode's title exchange no dialogue. The bitter contrast between the scene's pessimistic emotional tone and its optimistic morning-time mise-en-scène characterizes *Mad Men*'s critique of mid-century America's superficial normalcy and repression of the messier aspects of human behavior in the name of conformity to the dominant social order. The mess still exists, but it's been pushed below the surface. As the 1960s progressed, however, that repression became less and less tenable. *Mad Men* feeds on our understanding of what is to come in the latter part of the rebellious 1960s, looking backward and forward simultaneously.

The dressing of *Mad Men*'s sets with time-appropriate objects creates the viewing pleasure of picking out period details, like the rotary-dial phones and IBM Selectric typewriters shown in figure 5.1. Details from the 1960s are necessary to construct the program's general timeframe, but the program also uses objects in nuanced ways to anchor episodes to particular days in American history. "The Grown-Ups," for example, opens on an unspecified day in 1963. The year has been established earlier in the third season, and the characters complain about the lack of heat in the office, so we know it must be fall or winter. Then, in the background of a shot of Duck Phillips in a hotel room, we see the first of two televisions that are turned on and tuned to a live broadcast of *As the World Turns*. The sound is off and the television has less visual impact than the ostentatious glass lamps in the foreground of the room—although the shot has been carefully framed to include the TV screen. The very next scene shows us Pete and Harry Crane, the head of Sterling Cooper's media-buying department, in Harry's cluttered office. A television is on in the background here, too, its presence emphasized when Pete asks Harry, "Can you turn that off?" Harry replies, "Not really," though he does turn the volume down. As Pete and Harry talk, a CBS News bulletin comes on in the background, but they are oblivious to it. In his hotel room, Duck turns off the same bulletin when Peggy arrives for a lunchtime assignation. It's not until the Sterling Cooper employees crowd into Harry's office—one of the few with a television—that Harry and Pete realize what has happened and that we viewers begin to see the impact of the event on *Mad Men*'s fictional world.

FIGURE 5.2. *Mad Men*'s detailed mise-en-scène just barely contains the emotional upheaval below the surface of midcentury American "normalcy."

For the rest of the episode, televisions provide crucial narrative information and prompt characters to take, at times, extreme actions. Betty is particularly affected, with her confrontation of Don taking place beside a television tuned to funeral preparations (figure 5.2). Later, after seeing Lee Harvey Oswald killed on live television, she screams and exclaims, "What is going on?!" Motivated by the television violence she has witnessed and the collapse of her privileged world, she eventually leaves the house to meet Henry Francis, and he proposes to her. Thus, the television, an element of mise-en-scène, evolves in this episode from seemingly insignificant set dressing to major narrative catalyst, blending the personal crises of the characters with larger moments in American history.

The episode ends with one final comment on an object and its implicit reference to the assassination. After exiting the kitchen of his house in the scene discussed above, Don arrives at the empty and dark office, which is closed for a national day of mourning, and finds Peggy, who has come to escape her grieving roommate and relatives. The harsh, punishing florescent lights are off, and she is working by the natural light of a window, augmented by a desk lamp. Don examines the Aqua Net hairspray storyboards on her desk, one of which contains a high-angle view of four individuals in an open convertible (figure 5.3). Before he can offer an opinion, she anticipates his criticism: "It doesn't shoot until after Thanksgiving. We'll be okay." But Don authoritatively dismisses this delusion by shaking his head. The scene is rather elliptical unless the viewer is able to place

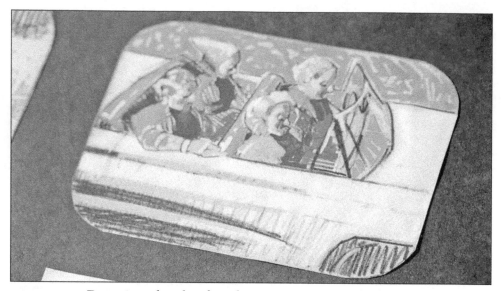

FIGURE 5.3. Don nixes the plan for a hairspray commercial after seeing a storyboard that evokes widely circulated photos of the convertible in which President Kennedy was shot.

this storyboard image within the iconography of 1963 and recognize how much it resembles widely circulated high-angle photos of the presidential convertible limousine in which Kennedy was shot (figure 5.4). Since none of those photos is shown in the episode, only viewers who associate the storyboard imagery with the visual vocabulary of 1963 will understand Don and Peggy's motivation for considering redoing the storyboard.

This short scene also illuminates *Mad Men*'s central preoccupation. It is a program about consumer products and the imagery attached to them through advertising. Moreover, *Mad Men* is obsessed with objects and their representation, and—by extension—with humans and their representations. Just as Don, who was born Richard "Dick" Whitman, has *styled* himself as "Don Draper," so has Don mastered the ability to style products in a way that satisfies his clients and increases their revenue. One could even say that Don is a designer of his own mise-en-scène (his clothing, hair style, walk, the spaces in which he chooses to live and work, and so on), but, of course, Weiner and his crew and cast have actually constructed the mise-en-scène for both Draper and *Mad Men*.

The way that *Mad Men* is filmed and cut is distinctive, but unlike the show's mise-en-scène, its cinematography and editing do not mimic 1960s television. "The Grown-Ups" calls attention to this difference by giving glimpses of live, black-and-white television from 1963: *Mad Men* clearly does not look anything

FIGURE 5.4. *Mad Men* relies on the viewer's associations with this photograph of the Kennedy motorcade.

like *As the World Turns*. Rather, it uses a mode of production associated with contemporary high-budget, primetime dramas (e.g., *Lost, The Sopranos*, and the *CSI* programs) and with theatrical films. This single-camera mode of production allows for more precise visual control than is possible in the multiple-camera mode of production that was used by *As the World Turns* throughout its long run. That precision is evident in the final shot of "The Grown-Ups," where cinematography is used both to build a mood and develop characterization. After saying goodnight to Peggy in the main Sterling Cooper office, Don enters his own private office and hangs up his hat while the camera shoots him through the doorway. The camera then arcs slightly to the left to reveal a liquor cabinet as Don walks into the room. Not bothering to remove his coat, Don reaches for a bottle and begins mixing a drink (figure 5.5). The scene then cuts to black and the end credits roll while Skeeter Davis is heard singing "The End of the World": "Don't they know it's the end of the world 'cause you don't love me anymore?"

Episode director Barbet Schroeder and episode director of photography Christopher Manley use framing and camera angle to signify Don's isolation. Keeping the camera outside the room and surrounding Don with the frosted-window walls of the doorway frame have the effect of both emphasizing his remoteness and distancing us from him. As shown above in figures 5.1 and 5.2, *Mad Men* often shoots from a low camera angle that incorporates the ceiling in the frame.

This shot is just below Don's eye-level, looking slightly up at him, which brings the ceiling into the top of the frame, blocking it off. The low-key lighting of the office—an aspect of mise-en-scène—works with the framing to blend Don into the darkness. In many TV programs and films, low angles emphasize the size and bulk and even heroic nature of a person or object, but in *Mad Men* the low angles more often make the ceiling close in on the characters, accentuating the repressiveness of their work and home spaces. In short, this scene's cinematography and mise-en-scène collaborate to generate an atmosphere of entrapment, despair, and alienation.

Mad Men's implementation of the single-camera mode of production allows for editing patterns that would be difficult or impossible in the multiple-camera mode used by soap operas. A breakdown of the kitchen scene previously described in which Don and Betty exchange no words (posted on criticalcommons .org) illustrates this point, and illuminates the narrative significance of characters looking at other characters.

As edited by Tom Wilson, the scene begins in the hallway as Don comes downstairs and walks through the dining room to the kitchen door. There, he pauses, unseen by his family. We see a point-of-view shot, over his shoulder into the kitchen. The next shot is a reverse angle from inside the kitchen, but not from anyone's point of view as he is still unobserved. We return to Don's point-of-view shot as he enters the kitchen and announces his presence: "Good morning." The children respond, but Betty pointedly does not. We cut to *her* point of view of Don even though she is looking down at the stove and not at him. The camera stays behind her, panning and tracking with Don as he crosses the room. During this short walk, he looks directly at her, but she does not return his gaze. The camera movement comes to a rest from nobody's point of view, showing Betty, Don, and the kids; she looks straight ahead, and he and the children look at each other. The camera stays objective for four medium shots, with the fourth shot offering a subtle bit of camerawork. Bobby looks at Sally, and when she turns around to look at Betty, the camera pulls focus from him to her—a distance of just a few feet. In terms of narrative motivation and the emotional rhythm of the scene, Sally needs to be sharply in focus as it is her look that motivates the next cut to Betty in a low-angle subjective shot where she looks back toward Sally and the camera. The scene concludes with a camera angle very close to the earlier one from Don's point of view, showing the entire kitchen as he sends one more unreturned look in Betty's direction before leaving.

This close examination of the ordering and framing of shots in the kitchen scene shows how important characters' looks—that is, whom they look at rather than how they look to others—are to this episode, the program, and television drama in general. And this dance of looks is achieved largely through editing,

FIGURE 5.5. Cinematography is used throughout *Mad Men* to build mood and add to characterization rather than to mimic the visual style of the multi-camera dramas of the day.

as in the eye-line match cut from Sally to Betty. Multiple-camera programs can also be fundamentally about looks, but this single-camera scene contains shots that would be too time-consuming or troublesome to capture during a multiple-camera shoot. Specifically, the camera has been moved to several positions well inside a four-walled set, showing us the Draper kitchen from virtually every angle. Multiple-camera shows, with their three-walled sets, cannot bring the camera as close to the characters' perspectives as *Mad Men* does. A seemingly simple shot such as the low-angle, medium close-up of Betty with a camera positioned deep inside the set would be nearly impossible to achieve in a multiple-camera production, whether that production be *As the World Turns* in 1963 or a twenty-first-century multiple-camera program such as *Two and a Half Men*.

Much like Douglas Sirk's melodramas in the 1950s, *Mad Men* makes sophisticated use of visual style—mise-en-scène, cinematography, and editing—to mount a critique of American consumer culture. The mise-en-scène of "The Grown-Ups," in particular, is about the significance of objects and about characters gazing at them and at each other. Built around looks at television sets, the episode provides an implicit commentary upon the medium's increasing social significance in the 1960s and the terrors that it would bring into our living rooms. Betty's horrified gaze as she watches the killing of Oswald from her suburban couch can be extrapolated to the viewing of televised violence of the Vietnam War and the assassinations to come in the later 1960s. On a personal level, the emotional and narrative power of looks—both returned and unreturned—is featured repeatedly in *Mad Men*. And its mode of production allows the program's crew to maximize that power through creative cinematography and editing. The sleek look of *Mad Men* and its reproduction of 1960s modernity might initially draw us to the program, but it is the characters' looks at one another that weave the emotional fabric of its stories. By dissecting the program's style, we can better understand *Mad Men*'s affective impact and its astute visual critique of mid-century America.

FURTHER READING

Bordwell, David, and Kristin Thompson. *Film Art: An Introduction.* 12th ed. New York: McGraw-Hill, 2019.

Butler, Jeremy G. *Television Style.* New York: Routledge, 2010.

Edgerton, Gary R. *Mad Men: Dream Come True TV.* London: Tauris, 2010.

NOTES

1. The Japanese woodcut is Hokusai's *The Dream of the Fisherman's Wife*, and the abstract painting is an untitled one by Mark Rothko.

6

Nip/Tuck
Popular Music

Abstract: Most analyses of television programs focus on a program's visual and narrative construction but neglect the vital element of sound that is crucial to any show's style and meaning. Ben Aslinger listens closely to the use of music in the FX series *Nip/Tuck*, exploring how it helps shape the program's aesthetics and cultural representations.

Nip/Tuck's pilot episode featured an extended sequence in which The Rolling Stones' "Paint It Black" plays as Sean McNamara and Christian Troy perform a facial reconstruction on a man who they find out later is a child molester trying to mask his identity. Most reviewers of the pilot drew attention to the importance of popular music to the program's style, noting "the eerie use of The Rolling Stones' 'Paint it Black' to dramatize a facial reconstruction even before mentioning the plot or the performances."[1] *Nip/Tuck*'s emphasis on surgery, style, and music was even reinforced in promotional materials, most notably the flash-based "Can you cut like a rock star?" game on the FX website. The uses of popular music in *Nip/Tuck* distinguish the series from older medical dramas such as *Dr. Kildare* and more recent series such as *ER*, as well as pointing to the ways that industrial imperatives surrounding popular music licensing affect the formal properties of contemporary television texts.

Some critics have argued that the tracks used in *Nip/Tuck* are perfect sonic illustrations of the skin-deep, youth-obsessed, superficial Miami culture chronicled by the program. However, television scholars should be skeptical of critical commentaries that sum up popular music licensing and scoring practices in broad strokes but fail to pay sufficient attention to specific production practices. While such trade and popular press pieces might work to get at a superficial sense of a show's use of music, they fail to address the complex ways that popular music

FIGURE 6.1. The fundamental link between music and *Nip/Tuck*'s "edgy" style was reinforced in promotional materials such as this game on the show's website.

interacts with visual elements to convey meanings, and the multiple ways that producers and music supervisors use licenses to strategically add weight to key plot points, visual sequences, and dialogue exchanges.

Feminist media scholars have analyzed the ways that *Nip/Tuck* works to define beauty in dominant terms that privilege whiteness and an unattainable size and shape.[2] These scholars have analyzed gender performances in *Nip/Tuck* and makeover shows that enlist the medical gaze in order to create aspirational narratives and police beauty standards; however, analyses of television textuality must take into account not just visual elements and scriptwriting practices, but also the ways that television sound is constructed for meaning-making effects. By addressing the popular music soundtrack in *Nip/Tuck*, I add to previous analyses centering on the visual culture of the program and further explore how program producers imagined surgical and embodied aesthetics in the series. Popular music tracks work in *Nip/Tuck* to initiate surgical sequences, to "soften" surgical sequences by aestheticizing the penetration of the body, and to bridge *Nip/Tuck*'s focus on appearance with psychological interiority and character identifications. In order to connect industrial imperatives to textual outcomes, I begin by discussing how executive producer Ryan Murphy's collaboration with music supervisor P. J. Bloom created strategies for deploying popular music tracks. I then draw on existing scholarly work on the soundtrack in order to analyze how specific examples of licensing work to complicate viewer perceptions of *Nip/Tuck*'s narrative and diegesis (the storyworld it creates and inhabits).

Critical to establishing *Nip/Tuck*'s "edge" was the way the series used popular music and editing strategies to turn surgeries into televisual spectacles.[3] Murphy had previously produced *Popular* for The WB, a network that was influential in establishing the importance of popular music to 1990s definitions of "quality" production practices and strategies for targeting niche demographics. By drafting P. J. Bloom as the series music supervisor, Murphy worked to make the series edgy and to emphasize the meaning-making capacity of the popular music soundtrack.[4]

According to Bloom, music supervision typically abides by certain norms and conventions that are defined by the producer and are specific to a particular series. Given the timeline needed to secure music licenses, prepare temp tracks, and create a final, polished soundtrack, a clear sonic palette expedites decision-making and the production process.

Bloom argued that setting up the "sonic fingerprint" and "musical tone" for the series was one of the strategies that guided his work as a music supervisor.[5] "Most of the time, we try to use songs that speak lyrically to the procedures being conducted in the operating room," he said. "On occasion, we'll use music that speaks to the characters' individual tastes; but most often the songs are a satirical look at whatever cosmetic procedure the patient is undergoing."[6]

According to Bloom, two major strategies for *Nip/Tuck* were to use "classic" rock tunes for ironic and/or satirical effect and to use "cool" newer tunes (mainly electronic music) to depict the superficial, slick world of South Beach and certain surgeries. Murphy and Bloom also repurposed songs that older audiences would remember from their original contexts and that could be viewed during the burgeoning 1970s and 1980s nostalgia trend by audiences too young to remember their original radio and MTV airplay. The series' Miami location and the use of classic rock and pop songs may have reminded older viewers of the strategic deployment in *Miami Vice* of popular songs such as Phil Collins's "In the Air Tonight," but *Nip/Tuck* depicted a much grittier Miami than the earlier "big three" network series, which was produced during the decline of the classic network system, whereas *Nip/Tuck* was produced during what Amanda Lotz calls the transition to a "post-network era."[7]

Bloom and Murphy decided to use the Bang Olufsen stereo in the operating room as a character of sorts in the series, and the music that the stereo plays is an important part of most surgical sequences.[8] These sequences often begin with either anesthesiologist Liz Cruz or one of the nurses waving a gloved hand in front of the device in order to activate it and then zoom in on a spinning CD that is also the sync point for the start of the master recording. In effect, the program's surgical sequences are set in motion by powering up audio technologies.

In addressing the textual and stylistic importance of highlighting the selection of music and the handling of listening technologies on the screen, Ken Garner

FIGURE 6.2.
Activation of the
Bang Olufsen ste-
reo in the operating
room draws atten-
tion to the series' use
of popular music to
help turn surgical
sequences into televi-
sual spectacles.

argues that Quentin Tarantino's films, especially *Reservoir Dogs, Pulp Fiction*, and *Jackie Brown*, devote screen-time to the act of musical selection in ways that heighten the meaning of the music played, linking the process of playing music more directly to on-screen actions, character identifications, and narrative incidents.[9] Extending Garner's point to television style in *Nip/Tuck*, we can see Murphy and Bloom employing the Bang Olufsen stereo to call attention to the visual and sound styles of each particular surgery. For viewers who might otherwise ignore the popular music soundtrack or miss its textual significations in other parts of the episode, the visual representation of the process of musical selection here emphasizes the role of popular music in establishing surgical aesthetics by incorporating audio technology in the diegesis. We pay more attention to the music because we see the moment that Garner describes, the particular circumstances in which music is played, and the way that music is activated; thus, we are visually primed to think about what we will hear during the surgical sequence. Activating the stereo sets the plastic surgery in motion and prepares viewers for shots of scalpels and medical technologies penetrating the surface of the body.

The sounds that emanate from the Bang Olufsen stereo directly affect our understanding of narrative and embodiment. The deployment of songs creates a critical commentary on what racialized, classed, and gendered bodies matter most in the cityscape of Miami, twists the meanings of pop and rock tunes, and calls attention to the construction of both the on-screen bodies and the televisual spectacle. In the episode "Montana/Sassy/Justice," Rod Stewart's "Hot Legs" plays during a surgery on a woman's "cankles." In the second season premiere, "Erica Naughton," the Bang Olufsen stereo plays Billy Idol's "Eyes Without a Face" during a facial reconstruction on Libby Zucker to repair some of the physical damage from a gunshot wound. These songs fit part of the "sonic fingerprint" of the series in that they use older songs for ironic/satirical effect; however, these songs may also work to treat surgical procedures as grotesque. The often upbeat songs, guitar riffs, and rock production aesthetic may render these sequences more disturbing and alienating for the viewer, as upbeat popular music achieves a contrapuntal quality when juxtaposed with the images.

Popular music gains some of its representational power from the lyrical allusion to embodiment, but this is not the only way that popular music affects meaning in the series. Popular songs that have been previously featured in high-profile soundtracks carry their previous significations into *Nip/Tuck*. For instance, during the third season premiere, "Momma Boone," "Stuck in the Middle with You" plays in the McNamara/Troy operating room as Sean performs a silicone implant replacement surgery. Sean takes over five hours to remove all the leaking silicone from just one breast and then has to put in a new implant before he can even move on to the other breast. Silicone sticks to his surgical gloves, forcing him to stop, put on new gloves, and continue to work. This sequence, with its disturbing visuals, encourages the viewer to link plastic surgery with mutilation. The song's prior usage in Quentin Tarantino's *Reservoir Dogs* further encourages this reading as Tarantino famously used the song to highlight a scene where one protagonist tortures a captured cop and cuts off the cop's ear. Thus, Murphy and Bloom draw not only on the 1970s classic rock hit, but also on intertextual allusions linking the song to forms of mutilation in the minds of many of *Nip/Tuck*'s audience members. Yet, even without knowledge of the intertextuality at work here, audience members are likely to be disturbed by the juxtaposition of the singer's throaty voice, danceable guitar rhythms, and early 1970s folk/rock sound with the visual track of the episode and be prompted to consider whether plastic surgeons are healers or carvers. This sequence can also be seen as setting up one of the central themes of the season, which features a serial killer called the Carver and openly questions what value should be attached to plastic surgeons and their craft.

The song lyrics themselves often remind us that we are watching bodies being opened and reconstructed on-screen. The use of "Poison Arrow" by the British New Wave 1980s band ABC in the episode "Antonia Ramos" further illustrates the role that lyrics in classic songs play in emphasizing the embodied aesthetics of surgery. Featured prominently in the first four minutes of the episode, the non-diegetic song plays as Sean and Christian are called to a hotel room on the seedy side of Miami to take care of a woman (Antonia Ramos) whose breast implants are leaking heroin. Ramos had agreed to smuggle heroin for drug lord Escobar Gallardo in exchange for a contract with what turns out to be a nonexistent Miami modeling agency. The lyrics of ABC's New Wave pop song are about romantic love and the potential for partners to hurt each other with the "poison arrow" of words. On one level, the placement of this song works to connect emotional and physical pain. For Antonia Ramos, the "poison arrow" is both a physical and a psychological one—surgery to have heroin-filled implants placed in her breast, unexpected complications that lead to her near death and a long recovery, surgery to have the implants removed, and imminent deportation once it is discovered that she has no work visa and the modeling agency doesn't exist. To sum up the textual role of "Poison Arrow" as ironic/satirical is to ignore the song's larger role in the narrative, where it further highlights the female, poor, and Latina bodies that "count" less in the Miami cityscape. While such bodies are marginalized within the real Miami, in *Nip/Tuck* they are also used as "exotic" plot points and "disposable" one-off characters in a series largely about the anxieties of middle-aged white heterosexual professionals.

Murphy and Bloom also make musical choices that take advantage of lyrical allusions and reward insider musical knowledge. Using music that is well known to target demographics deepens narrative comprehension for specific audiences and works to treat embodiment and plastic surgery as politically and socially contested terms within the series. In "Sophia Lopez, Part II," for example, the title of Tori Amos's "A Sorta Fairytale" is itself resonant, but Murphy and Bloom's choice of this song also draws on Amos's star positioning and her politicized fanbase. The music of Tori Amos, a recording artist with a huge gay, lesbian, and feminist audience who has done active political work for gender and sexual rights, is used to highlight Lopez's struggle for belonging and comfort in her own body. In the episode, Sophia Lopez, a recurring character, is undergoing gender reassignment surgery. Earlier in the season, Sophia had helped to expose Sean's mentor, who operated an unsafe and unsanitary practice and who had butchered members of the Miami transgender community. When Sophia expressed her misgivings about helping Sean try to shut down his mentor—namely, that for her and other working-class men and women this surgeon was their only option—Sean agreed to perform the rest of Lopez's surgeries pro bono.

Before the song begins, an operating room controversy erupts when a nurse tells Sean that Sophia has smuggled in something underneath her gown. Sophia confesses, revealing a picture of her son Raymond, and Sean tells the nurse to wrap the framed picture in a sterile bag and let Sophia hold it in the surgery. As Lopez counts back from ten while Liz administers the anesthesia, "A Sorta Fairytale" begins playing.

This sequence exhibits one common pattern of music licensing in contemporary television drama, where an extended song clip accompanies a montage to close the episode. Thus, while Amos's "A Sorta Fairytale" may be perceived as diegetic music, occurring within the fictional world of the program (although we don't always see the stereo being turned on in every surgery scene), the song becomes part of the nondiegetic soundtrack once we leave the operating room and we see Sean and Christian in their homes. In the operating room, Amos's song calls attention to the politically contested nature of embodiment. The content of the song, about an emotional breakup, is far from the romantic fairytale implied by the song title and refrain. Amos's performance on the Bosendorfer piano and backup musicians' performances on acoustic and electric guitar, bass, and drums work to create a kind of dreamy soundscape. While the refrain invokes Lopez's fantasy of social acceptance, the repetition of the lyrical refrain, "a sorta fairytale," along with the plaintive to wistful to morose quality of Amos's vocals call attention to the fact that even after this surgery, Sophia Lopez will have to fight for social acceptance and for bodies like hers to be valued in the public sphere.

The song, together with the visuals—the framed picture of the patient's son, our previous knowledge of Lopez as a recurring character in the series—highlight the economic, psychological, and physical struggles faced by transgender men and women, and calls attention to the precarious and ambivalent relationship transgender patients have historically had with the medical system.[10] Amos's star text and the lyrics of the song encourage audiences to consider Lopez's pursuit of gender reassignment surgery as a brave act and to consider whether Lopez will ever achieve social acceptance, what value will be placed on bodies like hers, or if, for contemporary America, Lopez's dream of equality is still "a sorta fairytale." My argument here is not that most audience members will extract this meaning from the sequence; rather, it is that music supervisors and executive producers can draw on lyrical allusions and discourses of musical meaning that are tied up in genre or artist/performer identity to create evocative effects for particular groups of the audience.

Occasionally, Murphy and Bloom decide to use classical music or no music to call attention to difficult and experimental surgeries in the series—surgeries that often fail. These exceptions bear out the rule that most of the music in the program is popular recorded music from the latter half of the twentieth century and highlight the ways that nonmusical forms of sound can be used for narrative and stylistic effect. Two examples of classical music include the surgery to separate Siamese twins attached at the head that ends in both girls dying on the table ("Rose and Raven Rosenberg") and the face transplant surgery on Hannah Tedesco ("Hannah Tedesco"). After Hannah's body rejects the transplant later in the episode and the transplant must be removed from the teen girl's face, Liz says, "I can't find any music that feels appropriate right now." This marks one of the few times the producers chose not to use music of any kind and instead incorporated the diegetic sounds of the operating room, particularly the respirator and the heart monitor, over flashes of the surgical sequence. This notable exception to the program's sonic style illustrates that while popular music licensing is the general trend in the program, producers do on occasion deviate in order to try something different. These deviations also illustrate that the sounds and images in all surgical sequences are carefully planned and that the musical choices in these sequences have much to tell us about the ways that *Nip/Tuck* constructs the embodied aesthetics of surgery.

The use of diegetic nonmusical sound in the surgery to remove the face transplant stands in stark contrast to most surgical sequences, where the volume of direct diegetic sounds is either lowered or muted. Popular music tracks played through the Bang Olufsen stereo are diegetically motivated, but as film music scholars Claudia Gorbman and Robynn J. Stilwell argue, music often crosses back and forth between the diegetic and the nondiegetic.[11] While music in the McNamara/Troy operating room is diegetically motivated, the music video–style editing and shot scale choices call attention to the camera shutter and the construction of particular shots as well as the disjunction between the passage of musical time and narrative time. Diegetic music is often viewed as more organic, as it belongs to the storyworld and the characters; in contrast, the nondiegetic score is sometimes interpreted as manipulative, as the nondiegetic score is used to establish preferred readings of on-screen action for the audience. In *Nip/Tuck*, thinking of the music as traversing the diegetic/nondiegetic boundary raises questions about how the sounds and images on-screen are being manipulated and brings into focus the tensions between organic bodies and bodies disciplined by plastic surgery. To see music cross the diegetic/nondiegetic boundary during surgery raises the question of what constitutes the organic, "real" body. That music in the series seems to cross this boundary as surgery ensues draws greater attention to the physical boundary crossing of the scalpel penetrating flesh.

By placing music strategically in surgical scenes, Murphy and Bloom use sound to think through the representation and politics of plastic surgery. *Nip/Tuck* provides an excellent example of how contemporary television producers and music supervisors craft musical sounds to fit a series and deploy popular music tracks for specific narrative effects. Series such as *Mad Men* or *The O.C.* may use popular music tracks to create a sense of a historical era or to appeal to a demographic market, but the shape and sound that music licensing takes depend on production norms and narratives. Television criticism must wrestle with the industrial norms and cultural connotations of licensed music to more fully understand how licensed tracks mobilize meaning.

FURTHER READING

Altman, Rick. "Television/Sound." In *Studies in Entertainment: Critical Approaches to Mass Culture*, edited by Tania Modleski. Bloomington: Indiana University Press, 1986.
Chion, Michel. *Audio-Vision*. Translated by Claudia Gorbman. New York: Columbia University Press, 1994.

Cook, Nicholas. *Analysing Musical Multimedia*. Oxford, UK: Clarendon Press, 1998.

Donnelly, K. J. *The Spectre of Sound: Music in Film and Television*. London: BFI, 2005.

Frith, Simon. "Look! Hear! The Uneasy Relationship of Music and Television." *Popular Music* 21 (2002): 277–90.

NOTES

1. Tom Lowry, "Finding Nirvana in a Music Catalog," *BusinessWeek*, October 2, 2006.
2. Kim Akass and Janet McCabe, "A Perfect Lie: Visual (Dis)Pleasures and Policing Femininity in *Nip/Tuck*," in *Makeover Television: Realities Remodeled*, ed. Dana Heller (London: Tauris, 2007).
3. Matthew Gilbert, "*Nip/Tuck* Is Not Afraid to Look the Ugly in the Eye; *Nip/Tuck* Diagnoses the Human Condition," *Boston Globe*, September 5, 2004.
4. P. J. Bloom, www.myspace.com/pjbloom.
5. "Exclusive Q&A with P. J. Bloom," www.niptuckforum.com.
6. "Exclusive: *Nip/Tuck* Music Supervisor P. J. Bloom Interview," January 11, 2008, http://rcrdlbl.com.
7. Amanda Lotz, *The Television Will Be Revolutionized* (New York: New York University Press, 2007).
8. "Exclusive: *Nip/Tuck* Music Supervisor P. J. Bloom Interview."
9. Ken Garner, "Would You Like to Hear Some Music?' Music In-and-Out-of-Control in the Films of Quentin Tarantino," *Film Music: Critical Approaches*, ed. K. J. Donnelly (New York: Continuum, 2001), 189.
10. Joanne Jay Meyerowitz, *How Sex Changed: A History of Transsexuality in the United States* (Cambridge, MA: Harvard University Press, 2002).
11. Claudia Gorbman, *Unheard Melodies: Narrative Film Music* (Bloomington: Indiana University Press, 1987); Robynn J. Stilwell, "The Fantastical Gap between Diegetic and Nondiegetic," in *Beyond the Soundtrack*, ed. Daniel Goldmark, Lawrence Kramer, and Richard Leppert (Berkeley: University of California Press, 2007).

7

One Life to Live
Soap Opera Storytelling

ABIGAIL DE KOSNIK

Abstract: Few genres are as associated with the television medium as the soap opera, which has populated daytime schedules for decades, often with the same shows running for more than the lifetimes of their characters. Abigail De Kosnik provides a long-term view of *One Life to Live* and the lifelong story of one character to highlight the unique narrative possibilities of soap operas and call attention to what might be lost if the genre continues to disappear from television.

In 2012, only four U.S. daytime dramas, or soap operas, remained in production, while as recently as 1999, twelve soap operas were broadcast daily. The last decade has witnessed a wave of cancellations of soaps, most of which enjoyed tremendous longevity, especially in comparison to primetime TV programs, which rarely reach a tenth season. In recent years, four of the most venerable soaps were terminated: *Guiding Light* ended after seventy-two years of continuous broadcast (fifteen years on the radio and fifty-seven years on television); *As the World Turns* concluded after fifty-four years; *All My Children* ran for forty-one years before its last episode aired; and *One Life to Live* was forty-four years old by its final broadcast. With four soap operas still airing daily on broadcast television (as of this writing in 2012), and soap-like genres growing in popularity outside the United States, the long-running serial television drama is not yet obsolete.

However, the cluster of recent forced finales indicates that U.S. television networks no longer believe that soaps are worth significant investment. The years 2009–2012 have been a "twilight" period for the American soap opera, with the genre's ranks diminishing swiftly and audiences beginning to accept that soaps, which had always presented themselves as "worlds without end," are headed for extinction. It is possible, even likely, that all U.S. daytime drama production will shut down in the next ten to twenty years.

Therefore, now may be an appropriate time to reflect on what soaps have been uniquely able to present in their extended runs—namely, *lifelong stories*, or stories that span some characters' entire lives. Even though soaps have large ensemble casts, and regular soap viewers follow the plot arcs of dozens of characters, only a handful of characters on each daytime drama have "lived" their entire lives on the show. These characters, in most cases played continuously by one actor, form the core of their respective soap operas, serving as touchstones for all other characters and the fulcrums for many major storylines. On *All My Children*, model-turned-mogul Erica Kane was the most prominent lifelong character; on *One Life to Live*, it was the aristocratic-but-tortured Victoria (Viki) Lord; *Guiding Light*'s most prominent lifelong character was probably attorney Tom Hughes. Erica and Viki were integral to their respective shows from the premieres, and Tom was born five years after the show's debut, but other lifelong characters appeared on their soaps at much later points in the shows' runs, such as *General Hospital*'s Robin Scorpio and Lucky Spencer, *Days of Our Lives*' Hope Williams Brady, and *Guiding Light*'s Lily Walsh Snyder. What defines lifelong characters is that they are featured on their shows for decades, so that many viewers have a sense of witnessing their entire lifetimes, or a very large portion it. Most of the aforementioned characters started as children or teens on their shows, so viewers feel as if they watched those characters "grow up," or, if they started watching soaps at an early age, that they grew up with the characters. Different generations of soap viewers may attach to different generations of soap characters, and people may miss out on several years of characters' lives if they stop watching soaps for a period of time and then resume regular viewing, but the intergenerational community of soap fans is available to fill in knowledge gaps. Oral histories relayed from fan to fan, as well as elaborate character histories published in book format and online, make it possible for a soap fan to follow, or retrospectively learn about, every major event in a soap character's life.

This essay focuses on the lifelong story of Viki Lord, the central character of ABC's *One Life to Live*. Viki's expansive narrative offers clear examples of three key elements of soap opera lifelong storytelling: (1) the *deep seed and long reveal*, (2) *continual reverberation*, and (3) *real-life temporality*. Each storytelling technique, as illustrated with examples from Viki's fictional life, highlights the unique narrative power and possibilities of the soap opera genre. Soap operas are best known for sudden and improbable plot twists, but not all revelations on soaps seemingly come from nowhere. Some "reveals" come after years of story-building and character development. I use the phrase "deep seed and long reveal" to refer to such plot arcs. Soaps have the ability to hint at plot points for decades, heightening tension around certain secrets or hidden aspects of characters' lives that the audience knows about, but that the characters are unaware of until at some point; often many years after a narrative arc begins, the secret explodes in a ferocious climax with severe narrative ramifications. On *One Life to Live*, the unveiling of the root cause of Viki Lord's psychological illness was the show's most notable deep seed and long reveal.

Viki was shown to suffer from Dissociative Identity Disorder (DID) from *One Life*'s start in 1968. Viki's most dominant "alter," the alternate personality that emerged and overtook Viki's life most often throughout the show's run, was called Niki Smith. Viki's father, millionaire newspaper magnate, Victor Lord, raised Viki strictly, with high expectations, as she was the heir to his fortune and his business empire. As a result, Viki grew up to be elegant, well-spoken, and incredibly responsible in all matters; in contrast, her alternate personality, Niki, was a loud-mouthed, manipulative, promiscuous party girl. Each time Niki surfaced, she wreaked havoc, and each time, Viki successfully suppressed her and repaired the social damage Niki had done. What caused Viki to develop such a destructive alter?

In the late 1960s, Viki uncovered a repressed memory of her mother accidentally falling down a staircase to her death. Viki believed that the trauma of witnessing this horrible event led her psyche to create "Niki." But in the 1990s, Victor Lord's widow and Viki's enemy, Dorian Lord, began to insinuate that the cause of Viki's DID lay in other childhood experiences involving her father, Victor, the memories of which lay buried in Viki's subconscious mind. For almost thirty years, *One Life to Live* viewers had seen Viki refer periodically to her domineering father's rigid expectations and impossibly high standards as sources of psychological pain. During those decades, the audience watched dozens of moments when Viki told stories about, or simply made mention of, Victor Lord, as well as numerous flashback scenes of a young Viki interacting with her father. Over this extended period of time, the viewer gathered many impressions of Viki's relationship with Victor, such as the fact that Victor was obsessed with his daughter, and had an unhealthy need to exercise complete control over every facet of Viki's life. Therefore, when Dorian began to imply that Viki was repressing memories about her father that led to her developing multiple personalities, most viewers heard Dorian's veiled warnings as confirmation of what they already suspected: that Victor had sexually abused Victoria.

In 1995, Dorian finally revealed the truth about Victor's having abused Viki during her childhood, and the knowledge shook Viki to her core. But for the longtime viewer, this reveal was an extraordinary reward for having faithfully followed *One Life to Live* for as many as twenty-seven years. For the possibility that Victor had been an abusive monster to Viki had been planted in the minds of audience members in the 1960s, and that seed of suspicion about Victor grew with every flashback that Viki had about her father, all through the 1970s and 1980s, until in the 1990s, the seed finally reached fruition as spoken dialogue between Dorian and Viki. As Dorian spoke the terrible secret of Viki's early years aloud, the long-time viewer likely thought, "I knew it all along! I always thought that's what must have happened to Viki."

Only long-running soaps can plant such a deep seed of plot, and then have it culminate in a satisfying reveal after such an attenuated length of time. Given the frequent changes in soap staff members, a long-arc plot might be initiated by one head writer or executive producer and then developed by entirely different sets of writers/producers. *One Life*'s decision to "reveal" Viki's childhood sexual abuse in the 1990s may have been motivated by writers of that time picking up on obvious plot threads left behind by earlier writers, or by fans' ongoing speculation about the origins of Viki's DID, or by an increasing awareness in American society of incest and the psychological disorders that often result. Whether the deep plot seed of Viki's victimization was intended from the start or not, it struck loyal viewers as faithful to what they knew of Viki's character and her past. A deep seed and long reveal need not have any "authorial" intent behind it, but the reveal must accord with viewers' recollection of characters' histories in order to ring true.

The multiple authoring of soap operas does not always culminate in a powerful plot twist that honors characters' histories while delivering fresh, shockingly dramatic scenes to viewers—some deep seeds and long reveals are better executed than others. But soaps accomplish this combination of history and surprise far more often than comic book reboots or James Bond recastings. Comics, comic-based cartoons and films, and the Bond movies are multiple-authored texts that depict the same moments in key characters' lives over and over (a superhero's origins, his early discovery of his powers, etc.), and *only* depict a limited range of years for characters (typically, the years when they are at their peak physical condition). No matter how long these male-oriented narratives remain a part of the popular cultural landscape, they rarely allow their core characters to substantially age, or to undergo the significant psychological and emotional crises that accompany different stages of life—by their emphasis on repetition rather than character growth, they lack the kind of narrative journey that *One Life to Live* writers were able to give viewers who followed Viki's advancement from youth into middle age.

Of course Viki's struggle with her mental illness did not end when she discovered its traumatic origins. Lifelong stories on soaps never conclude; as soon as a character resolves one long-running plot conflict, other related issues arise. I call this rippling narrative style "continual reverberation." On *One Life to Live*, after having lived for years with DID and repeatedly suffering the dire consequences of the devious actions of her red-headed alter, Niki Smith, Viki made a shocking discovery: her beloved daughter, Jessica, had actually been born a twin, and the twin had been kidnapped from the hospital before Viki even knew of her existence. The secret twin, Natalie, suddenly showed up in Llanview (the fictional Pennsylvania town where *One Life to Live* takes place) in 2001, and was an entirely different creature than the angelic Jessica. Jessica was blonde, and Natalie was a red-head. Jessica was a kind, polite, good-hearted young woman, and Natalie was a brash, self-centered, tough-talking hoyden. Jessica looked and sounded very much like her mother, Viki—but Natalie looked and sounded almost exactly like Viki's alter, Niki. Shortly after Natalie's appearance in Llanview, Natalie's claims to being Viki's biological child led Jessica to doubt that she was even related to Viki (Natalie suggested that perhaps she and Jessica had been switched at birth), and Viki attempted to reassure Jessica (and herself) that Jessica was indeed her child by standing beside Jessica in front of a mirror and forcing Jessica to look at the two of them, side by side. "You are my child!" said Viki. "Do you see how much you look like me?" Just at that moment, Natalie entered the room and paused behind Viki and Jessica, and in the mirror reflection of all three of them, Jessica did look very much like Viki, but Natalie's resemblance to Viki was equally strong.

Although Viki was initially loath to believe that rude, loud Natalie was as much her biological child as sweet, calm Jessica, *One Life*'s viewers recognized Natalie's significance right away. Natalie embodied the side of Viki that Viki could never bring herself to accept: the Niki side. For the progression of Viki's lifelong story, it was important that she be confronted with the physical incarnation, in two distinct bodies that were born of her body, of the "twin" aspects of her psyche. Jessica was a young Viki, but Natalie was a young Niki, and the girls' coexistence in Viki's life forced Viki to acknowledge and appreciate the two very different women as "hers."

The Jessica/Natalie story of the 2000s was not just any "evil twin" plotline, endemic to daytime dramas since the genre's beginnings; it held special resonance for viewers of *One Life to Live* because it provided a physical manifestation of the internal war that had been raging inside of Viki for so long. The Jessica/Natalie plot was a continuation of the Viki/Niki arc that spanned the entire duration of the soap's history. And although Jessica and Natalie became devoted to one another despite their differences, united in a way that Viki could never herself manage to unite the two halves of her personality, the story did not end there. A series of devastating events in 2005 led Jessica to experience a period of blackouts and memory-loss, and Jessica discovered that she, like her mother, suffered from DID. Jessica's wild and conniving alter, Tess, then repeated some of the

FIGURE 7.1. Viki's twin daughters, Natalie (left) and Jessica (right), embodied two sides of her personality that she could never reconcile.

same clashes that Viki/Niki had enacted years earlier: Tess loved a different man than Jess did; Tess had very different life goals than Jess; Tess's ideas of what constituted happiness and satisfaction were almost totally opposite to Jess's. Moreover, when a pregnant Tess found herself in a crisis, going into labor while totally alone in an abandoned vineyard, it was Niki Smith whom Tess hallucinated to help her through the delivery, as Tess claimed that Niki was the only "mother" that Tess had ever known. In fact, the traumatic event in Jessica's childhood that caused her to develop the Tess personality was an incident of sexual molestation that took place while Niki was running Viki's life (Niki routinely neglected young Jessica whenever she was in charge of Viki's household). The tragedy of Viki/Niki, never fully resolved for Viki, echoed in the tragedies suffered by her children and shaped the trajectories of their lives. For Viki, the knowledge that her beautiful daughter, her greatest accomplishment and joy, suffered from the same horrible illness that had forever plagued Viki was shattering.

Although the emergence of Jessica's alter was one of the more tragic pieces of fallout from Viki's ongoing struggle with DID, other plotlines that flowed from Viki's lifelong story yielded more positive outcomes. Natalie and Jessica's forming a sisterly bond, for instance, was rewarding for viewers who had often longed for Viki to be able to reconcile her dominant self with her Niki personality; the loving relationship that developed between Viki's twins felt like an analog or substitute for the Viki/Niki integration storyline that never played out. Also, the audience's (and Viki's) perception of Dorian shifted dramatically after Dorian informed Viki of her father's abusive behavior. Prior to the revelation about Victor in the 1990s, the audience had known Dorian only as Viki's wicked stepmother and archenemy, who had most likely killed Victor Lord while he was ill; although *One Life to Live* was vague on this plot point, Dorian was always singled out as the most likely murderer. But after Dorian told Viki the truth about Victor, the audience began to see that perhaps Dorian was not entirely a villainess. Perhaps Dorian had facilitated Victor's death, not only in order to inherit his millions, but also from a desire to enact justice. Perhaps Dorian had long felt animosity toward Viki because Dorian knew that she had avenged Viki's childhood suffering, but Viki did not know and always treated Dorian with disdain. The reverberations of Viki's ongoing multiple personality storyline reached far beyond Viki's life and shaped the stories of a number of other characters on *One Life*'s canvas. Martha Nochimson argues that the forced reconsideration of Dorian's nature and past acts had the added (potential) effect of raising women viewers' awareness of patriarchal stereotypes.[1] If viewers reevaluated Dorian's sometimes ethically questionable decisions as "complex," stemming from deep and various motives, rather than as the workings of a "simply" cruel woman typical of stereotyped female villains, then it is possible that the continual reverberations of Viki's long-arc story did more than entertain; they may have promoted a more feminist mode of interpreting media texts in fans of *One Life to Live*.

One reason that soaps' long-arc storylines, with their drawn-out plot reveals and unceasing reverberations, can affect soap viewers deeply is that "soap time" approximates "real time." Unlike the compressed temporalities of a two-hour film or a one-hour weekly series that runs for only a few years, soap opera events unfold in a timeline that mirrors viewers' lived time quite closely. A soap opera airs five days per week for fifty weeks of each year, usually for many decades, and so viewers have the sense that they live their lives alongside, or in tandem with, soap characters. Even though the events in soap characters' lives are usually far more dramatic than those taking place in viewers' lives, the parallel between soap time and real time gives soap operas a certain ongoing realism that other forms of drama rarely match. Viki uncovered her memories of her father's abuse, not twenty minutes or two hours after she began to manifest symptoms of DID (as would occur on a primetime television program or in a movie), but twenty-seven years later. The time that it took Viki to realize what had happened to her in her childhood is, according to Sigmund Freud, a normal amount of time for any adult to "remember, repeat, and work through" early trauma and heal psychologically.[2] Among TV genres, soaps alone have the ability to show an individual undergoing an intense psychological transformation over decades, which is often the time that people require to recover from the damage inflicted upon them during their youth.

Although soaps have often been criticized for their outlandish, unbelievable plots, in this respect, they are highly realistic fictions, resembling many women's actual experiences of psychological hurt and healing. The open-endedness, persistence, unevenness, and unpredictability of Viki's struggle against her inner demons, and the fact that it took her nearly thirty years to realize the most crucial truth of her own childhood, are what Nochimson values as realistic: a kind of realism that can be achieved in "soap time" far better than in any other narrative genre's timeframe.

The similitude of "soap time" to real time can lead viewers to feel close, even literally familiar, with soap characters. For example, media theorist Robyn Warhol writes of having moved thirty times in forty-six years and marveled at the fact that "in all those places, only one set of persons has been constantly present, continually and reliably 'there' no matter where: the characters who populate Oakdale, Illinois, the fictive setting of *As the World Turns*."[3] Similarly, Nancy Baym states that soap viewers can feel as if they have formed a strong bond with soap characters—a bond she calls "a parasocial relationship—a kind of family."[4] Neither Baym or Warhol claim that soap viewers are deluded that fictional people are, in fact, members of their family; although some studies of soap opera fans have speculated that fans confuse reality and fantasy, and although this stereotype of regular soap viewers remains popular today, numerous scholars have observed that the reality/fantasy conflation is experienced by only a small percentage of fans, and that the vast majority of viewers clearly understand the boundary between fictional lives and real lives.[5] Rather, Baym and Warhol point to an affective impact that soap operas can have on audiences that no other narrative genre can have by virtue of soaps' duration and the constancy of their casts of characters who come to feel like parts of viewers' families.

The sheer quantity of episodes that soaps produce every year, and the number of years that soaps air, allow soaps to tell "lifelong stories" about "lifelong characters," with deep seeds, long reveals, and continual reverberations of key plot arcs. These soap-specific narrative techniques can generate, in long-term viewers, an intensity of emotional response to plot twists that people usually feel only when they witness family members or close friends experiencing significant or sudden life changes. The unique temporality of soap storytelling, and its impact on audiences, was well understood by one of daytime drama's pioneers, Agnes Nixon, who created *All My Children*, *One Life to Live*, and several other soap operas. Nixon writes:

> The serial form imitates life in that, for its characters, the curtain rises with birth and does not ring down until death. . . . The ingredients are the same [as those] required for any good dramatic fare but with one basic difference: that the continuing form allows a fuller development of characterization while permitting the audience to become more and more involved with the story and its people.[6]

Some soap stories span fictional people's—and real people's—entire lives, and therein lies their effectiveness. If and when soap operas finally disappear from the American television landscape, the force and power of lifelong storytelling will die with them.[7]

FURTHER READING

Baym, Nancy K. *Tune In, Log On: Soaps, Fandom, and Online Community.* Thousand Oaks, CA: Sage, 2000.

Ford, Sam, Abigail De Kosnik, and C. Lee Harrington, eds. *The Survival of Soap Opera: Transformations for a New Media Era.* Jackson: University Press of Mississippi, 2011.

Harrington, C. Lee, and Denise D. Bielby. *Soap Fans: Pursuing Pleasure and Making Meaning in Everyday Life.* Philadelphia: Temple University Press, 1995.

Levine, Elana. *Her Stories: Daytime Soap Opera and US Television History.* Durham, NC: Duke University Press, 2020.

Warhol, Robyn R. *Having a Good Cry: Effeminate Feelings and Pop-Culture Forms.* Columbus: Ohio State University Press, 2003.

NOTES

1. Martha Nochimson, "Amnesia 'R' Us: The Retold Melodrama, Soap Opera, and the Representation of Reality," *Film Quarterly* 50, no. 3 (Spring 1997): 32.

2. Sigmund Freud, "Remembering, Repeating and Working Through," in *The Standard Edition of the Complete Psychological Works of Sigmund Freud*, vol. 12, trans. and ed. James Strachey (London: Hogarth Press, 1959), 145–56.

3. Robyn R. Warhol, *Having a Good Cry: Effeminate Feelings and Pop-Culture Forms* (Columbus: Ohio State University Press, 2003), 103.

4. Nancy Baym, "Perspective: Scholar Nancy Baym on Soaps after the O. J. Simpson Trial," in *The Survival of Soap Opera: Transformations for a New Media Era*, ed. Sam Ford, Abigail De Kosnik, and C. Lee Harrington (Jackson: University Press of Mississippi, 2011), 105.

5. Austin S. Babrow, "An Expectancy-Value Analysis of the Student Soap Opera Audience," *Communication Research* 16, no. 2 (April 1989): 155–78; Nancy Baym, *Tune In, Log On: Soaps, Fandom, and Online Community* (Thousand Oaks, CA: Sage, 2000), 36–37; Dannielle Blumenthal, *Women and Soap Opera: A Cultural Feminist Perspective* (Westport, CT: Praeger Publishers, 1997), 99–102; C. Lee Harrington and Denise D. Bielby, *Soap Fans: Pursuing Pleasure and Making Meaning in Everyday Life* (Philadelphia: Temple University Press, 1995), 101–8.

6. Agnes Nixon, "Coming of Age in Sudsville," *Television Quarterly* 9 (1970): 63.

7. In 2013, *One Life to Live* and *All My Children* were revived as web series available on Hulu and iTunes via The Online Network. Thus, as this book goes to press, the story of Viki Lord continues.

8

The Sopranos
Episodic Storytelling

SEAN O'SULLIVAN

Abstract: *The Sopranos* is one of television's most acclaimed series, ushering in the rise of the twenty-first-century primetime serial and helping to elevate the medium's cultural status. But Sean O'Sullivan problematizes our understanding of the show's seriality, highlighting episodes that function more as short stories than as chapters in a novel, and thus illuminating how the program's story structures and themes explore and challenge the norms of television narrative.

When Jennifer Egan discusses her inspirations for *A Visit from the Goon Squad*, the winner of the 2011 Pulitzer Prize for Fiction, she often cites *The Sopranos*. Egan's book has nothing to do with mobsters or federal agents. Rather, it is a loosely connected series of thirteen chapters, tracing over several decades a group of people affiliated with the music business. When it came out, there was considerable debate about whether the book should be called a novel or a collection of short stories. The style and point of view can vary drastically from chapter to chapter; characters that may have seemed "major" sometimes drop out and sometimes reappear, with "minor" characters at times taking over the reins. It was this structural restlessness, this ambivalence about linear connection, that Egan found appealing in the HBO show: "The lateral feeling of it, [and] not to have to always be focused on the forward thrust. There were whole episodes where you had no idea why this was going to be important in the bigger scheme of things, and yet it was fascinating; I loved the idea . . . of letting it feel meandering."[1] Egan points here to the powerful anti-serial riptide at the center of the most widely celebrated serial drama of the last decade, its resistance to the accumulative forces of consequence, continuity, and progression that nineteenth-century installment fiction and twentieth-century soap opera marketed as their defining features. This essay will spotlight two episodes from the show's initial season, each of which operates "laterally" in relation to the rest of that season. The first of these is the most highly praised of all episodes of *The Sopranos*; the second is one of the least beloved. That gulf in reception illustrates the attractions, perils, and effects of rupturing serial conventions.

Egan's diagnosis would undoubtedly please David Chase, creator and showrunner of *The Sopranos*, since his aversion to the traditional television business drove the design and ethos of the show. Chase described his early creative differences with the channel:

> There was a little bit of friction the first season between myself and HBO, because they were more interested in the serialized elements and I was not. "What's going to happen from one episode to the next?" "Are they going to kill Tony or not?" "Who planned it?" Or: "What's the result of what happened in episode 2?" I was more interested in discrete little movies.[2]

If Egan uses a metaphor of movement—the "lateral" rather than propulsive tendency of a narrative—Chase offers an arboreal image:

> If you look at a Christmas tree, people don't care about the trunk of a Christmas tree; they only care about the lights and the balls and the tinsel. But the trunk has to be there. So we always referred back to that; we had this continuing story, which people seemed to get involved in. I didn't intend to do a soap opera.[3]

Chase's notion of "people" here is helpfully contradictory. On the one hand, "people" got involved in the continuing story—namely the trunk of the tree; on the other hand, "people" care only about the surrounding baubles, those visual delights that make the trunk pleasingly invisible. This conflict between what "people" want—perhaps different kinds of people, or more likely the same people in different moods of narrative consumption—speaks directly to *The Sopranos'* self-conscious shifts between satisfaction and dissatisfaction.

The most famous hour of the series, and Exhibit A of Chase's stand-alone storytelling preferences, is "College," the show's fifth episode. Composed of just two storylines, rather than the typical model of three or four, "College" follows Tony and his daughter, Meadow, during her college tour in Maine and Tony's wife, Carmela, during her dangerous flirtation with Father Phil Intintola back in New Jersey. The dramatic core of the episode is Tony's discovery of a former mob informer, ensconced in rural New England thanks to the witness protection program; Tony tracks the "rat" down and garrotes him while Meadow is being interviewed at Colby College. *Time's* James Poniewozik reflected a critical consensus in 2007 when he ranked "College" as the best episode in the series' history, citing its riveting opposition "between the family and Family parts of Tony's life."[4] "College" precisely fits Egan's sense of *The Sopranos*' commitment to "lateral" movement, since the psychiatric environment and particular Mafia conflicts of the show's first four episodes are absent. Chase deemed it the show's "most successful episode . . . a film noir in and of itself"; critically, "it has nothing to do with anything that happened beforehand, and it has nothing to do with anything that happened later . . . To me, that was the ultimate *Sopranos* episode."[5]

In terms of the show's central figure, "College" produces ripples neither in the area of plot—there is no event-consequence to Tony's actions here—nor in the area of character—Tony does not "discover" something about himself at this point, and there appear to be no psychological aftershocks. But if we think of "character" not just as a fictional person's mental or emotional conditions, but as a relationship between that fictional person and a viewing audience, in fact "College" had significant ramifications for what "happened later." As Chase tells it, this storyline represented another major conflict with HBO in the inaugural season; channel executive Chris Albrecht worried that the gruesome, hands-on execution of the informant would harm Tony's "relatability," destroying the audience's ability to connect with the series' main character. Chase stuck to his guns, on the grounds of verisimilitude, saying that "if we're really gonna believe this guy is a credible mobster, he's gotta kill people. In real life, that's what these people do."[6] That conflict between creator and channel illustrated how "character" can mean something very different in two different contexts, whether in the show's internal world or diegesis, as championed by Chase, or in the world inhabited by the shows' viewers, foregrounded by HBO.

Five weeks after "College," another episode of *The Sopranos* would also enact the lateral move, Chase's preference for the "discrete little movie": "A Hit Is a Hit," the show's tenth hour. The chief preoccupation of "A Hit Is a Hit" is music, and specifically the music industry—as advertised by the title, which reflects the impossibility of understanding why some music succeeds commercially, and why some does not. The two chief storylines are bridged by the gangsta rapper Massive Genius—someone who truly has nothing to do with what happened beforehand, or with what happened later, since he appears nowhere else in *The Sopranos*. One of the two plots involves his attempts to get "reparations" from Tony's friend Hesh Rabkin, a Jewish mob associate who exploitatively managed R&B bands in the 1950s; the other involves Christopher Moltisanti's attempts to get his girlfriend, Adriana La Cerva, started as a music producer, with Massive operating as an advisor who is frankly more interested in Adriana herself. Massive essentially takes control of *The Sopranos* at this juncture, operating as the central agent of plot and serving as the focus of tension and desire. Structurally, the show borrows here from the anthology format, a televisual genre wherein each episode produces a self-contained story, with no relation to predecessor or successor episodes. Contemporary viewers of *The Sopranos* would have been uncertain about how much to invest in Massive's character and storylines. Does he matter, in the grand scheme of things? The answer to that question depends on what we imagine *The Sopranos* to be.

Given the central role of music in the episode, it is worth noting that music in *The Sopranos* was a defining authorial concern for David Chase. He made clear that getting a significant music budget was critical to his original deal with HBO, and that "music and this particular cast of actors" were his favorite parts of the series.[7] The show's use of diverse, preexisting musical sources—from Bruce Springsteen to Radiohead to opera—meant that each song or selection required no direct reference to the preceding or succeeding one; each musical cue was "discrete," just as Chase wanted for the episodes themselves. A familiar score in a series, with familiar melodies and practices, helps create continuity; we might think of the recurring musical intensification that typically led to commercial breaks on *Lost*, giving that show—which roamed across many genres and styles—an auditory serial thread for the audience, a welcome contact with the familiar. Chase's aversion to this kind of continuity even applied to his original plan for the title sequence, where he wanted to feature a different song every week. He characterized the televisual convention of using a single initial theme every week as "bourgeois"; but HBO insisted on "something identifiable" at the start of each episode, and he relented.[8] Music's ability to signal familiarity or change, in other words, represents another version of the continuous and the discontinuous. The cluster of material that we call an album offers a musical parallel to the structural tension between the novel and a series of short stories. A "concept album," like a novel, promotes connectivity, the promise that the order of the songs is crucial, that everything is linked—a start-to-end logic that mimics one version of serial drama. A collection of singles or separate pieces, like a series of short stories, fractures connectivity, minimizing the importance of sequence and allowing individual songs to be freely excerpted from the group. The first season of *The Sopranos* tested the boundaries between novel and short stories, between concept album and singles collection, and "A Hit Is a Hit" proved to be a particularly problematic case.

"A Hit Is a Hit" appears nowhere in any roll call of the show's most cherished moments. The *TV Guide Sopranos Companion* summarized and lamented it thusly: "Gangsta rapper meets boy gangster in this rather contrived episode of culture clash that pulls us away from the compelling intrigues of recent episodes."[9] This judgment expresses a typical way in which serial viewers compartmentalize and justify opinion and evaluation. "College" also depends on contrivance, and on pulling away—from the serendipitous reencounter with the mob rat to the circumstances under which Carmela and Father Phil spend a night under the same roof. But "contrivance" in that earlier context is forgiven because the payoff or pleasure trumps, for many viewers, the artifice of accident on which the plots of "College" rest. The schism of reaction between "College" and "A Hit Is a Hit" illustrates the risk/reward of abandoning televisual convention; Chase's inclination toward a "discrete" rather an integrated hour of events, topics, or people defines what we might call the conflicted or restless television serial, a twenty-first-century phenomenon of which *The Sopranos* has been the most vivid exponent. The most prominent successor, in the conflicted/restless vein, may be *Mad Men*. That show's creator, Matthew Weiner, was a staff writer for the final seasons of *The Sopranos*, and his series frequently disrupts expectations of serial momentum and narrative convention. "I don't want there to be a formula," Weiner has said. "I don't want people to know what to expect ever when they turn the show on."[10]

"A Hit Is a Hit" parallels "College" in terms of subject matter, and in terms of season placement. Both episodes obsessively examine art and culture, from an apt quotation from *The Scarlet Letter* that Tony sees on a wall at Bowdoin College during Meadow's interview to debates over authorship and musical inspiration that occupy the later episode. "A Hit Is a Hit" intensifies the attention to art that we see in "College," moving from a flurry of allusions to a focus on how art is made, and how art works. And structurally each episode functions as a break, interrupting a defined four-episode serial sequence. "College" follows the first quartet of shows, which depict the illness and death of acting boss Jackie Aprile and Tony's clever orchestration of Uncle Junior's rise to boss; "A Hit Is a Hit," meanwhile, appears just when the conflict between Tony and Uncle Junior is on the verge of exploding. Those two placements within the season, however, are not exactly analogous. One crucial difference is that of accumulation. Four hours into cooking a serial season, when the flavors have yet to take hold, we may be tolerant of something new. But after nine hours we are much more likely to grow impatient; Chase's commitment to the "discrete" film produces distinct problems at distinct points of a thirteen-episode story. A second difference is one of consequence, or aftermath. While "College" may have "nothing to do with" plot and character in terms of the major serial developments of the season, it has a great deal to do with character in terms of our relation to Tony; by contrast, "A Hit Is a Hit" will leave no wake of any kind. In many ways, it is the more radical of the two episodes, and the one that comes closer to performing the subversive job of rejecting serial conventions, within the guts of a singularly successful serial edifice, than anything else Chase and his team attempted. That struggle between freedom and form is explicitly addressed in "A Hit Is a Hit" when a record producer advocates for the clear, connective structure of a song like The Beatles'

"She Loves You" while the lead singer of Adriana's band, Visiting Day, argues for something "introspective" and unschematic—another version of serial conformity contrasted with a rejection of recognizable pattern.

Even more than music, one might say that the main topic of "A Hit Is a Hit" is performance—the performance not just of songs, but of identity categories like race, class, and ethnicity. Massive Genius performs a designated street persona but has a degree in Urban Planning; Hesh declares that, as a Jew, he was "the white man's nigger" long before hip-hop. In a third story, Tony feels that he is asked to put on a lower-class, goomba minstrel show in front of his rich neighbors, especially the Cusamanos, in order to gain access to their country club. The emphasis on performance, and on the instability of identity, connects to the episode's focus on the destabilized meanings of capitalism, status, and art in the postmodern world—the arbitrary value of money after the disappearance of the gold standard, of status after the 1960s social revolutions, and of art after the collapse of aesthetic hierarchies. "A Hit Is a Hit" is the first *Sopranos* episode to begin in New York City, the American epicenter of capitalism, status, and art, and the precipitating incident of the plot is the unexpected seizure of a huge pile of cash. Even the "D" story, the smallest element of the episodic interweave, touches on money and value as Carmela gets involved in the gossipy suburban world of hot stock tips. Each of these plots points to the fluctuating, possibly arbitrary nature of worth, meaning, and desire. Christopher offers another version of the problem of distinguishing how we know what matters, what fixed values things have or lack, when he laments the imponderables of Adriana's potential new business: "Music—it's not something you can hold in your hands, you know. Like football betting cards, or coke." Gambling chits and illegal drugs are the new gold standard; art, money, and status are an indecipherable mess.

"A Hit Is a Hit" essentially serves as a televisual essay on late twentieth-century culture more broadly, including treasured objects such as Murano glass, bidets, Versace clothing, and the *Godfather* films. *The Sopranos*, of course, would soon become such an object itself, a register of cultural acuity for those sharp enough to subscribe to HBO or purchase the DVDs; the episode, produced in the vacuum before the first season was aired, divined that a work of television might also turn into a valuable and tradable commodity, a nugget of knowledge that is worth something if we think it is worth something. "A Hit Is a Hit" ends with a clear gesture of viewer-teasing, as Tony—who is eventually frozen out of the Cusamanos' social circle—asks his neighbors to do him "a solid" by hiding a wrapped box, without revealing its contents. We know that the box is filled with sand, but they regard it with terror: "What is it? Heroin?" "A weapon? Could be anything." That box represents the uncertain condition of the entire episode, its immersion in the traumatic but inescapable state of American current affairs,

FIGURE 8.1. Just as Tony Soprano toyed with his neighbors by asking them to hide a mysterious box (harmlessly filled with sand), episodes of *The Sopranos* occasionally presented viewers with characters and plotlines whose relationship to the serial narrative was opaque.

where things mean what they mean only by context, or by shared guesswork. This is a world—both on- and off-screen—where the intrinsic seems opaque or antique, and we can know only by relation. Likewise, a serial episode of a television drama "means" what it means in relation to its seriality, to its relational context with preceding and succeeding episodes. An episode like "A Hit Is a Hit," which rejects its serial place, may seem to its detractors to create a void of meaning; "A Hit Is a Hit" is unbeloved precisely because it troubles our understanding of what *The Sopranos* is, as a serial narrative enterprise.

The episode shows us that *The Sopranos* is not a collection of characters, in the way that, say, *Six Feet Under* is a collection of characters; rather, *The Sopranos* is a way of thinking about serial narrative. That distillation of the show may be discomfiting. In a sense, "A Hit Is a Hit" is not so much the companion episode to "College" as its inversion. If that earlier episode appeared to institutionalize our relationship to Tony as the cornerstone of the show, the later one disrupts our sense that any single element, or even any stable cluster of elements, can define the show's essence. One legacy of "College" and "A Hit Is a Hit" is "Pine Barrens," a late third-season episode involving Christopher and Paulie's pursuit of a Russian through snowy woods—a Russian who disappears and is never found. "Pine Barrens" was number two on James Poniewozik's list of *The Sopranos'* greatest hits—a fact for which he apologized, calling it the "most un-*Sopranos*-like of *So-pranos* episodes," a "distinctly contained short story . . . in a series that unfolds like a novel."[11] As I have been claiming, *The Sopranos* does not unfold like a novel; it unfolds like *A Visit from the Goon Squad*, a text that hovers deliberately on the boundary between short story and novel. It is precisely the "un-*Sopranos*-like" episodes that most fully define the series' narrative interests.

Within the genre of the lateral move, "Pine Barrens" may be closer to "College"; both episodes feature familiar characters in a rural setting trying to kill, in alternately comic and grim fashion, a problematic foe whom the audience has never encountered before and will never see again. And both seem to be "about" a core territory of the show—underworld assassination—as opposed to being "about" something irrelevant—the world of music—even though David Chase manifestly cares a lot more about music than he does about underworld assassination. Perhaps the most radical consequence of withholding context and consequence can be found in a very different kind of *Sopranos* episode, one featuring a hugely important serial event. In the sixth-season "Kennedy and Heidi," a major character dies, and Tony ends up on a guilt-ridden, drug-driven escapade in Las Vegas; the episode concludes with him in a peyote haze, staring at a Western sunrise and proclaiming, "I get it!" This grand scene of epiphany suggests a moment of reckoning; surely we'll find out, a week later, what Tony "got." Instead, in the next episode, it's as if that epiphany never happened.

"Kennedy and Heidi" gives the lie to narrative nostrums of "arc" and "development," screenwriting-manual simplifications of how people operate and how lives happen; surely, it is more "real"—to use the key term that David Chase used to justify the central plot of "College"—to suggest that we as people often end up exactly where we started, that we change very little, that epiphanies are fleeting and delusive and ignored. And which is more "artificial": the episode that wanders off course, or the episode that obeys the authorial click-clack of plot sequencing? "A Hit Is a Hit" valorizes the disruption and the pause over the flow. Its model—the collection of singles—taps into our current moment of iTunes, and the crumbling of the album as a serial object. "A Hit Is a Hit," as an anti-serial serial episode, in 1999 anticipated the digital atomization of culture consumption. Is a season a concept album? Or is a season a collection of singles? Can it be both at the same time?

FURTHER READING

Chase, David. *The Sopranos: Selected Scripts from Three Seasons*. New York: Warner Books, 2002.
Lavery, David, ed. *Reading The Sopranos: Hit TV from HBO*. London: Tauris, 2006.
O'Sullivan, Sean. "Broken on Purpose: Poetry, Serial Television, and the Season." *Storyworlds* 2 (2010): 59–77.

Polan, Dana. *The Sopranos*. Durham, NC: Duke University Press, 2009.

Yacowar, Maurice. *The Sopranos on the Couch: The Ultimate Guide*. New York: Continuum, 2006.

NOTES

1. Boris Kachka, "*A Visit from the Goon Squad* Author Jennifer Egan on Reaping Awards and Dodging Literary Feuds," *New York*, May 11, 2011, www.vulture.com.
2. *The Sopranos*, "David Chase Interview" (season 1 DVD; HBO Video, 2001).
3. Ibid.
4. James Poniewozik, "Top 10 *Sopranos* Episodes," *Time*, www.time.com.
5. *The Sopranos*, "David Chase Interview."
6. Peter Biskind, "An American Family," *Vanity Fair* 560 (2007): 282–83.
7. David Chase, *The Sopranos: Selected Scripts from Three Seasons* (New York: Warner Books, 2002), x.
8. *The Sopranos*, "David Chase Interview."
9. *TV Guide Sopranos Companion* (New York: TV Guide, 2002), 47.
10. Alan Sepinwall, "*Mad Men*: Talking 'Out of Town' with Matthew Weiner," *What's Alan Watching?* (blog), August 16, 2009, http://sepinwall.blogspot.com/2009/08/mad-men -talking-out-of-town-with.html.
11. Poniewozik, "Top 10 *Sopranos* Episodes."

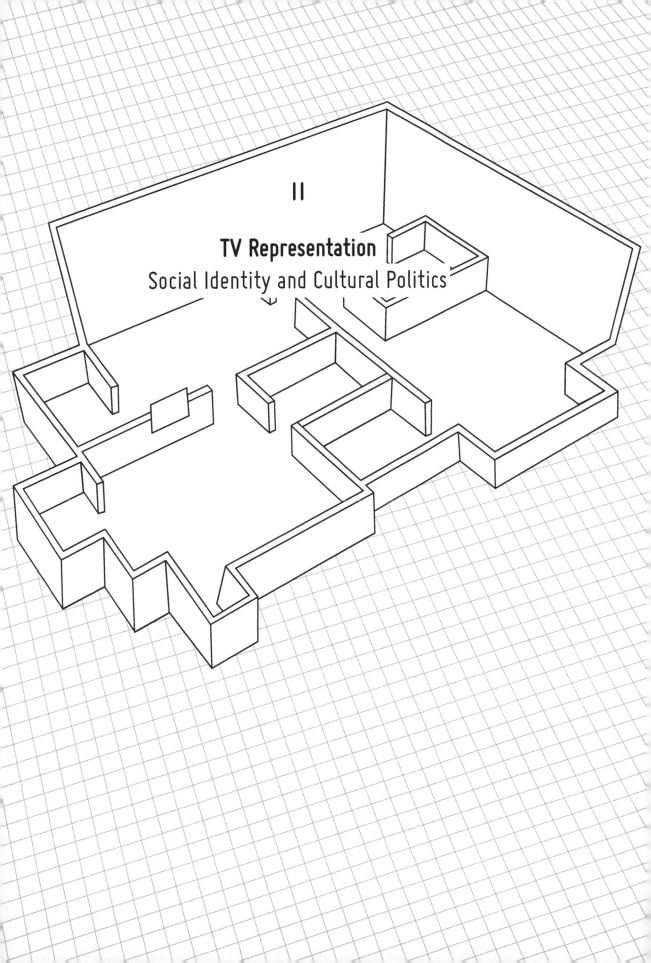

II

TV Representation
Social Identity and Cultural Politics

9

24

Challenging Stereotypes

EVELYN ALSULTANY

Abstract: Critical discussions about television's patterns of representation some-times devolve into reductive assessments of "positive" or "negative," "good" or "bad" images. In this essay, Evelyn Alsultany describes how the action-drama *24* employed innovative strategies to avoid stereotypes of Arab/Muslim terrorists but argues that sympathetic portrayals of individuals won't alleviate television's consistent representation of Arabs and Muslims primarily within the context of terrorism.

Since September 11, 2001, a number of TV dramas have been created with the War on Terror as their central theme, depicting U.S. government agencies and officials heroically working to make the nation safe by battling terrorism. Although initially created prior to the 9/11 attacks, Fox's *24* became the most popular of the fast-emerging cycle of terrorism dramas. The program centered on Jack Bauer, a brooding and embattled agent of the government's Counter-Terrorism Unit, who raced a ticking clock to subvert impending terrorist attacks on the United States.

In 2004, the Council on American-Islamic Relations (CAIR) accused *24* of perpetuating stereotypes of Arabs and Muslims. CAIR objected to the persistent portrayal of Arabs and Muslims within the context of terrorism, stating that "repeated association of acts of terrorism with Islam will only serve to increase anti-Muslim prejudice." Critics of CAIR retorted that programs like *24* reflected one of the most pressing social and political issues of the moment, the War on Terror, with some further contending that CAIR was trying to deflect the reality of Muslim terrorism by confining television writers to politically correct themes.

The writers and producers of *24* responded to CAIR's concerns in a number of ways. For one, the show included sympathetic portrayals of Arabs and Muslims, in which they were the "good guys," or in some way on the side of the United

States. Representatives of *24* said that the program "made a concerted effort to show ethnic, religious and political groups as multi-dimensional," and noted that "political issues" were "debated from multiple viewpoints." The villains on the eight seasons of *24* came from around the globe and included Russians, Germans, Latinos, Arabs/Muslims, Euro-Americans, Africans, and even the fictional president of the United States. Rotating the identity of the "bad guy" was one of the many strategies used by *24* to avoid reproducing the Arab/Muslim terrorist stereotype (or any other stereotypes, for that matter). *24*'s responsiveness to such criticism even extended to creating a public service announcement that was broadcast in February of 2005, during one of the program's commercial breaks, and featured lead actor Kiefer Sutherland staring into the camera, reminding viewers that "the American Muslim community stands firmly beside their fellow Americans in denouncing and resisting all forms of terrorism," as well as urging all viewers to "please, bear that in mind" while watching the program.

24 proved innovative in portraying the Arab/Muslim terrorist threat that has defined the War on Terror, while seeking not to reproduce the stereotype of the Arab/Muslim terrorist. This essay outlines some of the representational strategies *24* used to accomplish this, including portraying Arab and Muslim Americans as patriotic Americans or as innocent victims of post-9/11 hate crimes, humanizing Arab/Muslim terrorists, and presenting an array of terrorist identities. On the surface, such innovative strategies seem to effectively subvert stereotypes. However, a diversity of representations, even an abundance of sympathetic characters, does not in itself "solve" the problem of racial stereotyping. As Ella Shohat, Robert Stam, Herman Gray, and other scholars have shown, focusing on whether a particular image is either "good" or "bad" does not address the complexity of representation. Rather, it is important to examine the ideological work performed by images and storylines beyond such binaries. If we interpret an image as simply positive or negative, we can then conclude that the problem of racial stereotyping is over because of the appearance of sympathetic images of Arabs and Muslims during the War on Terror. The reality is much more complex, though, and an examination of such images in relation to their narrative context reveals how sympathetic portrayals themselves participate in a larger field of meaning about Arabs and Muslims. That is, combating stereotypes is more complex than including positive and nuanced Arab/Muslim characters and storylines. Such efforts can have only a minimal impact so long as the underlying premise of the story hinges on an Arab/Muslim terrorist threat.

The most common way that writers of *24* showed that they were sensitive to negative stereotyping was by creating "positive" Arab and Muslim characters. These characters generally take two forms: a patriotic Arab or Muslim American who assists the U.S. government in its fight against Arab/Muslim terrorism, either as a government agent or civilian; or an Arab or Muslim American who is the innocent victim of a post-9/11 hate crime or harassment. For example, on season six of *24*, Nadia Yassir, a Muslim woman from Pakistan who has lived in the United States since she was two years old, is a dedicated member of the Counter-Terrorism Unit, where she works to prevent a terrorist attack orchestrated by the Arab/Muslim Abu Fayad. In addition to her portrayal as a patriotic Muslim American, she is also framed as an innocent victim of the post-9/11 backlash against Arabs and Muslims when she is falsely suspected of leaking information to the terrorists, tortured by her colleagues during interrogation, and restricted access to the computer systems when she returns to work. Nadia is a "good" Muslim American: she is patriotic, likable, and we sympathize with her plight.

This strategy of representing Arabs and Muslims as patriotic Americans and as victims of violence and harassment is also evident in a fourth-season episode of *24*. Jack Bauer and Paul Raines, in the midst of a blackout and looting in Los Angeles, seek shelter in a gun shop while corporate commandos try to kill them. Two Arab American brothers own the gun shop. Tired of being unjustly blamed for the terrorist attacks, the brothers insist on helping to fight terrorism alongside Jack Bauer. "If you find the people who caused today's bloodshed, then we'll help you," they say. They are also given lines such as "You don't understand. For years we've been blamed for the attacks by these terrorists. We grew up in this neighborhood. This country is our home." This emphasis on victimization and sympathy challenges both long-standing representations of Arabs/Muslims as terrorists and a sense of celebration that otherwise surfaces when Arab/Muslim characters are killed.

Writers and producers of *24* also sought to diminish the Arab/Muslim terrorist stereotype by humanizing Arab/Muslim terrorist characters. Most Arab and Muslim terrorists in films or on television shows before 9/11 were stock villains, one-dimensional bad guys who were presumably bad because of their ethnic background or religious beliefs. In contrast, post-9/11 terrorist characters are shown in a familial context as loving fathers and husbands; they are given back-stories; we are offered a glimpse into the moments that have brought them to the precipice of terror. In 2005, *24* introduced viewers to a Middle Eastern family in a recurring role for the first time on U.S. network television; the family appeared for most of the season as opposed to a single episode. In their first scene they seem like an "ordinary" family eating breakfast together. The mother, Dina, and father, Navi, discuss how their son, Behrooz, is forbidden from dating an American girl. At first it appears that this is for religious or cultural reasons, but it is soon revealed that they are a sleeper cell and that the son is forbidden from dating the American girl because they do not want anything to get in the way of their mission.

FIGURE 9.1.
In *24*, terrorist characters are humanized by portraying them in a familial context.

Behrooz's task is to deliver a briefcase containing a device that will activate a nuclear power plant meltdown. If all 104 U.S. power plants melt down, they will release radiation that will kill millions and make regions of the United States uninhabitable for years. Portraying terrorists doing ordinary things like having a family discussion over breakfast helps make terrorist characters multidimensional. In the episodes to come, each family member's relationship to terrorism is explored. The father is willing to kill his wife and son in order to complete his mission; the mother will reconsider her involvement with terrorism only to protect her son; and the teenage son, raised in the United States, is portrayed as having an evolving sense of humanity that ultimately prevents him from being a terrorist. Such nuances show one means whereby writers and producers of *24* have tried to avoid reinscribing stereotypes.

They have also challenged the Arab/Muslim terrorist stereotype by "flipping the enemy," a strategy that leads the viewer to believe that Muslim terrorists are plotting to destroy the United States, and then reveals that those Muslims are not terrorists, or that they are merely a front for Euro-American or European terrorists or part of a larger network of international terrorists. During season two of *24*, Bauer spends the first half of the season tracking down a Middle Eastern terrorist cell, ultimately subverting a nuclear attack. One of the key terrorist suspects is Reza Naiyeer, who is Middle Eastern (though his country of origin is not named) and about to marry a blond white American woman, Marie Warner. Suspicious of Naiyeer, Warner's sister hires a private investigator to run a background check on him. The private investigator finds that he appears to know a man named Syed Ali, who has links to terrorist activities. Naiyeer is not a particularly likable character, which adds to his portrayal as a terrorist suspect. However, as Naiyeer seeks to prove his innocence, he discovers that his fiancée, Warner, the last person who would be suspected of terrorism, is the one collaborating with Syed Ali on a terrorist attack. In the second half of the season, we discover that European and Euro-American businessmen are behind the attack, attempting to goad the United States to declare a war on the Middle East and thereby themselves benefit from the increase in oil prices. Flipping the enemy operates first by confirming cultural assumptions that Arabs/Muslims are terrorists and then challenging that assumption by revealing an unsuspected terrorist identity. This strategy conveys that terrorism is not an Arab or Muslim monopoly.

Other common strategies *24* used to circumvent stereotyping include representing U.S. society as multicultural and leaving the country of the terrorist characters unnamed. For several seasons, the U.S. president was African American and his press secretary Asian American. The Counter-Terrorist Unit was equally diverse, peppered with Latinos and African Americans throughout the show's eight seasons. The sum total of these casting decisions created the impression of a United States in which multiculturalism abounds, people of different racial backgrounds work together, and racism is socially unacceptable. Fictionalizing or simply not naming the terrorists' country is another strategy that can give a show more latitude in creating salacious storylines that might be criticized if identified with an actual country. In season four of *24*, the terrorist family is from an unnamed Middle Eastern country; in season eight, the fictional country "Kamistan" is a source of terrorist plots. This strategy rests on the assumption that leaving the nationality of the villain blank eliminates potential offensiveness; if no specific country or ethnicity is named, then there is less reason for any particular group to be offended by the portrayal.

These representational strategies are not exhaustive, nor are they all new to our post-9/11 world. Rather, they collectively outline some of the ways in which writers and producers of *24* have sought to improve representations of Arabs (and other racial and ethnic groups). These strategies present an important departure from deploying stereotypes to creating more challenging stories and characters, and, in the process, reflecting a growing sensitivity to the potential negative impact of stereotyping. These strategies seek to make the point—indeed, often with strenuous effort—that not all Arabs are terrorists, and not all terrorists are Arabs. However, for all the show's innovations, *24* remains wedded to a script that represents Arabs and Muslims only within the context of terrorism and therefore does not effectively challenge the stereotypical representations of Arabs and Muslims.

Stuart Hall has claimed that even with the best of intentions, writers and producers who seek to subvert racial hierarchies can inadvertently participate in inferential racism, which Hall defines as "apparently naturalized representations of events and situations relating to race, whether 'factual' or 'fictional,' which have racist premises and propositions inscribed in them as a set of unquestioned assumptions." The persistent unquestioned assumption in these TV dramas is that Arabs and Muslims are terrorists or linked to terrorism, despite writers' efforts to create a wider range of Arab and Muslim characters. The primary objective of television writers and producers is not education, social justice, or social change. Rather, the goal is to keep as many viewers watching for as long as possible, thereby producing successful commercial entertainment. Television must therefore strike a balance between keeping its products as engaging as possible while not offending potential viewers. Writers thus seem to be constrained and influenced by two factors: audiences have been primed for many years to assume that Arabs/Muslims are terrorists, and therefore writers create what viewers expect and what will sell. At the same time, some viewers are particularly sensitive to and critical of stereotypes, and therefore writers are faced with the challenge of creating a more diverse world of characters. The results are some modifications to avoid being offensive, while still perpetuating core stereotypes that continue to have cultural resonance. Post-9/11 television is testimony to the fact that stereotypes that held sway for much of the twentieth century are no longer socially acceptable—at least in their most blatant forms. But this does not mean that such stereotypes (and viewers' taste for them) have actually gone away; they have only become covert.

Inserting a patriotic Arab or Muslim American or fictionalizing Middle Eastern countries are ineffectual devices if Arabs, Muslims, Arab Americans, and Muslim Americans continue to be portrayed solely through the narrow lens of good or bad in the fight against terrorism. The result of the good/bad coupling is startling: at its most effective, the strategy creates an illusion of post-racism that absolves viewers from confronting the persistence of institutionalized racism in a way that echoes Herman Gray's argument about how representations of the black middle class family in television sitcoms of the 1980s and 1990s contributed to an illusion of racial equality. Gray acknowledges *The Cosby Show* for successfully recoding blackness away from images of the "welfare queen" and the drug dealer, while simultaneously noting that it participated in rearticulating a new and more enlightened form of racism, and contributed to an illusion of "feel-good multiculturalism and racial cooperation." Similarly, while I acknowledge that *24* took important steps in diversifying its portrayal of Arabs and Muslims, we cannot go as far as assuming that such efforts actually solve stereotyping. Sympathetic images of Arabs and Muslims after 9/11 give the impression that racism is not tolerated in the United States, despite the slew of policies that have targeted and disproportionately affected Arabs and Muslims.

Many other post-9/11 TV shows use these strategies, from terrorist-themed shows like *Sleeper Cell* and *Homeland* to broader-themed shows with occasional terrorist motifs like *Law and Order* and *The Practice*. In effect, then, such strategies have become standardized. Nonetheless, while representational strategies that challenge the stereotyping of Arabs and Muslims were being broadcast, circulated, and consumed, real Arabs and Muslims were being detained, deported, held without due process, and tortured. According to the FBI, hate crimes against Arabs and Muslims multiplied by 1600 percent from 2000 to 2001. Across the decade following 9/11, hate crimes, workplace discrimination, bias incidents, and airline discrimination targeting Arab and Muslim Americans have persisted. In addition to individual citizens' taking the law into their own hands, the U.S. government passed legislation that targeted Arabs and Muslims (both inside and outside the United States) and legalized suspending their constitutional rights. The USA PATRIOT Act, passed by Congress in October 2001 and renewed multiple times since, legalized the following (previously illegal) acts and thus enabled anti-Arab and anti-Muslim racism: monitoring Arab and Muslim groups; granting the U.S. Attorney General the right to indefinitely detain noncitizens suspected of having ties to terrorism; searching and wiretapping secretly, without probable cause; arresting and holding a person whose testimony might assist in a case as a "material witness"; using secret evidence without granting the accused access to that evidence; trying those designated as "enemy combatants" in military tribunals (as opposed to civilian courts); and deportation based on guilt by association rather than actions. To put it mildly, the explicit targeting of Arabs and Muslims by government policies, based on their identity as opposed to their criminality, contradicts claims to racial progress.

Certainly not all Arabs and Muslims were subject to post-9/11 harassment. Nonetheless, these multiple representational strategies do not in themselves solve stereotyping and racism, and can actually perform the ideological work of producing the illusion of a post-race moment that obscures the severity and injustice of institutionalized racism as outlined above. Such TV dramas produce reassurance that racial sensitivity is the norm in U.S. society, while simultaneously perpetuating the dominant perception of Arabs and Muslims as threats to U.S. national security. So long as Arabs and Muslims are represented primarily in the context of terrorism, our current crop of representational strategies—for all of their apparent innovations—will have a minimal impact on viewers' perceptions of Arabs and Muslims, and far worse, will perpetuate a simplistic vision of good and evil under the guise of complexity and sensitivity.

Surely, one show alone cannot undo a history of stereotyping, even as the representational strategies employed by the creators of *24* did constitute steps toward subverting them. Nonetheless, although some television writers certainly have humane motives, and although some producers honestly desire to create innovative shows, devoid of stereotypes, such efforts are overwhelmed by the sheer momentum of our current representational scheme. Thus, representations of Arab and Muslim identities in contexts that have nothing to do with terrorism remain strikingly unusual in the U.S. commercial media. There have been a few sitcoms and one notable reality television show that have aimed to break out of prevailing molds: *Whoopi, Aliens in America, Community,* and *All-American Muslim* all offer broader portrayals of Arabs and Muslims. Three out of these four programs were short lived; still, they are examples of representations of Arabs and Muslims outside of the context of terrorism and homeland security. More recently Hulu's *Ramy* and other shows have begun to expand the field of representations. If there were a more diverse field of representations of Arab and Muslim identities in the U.S. media, then those representations in the context of terrorism as seen on *24* would not provoke as much concern over perpetuating stereotypes because they would no longer dominate the representational field. But despite a few exceptions, *24*'s model of framing Arabs and Muslims within the field of terrorism still is the dominant mode of media representation.

FURTHER READING

Alsultany, Evelyn. *Arabs and Muslims in the Media: Race and Representation after 9/11.* New York: New York University Press, 2012.

McAlister, Melani. *Epic Encounters: Culture, Media, and U.S. Interests in the Middle East since 1945.* 2nd ed. Berkeley: University of California Press, 2005.

Shaheen, Jack G. *Reel Bad Arabs: How Hollywood Vilifies a People.* Northampton, MA: Interlink Publishing Group, 2001.

Shohat, Ella, and Robert Stam. *Unthinking Eurocentrism: Multiculturalism and the Media.* New York: Routledge, 1994.

10

Bala Loca
Producing Representations

DAVID MIRANDA HARDY

Abstract: Cultural discussions about media representations of people with disabilities tend to either decry their absence in our narrative landscape or, when included, critique their misrepresentation. From narrative stereotypes to considerations about who should tell and embody these stories, producer David Miranda Hardy discusses how these conversations were at the inception of the Chilean drama series *Bala Loca*, which he wrote and produced, and how they informed the creative and executive decisions that gave it shape.

Telling stories often poses a challenge to balance the exploration of cultural issues and the dramatic need for specificity and individualization through characters and situations. Though what draws me to stories are their power to represent us collectively, in my own work as a storyteller, ideas often emerge in the form of a single character and a basic conflict. That was the case with *Bala Loca*, the drama series I created for Chilean Turner subsidiary Chilevision and the Chilean National Television Council. It is a ten-episode thriller written by Pablo Toro, Gonzalo Maza, and me; directed by Gabriel Diaz and Oscar Godoy; and produced by Marcos de Aguirre, my business and creative partner. It was broadcast in Chile in 2016 and later distributed by Netflix internationally, and was nominated for a Platino Award in 2017 and a Peabody Award in 2018. The Netflix-originated tagline reads, "A veteran journalist starting a news site about corruption in Chile stumbles on a big story when a fellow investigative reporter dies suspiciously." The fact that protagonist Mauro Murillo (Alejandro Goic) uses a wheelchair is not mentioned. Yet the origin of the project, first titled *Entero Quebrado* (*Broken*), was that simple idea: A man experiences a spinal-cord injury when he's at the top of his career. In this essay, I share the creative and practical decisions around that original desire: to represent a man and his wheelchair, and reflect on how those goals shifted throughout the production of the show, hopefully offering some insight on that tension between the specific and the general, the individual and the universal—or, in other words, how to represent disability to a mass audience through the experience of one character.

The origin of *Bala Loca* is easy to trace. Though I do not experience the world as someone with a disability, my aforementioned partner Marcos de Aguirre, the producer of the show, has been a disabled wheelchair user since he was thirty-one and has wanted to tell a story about a character in similar circumstances. In the twenty-five years I have been his friend, I have often witnessed the difference between who he is and the man people assume he should be. The impulse of nondisabled society to impose narratives upon people with apparent disabilities creates a friction that can be explored dramatically in ways that feel original, and that Marcos thought were sorely missing from film and television narratives. With such a kernel of an idea, my usual next step is to ask, "but what does it mean?"—to interrogate the premise beyond the individual character into broader, more universal issues. In this case, the premise may point toward prejudice and discrimination, otherness and alienation, and the many ways society structurally pits people against each other. The attempt to find meaning marks the first movement from the dramatic level to the thematic level, a dialectic process that goes back and forth multiple times while writing a story. Our hope, of course, is that we will end up with a great drama—compelling characters facing fascinating conflicts—that *means something* too.

Working at the dramatic level, I started by developing possible narrative premises, imagining our Mauro Murillo in different scenarios. In one, he is a TV actor finishing shooting a telenovela when an accident happens; in another one, he's a journalist working at a conservative newspaper where he is investigating a story about discrimination and corruption in the health industry, when he's the victim of a dubious hit-and-run. The aim was to find an environment and profession where the issues brought out by his acquired disability may connect with bigger themes. Entertainment television, often dismissed as a vapid image-centered milieu, could create an interesting contrast between Murillo's transformed life before and after his accident. The world of investigative journalism—the last-standing heroes uncovering injustices and prejudices—could also offer fascinating contradictions between the public moral stance of journalists and their private lives, between the noble search for the truth via slow, patient work and the sensationalism required in today's fast-paced media environment. Our final version combined both scenarios.

While developing a dramatic premise, I also explored the thematic level by researching issues of representation and disability in the media. One major factor is invisibility: Society's main strategy to deal with difference and otherness is to deny its existence or, in a more benign form, to relegate it to the periphery. This is not a sin exclusive to media makers but rather reflects forms of social discrimination that exist much more broadly with vital material consequences. In my home country of Chile, 17 percent of the population self-identifies as living with a disability, and they report experiencing two to three times more discrimination than nondisabled citizens.[1] Fictional representations of people with disabilities (or PWDs) are few and far between; characters with apparent disabilities are almost nonexistent in Chilean televised fiction, and international programming almost never features them as protagonists. In fact, when I first pitched ideas to network executives—in early 2013—their reaction was "interesting . . . but no thanks. A protagonist in a wheelchair is too *dark*."

Though representations of disabled characters are becoming more varied globally, long-standing disability stereotypes are still abundant, seen in the rare occasions PWDs appear in Chilean television and global imports alike. If the "angry misshapen villain" is now fortunately fading, the "innocent victim" placed in the narrative to elicit pity is not.[2] Beyond stereotypes, common narrative expectations restrict the possible dramatic arcs of characters with disabilities. An illustrative example of this form of discrimination came from Chile's top health provider, Clinica Las Condes, when we requested to use their facilities to shoot a scene for a proof-of-concept teaser of the series. After initially receiving a positive reaction from the medical staff, the clinic's marketing department decided they didn't want to associate their brand with a narrative in which the protagonist didn't "find a cure" for his disability. If we could make him walk in the end, they would be happy to participate. This blunt, if appalling, answer illustrates a common misconception about disability: that it is a problem in need of being fixed and that those experiencing it desperately seek a cure to overcome their disability. Under such misconceptions, fictional characters with disabilities will be dominated by their desire for a cure, such as to walk again, over any other human need or character trait.

In these stereotypical narrative tropes aimed at able-bodied viewers, PWDs need to either adapt to their tragic situation or fight heroically to overcome it. At their best, such stories use the thrill of fear, warning "it could happen to you" while providing an inspirational moment in the overcoming of a tragedy. At worst, they imply a life with disabilities is not a life worth living. Most importantly, whether portraying an innocent victim or a "supercrip," these narratives portray disability as a *problem of the individual*, the PWD's own capacity to adapt to or overcome their impairment, rather than a *societal construction*, an imposition from hegemonic systems and inaccessible infrastructures. This cultural logic enforces the expectation that PWDs must do all the adapting and overcoming, while it leaves the most pervasive forms of discrimination unchecked.

In writing *Bala Loca*, I realized I had to let go of the idea of portraying Murillo's accident. While it seemed at first like "story candy," a rich and obviously essential dramatic moment in the character's life, to use it as the inciting event would force a medicalization of the narrative and push the series down the same clichéd paths I just dismissed. To portray the accident, we would have to write scenes with doctors, the recovery, the rehabilitation process, and the mourning, all pushing the rehabilitation storyline to the foreground with inherent risks of excessive melodrama and overly didactic moments. This is not to say that these narrative tropes, like stereotypes, don't carry some truth: Acquiring a new disability will often trigger medical treatments, rehabilitation, adaptation, and so on. But focusing on the medical care would shortchange the complexities of the emotional processes involved and prevent *Bala Loca* from exploring other important events of PWDs' experiences. Disability civil rights activists and scholars have termed this approach the "medical model," one that focuses on disability primarily as a health issue, and thus a problem of the individual. Scholars and activists in this field have advocated instead for a "social model," one that frames disability as a collective issue that foregrounds the ways we organize our society, including design, interpersonal relations, and cultural representations.[3]

As an initial remedy, I decided to start the story a few years after Mauro Murillo's accident, so the first stage of his adaptation would be finished. Disability would not be the main storyline, but just a presence interacting with the different stories. The risk in this case is to perform an overcompensation, where the vicissitudes of being a PWD are entirely overlooked.[4] Some narratives use disability as texture and characterization, too far removed from the actual lived experiences of PWDs to be dramatically meaningful. To avoid these pitfalls, Marcos and I defined our goal in representing Mauro Murillo's disability: We wanted his experiences front and center, but we didn't want him to be defined by his impairment. Our hope was for audiences to witness his struggles, but not to construct him as the "dude in the wheelchair."

As a strategy to achieve this goal, we decided to avoid narrative conflicts for which the only possible explanation is Murillo's disability. He is presented in the beginning of the season as a man in crisis: dissatisfied at work, as the world of television and entertainment is abandoning him; in his family life, as he is estranged from his only son; and even in love, as he is sexually unhappy despite having a committed partner. But these crises are not reducible to his disability: Are TV executives ignoring Murillo because of his wheelchair, or because he is an insufferable know-it-all? Is he estranged from his son because he spent years depressed after the accident, or because he couldn't deal with the challenges of parenthood? Is his sexual impotence directly derived from his spinal injury, or a byproduct of alcohol abuse and age? The narrative refuses to offer simple answers to these dramatic questions. Even Murillo may blame his acquired disability for his shortcomings, but the narrative leaves the audience with alternative explanations, pointing to issues that nondisabled people also experience—in doing so, we aimed to craft a more complex context in which the character cannot be explained solely by his disability. Murillo shouldn't have to compensate for having a disability by becoming a saintly person or by acquiring preternatural clarity. Instead, the narrative should allow him to be contradictory: to be funny and depressed, to be abusive and kind, and to cheat and be loyal.

Another strategy we used to center disability was to find places within the storylines for what we called "how-to moments." We tried to portray as many of the procedural elements of dealing with a spinal cord injury as we could justify dramatically. Sometimes it worked really well, as in episode 6, when we see Murillo driving his Mustang with a hand-control lever, or in the pilot's portrayal of a sexual encounter between Murillo and his girlfriend Valeria (Fernanda Urrejola). This scene serves to portray the status of their relationship—love and companionship are high, but passion and joy are low—but it also works as a vehicle to display in detail some hurdles Murillo faces: the transition from wheelchair to bed, the body positioning, and the use of a penis pump. This device is used both by disabled and able-bodied people alike to treat erectile dysfunction, a condition that may affect some (but not all) men with spinal cord injuries. We felt that that exposure to the daily realities of PWDs increases perceived similarities within nondisabled viewers, creates points of identification and attraction, and works to counter stereotypes.[5]

Sometimes though, this how-to strategy failed us, as in the final sequence of episode 3. Throughout the episode, Murillo has been following retired army officer Ossorio Ruminot (Hugo Medina), recently released from prison, after serving time for the assassination of Murillo's brother during Pinochet's dictatorship. Having exhausted all legal and journalistic avenues, Murillo confronts Ruminot with a gun in hand, only to realize he won't be satisfied by revenge either. As a corollary to this painful arc, we thought it would be good to show, in an uncut long take, Murillo getting from his wheelchair into his car without help: the transition from chair to seat, removing the wheels, folding the chair, and the complicated maneuver to place the folded chair in the back seat. As wonderful as it read on paper—and still does to me—it fell flat in the editing room, disconnected from the dramatic tension accumulated in the storyline. The directing team provided a much more interesting final moment: a night scene where Murillo finally shoots the gun, only from an empty mountain lookout into an out-of-focus abstraction of Santiago in the distance, offering a metaphorical transition of responsibility and justice from the individual into the collective. I mention this failed choice because it's important to position issues of representation among the many other choices involved in producing a show. There are narrative, dramatic, political, and financial concerns, and the problems they present don't always align in neat ways.

It was important for us, too, to show disability as a collective issue, as much a result of the environment as of the physical conditions of individual PWDs. Throughout the show, Murillo has to contend with challenges imposed by a world that is not designed to include people with disabilities: from a handicapped parking spot used by an able-bodied television personality to the restaurant waiter that tries to forcibly help Murillo move without his consent; from the television executive that implies Murillo looks "too bitter" to get a new show to the many well-intended microaggressions Murillo receives, praising him for "his efforts." We wrote and planned most of these instances, but one of my favorites, for its visual clarity and almost-comedic appeal, was entirely imagined by the directing team. Mauro comes to meet a TV network executive, but at the lobby, the absurd height of the reception counter, clearly designed for nondisabled people, impedes any normal interaction between him and the receptionist.

In a couple of shots, the scene reveals whom we put at the center when we design our society. This emphasis on the collective is not to deny the individual implications of dealing with a physical impairment: Murillo goes to the doctor to treat his erectile dysfunction, he needs permanent medication, he sometimes dreams he can walk, and he is haunted by the pity he still sees in his own father's eyes. But it was essential for us to also address the collective role of society, the ways in which we relate to and interact with one another, in creating barriers and inequities that affect both material conditions and actual lived experiences.

In representing disability, the narrative—characters, events, conflicts, and relationships—may be the key concern but is not the only one. An important conversation has been becoming more mainstream regarding who should represent PWDs in fiction; recent data suggest that less than 5 percent of characters with disabilities are actually portrayed by actors who have a disability in their off-screen lives.[6] This conversation has parallels in other axes of power, particularly race, sexual orientation, and gender identity, though the parallels and analogies have limitations: Few people would defend the moral imperative to have only working-class actors represent working-class characters, for example, but few are willing to defend the decision to cast white actors portraying people of color. Regarding the representation of disability, some argue that actors should be allowed to act, regardless of ability status. For others, a time might come when we will perceive an able-bodied actor representing a character with a disability in the same light as we do blackface. If that's the case, *Bala Loca* won't age well: Marcos and I decided to cast able-bodied Alejandro Goic as Mauro Murillo. While representational considerations weighed on our minds, the reality is that *Bala Loca* was our first major production, and with a budget in the upper end of Chilean productions, there

FIGURES 10.1–4.
The sequence of shots in this scene communicates how normal interactions can be impossible in a world not designed to include people with disabilities.

were many demands placed upon casting: acting experience, name recognition, marketability, and even contractual agreements within networks, all depending on approval by the National Television Council and Turner/Chilevision. This is not to deny that we, as producers, also wanted the best possible actor, and Goic's talent was a gift to the character; his recognizable name in Chile also granted us more freedom to take the narrative wherever we wanted. It is nevertheless essential to acknowledge that we contributed to the problem: Actors with disabilities don't have the job opportunities to hone their craft and gain market appeal, making it more difficult for future productions to hire them. More effort remains to be done to cast actors with disabilities (and especially disabled actors of color, disabled trans actors, etc.) in all kinds of roles, not only for characters designed with their specific demographics in mind. And those efforts should also spread to diversify our writing rooms, production teams, and executive offices.

Notably, our interest in portraying a character with disabilities intersected with other issues of representation. Being mindful about one specific axis of power dynamics doesn't inoculate us against other entrenched representational biases. For instance, halfway through the casting stage of *Bala Loca*, I found myself disappointed with the way we were developing female roles in the show—hardly surprising since our writers' room was made up of three cisgendered men (albeit ones who self-identify as progressive and even *woke*). But ideology being the transparent water in which we swim, it permeates everything we do, and thus our female characters seemed a bit too simple and trite. As a last-ditch remedy, I proposed a gender switch for about half of our main characters, including the murdered journalist and their family, and Murillo's investigative team. It caused an immediate crisis, since we had been writing those characters for the good part of a year, and many actors had been already offered roles. Yet we soon realized we needed fewer changes than we thought we would, resulting in characters that seemed to push against stereotype.

The difficulties we experienced dealing with issues of representation didn't happen in a vacuum. These considerations interact and sometimes collide with narrative, financial, and production concerns. At times, we faced systemic or structural resistance, as diverting from the norm may scare financiers, advertisers, executives, and the other infrastructures essential to the material production of a drama series. But having Mauro Murillo and his disability as a compass guided our choices, and in the end, the show became better for it—not only better *politically* but also much better *dramatically*. Murillo's specific identity created many distinctive and underrepresented dramatic opportunities. For instance, his particular crisis of masculinity offered a different perspective of what power and vulnerability mean: a less-seen take on how we build romantic and parental relationships, with a fresher sense of intimacy, sex, and love. In summary, it gave us a window to show human conflicts and emotions from a distinct viewpoint. And this freshness spread into the other characters, making them less predictable, more specific, and more relatable. In a word, our fictional world became more complex.

As Chimamanda Adichie so succinctly expresses, the problem with the "single story" and stereotypes is not that they are necessarily untrue but that they are incomplete.[7] If we want to create stories that deepen our understanding of the world and our insight into the human experience, what writing *Bala Loca* taught us is that we can make progress by searching for that complexity. Whether you position yourself as a writer or an activist, an entertainer or a critic, such complexity offers a measure of whether you are being true to representing people and their lived experiences. The great news: It also makes for better stories.

FURTHER READING

Ellis, Katie, and Gerard Goggin. *Disability and the Media*. London: Palgrave Macmillan, 2015.

Norden, Martin F. "The Hollywood Discourse on Disability: Some Personal Reflections." In *Screening Disability: Essays on Cinema and Disability*, edited by Anthony Enns and Christopher R. Smith, 19–32. Lanham, MD: University Press of America, 2001.

Schalk, Sami. "Reevaluating the Supercrip." *Journal of Literary and Cultural Disability Studies* 10, no. 1 (2016): 71–86, 128.

NOTES

The author would like to thank Susan Burch and Carly Thomsen for generous feedback on this essay.

1. SENADIS Chile, *II Estudio Nacional de la Disacapacidad en Chile*, Servicio Nacional de la Discapacidad, Ministerio de Desarrollo Social de Chile (Santiago, Chile: SENADIS, 2015).

2. Martin F. Norden, "The Hollywood Discourse on Disability: Some Personal Reflections." In *Screening Disability: Essays on Cinema and Disability*, ed. Anthony Enns and Christopher R. Smith (Lanham, MD: University Press of America, 2001), 19–32; Charles A. Riley, *Disability and the Media: Prescriptions for Change* (Lebanon, NH: University Press of New England, 2012).

3. Katie Ellis and Gerard Goggin, *Disability and the Media* (London: Palgrave Macmillan, 2015).

4. Ibid.

5. This not only is intuitive but also has been long-supported by research. See, for instance, Nancy Weinberg, "Manipulating Attraction toward the Disabled: An Application of the Similarity-Attraction Model," *Rehabilitation Psychology* 20, no. 4 (1973): 156–64.

6. Bethonie Butler, "Almost All Disabled TV Characters Are Played by Able-Bodied Actors. Can We Fix That?" *Washington Post*, July 16, 2016, www.washingtonpost.com.

7. Chimamanda Ngozi Adichie, *TED TALKS: The Danger of a Single Story*, 2009, www.ted .com.

11

Being Mary Jane
Cultural Specificity

KRISTEN J. WARNER

Abstract: Through an analysis of the musical soundtrack as well as the narrative and stylistic devices throughout BET's *Being Mary Jane*, Kristen J. Warner explores how the series intentionally foregrounded black women's experiences. Warner illustrates how this act is a type of cultural specificity tied to the series' mantra "Black on Purpose" and ultimately results in crafting resonance with black audiences.

The second season of BET's critically acclaimed scripted series *Being Mary Jane* (*BMJ*) features an episode that uses solely neo-soul singer Erykah Badu's music as its soundtrack. For a series where the soundtrack guides the story as much as the embedded narrative conflicts, this choice not only sonically doubled down on the episode's drama but also reframed the importance of its targeted viewers and their musical tastes in some key ways. First, Badu's verses, with their wit and emphatic stances on being a black woman who finds herself in messy relationships time and time again, resonates with titular character Mary Jane Paul's circumstances within the episode. Second, while Badu is certainly an artist with mainstream appeal, part of her niche music style lies in a particular R&B aesthetic and tradition familiar to a predominantly black audience. Together, the messiness of the music and the characterization work to create a story steeped in a set of experiences that feels authentic to a specific niche of viewers.

BMJ's authenticity was not stumbled upon by accident. In fact, the realness of the characters and the attention to details in subject matter, community, and music are all the by-products of a mantra developed by the series creator and executive producer Mara Brock Akil. "Black on purpose" was coined by Brock Akil and her husband and co-producer Salim Akil to describe a strategic way of writing African American characters for their series that allows them to be seen as "unapologetically black." That is, through the writing, it is evident that these characters are black, and equally as important, are written by black folks. But what is this "black on purpose" ideology in reaction to, and why is it so important that the Akils make their ownership of the idea so explicit? The answer lies in an exploration of how racial representation has evolved in the television industry through specific innovations like colorblind casting that prioritize a critical mass of characters who are physically different but not necessarily culturally different or complex. As colorblind casting offered the illusion of a more level playing field, in reality the practice exposed actors of color to potentially more opportunity but also greater vulnerabilities of characterization. Enter "black on purpose." The Akils' approach, what I will refer to as "cultural specificity," presents a more active alternative to colorblind casting and insists that rather than the characters "happening to be black," it is more authentic and resonant if they are written as they are—with all the experiences, histories, and cultures that are tied to that identity marker. Thus, the goal of this essay is to unpack how cultural specificity operates as a more progressive type of casting strategy than its alternative of colorblind casting. Using *BMJ* as a case study, I will illustrate how the series embeds cultural specificity in its narrative, ultimately creating dimensionality for its characters and strong identification and resonance with its black audience.

When *BMJ* first premiered on BET in 2013, the world was introduced to Mary Jane Paul, a successful black Atlanta cable news personality, in her kitchen late at night baking with Mary J. Blige's "My Life" playing nondiegetically. Mary Jane, or MJ as her friends call her, wears a bandana head scarf, a baseball tee, and sweatpants as she answers the door holding a baseball bat for protection against a potential intruder. Seeing that it's her lover Andre, drunk but charismatic as he woos her to let him in, the soundtrack speedily switches to Rihanna's sex-charged anthem "Birthday Cake" as MJ quickly runs to clean up her bedroom and freshen up. Snatching off her bandana so her long locks can be on display and simultaneously ensuring her lingerie is right for the occasion, the scene switches to a love scene in her foyer with Andre. Seeing a black woman on television both as a normal homebody with her hair tied up in a protective style, and seconds later as a sexual being, is a rarity. This typical invisibility makes sense if we consider that since the inception of cinema and later television, black female representation has often been limited to specific types: the mammy, the tragic mulatta, the Jezebel, or the "loud-mouthed" Sapphire.[1] These women, because of the ways the film and television industries reinforced long-held racist ideologies about African Americans, were always rendered in extreme types. They were both asexual and hypersexual, their bodies in sum rendered undesirable except for specific parts of their anatomies that were fetishized such as Sarah Baartman's buttocks in the nineteenth century.

FIGURE 11.1.
Mary Jane's headscarf
points toward a specific-
ity of black women's hair
culture that resonates with
those viewers.

In addition, these black women types were depicted as wanting nothing for themselves, but only existing at the service of their white employers and friends. When they did desire more for themselves, as was the case with the tragic mulattas, they were punished and taught to want less.[2] As time goes on, these characterizations become identified as "stereotypes": a representational practice that, defined by Stuart Hall, "reduces people to a few, simple, essential characteristics, which are fixed by Nature."[3] Put simply, these types become a kind of eternally fixed essence of who *all* black women are, regardless of culture, experiences, and individual background. In reaction, black filmmakers and audiences thought of these types as "negative" because they were believed to stunt the progress of African Americans in society, and sought to locate more "positive" representations. The problem with that plan was that defining positive is much more difficult than defining negative. Would positive be depicted through costuming, through occupation, or through characterization?

Further complicating this positive/negative binary were the social contexts that reinforced their necessity. Herman Gray argues that representation functions as a discursive strategy that could potentially rally citizens around more progressive notions of racial equality. For example, in what he characterizes as the assimilationist era, narratives distilled racial equality as not a systemic issue but an individualized one that could be corrected if only people thought differently.[4] And of course, who better to teach them than a "positive" black character who, outside of a specific episode's problem-of-the-week, rarely acknowledged race or her own racialization? NBC's 1968 hit *Julia* starring legendary black actress Diahann Carroll epitomized this phenomenon. As Beretta E. Smith-Shomade asserts, "*Julia* never alluded explicitly . . . to the civil and social unrest raging on American streets. The show implied that . . . harmony could be achieved if we could all just get along."[5] This strategy may have helped black actors avoid specific stereotypical tropes, but its insistence on a sameness of all characters, regardless of racial history, opened the door for a new strategy with just as many problems: colorblind casting.

Colorblind casting, or blindcasting, is the process of casting where race is not written into the script. Originally a theater practice emerging in the 1950s, blindcasting sought to correct the underrepresentation of minority actors on the stage. Colorblind casting operates under the guiding principle that since acting is fiction, the best actor for the role should earn it regardless of their race. Combining this principle with the assimilationist approach, transferring blindcasting to television and film became a wise decision for media professionals at both the producing level and those in the executive suites. And indeed, the surface goals of blindcasting are well intentioned: opening auditions to a multitude of types in search of the best actor for the job is an admirable and sensible choice. However, the drawbacks to this casting approach are numerous. At the level of characterization, blindcasting does not factor in that although the actor hired may be best for the role, the part must be adjusted to accommodate the diverse histories and experiences that are encompassed in her body. To the contrary, blindcasting assumes a normativity, or sameness, to the characters as those traits are what they had planned for the character. Normativity here is often code for whiteness, that is, an identity deemed so culturally natural, it becomes the norm that all other identities must be compared to. As a result of the parts not being adjusted to fit the actor's racialized history, the person of color who takes a role may unintentionally be placed in a situation that makes them vulnerable to being read as a stereotype. The pitfalls of colorblindness are the unintentional consequences of not thinking through the cultural experiences attached to the body of the actor hired, and instead only considering the viewpoints and experiences of what is valued in predominantly white male writers' rooms—or rooms where although the racial makeup may be different, the same normative expectations are still in play.

This phenomena explains, for example, how as a result of ABC's *Grey's Anatomy* blindcasting its lead and supporting roles, Dr. Miranda Bailey, played by African American actress Chandra Wilson, both exists as the irascible yet caring chief resident of the predominantly white interns she supervises, which was required for the role regardless of who played it and is simultaneously tethered to stereotypes of black women as mammies by virtue of her racialized body being placed in that role. The issue in this case is not that Wilson was hired for the part; rather, the issue is that once she took the role, nothing about her characterization was adjusted in consideration of the historical experiences associated with black womanhood, ultimately placing her character in a vulnerable pitfall in the name of sameness.

Blindcasting creates a vulnerable position not only for the character but also for racially marginalized audience members who wish to find characteristics they can identify with in the person on screen who looks like them. Part of the rationale for blindcasting is that through normalizing all racial and ethnic types, mainstream (read: white) audiences could accept on-screen visual differences more easily. Nevertheless, in pursuit of this mainstream tolerance of physical diversity, marginalized audiences are left to stitch together meaningful representations that resonate and connect with their own experiences. Brock Akil confirms this point: "What's interesting to me is that when it comes to sometimes getting things made, we have to [cast color-blind]. I'm like, 'No, I'm not fucking color-blind! I have a rich history, can you include that?'"[6] Her frustration with this normative industry policy stems from the dismissal of black experience as rich and valuable, in favor of a stripped-down universal one. Of course, Brock Akil's point begs the question: Is this kind of "make do" construction the only way for black audiences to have representation?

Indeed, it is not. Cultural specificity involves intentionally writing characters as complex racialized individuals that exceed the boundaries of positive and negative, so that their familiarity, relatability, and humanity can draw audiences seeking out that kind of visibility. Cultural specificity speaks to a more genuine and meaningful diversity because it allows for audiences to see a fully dimensional view of themselves on screen, since the character is created and performed as a person based on real identities, experiences, and culture. Cultural specificity is the means by which writers immerse their characters into a particular set of traditions and experiences that are recognizable to audiences who identify with those identities. These visual and aural techniques ultimately connect the viewer to the creative work because such shared experiences resonate. When asked if *BMJ* was intentionally written for a black audience, Brock Akil asserted, "I believe in approaching writing through the specific; the details of a particular culture. So, yes, black people are going to recognize themselves first, and they're going to be the first ones to validate it. 'Yep, you got that right.' There's an authenticity."[7] Brock Akil affirms that black audiences are the first targets she tries to reach through her characterizations, but she does not suggest that they are the last. In fact, specificity can still draw a host of diverse viewers even while it zeroes in on trying to cultivate authenticity.[8] A benefit for *BMJ* is that it is housed on BET, a cable network designed to create programming for a niche audience—in this instance, black viewers. This then begs the question: In what ways is *BMJ* a culturally specific text?

As part of the credits of the *BMJ* pilot, the world of the series is introduced through words typed onto a black screen: "42% of Black women have never been married. This is one Black woman's story. . . . Not meant to represent all Black women. Being Mary Jane."[9] According to a *New York Times* interview, the premise of the entire series hinged upon the above title cards, as Brock Akil wanted to explore the "human side of that number and wanted each episode to follow Mary Jane through a day in her life."[10] In addition, the claim that this is one black

FIGURE 11.2.
Mary Jane panics when she learns her hairdresser isn't able to install her new hair extensions after she's taken out her old ones—another nod to Akil's "black on purpose" mantra.

woman's story, "not meant to represent all Black women," is an explicit tactic of reminding viewers that this is a *specific* story, that the totality of Mary Jane's experiences are not universal to all black women or women in general. Put simply, the show asserts that Mary Jane's black womanness is specific but not monolithic—a position that reminds audiences that while the lead character may be relatable and familiar, she is not the only acceptable version.

It's the details of Mary Jane's characterization that make her "black on purpose." Journalist Jada F. Smith describes the attributes that center Mary Jane as a specific kind of black woman: "Viewers see her scroll through Twitter while using the restroom, smoothing down the edges of her hair with a warm curling iron . . . and conflicted over whether to expose a fellow black journalist who fudged some facts in a story but whose articles led to widespread prison reform."[11] These examples operate as traits readily identifiable for any woman; however, if Brock Akil's point about targeting black audiences first is true, then these moments have discernibly different meanings for those viewers. Black hair culture in particular is always considered central to Mary Jane's (and viewers) identities. Smoothing down her edges, freaking out when she learns her hairdresser isn't able to install her weave after she's detached her old weave from her scalp, or wearing a plastic shower cap as she prepares to shower at the gym because she cannot get her hair wet are all gestures that point to cultural specificity. Her hair is not like her white female counterparts, and the acknowledgment of such differences in these familiar ways gestures to a "black on purpose" point of view.

Also of note is that Mary Jane Paul is not the character's real name. Changing her name from Pauletta Patterson to her new moniker functions within the narrative in two key ways. In the first instance, it reveals the duality of what it means to be a contemporary black woman. Pauletta Patterson, a name that tethers her to a particular kind of southern black identity, is not a "respectable" name for a mainstream news personality. On the contrary, Mary Jane Paul takes some of the spirit of her real name but neutralizes it into something far more palatable and normative. The second way the name change functions within the narrative is how it offers a meta-commentary on the actual split between the notion of color-blindness and that of cultural specificity. Mary Jane Paul, the consummate cable news anchor who blends into her workplace without creating tension because of her difference, offers a glance at a type who to some "happens to be black," while Pauletta Patterson becomes the name she is called by her family when she sings the Stevie Wonder version of "Happy Birthday"—a culturally specific act often described as the "Black Happy Birthday song"—with them. Considering how her names act as a lens to understand how she operates in the world reinforces her relatability and familiarity with black women who have to do the same.

The cultural specificity of Mary Jane's family life is essential to understanding how the show resonates with black audiences. As the middle and most financially successful of three children in the pilot, MJ's rapport with her family is located in a particular southern black vernacular. Watching MJ just arriving to work while on the phone with her mother Helen, who is fussing about one of her siblings, offers yet another opportunity to see the split between colorblindness and cultural specificity. Helen describes to Mary Jane how her youngest son PJ who lives at home brought a young woman over to spend the night. The specificity in this scene is located in the dialogue. Helen rants, "He brought a fast-tail gal in my house. Now, he can't pay a bill or even buy a loaf of bread, but he has the nerve to screw some tramp in my house. I'm telling you—in MY house." MJ, needing to maintain an acceptable presentation to those around her, does not react to her mother but instead deploys her "professional" vocal register to end the call. Helen's dialogue in tandem with Margaret Avery's performance of the lines resonates because of the oral tradition so much a part of the histories of African Americans.[12]

In sum, be it through costuming, the visuals, or the very particular soundtracks that feature R&B singers like Mary J. Blige, Jill Scott, and Erykah Badu who complement the narratives of success and distress that feature so prominently in *BMJ*, cultural specificity marks this show as one that seeks to gain the viewership of black women viewers. The black on purpose strategy has been successful for the Akils: *BMJ*'s first season finale was watched by 5.8 million live-and-same-day viewers and became BET's number one series by its third season. The success of the show can be attributed to a host of factors, from its placement on the Viacom-owned network to the star persona of Mary Jane's lead actress Gabrielle Union. But I argue that it's the cultural specificity that connects the audience to the characters who, despite their flaws, have enough identifiable qualities that they feel familiar and real to viewers. *BMJ*'s black on purpose mantra allows the characters to exceed the stereotypes that surround their black identities.

Brock Akil suggests that the show's tagline, "beautifully flawed," moves the performances beyond the mediated images of black identity that can only be understood through the lens of "positive versus negative" language: "I think [beautifully flawed] that's what [humanity] is. Oftentimes the African American audience will ask for a positive image because so much of the stereotype has been what gets in the landscape of our image. They want to counteract that with a positive image, but I personally believe strongly that the positive image is just as damaging as the negative image. Humanity does not exist in those extremes."[13] Cultural specificity as a strategy sidesteps that conversation of positive and negative, focusing instead on what makes the characters true, laying out their experiences meticulously so as to call out to viewers to see and relate. Creating that visibility allows for black viewers, who are rarely given the opportunity to see themselves with such complexity on screen, to have that humanity that Brock Akil describes.

FURTHER READING

Hall, Stuart. "Stereotyping as a Signifying Practice." In *Representation*, edited by Stuart Hall, Jessica Evans, and Sean Nixon. London: SAGE, 2013.

Smith-Shomade, Beretta E. *Shaded Lives: African-American Women and Television* (New Brunswick, NJ: Rutgers University Press, 2002).

Warner, Kristen J. "In the Time of Plastic Representation." *Film Quarterly* 71, no. 2 (December 2017).

NOTES

1. For more on mediated histories of African American stereotypes, see Donald Bogle, *Toms, Coons, Mammies, Mulattoes and Bucks: An Interpretive History of Blacks in American Films* (New York: Continuum, 1991); Patricia Hill Collins, *Black Feminist Thought: Knowledge, Consciousness, and the Politics of Empowerment* (New York: Routledge, 2002); and Beretta E. Smith-Shomade, *Shaded Lives: African-American Women and Television* (New Brunswick, NJ: Rutgers University Press, 2002).

2. Both the 1934 and 1959 versions of *Imitation of Life* illustrate the punishment of the tragic mulatta.

3. Stuart Hall, "Stereotyping as a Signifying Practice," in *Representation*, ed. Stuart Hall, Jessica Evans, and Sean Nixon (London: SAGE, 2013), 247.

4. Herman Gray, *Watching Race: Television and the Struggle for Blackness* (Minneapolis: University of Minnesota Press, 2004).

5. Smith-Shomade, *Shaded Lives*, 14–15.

6. Adrienne Gaffney, "*Being Mary Jane* Creator Mara Brock Akil on Her Flawed Heroine, the Rise of Diverse TV, and Why She Hates Color-blind Casting," *Vulture*, February 3, 2015.

7. "*Being Mary Jane*'s Gabrielle Union Grills Her Bosses about Writing for a Black Audience: 'We Actually Do Black on Purpose,'" *Hollywood Reporter*, October 17, 2014.

8. As another example of specificity gaining a larger audience, consider BET's *Real Husbands*

of Hollywood, which in its first season became cable's number one sitcom among 18–49-year-olds. Craig D. Lindsey, "Cable's Number One Sitcom? 'Real Husbands of Hollywood,'" Balder and Dash, October 15, 2015, www.rogerebert.com.

9. *Being Mary Jane*, pilot, BET, July 2, 2013.

10. Jada F. Smith, "With *Being Mary Jane*, Mara Brock Akil Specializes in Portraits of Black Women," *New York Times*, October 20, 2015.

11. Smith, "With *Being Mary Jane*."

12. For more reading on African American oral traditions, see Henry Louis Gates Jr., *The Signifying Monkey: A Theory of African American Literary Criticism* (Oxford: Oxford University Press, 2014).

13. Gaffney, "*Being Mary Jane* Creator."

12

Buckwild

Performing Whiteness

AMANDA ANN KLEIN

Abstract: Throughout the 2000s, MTV released a series of reality programs focusing on identities like *Jersey Shore*'s guidos and the young mothers of *Teen Mom*. In this essay, Amanda Ann Klein argues that MTV's *Buckwild*, which focuses on the antics of working-class, white, West Virginia youth who identify as "rednecks," illustrates the importance of whiteness as a performative identity category in contemporary America. The series provides a venue for white audiences to offer resistance against a perceived, symbolic loss in white hegemony.

Beginning in 2004 with *Laguna Beach*, and continuing on with series such as *Catfish*, MTV has aired more than a dozen identity-focused reality shows focusing on and highlighting a variety of American youth identities.[1] In series such as *The Hills, Jersey Shore, Sixteen and Pregnant, Virgin Territory, The Real World, Washington Heights, Floribama Shore*, and others, millennial audiences have the opportunity to take up what Herbert Gans has called a "symbolic ethnicity," an identity they choose for themselves, which they perform before MTV's cameras.[2] For contemporary youth audiences, who regularly document and project their selfhood via social media and smartphones, MTV's reality programming functions as an "identity workbook," showcasing a variety of ways of being in the world. These reality TV programs offer a financial and social reward in exchange for the cast members' willingness to appear on camera to perform a particular, codified version of their selected identity. Benjamin Wallace calls contemporary reality television "an extractive industry," taking the recording, amplification, and repetition of identities and converting them from lived experiences into "corporate brands": *Jersey Shore*'s guidos, *Teen Mom*'s teenage mothers, and *Buckwild*'s rednecks.[3] In other words, prospective MTV cast members are encouraged—through money and the taste of fame—to self-script their identities and then perform them on screen. Youth audiences are invited to self-script their identities on camera in exchange for the opportunity to be on television. This essay explores one example of this self-scripting of youth identities on MTV—the cultivation and celebration of rural white identities on *Buckwild*, a short-lived reality series focusing on the *Jackass*-style antics of West Virginia youth.

For most of Western history, whiteness, as a racial category, has been invisible. In his canonical study of whiteness, Richard Dyer explains that "the invisibility of whiteness as a racial position" goes hand in hand with its ubiquity.[4] That is, because whiteness has been the default race, the starting point, the blank slate, it has escaped analysis and critique within Western culture, recognized not as a raced identity but rather as the *absence* of race or identity. But whiteness has steadily lost its dominant demographic hold on the United States over the last few decades; in thirty years, people who identify as white in America will be a minority, behind those who identify as Latino.[5] The less hegemonic power white people hold in the United States, the *more* visible whiteness has become in the American popular imagination. Specifically, there has been a rising interest in films, television series, novels, music, and political ideologies that examine whiteness as an explicit racial category. It is now possible to speak of whiteness and white privilege, and with that possibility comes the need to rebrand whiteness and take ownership of its meaning. Furthermore, in the wake of the Great Recession of 2008, poor, white Americans became the focus of a number of sociological tomes and hand-wringing profiles exploring the financial and political sea changes of this demographic.[6] This interest in whiteness as something that was both fragile and proud reached an apex with Donald Trump's successful bid for president of the United States in 2016. While Trump's anti-immigrant and antiminority rhetoric mobilized this white, working-class voting base by capitalizing on white America's fears about a loss of racial hegemony, dozens and dozens of investigative articles and polarizing think pieces published in the wake of the 2016 election attributed this demographic's Trumpism to an amorphous "economic anxiety." Thus, even when many Trump supporters were publicly proclaiming their white supremacist and neo-Nazi rhetoric—on the Internet and on live television—it was difficult for American media outlets to accuse white America of racial bias.[7]

In the last decade, dozens of reality shows have portrayed "white trash" America, in which the poor, white subjects have made a choice to appear on television and have their lives documented through the particular lens of the "hillbilly" or "redneck," a production cycle that Andrew Scahill calls "white trash spectacle."[8] In these series, the label is taken on as a badge of honor. To be a hillbilly or redneck is to be proud of one's modest upbringing.[9] For example, Kristen Hatch argues

FIGURE 12.1. *Buckwild* suggests that being poor and white isn't all that bad as long as you can still have fun.

that in *Here Comes Honey Boo Boo*, the term "redneck" becomes shorthand for rebelliousness against restrictive norms of modern capitalism. Poverty is "celebrated as self-acceptance" with pleasure "derived from witnessing the family's excesses and their unwillingness to embrace middle-class behaviors or succumb to the dictates of neoliberal citizenship."[10] While middle-class audiences might view the cost-saving behaviors exhibited in "hillbillysploitation" series like *Here Comes Honey Boo Boo* or *Duck Dynasty*, including extreme couponing and the cooking and eating of roadkill, as low-class or even gross behaviors, the series' stars took pride in their own inventiveness. In the midst of this so-called crisis of whiteness, *Buckwild* likewise offers a model of whiteness emblematic of resilience and resourcefulness in the face of economic hardship. The *Buckwild* cast works menial jobs (or in some cases, no jobs at all) but embraces and celebrates the freedom this unfettered lifestyle provides. They engage in a kind of rural *bricolage*, turning old pickup trucks into swimming pools and "skiing" on old garbage can lids tied to the back of RTVs; such resourcefulness suggests that being poor and white isn't all that bad as long as you can still have fun. Furthermore, the series effectively rebrands whiteness as freedom, ingenuity, and bravery, thus reclaiming it from negative signifiers like poverty, racism, and lack of education.

Scahill argues that hillbillysploitation reality series rhetorically mirror the Victorian freakshow in that they encourage a derisive gaze on the part of the spectator. Only in this case, "the assumed white spectator assumes his/her 'good white' status through deriding spectacles of 'bad whiteness.'"[11] J. D. Vance, author of the best-selling memoir, *Hillbilly Elegy*, discusses his rural Ohio upbringing and how so-called white trash have been understood in the American imagination by quoting his grandmother: "We [hillbillies] are the only group of people you don't have to be ashamed to look down upon."[12] One of Vance's arguments is that all people feel a need to look down upon another social group as a way to shore up their own superiority; for wealthy, educated whites, looking down on other white people, so-called hillbillies or rednecks, fulfills that need without the nasty baggage of feeling like a racist or a xenophobe. Hillbillysploitation capitalizes on this particular brand of *schadenfreude*. It is in this environment of visible whiteness that MTV turned its cameras to West Virginia.

Nonwhite, non-middle-to-upper-middle-class characters in the media tend to stand in as representatives for their race, ethnicity, or class. A black person who appears on a reality series, for example, is frequently saddled with the expectation to "speak" for his or her race. By contrast, middle- and upper-class white characters have, to quote Richard Dyer, the "right to be various."[13] Representations of white characters on television run the gamut from rich to poor, old to young, and criminal to saint, all without any assumption that one of these character traits is definitive of the white race. Dyer further explains, "The uncertainties of whiteness as a hue, a color and yet not a colour, make it possible to see the bearers of white skin as nonspecific, ordinary and mere, and it just so happens the only people whose color permits this perception."[14] However, the whiteness of the *Buckwild* cast is not invisible. *Buckwild*'s portrayal of whiteness is bound to region, to West Virginia and to redneck culture. The white characters in *Buckwild* are marked and made visible, and therefore the dangerous behaviors, cursing, drinking, and screwing they engage in, are *all* tied to West Virginia and West Virginians. Indeed, characters frequently preface their behaviors with the phrase "'Round here we . . . ," as if every activity featured on the series is a West Virginia tradition. *Buckwild* not only makes the part stand in for the whole but also places whiteness in a category it rarely occupies: visibility. It is worth pausing here to note that there is one person of color in the *Buckwild* cast, Salwa Amin, who identifies as South Asian. Her nickname, "Bengali in Boots," highlights the incongruity of her ethnic heritage with the region in which she lives. While Salwa's presence in the otherwise all-white *Buckwild* cast might signal the fact that ethnicity is not a barrier to entry into Sissonville's redneck community, her marginal presence on the series indicates otherwise. Salwa barely appears in the series' 2013 promotional trailers and is not even given her own introduction (complete with block letters displaying her first name) in the pilot's opening credits sequence. Salwa appears in multiple episodes as a secondary character who comments on main plot arcs but who is rarely in the spotlight herself.

Buckwild's breakout star and frequent narrator is Shain Gandee, the ideal subject for a series interested in "rednecks" in West Virginia. Shain performs his West Virginia-ness through his heavy accent, his love of the state, and his staunch refusal of urban life and technology. For example, Gandee refused to carry a cell phone, even after the show's producers bought him one and asked him to carry it, and his first time on an airplane was when MTV flew him to New York City to promote *Buckwild*. Shain is danger-loving, laconic, frightened of the big city, and

FIGURE 12.2.
Breakout star and
frequent narrator
of *Buckwild*, Shain
Gandee.

filled with amusing insights about what it *really* means to be a West Virginian, leading viewers by the hand, taking them into his world, and showing them how things are done "round here." He is usually the inventor of the redneck leisure sports featured on the series and is usually the first to suggest or to engage in a dangerous activity. Shain's segments in the series are frequently preceded with footage of him riding a motorized vehicle—a bike, an ATV (all-terrain vehicle), a truck—at an alarming speed through a natural backdrop. Sometimes this footage is filtered through a mud-speckled Go-Pro camera strapped to the vehicle, thus taking the audience along for the ride. Shain tells the cameras, "If you wanna be a man, you can't be scared of anything." At a time when the very categories of gender identity and what it means to be a "man" or a "woman" are becoming less concrete and more fluid, the need to assert gender becomes all the more important. Embracing danger, seeking it out, and subjecting one's body to it is a simple litmus test for masculinity in *Buckwild*.

The relative danger of activities is constantly assessed, debated, and celebrated by *Buckwild*'s cast members. In episode 3, for example, Shain and his friend, Joey Mulcahy, haze Tyler Boulet into riding a motorized bike for the first time. Tyler ultimately crashes the bike during his last lap, much to the delight of his friends, who whoop and high five each other. But Shain's father is not amused and chastises the boys: "If you ride the bike, put the helmet on!" But the boys never do, because they are never scared. In episode 11, Shain and Tyler take Katie Saria, the new girl in town, for her first "muddin'" experience. The object of muddin', according to the show's cast, is to drive a pickup truck directly into mud holes, which creates a doubled effect: the bump and crash of the truck going into and out of a hole, and the splash of mud generated by the impact. As Shain's truck backs out of the driveway, Katie asks, fear creeping into her voice, "Why are there no seatbelts?" They drive her out to the middle of the woods, where sinkholes can accumulate puddles of mud without disturbance. The cinematography alternates from long shots outside of the truck and medium close-ups taken inside the truck's cabin. The diegetic sounds of the trucks revving engines are amplified, thus enhancing the impression of their mechanical largess and thus the masculinity of the men operating the vehicles.

Buckwild also promotes the idea that West Virginia-ness is synonymous with freedom, a belief that dates back to the state's founding in 1862, when it succeeded from Virginia. The state's motto, *Montani Semper Liberi*, translates to "Mountaineers are always free."[15] Perhaps in a nod to this history, *Buckwild's* opening credits narrator explains, "West Virginia is a place founded on freedom. For me and my friends, it's to do whatever the fuck we want!" The characters in *Buckwild* are free because they are able to seemingly control their own environments, treating West Virginia like "one big playground." Their inventive use of leisure time is transformed, through the industry of reality television, into productive labor: the performance of West Virginia-ness. *Buckwild's* cast members take seemingly useless, abandoned objects from their environment—garbage can lids, plastic oil drums, and PVC piping—and convert them into useful objects of leisure and entertainment. In episode 7, the kids actually construct a "bull" out of a plastic oil drum suspended from four poles by ropes. *Buckwild's* cast demonstrates its freedom, as neoliberal citizenry, to make the most of their limited means. Like the cast on series such as *The Biggest Loser*, the *Buckwild* cast is taking ownership of and pleasure in the care of the self.

Although the behaviors on display in *Buckwild* are dangerous and reckless, the product of boredom combined with a lack of money, audiences are never supposed to see the cast's behaviors are pitiable or in need of reformation. Indeed, this image of unfettered American freedom is explicitly tied to whiteness, which functions to make these behaviors appear as good-natured hijinks, rather than threating. In another context, and with young characters of a different race, the drinking, fistfights, and dangerous, ad hoc extreme sports practiced by the cast would be something to discourage. But these behaviors are not framed as problems in need of a solution. For the cast of *Buckwild*, the "problems" associated with living in rural West Virginia, including a lack of entertainment or gainful employment, are solved with the appearance of MTV's cameras. The group's reaction to their life circumstances—to go muddin' or make a swimming pool out of an abandoned dump truck—are ways of not only making lemonade out of lemons but also monetizing these lemons via MTV. This neoliberal arrangement makes "the borders between the time and space of life and those of so-called 'productive' labor seem to disappear, in order to account for the phenomenon of 'setting affect to work' or 'setting life to work.'"[16] In this context, the term "neoliberal" is used to describe the way that certain strains of reality television appear to provide goods and services, such as home repairs or health care, that the government has failed to provide. As Laurie Ouellette explains in her discussion of series like *Extreme Makeover: Home Edition*, "At a time when low-income housing programs are strapped for funding and welfare as we know it doesn't exist, the program epitomizes television's literal (not merely symbolic) role in the privatization of social services."[17] *Buckwild* not only provides a model of whiteness for youth audiences that celebrates rural living, the value of American machinery, and postrecession resilience but also implies that that this identity is productive and generates an income. *Buckwild* suggests that being poor isn't all that bad as long as you can still have fun, and once you start having fun, MTV might come to your town and film you and your friends.

As the show began to take off in the ratings—*Buckwild* had an average of three million viewers per episode and ranked eighth among all cable series in 2013—many of the cast members were hopeful about making more money.[18] Indeed, the casts' salaries were reportedly increased by 400 percent for season 2. But the casts' hopes for season 2 salaries were cut abruptly short in April 2013, when the *Buckwild* cast and crew were given the weekend off for Easter. To celebrate the holiday weekend, Shain and two friends drove off in Shain's truck for some muddin' and off-roading activities. They disappeared for thirty-one hours. After an exhaustive search, Shain's family eventually found his Bronco on its side in a mudhole, with the tailpipe stuck in the mud. The three men inside, including Shain, had died of carbon monoxide poisoning. As Shain was the show's central figure—the most West Virginian, the most reckless, and the most *Buckwild*—it's significant that he died while muddin', one of the casts' favorite activities showcased in much of the series' press materials and trailers. Although four episodes of season 2 were shot and in the can, MTV ultimately decided to cancel the series, a move that angered and disappointed the cast. Susanne Daniels, MTV's head of programming, explained: "This is a show that for me is about *joie de vivre*, about youth and having fun and throwing caution to the wind and taking chances and playfulness and partying. . . . So how do you continue with the show when you've lost the heart of that show?"[19] In other words, Gandee's untimely death had polluted the series' brand. It was no longer fun and games now that someone was dead.

The *Buckwild* cast labored to redefine their identities from that of poor, disenfranchised, white West Virginians to a group of individuals who are free to endanger their bodies and to make a paycheck doing so. Instead of a source of shame, their West Virginian identities became something to celebrate and even emulate. But the symbolic value of the West Virginian redneck identity—a person who is unfettered by the regulations and rules that the rest of society must follow—ultimately collided with the material reality of this self-scripted identity in April 2013. For while it is true that Shain Gandee and his friends would have gone muddin' on that fateful Easter morning with or without the presence of MTV's cameras, their deaths—*a result of performing West Virginia-ness*—highlights the danger in building a career out of one's identity, especially an identity that is at odds with physical safety. Indeed, *Buckwild*'s tragic ending highlights how on-screen identities and material bodies are bound tightly together in MTV's identity cycle. When your job is to play yourself, you are never not working. And when being yourself means endangering your body, then both work and being yourself is a never-ending state of precarity. The premiere, as well as the untimely cancellation, of *Buckwild* highlights the importance of whiteness as a performative identity in contemporary America. In the context of the series, whiteness is both a point of pride and an obstacle to overcome with clever redneck ingenuity, even though race and whiteness is never explicitly discussed or evoked within the series. Much like "economic anxiety," in the context of *Buckwild*, "redneck" is a deracinated term for pride in white identity and resilience against a perceived loss in white hegemony.

FURTHER READING

Dyer, Richard. *White*. London: Routledge, 1997.

Gans, Herbert. "Symbolic Ethnicity: The Future of Ethnic Groups and Cultures in America." *Ethnic and Racial Studies* 2, no. 1 (1979): 1–20.

Scahill, Andrew. "Pigmalion: Animality and Failure in *Here Comes Honey Boo Boo*." *Flow: A Critical Forum on Television and Media Culture*, May 6, 2013.

NOTES

1. MTV's interest in reality identity programming dates back to the premiere of *The Real World* in 1992, but this series was an isolated example of this phenomenon at a time when MTV was still invested in the music video format. It is not until 2004, when *Laguna Beach* premieres, that MTV's identity-focused reality series become an established cycle on the channel.
2. Herbert Gans, "Symbolic Ethnicity: The Future of Ethnic Groups and Cultures in America," *Ethnic and Racial Studies* 2, no. 1 (1979): 1.
3. Benjamin Wallace, "Diamond in the Mud: The Death of *Buckwild* Star Shain Gandee and the Search for Authenticity in Reality TV," *Vulture*, September 15, 2013.
4. Richard Dyer, *White* (London: Routledge, 1997), 3.
5. Haya El Nasser, "US Birthrate Continues to Slow Because of Recession," *Aljazeera America* December 10, 2014.
6. Charles Murray's *Coming Apart: The State of White America, 1960–2010* (2012), Robert D. Putnam's *Our Kids: The American Dream in Crisis* (2015), J. D. Vance's *Hillbilly Elegy* (2016), Nancy Isenberg's *White Trash: The 400-Year Untold History of Class in America* (2016), and so forth.
7. See, for example, the "Unity the Right" rally in Charlottesville, Virginia, in the fall of 2017, that featured antiblack and anti-Jew chants, and which culminated in the death of a white woman who was counterprotesting the event.

8. Andrew Scahill, "Pigmalion: Animality and Failure in *Here Comes Honey Boo Boo*," *Flow: A Critical Forum on Television and Media Culture*, May 6, 2013.

9. Titles include *Hillbilly Handfishing, Swamp People, Bayou Billionaires, Rocket City Rednecks, Redneck Island, Rocket City Rednecks, My Big Redneck Wedding, Redneck Intervention, Cajun Pawn Stars, River Monsters, Bayou Billionaires, Moonshiners, American Hoggers, Lady Hoggers, The Legend of Shelby the Swamp Man, Pit Bulls and Parolees, Call of the Wildman, Backyard Oil, Street Outlaws, Lizard Lick Towing, Welcome to Myrtle Manor,* and *Here Comes Honey Boo Boo.*

10. Kristen Hatch, "*Here Comes Honey Boo Boo* and the Spectacle of the Ungovernable Child," *Flow: A Critical Forum on Television ad Media Culture*, September 10, 2012.

11. Scahill, "Pigmalion."

12. Quoted in Rod Dreher, "Trump: Tribune of Poor White People," *American Conservative*, July 22, 2016.

13. Dyer, *White*, 49.

14. Ibid., 60.

15. Gerald D. Swick, "Virginia's Great Divorce," *HistoryNet*, March 5, 2013, www.historynet.com.

16. Antonella Corsani, "Beyond the Myth of Woman: The Becoming-Transfeminist of (Post-) Marxism," *Italian Post-Workerist Thought* 36, no. 1 (2007): 124.

17. Laurie Ouellette, "Do Good TV?" *Flow: A Critical Forum on Television and Media Culture*, February 24, 2006, www.flowjournal.org.

18. Quoted in Wallace, "Diamond in the Mud."

19. Ibid.

13

Glee/House Hunters International
Gay Narratives

RON BECKER

Abstract: One key cultural function of television is to represent different identities, especially marginalized groups; here Ron Becker considers one interesting type of contemporary gay representation. By connecting seemingly disparate texts of *Glee*, *House Hunters International*, and the online It Gets Better movement, we can see how media construct messages of optimism and hope that can have powerful impacts on viewers.

In 2010, syndicated advice columnist Dan Savage and his partner, Terry Miller, posted a video to YouTube in an effort to reach out to teenagers dealing with anti-gay bullying and thoughts of suicide. The fortysomething couple shared their own painful experiences being consistently harassed and feeling ostracized at school. Their main goal, however, was to provide hope for gay teenagers by assuring them that things will improve. "It gets better," Savage avowed, "and it can get great and it can get awesome. Your life can be amazing, but you have to tough this period of it out and you have to live your life so you're around for it to get amazing. And it can and it will." The video went viral and kick-started a social movement that brought unprecedented national attention to the problems of gay teen suicide and anti-gay bullying. Thousands of people posted videos to the It Gets Better Project website, and millions viewed the videos and donated money.

This essay is not about the It Gets Better campaign per se, but rather the fundamentally optimistic social message at its core. Most of this essay will, in fact, focus on two television series: *Glee*, Fox's campy musical "melodramedy" about the joys and pains of a high school glee club in Lima, Ohio, and *House Hunters International*, HGTV's formulaic, real-estate reality show in which people looking to relocate to distant places like Dubai or buy second homes in tropical spots like

St. Lucia tour three homes before deciding which one to buy. I connect these two disparate programs—one, a primetime network mega-hit that had as much buzz as any show during the 2010–2011 season; the other, just one of a dozen inexpensive, home-centered, lifestyle shows steadily repeated on cable networks like HGTV, TLC, and Bravo—because I believe that they work together to support the same optimistic vision of contemporary gay life as the It Get Better Project does. While *Glee* portrays the pathos of gay teens seeking a better life, *House Hunters International* gives viewers an aspirational glimpse of what that life could be.

Chris Colfer, the openly gay actor who plays Kurt Hummel, the openly gay high school student on *Glee*, was one of the first celebrities to post a video to ItGetsBetter.org. His prominent participation seemed appropriate. By the fall of 2010, the hit FOX series had become well known for its depiction of high school bullying and as a champion of kids who don't fit in—themes that are firmly established in the pilot episode. In fact, Kurt is introduced to viewers as a bullying victim in one of the series' first scenes. As the pilot's narrative opens, we see Kurt, a look of panic on his face, standing next to a dumpster and surrounded by nine tall jocks in letterman's jackets ("Pilot"). Kurt seems to know the drill, but insists that they wait for him to take off his Marc Jacobs jacket before throwing him in the garbage. The scene also introduces viewers to the unique mix of melodrama and satiric comedy that *Glee* would become known for. While Kurt's ashen face at the start of the scene suggests real fear, the upbeat score, the sunny lighting, and the bullies' seeming respect for designer couture give the scene a comedic incongruity.

Our introduction to Rachel Berry (Kurt's soon-to-be glee club teammate) captures the anguish of being an outsider at McKinley even more powerfully. We get to know Rachel through a flashback montage that juxtaposes her self-confident optimism and ambition to be a star against the cruel abuse she experiences at school. The sequence is framed by Rachel's audition for glee club in which she sings the pathos-filled ballad "On My Own" (from the "seminal Broadway classic *Les Mis*"). In voiceover narration, Rachel enthusiastically explains her rich life (e.g., she was "born out of love" by two gay dads who "spoiled her in the arts"; she doesn't have time for boys because she posts videos of her performances to her MySpace page every night to hone her skills). Alongside Rachel's description, however, viewers see that there is more to the story. Rachel's earnest MySpace video, for example, becomes fodder for cyber-bullying by cheerleaders who post comments like "Please get sterilized." As the sequence ends, we return to Rachel's audition at its emotional climax, the lyrics now connected to Rachel's own story. While Rachel belts out the line "A world that's full of happiness that I have never known," we see a flashback of her reading the mean girls' comments. The hurt expression on her face and the pathos of her performance of the lyric belie her bravado. The moment, however, is disrupted by a somewhat violent exclamation point. Just as Rachel ends the lyric's final note, the scene abruptly cuts to a shot of Rachel having a slushie thrown in her face as she turns around. The scene is traumatic—certainly to Rachel, but it might also be for the viewer who is meant to be startled by the unexpected edit and the sudden silence of the scene.

While bullying becomes endemic at McKinley High (e.g., all of the glee club members eventually get slushied), Kurt is singled out for special abuse because of his sexuality and his refusal to conform to traditional gender norms. In a later first season episode, when word gets out that Kurt is competing for the chance to sing "Defying Gravity" (a song traditionally sung by a woman), his father receives an anonymous phone call from a guy who states, "Your son's a fag." Although his dad is worried, Kurt is not so shaken; he tells his dad, "I get that all the time" ("Wheels"). The anti-gay bulling increases in season 2, however, when Kurt is repeatedly harassed by Dave Karofsky, a football player who we eventually learn is gay himself, although highly closeted. The harassment intensifies over the course of several episodes, with Karofsky even threatening to kill Kurt. When official policy limits what school officials can do, Kurt's father decides to pull him from McKinley and the glee club. As the series developed, Kurt's storyline became perhaps the most powerful way for the series to explore the central themes of high school bullying and the pain of being an outsider. "When we did the 'Preggers' episode, when Kurt tries out for the football team," remembers Brad Falchuk, *Glee* co-creator and executive producer, "that's where I think we really understood who Kurt was and how much of an emotional anchor he was going to be for the show."[1] As stories about gay-teen bullying and suicides grew in the 2010, Kurt's story and *Glee* gained even wider resonance.

Glee doesn't simply focus on the problem of high school bullying, however. In describing the series' narrative philosophy, executive producer Ryan Murphy explained: "It's four acts of darkness that take a turn and have two acts of sweetness. It's about there being great joy to being different, and great pain."[2] The series' sweetness, of course, is written into the optimism of its underlying premise: that the glee club is a safe space where you can embrace who you really are despite the bullies. It is also woven into the series' longer-term story arc—the idea that this ragtag group of misfits can win nationals and in the process create a future for themselves where things are better. As Kurt explains to his father, "Being different made me stronger. At the end of the day, it's what's going to get me out of this cow town" ("Wheels").

Glee includes more specific scenes of sweetness—elements one might describe as moments of magical-musical realism. "Preggers," for example, provides a joyously queer version of a high school narrative cliché. In an effort to impress his father, Kurt joins the football team and discovers an innate talent for kicking the ball. Meanwhile, the football coach believes that learning choreography from Mr. Schuster might make the football team (the glee club's repeated tormentors) "perform" better on the field and help them end their embarrassing losing streak. The players resist, fearing they will look "gay." But down six points in the final second of the big game, they decide to go with it. As Beyoncé's "Single Ladies" blares over the speaker system, the team breaks into a choreographed dance routine, confusing their opponents enough to help them score a dramatic touchdown. It is then up to Kurt, who dances up to the ball Beyoncé-style and kicks the winning field goal. The crowd erupts, and for a moment, the effeminate gay kid is the high school football hero.

Many of the musical numbers have such magically joyous qualities and seem to function as wish fulfillments. In "Born This Way," for example, Kurt returns to McKinley High from Dalton Academy, the idyllic, gay-embracing, all-boys private school Kurt had transferred to when he needed to escape Karofsky's harassment. As Kurt is welcomed back by his glee club friends on the steps outside McKinley, his boyfriend, Blaine, and the other members of Dalton's all-boy show choir make a surprise appearance and serenade him with an emotional rendition of "Somewhere Only We Know." For the length of the performance, the narrative and "normal" life at McKinley High are suspended, and the scene offers a vision of the world where things are better.

In *Glee*, such scenes are momentary; the music ends, and life returns to "normal." Kurt and the power of dance may have helped win the game on Friday, but the football players will slushie the glee kids on Monday. Blaine may get to declare his love for Kurt through a choreographed Keane song in the schoolyard, but homophobia doesn't disappear. At prom, for example, Kurt is elected prom queen as a practical joke. "Don't you get how stupid we were?" Kurt asks Blaine, in tears. "We thought that because no one was teasing us or beating us up that no one cared. Like some kind of progress had been made. But it's still the same . . . all that hate. They were just afraid to say it out loud, so they did it by secret ballot" ("Prom Queen"). Such reversals are narrative necessities. As a continuing series, *Glee* needs to keep its antagonists as important sources of narrative tension. If a series predicated upon the struggle for a better future is to come back for another season, that better life must continually be deferred.

Observers have criticized the series for what they see as poor writing, pointing to episodes with incoherent plot developments, jarring shifts in tone, or inconsistent character motivations.[3] While I sympathize with some of this criticism, for me the pleasures offered by the pathos of such narrative reversals and the anticipation of more magical realism compensate for any sense of contrivance or narrative inconsistency. I would also argue that such inconsistency might actually speak to the disorienting experience of homophobia and the indirect and

FIGURE 13.1. Openly gay actor Chris Colfer, seen here in the *Glee* pilot, was one of the first celebrities to post an It Gets Better video.

ultimately uncertain path of progress. In fact, part of *Glee*'s appeal, I think, is that alongside its peppy musical score, campy comedy, and upbeat musical numbers, there is an underlying "darkness" that suggests that things don't always get better.[4]

While *Glee* invokes hope in a future where things get better for gay kids like Kurt, home-centered reality shows like *House Hunters International* present an already existing world where things aren't only better for gay men and women, they are actually terrific. Gay people are commonly included as designers and clients on makeover design shows like *Curb Appeal: The Block, Design Star, Flipping Out*, and *Color Splash*, and as homeowners and house seekers on real-estate shows like *Million Dollar Listing, Selling L.A., Bang for Your Buck*, and *Income Property*. Although gay people are often central characters in these programs, the narrative tension never relies on the struggles they face because they are gay. Instead, viewer interest is maintained through anticipation: Will Jane and Mary love their newly landscaped backyard? How excited will the family be by the re-modeled kitchen the show's gay host David designed? Which house will Patrick and Brian purchase? Given the format of these shows, we always get our answer by the end of the episodes, and the answers to such questions are typically "yes," "yes," and "the house of their dreams."

The fact that such shows are edited to guarantee happy endings is not sur-prising. After all, they rely heavily on sponsorship from the home improvement industry, a sector deeply interested in making home renovation and ownership look appealingly effortless. Such shows also tend to represent a decidedly up-scale sector of home ownership; for instance, *Bang for Your Buck* might compare three $75,000 master suite renovations, *Flipping Out*'s Jeff Lewis renovates only million-dollar LA homes, and *Curb Appeal: The Block* spends $20,000 on each front yard make-over. It is likely much easier for the producers and network executives to attract both advertisers and viewers (especially those viewers advertisers most want to reach) with aspirational images of home ownership. Thus, the gays and lesbians featured in these programs are almost always successful professionals and relatively affluent homeowners living the dream.

A 2011 episode of *House Hunters International*, entitled "Family-Friendly Living in Hellerup, Denmark," illustrates these points well. The family in question includes "lifetime partners" Paul and Meinhard St. John. According to the host's voiceover commentary, Paul, a software engineer from Colorado, and Meinhard, a part-time actor and model from Denmark, "started off worlds apart, but destiny brought them together." As we watch the two tall, thin, attractive middle-aged men stroll down the cobblestoned streets of Stockholm, Sweden, purchase cheese from a deli, and drink beer with a circle of friends, the host explains that the couple is adopting a baby boy, Liam, and has decided to move to Denmark to start their new family. The couple looks blissfully happy, but the host informs us that trouble may be brewing. It seems that the couple has different priorities when it comes to picking their dream house. "Will disputes over location versus renovation create a divide? Or will they find happiness in the perfect home?" the host asks, establishing the episode's narrative tension. "Find out when *House Hunters International* heads to Hellerup, Denmark."

Consistent with the series' rosy representation of home ownership, Paul and Meinhard's story ends happily. Although their real estate agent warns us that the couple's seemingly ample $2 million budget might make it tough to find the perfect home in Denmark's hot housing market, the couple tours three massive homes in an affluent Copenhagen suburb. As the host anticipated, the couple does disagree. Paul doesn't like the closed-off kitchen in the first house. Meinhard doesn't like the casement windows in the second house. Both love the third house, but Paul hates the fact that it sits next to a busy freeway. In the end, however, Paul and Meinhard agree completely and purchase the third house for "only" $1.8 million. In the episode's coda, we get to check in on the couple eight months later. Liam has arrived, and the family has settled into their dream house. As we watch idyllic images of the couple feeding their chubby-cheeked son and entertaining friends, Meinhard describes their new life as a family: "You think that you're prepared, but it's never what you imagined. It's been a gift. It's been a blessing."

FIGURE 13.2.
"Lifetime partners" Paul and Meinhard reflect on *House Hunters International* how good their life is in Denmark.

Glee and *House Hunters International* intersect with the It Gets Better campaign in various ways. When put together, these gay characters (Kurt's fictional story and Paul and Meinhard's reality-edited story) create a larger narrative that echoes Dan Savage and Terry Miller's personal story and those of many of the people who contributed to the website. Many It Gets Better video testimonials follow the same narrative structure. In act one, they recount painful memories of being bullied as a teenager; in act two, they describe when things started to get better; and in act three, they explain how good their current life is. In this context, one can read Paul's successful family and house hunt as the culmination of the journey Kurt is starting. The last shot of the couple—they are framed in a two shot sitting beside each other in their living room, reflecting on the joys of family life in their new home—strongly recalls the visual look and themes of the video testimonials. Kurt Hummel's dream of escaping the oppressive homophobia of Lima, Ohio, is realized in the globe-hopping life of Colorado-native Paul St. John.

Kurt's dream is also realized in the real-life experience of Chris Colfer. As Colfer's video testimonial makes clear, he had a very painful experience as a gay kid growing up in Clovis, California. His high voice made him a target of bullies; his only friends were the high school lunch ladies. Since getting cast on *Glee*, however, his life has improved dramatically. "It's very therapeutic," Colfer explains. "Outside of work I'm getting the praise and acceptance I've always wanted. And at work, I've got my first set of friends ever. What I am is a true Cinderella story."[5] Thus Colfer's real-life path working on *Glee* supports the show's underlying optimism that being true to yourself will eventually pay off, and the message that things get better.[6]

My training in media criticism encourages me to be skeptical of television's images of gay life. Media scholars, myself included, have been understandably hesitant to equate the increased number of gay men and lesbians on television with political progress, arguing that increased cultural visibility doesn't mean that discriminatory public policies have been overturned or that anti-gay attitudes have disappeared. Critics have also been right to point out how television's images of gay life are problematically shaped by commercial imperatives; *House Hunters International*'s representation of an affluent global gay elite serves as one clear example of this dynamic.[7]

While it is always important to be skeptical, the It Gets Better campaign encourages me to value the importance of strategic optimism as well. Things don't always get better for gay people, of course. Gay adults sometimes face intense discrimination at work, rejection by friends and family, and an underlying social system that disadvantages nonheterosexual people (especially those who aren't white, upscale, or gender normative). Yet the It Gets Better campaign is predicated on the idea that struggling gay kids can find real emotional support by hearing from people who survived such challenges. Television images of gay life can play a similar role. Colfer, for example, recounts the many moving letters he receives from gay viewers explaining how Kurt helps them feel that it is okay to be who they are. "With all due respects to my castmates," Colfer states, "they don't get the letters like I get—the letters that not only say 'I'm your biggest fan' but also 'Kurt saved my life' and 'Kurt doesn't make me feel alone' from 7-year-olds in Nebraska."[8] The emotional impact of the It Gets Better videos and *Glee* encourages me to consider programs like *House Hunters International* in another light. Yes, few gay people have access to the web of socio-economic privileges that helped Paul and Meinhard build their happy family in their $1.8 million Danish house. And I have no idea whether the perfect family life promised by the end of the episode is actually real or just the product of effective editing. At the same time, programs that normalize idealized images of gay life can offer real hope and emotional support for gay viewers who live in a culture where inspiring role models and positive reinforcements may be lacking.

The line between being delusional and being optimistic can be a very fine one. American commercial television can be decidedly delusional. It is subsidized, after all, by a commercial logic that claims that there is a product out there to solve any problem you might have. It is important to be highly skeptical of that logic—to interrogate its claims and to call out the delusions it supports. At the same time, our critical approach to the media's distorted representation of the world shouldn't lead us to discount the strategic value of television's optimism and to believe that things can, and are, getting better.

FURTHER READING

Becker, Ron. *Gay TV and Straight America*. New Brunswick, NJ: Rutgers University Press, 2006.

Gorman-Murray, Andrew. "Queering Home or Domesticating Deviance? Interrogating Gay Domesticity through Lifestyle Television." *International Journal of Cultural Studies* 9, no. 2 (2006): 227–47.

Walters, Suzanna Duanta. *All the Rage: The Story of Gay Visibility in America*. Chicago: University of Chicago Press, 2001.

NOTES

1. Tim Stack, "Chris Colfer Makes Some Noise," *Entertainment Weekly*, November 12, 2010, 46–48.

2. Erik Hedegaard, "*Glee* Gone Wild," *Rolling Stone*, April 15, 2010, 42–49.

3. See, for example, Robert Bianco, "*Glee* Loses Its Voice in the Chaos," *USA Today*, March 3, 2011, D1.

4. At the pilot's main narrative turning point, quarterback Finn Hudson stands up to his football teammates when they try to force him to quit glee club. "Don't you get it, man? We're all losers," he tells them. "Everyone in this school. Hell, everyone in this town. Out of all the kids who graduate, maybe half will go to college and two will leave the state to do it. I'm not afraid of being called a loser, because that's what I am. But I am afraid of turning my back on something that actually made me happy for the first time in my sorry life." Although the speech helps deconstruct the kind of hierarchy that enables bullying, it also has a certain fatalism, a recognition that not everyone will get to leave Lima. In this regard, Finn serves as a counter-balance to Rachel and her insistent optimism that she will become a star. So too do many of the show's adult characters—none of whom seem to be living out their dreams. Whether or not the show sustains this balance through later season is debatable.

5. Hedegaard, "*Glee* Gone Wild."

6. That Chris Colfer's and Kurt Hummel's lives would merge in this way is not surprising since *Glee* producers created the role for Colfer and used specific experiences Colfer had in crafting storylines for Hummel.

7. See Ron Becker, *Gay TV and Straight America* (New Brunswick, NJ: Rutgers University Press, 2006); Suzanna Duanta Walters, *All the Rage: The Story of Gay Visibility in America* (Chicago: University of Chicago Press, 2001).

8. Stack, "Chris Colfer Makes Some Noise."

14

Grey's Anatomy
Feminism

ELANA LEVINE

Abstract: Looking at how *Grey's Anatomy*'s representations of gender and race go beyond simple notions of positive or negative images, Elana Levine argues that the hit medical drama serves as a fantasy space for imagining a world free of discrimination and power imbalances, and thus offers a more nuanced set of representations than might first appear.

Contemporary entertainment television often tells stories of professionally accomplished women who, despite their successes, lament the missing men, children, or home life that would make them feel complete. Whether in Ally McBeal's dancing baby dreams of the 1990s or *Sex and the City*'s Carrie Bradshaw's boyfriend troubles in the early 2000s, female characters have frequently expressed frustration with the lack of "balance" between their personal and professional lives. At the same time as they have faced such struggles, many of these same characters have found empowerment, whether by embracing a (hetero)sexually attractive appearance and the command it allows them over men, or by enjoying confidence boosts and pleasure through shopping and other forms of decadent consumerism made possible by their privileged economic status.

While viewers have found such depictions entertaining, some audiences, including some media scholars, have criticized these representations for the ways that they implicitly—and sometimes explicitly—suggest that our society no longer needs the critical take on gender roles provided by the feminist movement. In this sort of "postfeminist" mindset, either feminism is identified as the cause of women's problems, in that the movement's embrace of women taking on greater professional roles purportedly failed to account for how to fit a personal life within such accomplishments, or feminism has succeeded so well that it no longer applies. For example, according to this line of thinking, women who present themselves as sexual objects do so by their own choosing and not due to societal pressures to appear attractive to men, as feminism has supposedly erased those kinds of gender inequalities. Media scholars and other critics have charged that such assumptions that feminism is "done" actually work in the interests of the male-dominated social structure known as patriarchy.[1] Such postfeminist thinking makes even the suggestion of gender inequalities seem outdated or even discriminatory in its own right, and fails to account for the experiences of under-privileged women, especially in terms of class status. As a result, many persistent inequalities are allowed to continue all the more powerfully, with little hope of challenge to their power.

ABC's hit medical drama *Grey's Anatomy* is a product of this postfeminist cultural environment. The world it presents is in many ways one that has been changed by feminism. But instead of suffering from these changes, or using such changes as a means of revalidating conventional expectations of gender, sexuality, and also race, *Grey's* provides a feminist-friendly fiction or *fantasy*, allowing us to imagine a world in which identity-based discrimination has been defeated to women's benefit, rather than at their expense. In its early seasons, *Grey's* overtly tapped into the postfeminist cultural context that had helped make programs like *Sex and the City* into hits. This is most clear in the early seasons' opening credit sequence, which paired markers of medical expertise with those of sexualized femininity: a pair of red stiletto heels disrupts a row of surgical booties, an eye-lash curler is laid alongside surgical instruments, an IV drip dissolves into a mar-tini being poured into a glass, intertwined male and female feet caress at the edge of a gurney. The sequence characterized the fictional world as more concerned with sexual hijinks than medical drama, one in which the sexualized femininity of the female leads would supersede, or at least always accompany, their profes-sional endeavors.

But the fictional world that actually follows the opening credits does not ad-here to such a model; instead, this world leans more toward a feminist fantasy than a typical postfeminist compromise. While the characters' sexual relation-ships are central from the beginning, none of the female leads are convention-ally sexualized. All of the characters wear scrubs in most of their scenes, and the flowing tresses of characters like Cristina and Izzie are typically tightly secured in knots and ponytails. The sexual attractiveness of former lingerie model Izzie is deliberately downplayed—she wears little visible make-up and her body is most overtly displayed when she blows up in anger at her colleagues for ogling a modeling spread she posed for as a medical student. Angrily stripping down to her underwear to show the mundaneness of exposed flesh, she pointedly notes that working as a model has left her debt-free while her fellow interns deal with

FIGURE 14.1. The first-season credit sequence of *Grey's Anatomy* included images of sexualized femininity (like these red heels alongside surgical booties) that were contrary to the show's depiction of women doctors as medical professionals ahead of sexualized beings.

hundreds of thousands of dollars in loans ("No Man's Land"). While many representations of women in postfeminist culture depict femininity and sexual attractiveness as women's foremost sources of liberation, in *Grey's Anatomy*, empowerment comes when the women doctors are seen as medical professionals ahead of sexualized beings. Izzie's victory is in getting her colleagues to take seriously her skills as a doctor, despite her modeling; she does not need her work as a model to prove her sexual appeal despite her professional success.

As much as the series traffics in the personal travails and romantic dramas of its characters, the female protagonists nearly always privilege their careers over their personal lives. This is in opposition to many of the male characters, who openly yearn for love and family in a characterization directly descended from daytime soap opera, where male characters tend to have similar desires. In many instances of postfeminist culture, women who are excessively invested in their careers must "pay" for this investment with some kind of debilitated or dysfunctional personal life, as on the aforementioned *Ally McBeal*. Yet the women of *Grey's* are rarely punished for their professional focus. As the most aggressively careerist of her peers, Cristina repeatedly rejects her male partners' efforts to get her to devote more time and attention to her personal life, whether this be in her initial reluctance to marry Burke or in her unambiguous decision to have an abortion following each of two unplanned pregnancies. Meredith, the title character of this ensemble show, is equally career-focused. She insists that Derek treat her as a resident, not as his wife, when she expresses discomfort at dealing with a patient; she puts off attending to her (even more careerist) mother who is suffering from Alzheimer's; and she long resists Derek's efforts to get her to marry him. The active and satisfying sexual and romantic lives of these characters challenge the postfeminist assumption that career and interpersonal happiness are either incompatible or that they require super-woman perfection. The female characters of *Grey's* are flawed, beset with troubles, and frequently unhappy, but their work as surgeons is never represented as a mistake or even as a particularly costly choice. It defines them and makes them proud, another nod to daytime soap opera, with its accomplished career women who suffer unrelated personal travails.

Part of the way that *Grey's* makes such a nonjudgmental representation of career-focused women possible is that it presents a fantasy world nearly free of discrimination of all kinds. In the first season, Cristina wryly notes the gender imbalance amongst surgeons ("A Hard Day's Night"), Meredith attacks the sexist Alex for his assumptions ("Winning a Battle, Losing the War"), and Izzie has to prove herself as more than a pretty face and voluptuous body. But such overt attention to inequalities quickly fades, and the series spends very little time concerned with such obstacles. The program even more overtly resists any acknowledgement of racial inequalities or differences. The series has been well publicized for having an unusually high number of racial minorities amongst its cast and for "blindcasting" many roles, such that actors of different races might have been cast as particular characters. On-screen, interracial romantic relationships are common, and the characters' racial differences are never an issue between them. When the Asian-American Cristina and the African American Burke are forced to confront their differences, the show focuses on his neatness and her slovenliness, amongst other nonracially marked qualities.[2] Their racial difference is unnamed, as is that between Cristina and her white husband, Owen, in the program's later seasons.

Critics of postfeminist and "post-racial" thinking would argue that the denial of gender- and race-based discrimination in the world of *Grey's* ultimately works to excuse or diminish the significance of the real-world discriminations that continue to exist, particularly those faced by people less privileged than the typical characters of primetime TV, such as racial profiling by law enforcement or unequal treatment by employers. While largely blind to the problems (and the pleasures) of difference, the program does not condemn or dismiss the efforts of past (or present) feminist or civil rights movements. Instead, it presents a world in which such efforts would be unnecessary, in which the politicizing of identity is not needed. In this respect the program offers a fantasy space—what we might think of as a feminist fantasy of a world beyond inequalities of gender, sexuality, and race. In this respect, the program matches a conception of popular entertainment as offering utopian fantasies responding to "real needs *created by society*." When film scholar Richard Dyer used this concept to explain the appeal of Hollywood musicals, he also argued that the utopia offered by such entertainments leaves out real world dissatisfactions of class, race, and patriarchy.[3] In the case of *Grey's*, however, the utopic view on offer in fact engages with some of those very dissatisfactions, albeit in compromised ways.

An imagined world beyond such dissatisfactions is taken for granted in most *Grey's* episodes. However, select episodes and moments highlight these inequalities, placing them safely in the past or in a world apart from that of the surgeon protagonists, preserving the hospital itself and the work of medicine as a utopic sphere. For instance, the series seems to blame Meredith's mother, Ellis, for being selfish and career-obsessed, as Meredith's own fears of commitment and motherhood seem to stem from her mother's hurtful influence. Yet as the series proceeds, we learn that Meredith's father was also to blame for her dysfunctional home life, and that Ellis did the best she could to mother Meredith while also succeeding in the cutthroat and male-dominated world of surgery.

The sexism—and racism—of the past, as well as Ellis's struggle to deal with her competing roles, are made most clear when former chief of surgery Richard Weber recounts to the staff his and Ellis's experience with an AIDS patient in 1982, before the disease was named or understood ("The Time Warp"). In the ensuing flashbacks, we learn more about Richard's affair with Ellis, about the racism and sexism each faced in their training (Richard is the sole person of color amongst his cohort; Ellis the only woman), and about the presence of discrimination more broadly, as most of the staff refuses to treat the AIDS patient. While we see Ellis walk away from a needy, young Meredith, we also see that this is not easy for her, and that Meredith's father is in part to blame. Ellis's position is made especially sympathetic when she and Richard argue after he tells her she cannot leave her husband because of Meredith, and that he will handle their surgery so that she can attend to her distraught daughter. At this, Ellis declares, "I gave birth to a child, Richard. That makes me a mother. It doesn't make me inept; it doesn't make me less of a woman. It doesn't make me less of a surgeon. No matter how much everyone wants it to." Ellis's fury and her refusal to see her roles as incompatible are feminist responses to a discriminatory situation. That she nonetheless thrives and that Meredith comes to follow in her path suggest that—for all their tensions—the feminist struggles of the earlier generation have made for a better world.

The feminist fantasy of the hospital-centered world of *Grey's* manifests itself in multiple ways. The final three episodes of season 7 in 2011 amply demonstrate these tendencies ("White Wedding"; "I Will Survive"; "Unaccompanied Minor"). In this set of episodes, Derek and Meredith decide to adopt an orphaned African baby who has been brought to the hospital for treatment; lesbian partners Callie and Arizona get married; and Cristina discovers she is pregnant and plans

FIGURE 14.2.
One way in which *Grey's Anatomy* functions as a "feminist fantasy space" is through its dramatization of nontraditional conceptions of marriage, such as that between characters Callie and Arizona.

to have an abortion. These events, and the developments surrounding them, are representative of the program's handling of three matters that contribute to its functioning as a feminist fantasy space and that resonate with the historically feminized genre of soap opera: straight men's commitments to women and family, nontraditional conceptions of marriage, and women's connections to one another as mothers, daughters, and friends.

Throughout the series, many of the lead male characters assert their commitments to the women they love and their willingness to devote time and attention to rearing a family. Derek, nicknamed "McDreamy" by the women interns in the early seasons, is not only a star surgeon and a handsome charmer; he is also a devoted partner and, we determine in these episodes, a dedicated father. Unlike other male characters, Derek is never unfaithful to his romantic partners and easily commits to Meredith; in their relationship, she is the one with commitment issues. When he treats baby Zola, he feels an instant bond and persuades Meredith that they should adopt her ("White Wedding"). That it is Derek's connection to the baby, not Meredith's, motivating the adoption makes the character even more appealing as a romantic, yet feminist-friendly, fantasy figure.

When Cristina's husband, Owen, tells her how committed he would be to the child they have unintentionally conceived and offers to interrupt his career as a surgeon both to care for the child and to preserve Cristina's commitment to her own (less advanced) career, he, too, demonstrates such fantasy qualities. While he tries to persuade Cristina to have the baby, he does not try to persuade her to change her ambitions as a result. When she schedules the abortion without discussing it with him, his anger is not directed at her unwillingness to fulfill a traditional role ("Unaccompanied Minor"). Rather it comes from her unwillingness to engage in a full, equal partnership that would consider his concerns and commitments as equal to hers. Not only does this story represent another straight man wholly invested in an equal partnership and primary child-raising duties, but it also depicts a woman who does not want to be a mother, a stance for which she is not villainized.

The conceptions of marital partnership and parenting at the center of Owen and Cristina's dispute are also central to these episodes' feminist tendencies. This three-episode sequence begins with the lavish wedding of Callie and Arizona, a couple whose tribulations had been central to major storylines of season 7. When the two were broken up, the bisexual Callie slept with her best friend, Mark, with whom she had been involved previously. While their sexual involvement did not indicate a romantic relationship to either of them, they accidentally conceived a child and decide to raise that child together. Once Arizona and Callie reunited, Arizona also agreed to parent the child. The program offers this unconventional arrangement as an ideal situation all around, allowing Arizona and Callie to build a home together with their daughter while allowing Mark to be a devoted father, a newfound passion for the former playboy—in this storyline, Mark becomes yet another of the series' handsome men devoted to child-rearing. Callie's mother's disapproval of her out-of-wedlock child and her same-sex relationship provides the central conflict in the wedding episode, demonstrating that the show does occasionally represent identity-based prejudices, though typically roots them in an older generation.

Still, the episode centers on the joyful connection between Callie and Arizona, with Mark and their daughter key members of their newly configured family. That the brides' white gowns and traditional ceremony are juxtaposed with the wedding of Derek and Meredith, who realize that being legally married will assist their adoption of Zola, further accentuates the program's progressive conception of marriage and commitment. Derek and Meredith's wedding, held at City Hall, in their street clothes, in front of a judge, at the end of a busy work day, provides a compelling contrast with Callie and Arizona's ("White Wedding"). When the straight, white couple treats legal marriage as little more than a procedural matter while the interracial lesbian couple treats their not-legally-sanctioned wedding as a celebratory ritual, the program presents a fantasy world in which convention, tradition, and even law become insignificant in light of the bonds of love and commitment.

These episodes also highlight another ongoing theme of the series—women's relationships to other women, especially as mothers, daughters, and friends. While the storylines that occupy these episodes are centered on romantic relationships (as well as workplace drama), kinship and friendship connections between women also play significant roles. When Callie is devastated by her mother's rejection of her life, her friend and colleague Miranda helps her to move forward with her plans. Meredith's series-long struggle to come to terms with her own now-deceased mother comes to a head as she begins to identify as Zola's potential mother. We see Meredith's anxiety about her own maternal worth and see her carry on Ellis's legacy when she tells Zola's social worker, "I'm a surgeon. And I'm a good surgeon. And I want to be a good mother. Honestly, I don't know much about it. But I am ready to learn, and I'm a fast learner. And I will do whatever it takes to be a good mom" ("I Will Survive").

Meredith's tentative effort to be a mother and a surgeon comes to a head in "Unaccompanied Minor," when the ties between Meredith and Cristina and that between Meredith and Zola intertwine. In the second season, when Meredith agrees to be Cristina's "person"—the support person required by the clinic where Cristina is to receive her abortion—the two form a lasting bond, even as they compete with each other for access to surgeries and other workplace honors ("Raindrops Keep Falling on My Head"). While the two eschew hugging and other conventional markers of female friendship, they support one another unconditionally, and often rely on one another before and apart from their romantic relationships with men. As season 7 concludes, not only have Owen and Cristina broken up, but so too have Meredith and Derek, after Derek discovers a work-related choice Meredith made that potentially jeopardizes both of their careers and the hospital. Just after Meredith and Derek's split, Meredith is permitted to take Zola home on her own. Cristina also comes "home" to Meredith's house, seeking comfort and security. The season ends with the two women together again, bonded more to each other than to their male partners, each in her own way facing the daunting task of choosing to be a mother, or not. The season ends with its two female leads simultaneously quite lost and calling upon their inner strengths, leaning upon each other and the traditions of the many women before them.

If we can agree that *Grey's* offers this vision of a space beyond the inequalities of gender, sexuality, and race, how might we account for this fantasy? American television is hardly known for its progressiveness of outlook, and most often contemporary popular culture pairs some sort of backlash with its representation of a world changed by feminism and other progressive social movements. We might account for *Grey's Anatomy*'s vision by considering the perspective of the program's creator and showrunner, Shonda Rhimes, one of the few women, and few African Americans, to head a primetime network drama series in television history. While the identity of a program's leader is only one of many factors that shape it, we have so few examples in television of an African American woman's leadership that it is difficult to know what impact Rhimes's particular perspective may have. The program's outlook may also be the product of a new phase in post-feminist culture, one that is finally able to let go of the many recriminations and costs that more typically have accompanied media tales of women's empowerment and independence. *Grey's* does not present a perfect feminist picture, but it does provide a fantasy of a world truly changed by feminism—a welcome relief in a reality that too often fails to live up to such promise.

FURTHER READING

Banet-Weiser, Sarah. *Empowered: Popular Feminism and Popular Misogyny*. Durham, NC: Duke University Press, 2018.

Gill, Rosalind. "The Affective, Cultural and Psychic Life of Postfeminism: A Postfeminist Sensibility 10 Years On," *European Journal of Cultural Studies* 20, no. 6 (2017): 606–26.

Levine, Elana. "*Buffy* and the 'New Girl Order': Defining Feminism and Femininity." In *Undead TV: Essays on Buffy the Vampire Slayer*, edited by Elana Levine and Lisa Parks. Durham, NC: Duke University Press, 2007.

Tasker, Yvonne, and Diane Negra, eds. *Interrogating Postfeminism: Gender and the Politics of Popular Culture*. Durham, NC: Duke University Press, 2007.

NOTES

1. For example, see Angela McRobbie, "Postfeminism and Popular Culture: *Bridget Jones* and the New Gender Regime," in *Interrogating Postfeminism: Gender and the Politics of Popular Culture*, ed. Yvonne Tasker and Diane Negra (Durham, NC: Duke University Press, 2007), 27–39; and Rosalind Gill, *Gender and the Media* (Cambridge, UK: Polity, 2007).

2. For more on the series' use of blindcasting, see Kristen Warner, "Colorblind TV: Prime-Time Politics of Race in Television Casting" (PhD diss., University of Texas at Austin, 2010).

3. Richard Dyer, "Entertainment and Utopia," in *Genre: The Musical*, ed. Rick Altman (London: Routledge, 1981), 184.

15

Master of None
Negotiated Decoding

RITESH MEHTA

Abstract: South Asians have rarely been depicted on American television as having normal, fully realized romantic relationships and sexual lives, but Ritesh Mehta explores how Aziz Ansari's *Master of None* is a breakthrough exception in this regard. Using Stuart Hall's theory of decoding to examine protagonist Dev Shah's relationships, Mehta encourages audiences to consider what constitutes "normal" and how their unique readings of TV programs reflect their position vis-à-vis society's dominant ideology.

The highly lauded Netflix series *Master of None* opens with a bang. More accurately, a bust. In the pilot episode, "Plan B," the camera, positioned in the living room of a dark apartment, distantly observes a heterosexual couple engaged in sex through the glass bedroom door. Suddenly, the dude, Dev Shah, exclaims, "The condom broke!" The duo then Googles whether pre-ejaculation fluid can cause pregnancy. After Dev buys the woman, Rachel, the Plan B brand of contraceptives, they say goodbye as an Uber's door closes awkwardly between them. We sense that the two may never meet again, that this was just another hookup in New York City.

What's immediately notable, even remarkable, is that a popular TV show opens with a South Asian man having sex. In November 2015, when *Master of None* debuted on Netflix, this was a first for American TV. And it wasn't a fluke either. In later episodes, Dev—played by stand-up comedian and actor Aziz Ansari, who along with Alan Yang created the series and wrote a majority of its episodes—is depicted having sex with other traditionally attractive women and generally is quite proactive in the dating scene. What's more, it's not just about casual sex. The central narrative arc of *Master of None*'s second season is Dev's romantic connection to an Italian woman, Francesca; alongside his relationship with Rachel in the first season, the series showcases his intimate life to be rich and multidimensional. Thanks to *Master*, a South Asian American man is finally portrayed as unrepressed, as sexual, as eager to "settle down" with the woman of his dreams. An Indian on TV is good at love!

Previously, this "success" had been the purview of white men and, to a smaller extent, black and Latino men. By stark contrast, depictions of romance, sexuality, and relationships have largely eluded South Asian, East Asian, Arab, and Native American characters on TV. Consider the character of Rajesh Koothrappali on CBS's *The Big Bang Theory*, who in early seasons is literally mute in front of women; or Jonathan on NBC's *30 Rock*, who apparently has no sex drive other than a queer obsession with his boss; or even Ansari's own Tom Haverford on NBC's *Parks and Recreation*, who is portrayed as a superficial flirt but actually either is scared to commit to women who show genuine interest or is an annoyance to women whom he endlessly pursues. Dev Shah, by contrast, has his head more squarely on his shoulders, as a boy next door whom women want, and who even when he falters isn't the sole responsible party.

Master of None, in portraying a South Asian character that is "normal" in the romantic, sexual, and relationships aspects of his life, is thus a breakthrough program in making experiences of masculinity more visible and accessible that have been largely absent on television. Furthermore, in doing so, it allows audiences to productively discuss cultural notions of "normal" and "traditional." For comparison, NBC's internationally hailed 1990s sitcom *Friends* is about six twenty-somethings in New York City who over the course of a decade turn the pages of friendship, romance, marriage, and family. However, the fact that all characters are white in an extremely diverse New York City constructs these attributes solely as the experiences and stories of white Americans, thereby making those the "dominant" or baseline narrative by which global media audiences form their cultural understandings about love and friendship. Particularly, the famous ballad of Ross and Rachel—the comic-dramatic turns in their relationship and how the show's gender politics influenced interpretations about the couple's sexuality and romance—makes for an illuminating comparison to Dev's two main relationships on *Master* with Rachel and Francesca.

After the condom-breaking fiasco, Dev does not see Rachel again until the show's third episode. They run into each other at a concert, where their goofy chemistry is evident (thanks to an appealingly natural performance by Noël Wells). Dev is disappointed to learn that she is back with her ex, as the scene ends with a shot of Dev looking at Rachel as though she was "the one that got away." In episode 5, Dev hooks up with Nina (portrayed by Claire Danes) and constantly interrupts their kissing to express his incredulity that a hot woman actually wants him: "You're the coolest thing that's ever happened to me." In differentiating between Dev's reactions to Rachel and Nina, Dev appears to subscribe to standardized ideas about female beauty: Nina has blonde streaks, is fuller bodied, and is overtly flirtatious, whereas Rachel is cute, nerdy, and petite. This episode is the first time we properly see Dev having sex. From Nina's perspective, he appears to be an unlikely hookup, since he isn't virile and is physically smaller than her. His thrusting motions seem bumpy, comical, and lacking in technique, compared to the trail of conquest blazed by TV's more assured masculine and predominantly white characters. Yet, as asserted above, a South Asian man is finally shown as successful in desiring and being desired. Later, Dev begins dating a newly single Rachel again, making a "bold" move by taking her to Nashville for the weekend in the season's most dashingly romantic episode, brimming with country music and postcard-perfect moments.

These story points give weight to certain widely accepted ideas in mainstream culture: that hooking up, dating, and being in relationships is the norm; that dating should lead to long-term relationships and potentially marriage; that men often make the "first move"; and that there is one "right person" out there for everyone. Many series and film genres, such as rom-coms, melodramas, and soap operas, proliferate these ideas. In *Friends*, Ross and Rachel's relationship dramatized all these steps: while Ross dated several women and even married two women other than Rachel, at key moments, the show's writers make it a point to highlight how he and Rachel were truly meant to be together. Fellow friend Phoebe memorably articulated their destiny with her line "She's your lobster"; as Phoebe reasons, "It's a known fact that lobsters fall in love and mate for life." In *Master*, these "stages" are teased out with more subtlety and nuance, per the tone and genre of the show—*Friends* was a multicamera sitcom and decidedly mainstream fare; *Master* is a single-camera romantic dramedy with more highbrow and "quality TV" inclinations. Dev and Rachel hook up, separate, remain friends, begin a new romance, and eventually live together. In repeatedly crafting such stories, television producers valorize society's dominant ideology of monogamy and heteronormativity.

Ross and Dev share certain norms of masculinity and traits within relationships. For instance, both make their fair share of "boyfriend" mistakes. Corresponding to Dev's condom breaking is a key storyline in *Friends* in which Ross gets Rachel pregnant because he didn't know that condoms are only 97 percent effective. A fan of both shows might interpret Dev, a minority character and a son of South Asian immigrants, as being more well informed than Ross, an "all-American" guy with a PhD to boot. On one hand, this constitutes a local, situational interpretation that shows a brown man to be more upstanding in the relationship game. On the other, it reinforces an even more dominant social norm surrounding dating, that men who take responsibility for birth control can date to their heart's delight, maximize "fishing in the sea," before "getting the girl" and settling down.

One of the most influential approaches to understanding the ways that audiences make sense of media comes from Jamaican-British cultural studies scholar Stuart Hall's theory of decoding: Hall argues that audiences have multiple readings of media, of characters and stories, some of which align with what he calls "dominant" ideology, and others that play around with or downright flip those ideas.[1] Viewed through Hall's paradigm, *Master* helps audiences fathom a *new* normal for television's minority characters, while generating conversation about a society's shifting ideological hierarchies. First, for Hall, an "audience" is not an abstract entity but consists of flesh-and-blood individuals, located in specific relations to each other within a culture, nation, or region. Second, any media text has a range of cultural meanings that different viewers might latch onto, as all audience members can access various interpretations that derive from each viewer's particular social contexts and experiences. Hall differentiates these more varied meanings tied to a viewer's specific context from a culture's more widespread, mainstream meanings that often reflect a society's prevailing ideology, or what he calls "dominant culture." Every symbol or code—for instance, the face of a South Asian man—has dominant meanings that appear normal—the stereotype that Asian men are more intellectual than physical. Such pervasive stereotypes and norms of representation form the web of dominant meanings that run through all media and are often critiqued as products of ideology.

However, Hall's key argument is that dominant meanings are not necessarily accepted by viewers. Television's images, characters, and plots are frequently interpreted or "read" as something more local, idiosyncratic, or communal, negotiating between texts and viewers' contexts and experiences—such varying readings can even be "oppositional" or wholly contradictory. Thus, Hall proposes three types of decodings: "dominant," "negotiated," and "oppositional." Various audience members and the communities they identify with have different relationships to the dominant "system" of codes and meanings that support entities in power, such as corporations, governments, and cultural norms. Viewers watching a love story between an interracial couple—an Asian man and a white woman, for instance—can have a varied set of reactions. Some with a "dominant reading" might outright reject the very possibility of a real relationship between people of different races, as the underlying ideology of American society still regards interracial couples as exceptional more than typical. By contrast, those with an "oppositional reading" might also strongly critique the relationship but on different grounds, perhaps pushing against how heterosexuality and romance are accepted as common sense by the show. However, for Hall, the vast majority of audiences will have a "negotiated reading," one that accepts new meanings—interracial marriages as gradually becoming more welcome—but rejecting others—women making the first move.

Considering dominant and negotiated readings of Dev and Rachel, it is instructive to compare *Master*'s ninth episode of season 1, which narrates an important period of Dev and Rachel's relationship, with the ninth episode of season 2, which delineates an important period of Dev and Francesca's. Both episodes are deeply layered in subtle codes about friendship, romance, desire, sexuality, and partnership. I argue that audiences will find more "traditional," dominant, and mainstream representations of romance and masculinity in the Dev-Francesca relationship than in the Dev-Rachel relationship.

In "Mornings," one of the first season's more unusually structured and evocatively shot and edited episodes, Dev and Rachel are now living together and we glimpse vignettes of mornings over eleven months in his hip apartment. We see no other characters (save Dev's parents), we stay mostly in the bedroom, and we witness three major conflicts play out. As relaxed as the lilting naturalism of the filmmaking lends to the episode's sense of space, the passage of time, denoted by a sturdy calendar clock, feels equally luxurious. From a July to a June, the story told on screen has the beats TV audiences have been led to expect of a cohabitating couple: (1) the excitement of moving in; (2) the initial, enthusiastic sex; (3) the playful jibes about untidiness that turn more personal and pointed, even as the sex becomes more routine, tired; (4) the giving of gifts to make up for miscommunications, which lead only to greater misunderstanding; (5) the realization that one of them has shared nothing about their relationship with his parents; (6) the broaching of doing the relationship long distance when the other's work might lead her away; (7) meeting the parents; and (8) a career compromise that leads to a period of stability. Ross and Rachel on *Friends* went through the exact same beats (albeit in a different order). Yet the predictability of the steps feels novel in *Master*: The episode is a technical marvel, compared to the conventional multicamera attributes (including a laugh track) of *Friends*; Ansari and Yang's dialog is lively and specific, and most importantly, Dev and Rachel don't look or act like your everyday TV couple.

Audiences thus have much to parse. We are invited to wonder: Will a South Asian man and a white woman living together behave differently, as dominant cultural norms might suggest? In a sense, the standard relationship manual feels not oppressive, boring, or inevitable but pleasant, organic, and desirable. Dev and Rachel make the ups and downs of living together endearing. Dev photographs Rachel posing cutely inside their fireplace. Dev makes Rachel fresh pasta from their pasta maker. To avoid the bickering that often plagues relationships in the middle stages, the two come to an agreement that the person who leaves the

FIGURE 15.1.
With its portrayal of the ups and downs of living together, "Mornings" challenges dominant skepticism over interracial couples.

bedroom floor dirty must perform oral sex on the other. The episode portrays Dev and Rachel as special, goofy, and reasonable—in doing so, the couple's journey challenges dominant skepticism over interracial couples.

However, in the season 1 finale, Rachel calls things off, stating, "The time in our lives to do crazy shit is winding down." What are examples of Hall's three readings here? A dominant reading would dismiss Dev: The relationship was doomed from the start because Dev is brown and interracial relationships are nonnormative. Others might form an "oppositional" reading: Not only would these audience members strongly reject any stereotypes against interracial dating, but also they might push against heteronormativity by wanting a romantic relationship to develop between Dev and his male best friend, Arnold. Most audiences, though, will have a range of negotiated readings, which combine dominant and oppositional elements and meanings according to the social situation of viewers. For instance, a dominant meaning could involve the widely held cultural notion privileged Americans hold about their twenties being the last frontier of self-discovery. At the same time, the fact that a woman rather than the man is doing the breaking up goes against dominant patriarchal culture. Thus one potential negotiated reading is, "Rachel is surprisingly independent for a woman, which is great, but it's appropriate that given her age, she doesn't want to settle down yet." A different potential negotiation would emphasize other readings and meanings in play: "Rachel's desire for 'crazy shit' is the by-product of economic and racial privilege, but clearly they are ultimately incompatible given their cultural differences."

The Dev-Rachel relationship gives itself to plentiful negotiated readings, but Dev's relationship with Francesca in season 2 and the kind of masculinity Dev enacts hit a lot more of the standard dominant beats in a more predictable manner. Rachel's departure to Japan precipitates Dev's to Italy, so season 2 begins with him as an apprentice in a tiny pasta shop in an idyllic small town. There he rides bicycles, keeps exclaiming "Allora," and strikes a warm, fuzzy friendship with the shop owner's beautiful daughter, Francesca, who has a boyfriend of ten years, Pino. The show offers close-ups of Francesca's face, suggesting that somewhere within, she is unhappy with her small-town life and is intrigued by Dev's Big Apple world. In the fifth episode, Francesca visits New York for the first time and Dev realizes that he has feelings for her after they go out for a classy dinner at which John Legend performs. The episode executes this story point poignantly with the camera staying on Dev for three whole minutes after he drops Francesca off. When Dev learns via Skype that Francesca and Pino are engaged, he must feign a smile. Another one got away.

Thus, leading up to "Amarsi Un Po," the season's nearly hour-long centerpiece episode, we see traditional tropes that play along dominant gendered lines: Francesca enacts ambivalence about her relationship with Pino by constantly seeking Dev's company, while maintaining her distance. This brings up the dominant cultural motif of women being coy. By contrast, Dev channels a deep-seated longing, a demeanor that invites audiences to think that he has found the woman of his dreams. But he continues to play the "nice guy" trope and doesn't act on it.

In "Amarsi Un Po," these themes and emotional aches are ratcheted up several notches, increasing audience investment as well as frustration. Early on, the writers telegraph that Dev-Francesca are an exotic item. A man on the street catcalls, "Damn, your girl fine, . . . Got you an Indian dude. I like it." Francesca laughs this off. We follow the couple inside a pharmacy where there is lots of touching, Francesca aah-ing over tiny chocolate Vaseline (a line reading that audience members might decode as sexual attraction to Dev), and her admitting that Pino has begun to take her for granted since their engagement. Later, as they promenade around trees in Washington Square Park, Francesca muses, "This is what you do, right? Ten years with a person. You just get married." Most audience members would recognize that line as clearly from the dominant cultural manual about the logic behind marriage, even if they were to have a more local, negotiated reading about Francesca's motivation.

Dev, meanwhile, struggles with Francesca's mixed signals. When she suggests coming over to watch a movie at his apartment one night when her fiancé is out of town, her ambivalence becomes unbearable for Dev (and the audience) to interpret. The sequence forms the crux of the episode: staying with the couple in Dev's living room and later moving to the bedroom, forming a compelling stylistic complement to "Mornings." Narrative codes encourage a dominant reading that Francesca has "traditional feminine" emotions and casts second-season Dev as a traditional South Asian man who doesn't push boundaries in relationships, thereby going against the more proactive, lighthearted Dev of the first season. On Dev's living room couch, as they watch an Italian film where the couple is making out on the screen, Francesca asks for a blanket they both get under. Francesca suggests a pajama dance party, where she shows Dev the "Twist" while wearing only an over-large top. She confides silkily that Pino is the only guy she has slept

FIGURE 15.2.
Dev struggles over how far (and when) to push boundaries in his relationship with Francesca in season 2.

with, but with another wink to *Friends*, Francesca has a list of celebrities she is allowed to sleep with; when Dev mentions his, she murmurs, "You like the Italians." The next morning, after having slept on the same bed, Dev decides they need to have a proper talk and Francesca leans in and says, "I am *really* going to miss you," which Dev misinterprets as a cue to kiss her. Some days later, they go on a helicopter tour of NYC, where Dev finally divulges his feelings and Francesca says, "But I'm with Pino and I can't do anything about it," one of the most overused conflicts in romantic dramas.

Global television audiences, positioned in dazzlingly diverse arrays of lived experiences, ideologies, affect, and socioeconomics, are bound to have divergent readings of media narratives. However, it's worth remembering that in any given sociocultural context, there is a prevalent dominant ideology. Compared to Dev-Rachel's more offbeat relationship, which *Master* refreshingly normalizes, the ambivalence and blurring of lines in Dev-Francesca's relationship can be interpreted along patriarchal and heteronormative lines via a dominant decoding. While certainly viewers will negotiate their own meanings out of this storyline, the second season is encoded with more dominant meanings, privileging patriarchal and racial norms.

While I was writing this essay, allegations against Aziz Ansari were published by *Babe* magazine, wherein a female cinematographer narrated her terrible date during which Ansari constantly demanded sexual acts even though she felt unsure she wanted to carry them through.[2] In the wake of the powerful cultural context of the #MeToo movement, with women demanding autonomy over their bodies and policies to ensure accountability for harassment and assault, it is likely that several audience members—me included—form drastically different readings about Dev. They might reframe everything Dev did as alluding to actor/writer *Ansari*, the real-life creep. In this reading, Dev and Ansari are hard to separate. Dev's agreeing to take up Francesca's offer to sleep under the same blanket, or his misinterpreting a cue to kiss her, or finally, his blaming Francesca in the season 2 finale, might be read as Ansari's tacit predatory intentions and his typical spurned male chauvinist. Thus, Dev can be decoded as a pig because Ansari seems to be.

Startlingly different and incompatible readings of a television program do exist in culture. Often, life experiences reshape or even disrupt audiences' understanding of the text, even in retrospect. Television watching never happens in a vacuum, and audiences not just are aware of a culture's dominant codes but also negotiate and invert story and character arcs in a constantly unfurling, highly complicated set of cultural contexts. Whatever conclusions you draw from Dev-Francesca and Dev-Rachel, Hall would suggest that your reading speaks volumes about how you see your place in a changing society and how you relate to dominant ideology and codes.

FURTHER READING

Durham, Meenakshi Gigi. "Constructing the 'New Ethnicities': Media, Sexuality, and Diaspora Identity in the Lives of South Asian Immigrant Girls." *Critical Studies in Media Communication* 21, no. 2 (2004): 140–61.

Hall, Stuart. "Encoding/Decoding." In *Culture, Media, Language*, edited by Stuart Hall et al., 128–40. London: Hutchinson, 1980.

Lopez, Lori Kido. *Asian American Media Activism: Fighting for Cultural Citizenship*. New York: New York University Press, 2016.

Pillai, Poonam. "Rereading Stuart Hall's Encoding/Decoding Model." *Communication Theory* 2, no. 3 (1992): 221–33.

NOTES

1. Stuart Hall, "Encoding/Decoding," in *Culture, Media, Language*, ed. Stuart Hall et al. (London: Hutchinson, 1980), 128–40.
2. Katie Way, "I Went on a Date with Aziz Ansari. It Turned into the Worst Night of My Life," *Babe*, https://babe.net.

16

Orange Is the New Black
Intersectional Analysis

MARY CELESTE KEARNEY

Abstract: Like all human beings, television characters are intersectional, meaning that each of the identity categories ascribed to and performed by them, such as race, gender, age, and sexuality, are interdependent and thus mutually informing. In this essay, Mary Celeste Kearney demonstrates the use of intersectional television analysis via a close study of one episode and one character from *Orange Is the New Black*.

Orange Is the New Black, Netflix's dramedy series, has received much attention for its portrayal of women prisoners in a federal penitentiary. Creator Jenji Kohan based the series on Piper Kerman's memoir, *Orange Is the New Black: My Year in a Women's Prison*, which she wrote following her incarceration for drug smuggling with a former girlfriend. At the beginning of the TV series, Piper Chapman, a thirtysomething, white, Anglo American, upper-middle-class cisgender woman, is engaged to Larry Bloom, a Jewish American cisgender man of the same privileged class, age, and race. Like Larry, Piper's family members have no knowledge of her criminal past. Thus, their understanding of Piper is upended when she is convicted.

If *Orange Is the New Black* (*OITNB*) were a conventional TV drama, it would likely focus on Piper and those closest to her, with less attention to other characters. But that is not Kohan's objective. The show does follow Piper as she navigates the federal prison system and the effects of her incarceration on her family and friends, but it broadens out to explore the lives of the other prisoners, as well as the prison guards and administrators who supervise and discipline them. As a result of its numerous and considerably diverse characters, *OITNB* lends itself well to intersectional analysis.

First named as a critical concept in the 1980s, intersectionality is now the dominant lens used to analyze identity within virtually all academic fields, including television studies.[1] Intersectionality has four primary components. *First, human identities are multiple rather than singular, and each person's identities are interdependent, working together to create a person's overall identity.*[2] Students first using an intersectional approach often focus on one specific identity at a time, building their analysis in a cumulative fashion (e.g., race plus gender plus class, etc.). But the goal is to consider how such identities exist in unison, creating a sum that is greater than its parts. For example, we cannot understand Michelle Obama's identity by focusing only on her gender or race. We must take both into consideration, as well as her age, class, sexuality, nationality, religion, and other aspects of her identity. Analyzing the intersectional identities of TV characters (or producers or viewers) can take considerable time and effort, and not only because of the multiple categories constituting an individual's identity. All TV series involve numerous characters, not just one, and some TV genres, particularly serial dramas, involve characters with complex identities built up over a long period of time. To create more manageable research projects, television scholars interested in intersectional identities will often focus on just a few characters (or producers or viewers) that meet their study's particular criteria (e.g., the three Taiwanese American boys on *Fresh Off the Boat*).

Second, identities are forms of human classification produced via social interaction and in relation to systems of power, not predetermined or natural categories. Human beings do not exist autonomously, performing our identities in a vacuum. Rather, we interact regularly with others, who hold us accountable for such performances.[3] Those judgments are based on ideas and values used by various social institutions (e.g., politics, religion, and education) to define and rate our identities. Where our interlocking identities rank on such cultural hierarchies influences the amount of privilege—opportunity, agency, and status—we have, or don't have. For instance, despite being a black woman (a relatively deprivileged identity in white male-dominated societies), Michelle Obama has had multiple opportunities for a good life as a result of her straight cisgendered identity, middle-class background, and U.S. citizenship, all of which have converged to give her advantages many other American black women do not have. Michelle's privilege increased considerably when her husband became president of the United States of America. When using the intersectional approach to study television characters (or producers or viewers), we examine how each character's intersecting identities are produced in relation to other characters and social institutions, which in turn suggests the amount of status and power they have within their storyworld.

Third, interlocking identities must be considered within the historical period and geographic context in which they are located. How identities are understood and valued differs across space and time. Thus, privilege is affected by where a person is located geographically and temporally. Michelle Obama, a black woman born in the United States in 1964, would not have had the same status, opportunities, and agency had she been born in Afghanistan or during the eighteenth century. Time and place are therefore indispensable to understanding the intersecting identities of TV characters, producers, and audiences.

Fourth, the ultimate goal of intersectional analysis is assisting in the elimination of oppression and establishing equality for all human beings. Part of the intersectional project is to compare a person's interlocking identities with those of other people (both similar and dissimilar) to discern how those identities differently affect experiences, opportunities, and agency. If research reveals social marginalization and oppression, scholars discuss strategies to bring about social justice. In television studies, this means analyzing characters' intersecting identities to determine how they measure up to dominant values related to those identities, as well as to the experiences of real people who identify with them. When demeaning portrayals are found, researchers suggest ways to develop respectful representations that can influence public opinion and social policies. Studying TV producers' and viewers' intersecting identities can help us to achieve a more democratic media culture as well, since who makes media, who consumes media, and how they engage in such practices all matter.

As a serial dramedy about a diverse group of prisoners, guards, and administrators commingling in an environment structured by issues of status, agency, containment, and oppression, *OITNB* offers an excellent opportunity to examine intersectional identities and their social effects. Optimally, conducting an intersectional analysis would explore the program's multiple characters' identities, as well as those of its production team and viewing audience, over all of its seasons—a massive project that would fill an entire book. Instead, I have selected the third episode, "Lesbian Request Denied," to model intersectional representation analysis.[4]

"Lesbian Request Denied" features the backstory of Sophia Burset, played by Laverne Cox.[5] Sophia is introduced in the first episode as a complex character. She is marked as both black and female due to Cox's physical features, as a prisoner by her costume and location, and as an American through her use of language. Yet such demographic characteristics do not alone define her. Sophia is also presented as a kind, helpful, and stylish person who works as a hairdresser in the prison's salon. These latter traits construct her as highly feminine, a trait rarely associated with black women prisoners in media. As this episode delves into Sophia's past, it reveals more about her background as a working-class transwoman who must navigate the binary gender order of prison and beyond.[6] Significantly, *OITNB* does not depict transgender as an autonomous identity, as many other trans representations have done, but one that is complexly intersected with other identities. The episode also avoids representing transgender as just a medical/physical identity. Although Sophia's medical treatment is a topic, "Lesbian Request Denied" largely portrays her transgender identity as socially developed in conjunction with other identities, as well as via interpersonal relationships and larger social structures.

Because "Lesbian Request Denied" continues the development of Piper's backstory and transition to prison life, and because Sophia and Piper are both in their early thirties and the most conventionally feminine prisoners, this episode encourages viewers to compare the two characters as they deal with a masculine prison environment and the men who supervise them. As a result, this text provides an opportunity to witness the different effects of their intersectional identities: Sophia's have resulted in her devalued social status, limited opportunities, and lack of conventional forms of power, while Piper's have ensured her privilege (at least before she was convicted).[7] Piper has more than race to her advantage. She is cisgender and presented as sexually attractive to both men and women. Because the episode does not focus on the construction of Piper's appearance, she is portrayed as a "natural" beauty, someone who does not need to work on her appearance to be seen as attractive by a broad range of people. In contrast, Sophia's constructed femininity and trans identity are repeatedly foregrounded via attention to her body, makeup, clothing, hormones, and surgery. Piper's privilege also comes from her upper-middle-class family, which has provided her with a stable home life, a college education, and financial security. Yet despite Piper being normative in virtually all ways other than her bisexuality, she is out of her element in a prison dominated by poor Latinas and black women. Indeed, she is as much of an anomaly in Litchfield Prison as is Sophia.

"Lesbian Request Denied" opens with a flashback sequence wherein Sophia appears in her pre-transition identity as a firefighter named Marcus, played by M. Lamar, Cox's cisgender twin brother. Marcus's masculinity is emphasized by his job and interactions with male colleagues, as well as a later revelation that he is a husband and a father to a son. However, the pink and lacey lingerie he wears under his work clothes marks his gender identity as nonnormative. While Marcus's class status is never stated, because he has a physically demanding job and because he steals other people's credit card information to pay for medical treatments, the show implies that he is working class. Such a vague characterization suggests that the series' mostly white, middle-class writers may have relied on the common conflation of blackness and lower socioeconomic status when developing this character.[8]

Once Marcus presents as Sophia, the intersections of her gender, race, and class produce different meanings and effects. For example, in a flashback, Sophia

FIGURE 16.1.
A scene in which
Sophia hesitates to purchase
$300 shoes for her son
marks her class status and
suggests her hesitance is
related to saving money for
her genital reconstruction
surgery.

is shown as hesitant to purchase a $300 pair of athletic shoes for her son. In addition to marking her class status, this scene suggests that her hesitance is related to concerns about saving money for her genital reconstruction surgery. Sophia is no longer a firefighter by this scene, and the show has not represented her in a new job. Therefore, the episode may be commenting on the widespread unemployment of real trans people, especially those of color, who are excessively disadvantaged because of their interlocking gender and racial identities.

The episode's exploration of Sophia's intersectional identities continues during scenes of her in prison. With minimal means to accrue income, Sophia is now truly poor, and her wife, Crystal, complains about needing to hold down two jobs. In comparison, Piper's privileged class status is highlighted several times, including via a reference to her as a Smith College graduate, as well as her purchase of gifts for other prisoners. Nevertheless, despite Sophia's general lack of agency, she demonstrates considerable initiative and creativity by developing work-around tactics for goods and services she desires but cannot afford, such as making duct-tape sandals and Kool-Aid/Vaseline lipstick. Sophia's crime of credit card theft can also be read as a work-around tactic. As with Marcus, her blackness is not explored to the same degree as her class, especially in comparison to other African American characters in media. Yet the show's foregrounding of the broken, female-headed family that results from Sophia's imprisonment could be understood as reproducing stereotypes of black people.

How Sophia's intersecting identities affect the people closest to her is perhaps best represented in a flashback scene that highlights the performativity of identity, as well as the difficulty some transgender people have in expressing their subjectivity through clothing. The scene begins with preoperative Sophia asking Crystal to assess the stylishness of a new outfit. Crystal does not hold back her criticism, describing Sophia as both "Hannah Montana" and "a two-dollar hooker," because of the frayed jean mini skirt, sparkly top, and cowboy boots. Crystal's dialogue

FIGURE 16.2.
Crystal advises Sophia to dress like a "classy, grown-up lady," demonstrating the respectability politics that black people living in a white-dominated society are encouraged to adopt.

further intersects gender with class, race, and age as she encourages Sophia to dress like a "classy, grown-up lady." Consulting her own wardrobe, Crystal finds a dark purple dress, which both women agree is more appropriate. This scene demonstrates the respectability politics that black people living in a white-dominated society are encouraged to adopt to deflect attention from their racial difference and lessen the possibility of discrimination.[9] When we consider how class and gender function alongside race in such respectability politics, the scene and Sophia's identity become significantly more complex.

A respectable appearance is not the only issue with which the couple grapples, however. Helping Sophia to undress, Crystal notices the bulge in Sophia's underwear, which prompts Crystal to discuss Sophia's planned genital reconstruction surgery. While Crystal says she's supportive of Sophia's superficial transition to femininity (e.g., clothes, makeup, and gestures), she does not want Sophia to remove her penis, which suggests that Crystal would prefer their relationship, and her own identity, to remain heterosexual.[10] Sophia does not argue with Crystal but reminds her that "[she] can leave," which suggests Sophia's determination to have the surgery. Crystal's request and Sophia's response gesture toward the differential power dynamics of patriarchal heterosexual relationships that may have underlined their relationship as wife and husband, thus demonstrating gender and sexuality as intersected.

As the couple reconciles and kisses, the camera cuts to their young son Michael, who walks in on them, scowls, and turns away before slamming the door behind him. Such actions suggest that, from his perspective, his parents are now a lesbian couple, which he finds undesirable. In other flashbacks, Michael's transphobia becomes apparent, resulting in him being revealed as the person who reported Sophia to the police. "Lesbian Request Denied" thus lays bare the complex challenges trans people have in maintaining relationships during and after transition, as gender is deeply intersected with sexual identity and desire, not to mention family roles.

While this episode demonstrates intersectionality and power struggles within the family unit, it also explores them within another power-laden social institution: prison. *OITNB*'s prison scenes depict the oppression Sophia faces as a black transwoman of little means within an institution run primarily by white, cisgender, heterosexual, middle-class men. For instance, Sophia becomes the victim of the prison's new regulations on medication, which preclude her from receiving the regular dose of hormones she needs to maintain her female identity. Via an alleged cost-cutting strategy, the prison reduces her dosage by half, thus compromising her health. When Sophia receives no help from her white, straight, cisgender male correctional officer, she swallows part of a toy so that she can be sent to the infirmary and ask for an exception to the new policy—another demonstration of her tactical maneuvering within a system where she has no power. Yet the attending white, cisgender, female doctor says she has concerns about Sophia's liver, takes her off hormones, and offers her an antidepressant instead.

Given Sophia's multiple, interlocking forms of nonnormative identity and thus lack of opportunities for conventional agency, it is no surprise that she seeks other means for obtaining medication. She first asks the white, straight, cisgender female head cook to smuggle in hormones via the prison's grocery delivery. But the cook refuses and refers her to a white, straight, cisgender male prison guard, George Mendez, who is known to trade goods for sex with prisoners. Refusing to pursue that route, Sophia's next asks her wife to smuggle in the hormones during prison visits. Crystal refuses, noting that smuggling is illegal and, if she were caught and arrested, neither of them would be available to raise their son. Deeply frustrated by the request, not to mention the pressures facing her family and work life resulting from Sophia's transition and imprisonment, Crystal resorts to an offensive tactic of the disempowered, yelling in anger, "Get out of here so you can be a father to your son. Man up!" Sophia's last scene in this episode shows her plucking out chin hairs.

Such depictions of the prison system constraining Sophia's poor, black, transgender womanhood work in tandem with others where she is demeaned or disrespected, such as when she is sexually harassed by Mendez, who is excited by the prospects of having sex with a transwoman. Other guards and prisoners refer to Sophia as "freaky deaky," "he/she," and "tranny," and a white, heterosexual, cisgender, female supervisor asks, "Why would anyone ever give up being a man? It's like winning the lottery and giving the ticket back." Although this latter comment explicitly points to male privilege, it nevertheless reveals a misunderstanding of transwomen's relationships to that form of privilege, not to mention the collective impact of nonnormative racial and class status on male privilege. In contrast to Sophia's multiply devalued identities, Piper's gender is bolstered by her whiteness and wealth and compromised only, and only slightly, by the unfashionable prison uniform she is forced to wear.

Via its focus on these two characters, "Lesbian Request Denied" demonstrates how intersecting identities are constructed in relation to other people, social institutions, and systems of power. Yet as students of intersectionality, we are compelled to move beyond the text to consider how its representations connect with real life and popular notions of identity. While as a series *OITNB* complicates the normativity and privilege associated with Piper, this is not evident by its third episode. In comparison, Sophia's representation improves upon previous depictions of poor transwomen of color as a result of her somewhat stable family life and the fact that she is not portrayed as mentally unstable or a sex worker. Moreover, this episode contributes to a greater understanding of transgender people by focusing on the multiple, overlapping forms of oppression Sophia experiences as a result of her intersecting identities. Nonetheless, her character repeats some conventional elements of trans representation: Like most trans characters, she identifies as a woman, she is the series' only trans character, and she appears as a recurring rather than regular cast member. I would suggest, therefore, that the writers and producers of *OITNB* reflect critically on these elements when developing new storylines for Sophia, and that other media professionals consider them when shaping their own narratives about transgender people.

Deep divisions exist today in U.S. society around all forms of identity, especially race and gender. If we are to overcome such social strife, the systematic mechanisms of oppression and privilege that give rise to those divisions must be studied carefully. For students of television, this means that the powerful discourses of identity that circulate within media culture demand our close attention. An intersectional approach to representation offers us an opportunity to think more critically about how certain ideas and values about identity shape TV characters' relations to power, which in turn allows us to consider how such dynamics play out in real life. Although not explored here, the concept of intersectionality is useful also for examining the identities of television producers and viewers, for all of us are caught up in a complex system whereby the combination of our individual identities affects the amount of status, opportunity, and agency we have, which in turn influences the television representations we make and consume.

FURTHER READING

Cho, Sumi, Kimberlé Williams Crenshaw, and Leslie McCall. "Toward a Field of Intersectionality Studies: Theory, Applications, and Praxis." *Signs: Journal of Women in Culture and Society* 38, no. 4 (2013): 785–810.

Collins, Patricia Hill, and Sirma Bilge. *Intersectionality*. Malden, MA: Polity Press, 2016.

Nash, Jennifer C. "Re-thinking Intersectionality." *Feminist Review* 89, no. 1 (2008): 1–15.

NOTES

1. Kimberlé Crenshaw, "Demarginalizing the Intersection of Race and Sex: A Black Feminist Critique of Antidiscrimination Doctrine, Feminist Theory and Antiracist Politics," *University of Chicago Legal Forum* 1, no. 8 (1989): 139–67.
2. Because feminists of color introduced this concept, intersectionality is often mistakenly conflated with racial minorities. Yet every human being's identities are intersectional. Intersectionality is also incorrectly connected with racial diversity, which describes a variety of raced people in one community.
3. See Candace West and Don H. Zimmerman, "Doing Gender," *Gender and Society* 1, no. 2 (1987): 125–51.
4. The episode was written by Sian Heder and directed by Jodie Foster. The first season debuted on Netflix on July 11, 2013.
5. A character's traits and actions as represented in one episode may be interpreted differently when considered in relation to other episodes and the series as a whole. Therefore, the analysis I offer here should not be taken as an interpretation of Sophia's representation during the entire series.
6. In contrast to many actors playing transgender characters, Cox is trans.
7. Because of the common privileging of such women in U.S. society and culture, Kohan has been criticized for placing Piper in the protagonist role. However, the creator has argued that the character worked as Kohan's "Trojan horse," offering white, straight, middle-class TV executives and audiences a point of identification when Kohan's ultimate goal is to share the stories of a considerably diverse group of incarcerated women. See "'Orange' Creator Jenji Kohan: 'Piper Was My Trojan Horse,'" NPR, August 13, 2013, www.npr.org.
8. The show's almost all-white writers' room has received considerable criticism from viewers and critics of color. For example, see Ellen McGirt, "An Uproar Over 'Orange Is the New Black' Shows the Problem with Diversity," *Fortune*, June 22, 2016, http://fortune.com.
9. See Evelyn Brooks Higginbotham, *Righteous Discontent: The Women's Movement in the Black Baptist Church, 1880–1920* (Cambridge, MA: Harvard University Press, 1993).
10. This scene thus gives another meaning to the episode's title, "Lesbian Request Denied," which some might interpret as relating primarily to Piper's rejection of sexual advances from another female prisoner.

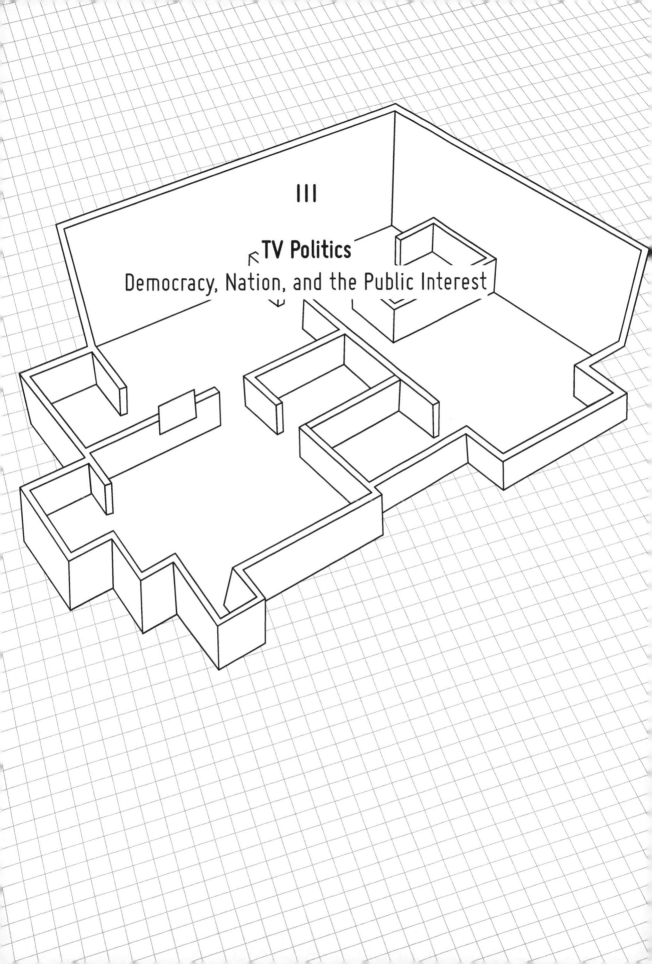

III

TV Politics

Democracy, Nation, and the Public Interest

17

The Amazing Race
Global Othering

JONATHAN GRAY

Abstract: *The Amazing Race* is one of the most successful reality shows in American television history, and arguably no other program has spent so much time outside of the United States or introduced U.S. audiences to so many non-Americans. Jonathan Gray applies a postcolonialist critique to the show's images and characters, finding plenty to criticize, while also pointing to moments that suggest the potential to challenge age-old images of crazy and exotic foreigners.

American television was never just American, but in recent years, its production, distribution, and reception have all globalized in a more concerted way. In terms of American television's on-screen representations, though, its interest in and use of the rest of the world are still starkly limited. Vancouver and Toronto stand in for American cities when Canadian tax breaks help Hollywood out. *Law and Order: SVU*'s Elliot Stabler takes a trip to Prague to bust a child pornography ring and spy or military shows jaunt around the globe to capture nefarious evil-doers, portraying the globe as a problem to be fixed by American law enforcement. Reality television and the news, meanwhile, also seem most interested in the world at large when it is corrupt and violent, corrupt and dying, corrupt and depraved, and/or willing to supply a judge for a competition reality show. Or occasionally the rest of the world justifies coverage when it is stunningly beautiful, exotic, and free of people, as in *Survivor* and many nature shows or documentaries.

I generalize, of course, but so does American television. Exceptions can be found, but they are few and far between, largely because depictions of the rest of the world are themselves few and far between. In the 2011–2012 television season, for instance, every scripted program on American primetime network television was set in America, with only the retro airline drama *Pan Am* and the spy shows

Chuck and *Nikita* leaving American shores even occasionally. Network reality programming offered us a quick trip overseas on *America's Next Top Model*; it gave us a lush yet unpopulated South Pacific in *Survivor*, and *The Amazing Race*. As is often the case, and as had become de rigueur by the show's nineteenth season (in its eleventh year on television as of this writing in 2012), the heavy lifting of representing the world and its people on network television was left to *The Amazing Race*.

Over those nineteen seasons, *The Amazing Race* regularly brought in 10–12 million viewers a week, according to Nielsen ratings, and won the Primetime Emmy for Outstanding Reality-Competition Program nine out of ten times after the award was introduced in 2003. The show's format is relatively simple, filming several teams on a race around the world. The race is broken into legs in different countries with tasks to be completed before advancing, movement by all manner of modes of transport, and ultimately a footrace at the end of each leg to the *Amazing Race* mat where host Phil Keoghan and a festively costumed local await, ready to eliminate the last-placed team in most instances. The teams set out from the United States, and the first team back to the final mat in the United States wins a million dollars. The race requires the competitors to interact with locals to get ahead, and the series regularly portrays the competitors' thoughts and opinions on the places they visit. As a result, it is a remarkably rare entity on American network television in this supposedly globalized era: a program that spends time in other countries, depicting the locals of those countries while doing so, and showing an interest, however fleeting and caricatured at times, in the rest of the world. As one of the few shows on American television to do so, it carries significant representational "weight" in speaking of, for, and about the world at large.[1] Like it or not, outside of the news, the *Amazing Race* crew are one of the key sources on American primetime television for messages about the world and its various citizens.

What, then, does it say about the world? Jordan Harvey argues that its depiction is mostly without merit, stereotypical, and Orientalized.[2] I agree to a point and will illustrate how deeply nationally chauvinist the program can be, through analyzing season seven, broadcast from March to May 2005. However, I will not "only" critique *The Amazing Race*; I will also focus on moments in season seven when it realizes progressive potential for depiction and challenges rather than reiterates tired clichés about the rest of the world in ways that highlight the multiplicity inherent in most television representations.

In his groundbreaking analysis of the discursive conquest of the Middle East by centuries of Western writing about the area and its peoples, Edward Said notes how this conquest happened in part by denying non-Westerners the right to speak for themselves, as knowledge was constructed for and about them in the West instead.[3] While everyday discussion about depictions and representation can often turn to noting the presence of "stereotypes" and to the rating of depictions as either "good" or "bad," one of Said's most helpful offerings was to remind us that much of the symbolic violence done to those being depicted begins when they are denied the right to speak for and of themselves and is exacerbated by the need to reduce complex, varied cultures to singular signs that take on the status of representativeness. Significant cultural diversity is thus reduced, for instance, to the singular depiction of the angry, irrational, despotic, and barbaric "Arab" seen in fictional texts written by non-Arabs. However, cultural identity is always in such flux, characterized by variation and difference, that any attempt to depict a group of people will at the least prove inadequate, and at the worst do great damage to an understanding of the diversity of identity. Said observes how large swathes of Western literature, "science," and travel accounts engaged in a process by which cultural differences within the Middle East were flattened out and reduced to a monolithic group ("the Oriental") that was then regarded as a knowable, singular entity and to a rhetoric that justified colonization and subjugation. And though Said's initial work was primarily historical and concerned with the Middle East, subsequent work by Said and others shows the continuation of this into the present day (witness how rarely, for instance, Iraqis are invited to discuss Iraqi culture or society on American cable news), and the extension of Orientalism to multiple foreign groups. If the nation is, as Benedict Anderson famously notes, "an imagined community,"[4] much of the work that goes into nation-building takes the form of imagining those who are not like us and projecting onto them all manner of unsavory attributes, so that we can then flatter ourselves with the contrast we see between the savage them and the noble us.

In many ways, *The Amazing Race* takes an active part in this process of nationally chauvinistic projection, all the more so because it wears the badge of being "reality." Yet many of the show's more egregious moments of representation let us see how such depiction has often become a self-confirming process. The premise of *The Amazing Race* suggests that we will see competitors in "real" situations with "real" people around the world, but instead they are often interacting in highly contrived situations. In an early leg of season seven, for instance, teams face a challenge in which they must lead llamas a short distance in Peru. Rather than read this instruction in the Lima airport and be forced to find llamas, llama herders, and so forth, the teams are guided to a specific location in the countryside where the llamas await them, and where only those Peruvians hired or otherwise allowed "on set" by the producers may interact with them. The producers often hire the locals beforehand; for example, the bushmen from whom the teams can select for lessons on spearing a swinging sack in South Africa were preselected by the producers. While we can understand this choice for logistical reasons, the result is that the producers have *chosen* many of the locals to whom both the teams and we as viewers are introduced to represent their culture, and we would be naïve to assume they were chosen at random. *The Amazing Race* requires an amazing feat of international organization and stage design (hence its many Emmy awards); before the cameras even arrive, therefore, the producers have already played a key role in deciding exactly what we will or even *can* see. They decide what is worth depicting from a country, and hence they decide what should be represented, leaving the country and its people little and sometimes no room to speak for themselves.

This stage design is especially notable in the challenges, as complex cultures are reduced to a small set of tasks that are habitually described as "common" and "traditional" by Keoghan. South Africa, for instance, gives us a "Tunnels or Tribes" Detour challenge, introducing South Africans to us literally as cavemen, or as primitive tribal elders who demand those most stereotypical of tribal belongings: necklaces, drums, pipes, and bowls (rather than iPods, say). In Botswana, the "Food or Water" Detour challenge reductively implies that the people are so poor that their life and cultural being has been reduced largely to the search for food and water. And India gives us "Trunk or Drunk," exoticizing the country as a land of elephants, vibrant color, and mysticism. Of course, producers also decide *where* in different countries the teams will visit, and these decisions have considerable impact on the resulting image of the country and its people as well. Whether the nation is presented as traditional, simple, and rural, or as commercially vibrant, modernized, and urban comes down entirely to the producers' choice. And then there is the mat, where Keoghan waits sternly for the teams, flanked by a local who is usually in traditional dress and limited in task to waiting several hours with the host before turning on a smile and welcoming the teams to their country. "Mat talk" will often ensue between Phil and the racers, and this usually entails retrospective commentary on the day's tasks, yet the "native" welcomers are never invited to contribute to these discussions, nor to provide further context or additional information. Moreover, because of the speed of the race, many interactions with locals along the way reduce them to passive pointers; we rarely see or hear a local rise even to the level of supporting character in an episode. Surely more interactions occur along the way during the race, but the editing leaves audiences with heavily restricted *and directed* vision.

The locals quite often function as backdrops alone. One reply to the criticism that we learn so little about the locals is that the show ultimately isn't about them—it's about the American racers. Interpersonal dynamics between the racers, both within groups (witness Ray and Deanna's spats in season seven) and between them (witness Alex and Lynn's hatred of Rob and Amber), frequently take center stage, and the locals are merely obstacles around which the racers and their attitudes must maneuver. This reduction of "the Other" to backdrop, though, has been a key component of the simplistic rendering of foreign cultures for centuries. Thus, for example, Chinua Achebe notes critically of Joseph Conrad's *Heart of Darkness* that the Africans are poorly rendered in order to make them more ideal as backdrop for the central concern with the hero Marlow's psyche.[5] Conrad's novel may be critical of colonial governance, as such, but it never shows a true interest in colonial *subjects* of that governance; instead, the novel renders them in broad, crude strokes. Similarly, in *The Amazing Race*, non-Americans are rarely if ever allowed to become true characters. Rather, the world becomes a sounding board for the American subject, and the world's people appear as objects to be looked at, smiled at, or occasionally frowned at, yet never fully fleshed-out individuals.

Season 7's episode entitled "We Have a Bad Elephant!" offers one case in point, with editing and stage design forcing the various Indians on the show into a series of unsavory positions. Rob claims ownership over a local serving as guide, worrying that another team might "steal" him. A challenge requires teams to push ornately decorated wooden elephants through the streets, co-opting locals to push for them. Gretchen ends up atop the elephant, yelling at Indian children to push harder, presenting us with a shocking colonial era tableau. Later, a Fast Forward challenge requires Joyce to submit to having her head shaved, which leads to shots of an Indian man standing above the prone, crying Joyce, cutting off her hair, in a disturbing image that evokes countless tales of foreign male sexual aggression against "our" women. Finally, after a camel race with dancing, colorfully dressed Indians looking on, the teams arrive at the mat, where they are greeted by an old Indian man whose moustache connects to his sideburns, and whose welcome suggests little command of English. Few of these subalterns are allowed to speak, save to confirm their ownership by Rob in the former case, or to welcome racers in the latter, and none serves as anything more than local color.

As this criticism suggests, a key disappointment with *The Amazing Race* is its failure to live up to its potential to offer better chances to hear from and of non-Americans. Small modifications could make for such interesting moves forward in the presentation of foreign nationals to the viewing audience. What if, for example, Phil's companions on the mat debriefed the racers instead of Phil? What if locals joined the team members for an entire leg? What if not all teams were American? What if they were rewarded more systematically and significantly for learning about the cultures and people around them? And what if less of the action was staged?

Certainly, when the race finds itself in spaces that the producers cannot control, we often see the show working at its best. Throughout the show's many seasons, passersby in markets have fueled some of the more captivating interactions, as they speak for themselves and not according to script. In season seventeen, one task involving a set of Russian babushka potato farmers was brought to life by subtitled translations of the babushkas' plucky commentary and mockery of the racers. Camera work and editing in the cracks between challenges often give us better, if fleeting, access to the locals' perspectives as well. As with all reality shows, one risks falling into a trap by focusing on the set-up of *The Amazing Race* alone, as much of the art of reality television lies in its editing. Reality as genre specializes in judgment by editing, wherein insensitive and stupid comments are rendered as such by a quick cut to someone else's judgmental glare. Here, the show's editing regularly rewards the culturally sensitive and interested racers, and chastises the insensitive and ignorant. In many of these brief moments, viewers are invited to identify with the locals, not the racers, and to see the Americans and their behavior as the spectacle. Thus, for example, when "the hillbillies" boisterously start singing on a pickup truck serving as a bus in Peru, the camera captures numerous scornful and bemused looks from their fellow Peruvian passengers. And throughout season seven, Lynn's derogatory comments about, for instance, Peru being "donkeys and blankets" or Johannesburg being "a real city" and not just "like chickens and camels and whatever" are habitually met either by admonishment from his partner Alex or with a quick cut to a disapproving local taxi driver. In such moments, the show can break from offering a racer's eye-view of the race, and it often becomes most amusing when doing so.

The show works against stereotype at other points, too. Season seven, after all, is not all llamas and bushmen. Rather, Keoghan and the camera introduce several cities by focusing on their outstanding architecture, commercial centers, technology, and modernization, hence refusing to label those attributes as American only. Occasionally, the show also gives cultural and political history in ways that could expand its audience's understanding of a country. One of the tasks in Chile, for example, begins with Keoghan noting the country's many award-winning novelists, while a visit to Soweto leads to a history lesson (albeit extremely brief) on the city's political past. Lynn's comment that Johannesburg isn't just "chickens and camels and whatever" may be especially cringe-worthy, but it stands alongside many moments in the run of *The Amazing Race* when racers have commented with awe at how a place or people have defied their expectations and stereotypes. Such moments may be offset and outnumbered by tasks that play into stereotype, but here we see how easy it is and would be for the show to more systematically *challenge* received knowledge about the rest of the world and give us an expanded sense of what to expect outside the United States.

Meanwhile, the show's initial and final legs always take the teams through the United States, where we see American passersby treated entirely akin to foreign passersby. American cabbies' incompetence can often decide the race as much as

FIGURE 17.1. A competitor yells from atop her elephant at locals to push harder.

(or, due to placement at the end of the race, seemingly more than) foreign cabbies; Americans become backdrop and passive pointers; American cities and regions are reduced to simplistic tasks; and each season therefore ends with Americans filling in the same roles as their foreign counterparts. The representational weight of such in-country depictions are lighter than those of foreign locations, of course, as most viewers have likely seen countless other depictions of Miami (in the case of season seven), but astute viewers may at least be taught in these final legs that the show's depictional mode is just that—a mode and a visual grammar—rather than accurate representation.

Everything happens so quickly on *The Amazing Race* that racers often voice a desire to return to the country and "really" see it later. Such moments actively frame the show's depictional mode as superficial, and thereby gesture to depths of cultures and countries that *The Amazing Race* is not showing. While this framing does not excuse the show's choice to paint in broad strokes, and while we still might be left wondering why, for instance, the show doesn't offer us an entire race in only one country in order to allow for more depth, the acknowledgment of the show's inability to represent the world is still important. Just as we are all surely aware by this point in reality television's history that the camera doesn't show us everything about each person, *The Amazing Race* invites us to realize that we haven't seen everything about the countries it visits. Moreover, as evidenced by Travelocity's multiseason sponsorship of *The Amazing Race*, the show encourages viewers to fill in the gaps themselves by traveling more and seeing more. A glance at most *Amazing Race* fan discussion boards also indicates that the show offers viewers the chance to sit back in judgment both of its representations, as fans often compare what they saw in their own travels in a featured country to what the show depicts, and its racers' social strategies in interacting with locals, as such behavior is commonly central to fan reactions to cast members. And as with its CBS reality partner, *Survivor*, the show invites us to imagine how much better we'd be as contestants in terms of both speed and ethics.

Where are we left, then? With a show that can easily fall into an age-old rut of belittling other people and cultures in an attempt to lift up America and Americans, and yet one that is also capable of subverting elements of that process. As one of the few American primetime shows that regularly takes Americans outside of their own country, it is therefore simultaneously disappointing and promising. While it would be "neater" to conclude with either condemnation of the show or praise, it deserves both, albeit at different moments. More broadly, though, its failures point to a larger shared failure of American network television to cope representationally with globalization. After all, while *The Amazing Race* deserves criticism for its worse moments and for frustratingly falling short of its potential, its colleagues on primetime television deserve criticism for not even bothering. Hollywood is happy to take the world's money, it seems, and to export its American-centric brand of television far and wide, but it is still largely disinterested in creating a truly global television. When representations of the world at large and of the billions of people outside of America are restricted to *The Amazing Race*, the news, rewards on *Survivor*, nature shows, images of Anthony Bourdain eating in other countries, the imported *Locked Up Abroad*, and little more, U.S. television is failing both the world and the United States.

FURTHER READING

Hall, Stuart, ed. *Representation: Cultural Representations and Signifying Practices.* Thousand Oaks, CA: Sage, 1997.
Harvey, Jordan. "*The Amazing 'Race':* Discovering a True American." In *How Real Is Reality TV? Essays on Representation and Truth*, edited by David S. Escoffery. Jefferson, NC: McFarland, 2006.
Havens, Timothy. *Global Television Marketplace.* London: British Film Institute, 2008.

Ouellette, Laurie. *A Companion to Reality Television*. Malden, MA: Wiley-Blackwell, 2016.

Roy, Ishita Sinha. "*Worlds Apart*: Nation-Branding on the National Geographic Channel." *Media, Culture and Society* 29, no. 4 (2007): 569–92.

NOTES

1. See Jonathan Gray, *Television Entertainment* (New York: Routledge, 2008), 109.

2. Jordan Harvey, "*The Amazing 'Race*': Discovering a True American," in *How Real Is Reality TV? Essays on Representation and Truth*, ed. David S. Escoffery (Jefferson, NC: McFarland, 2006), 212–29.

3. Edward Said, *Orientalism* (New York: Vintage, 1979).

4. Benedict Anderson, *Imagined Communities: Reflections on the Origin and Spread of Nationalism* (New York: Verso, 1993).

5. Chinua Achebe, "An Image of Africa: Racism in Conrad's *Heart of Darkness*," in *Hopes and Impediments: Selected Essays, 1965–1987* (Portsmouth, NH: Heinemann, 1988).

18

America's Next Top Model
Neoliberal Labor

LAURIE OUELLETTE

Abstract: Reality competitions have emerged as one of the most popular and prevalent formats on contemporary television, typified here by *America's Next Top Model*. Laurie Ouellette argues that through the lens of social theory, we can see how such programs enact a version of contemporary labor practices, helping to train viewers as workers within new economic realities.

America's Next Top Model is a reality series in which ten to twelve young women take part in a "highly accelerated boot camp to see if they have what it takes to make it in the high-profile modeling industry."[1] Fusing the conventions of the televised makeover, the internship, and the talent competition, the show immerses the women in lessons, tests, and challenges deemed integral to their success in the competitive modeling business. This skill set includes posing for the camera, improvising and performing scripts, body management, self-stylizing, and emoting on command, as well as less obvious job requirements such as social networking, self-esteem, adaptability, and self-promotion. Stylists, former models, photographers, and other industry intermediaries coach and evaluate the aspiring models while the cameras roll, and a panel of judges led by former supermodel and *ANTM* creator Tyra Banks sends one contestant home each week until the winner is revealed.

The prize is a $100,000 contract with Cover Girl cosmetics, a referral to the Elite Model Management agency, and an appearance in *Seventeen* magazine. While there can be only one Top Model per "cycle," the series claims to help all the contestants by providing vocational training. Most, in fact, do not become professional models, and even the winners tend to fade from sight postcompetition. Nonetheless, *ANTM* flourishes as a televised stage for learning to labor in a field that demands a high degree of "to-be-looked-at-ness," performativity, flexibility, and self-enterprise from its aspirants.[2] At a time when many workers are facing similar requirements, particularly in the service industries, its curriculum extends to TV viewers at home, even as we watch for entertainment purposes. Just as schools facilitated the social reproduction of the (mostly male) factory workers needed by industrial capitalism, reality games like *ANTM* help socialize today's postindustrial workforce, with the help of informal teachers including coaches, stylists, photographers, and business moguls. As a feminized "display" profession set in the cultural industries, modeling provides the perfect context for this schooling. Illustrating the dos and don'ts of the modeling profession, *ANTM* teaches us all to navigate the changing demands of twenty-first-century work.

This essay uses social theories to analyze *ANTM* as a case study of reality television's labor politics. I show how a television production about "real life" amateur models intersects with broader trends, including cheaper modes of production, the rise of aesthetic labor, the feminization of job skills in postindustrial societies, and the extent to which today's workers are encouraged to envision themselves as "entrepreneurs of the self" rather than relying on unions or long-term job security. While *ANTM* exploits the labor of unpaid female contestants who are often lower income and women of color, it also constitutes the young women as the ultimate beneficiaries of their own self-enterprising activities. In this version of a labor market without guarantees, the winner is never simply a passive beauty or an obedient worker—she is the contestant who transforms herself into her own best asset. She is cruelly subjected to others (producers, experts, cultural intermediaries, judges) who profit from her labor, but is also invited to "maximize" herself for her own gain. *ANTM* does not conceal the predicament of the aspiring model, as much as it uses her double experience to demonstrate the rules of the game.

To analyze *ANTM* requires a critical understanding of labor. We begin with *commodity fetishism*, defined by Marx as the erasure of labor power and the signs of production as the source of a commodity's value, or an elimination of "any trace of the grime of the factory, the mass molding of the machine, and most of all, the exploitation of the worker," as Laura Mulvey explains. The commodity is instead endowed with a "seductive sheen," competing to be desired on the market.[3] While reality television production shifts away from the traditional Fordist factory, its commercial "sheen" is similarly divorced from behind-the-scenes labor practices. Encouraged by media deregulation, the proliferation of channels, and a desire to minimize labor costs, the television industry has come to rely on unpaid amateur talent and on nonunionized and freelance production crews who can be denied routine benefits, long-term employment contracts, overtime wages, and residuals.[4] *ANTM* exemplifies these trends, and like most reality productions, it also avoids hiring professional writers on the grounds that the competition isn't written. When the mostly female staffers responsible for shaping characters and devising story arcs from hours of footage went on strike to obtain better pay, health coverage, and Writers Guild representation in 2006, they were fired and replaced by a new crop of workers.[5]

Just as the "erasure of the mechanics of production in Hollywood" constitutes a form of commodity fetishism, *ANTM* expunges the labor of camera operators, editors, and craft services workers from the "reality" captured on screen.[6] *ANTM* does however expose the mechanics of commercial image production, going behind the scenes of fashion modeling and advertising to witness the rehearsing, staging, direction, and reshooting that produces "desirable" women in magazines and TV commercials. *ANTM* demystifies the process whereby women are objectified, put on display, and fetishized for profit-making purposes. The female contestants not only resemble the commodity form—they literally are commodities. Indeed, the competition revolves around the market calculations of image-makers and the labor of the aspiring models, who must learn to create and perform salable versions of femininity.

Exposing the manufacture of the female object destroys some of the power and pleasure associated with the "male gaze." It is difficult to revel in a fantasy about the female body when the production of that fantasy is exposed, disrupting the dreamlike conditions of voyeurism. The labor required to produce femininity that sells—endless makeup and dieting, Brazilian waxes and hair extensions—is also made visible, disrupting the "sheen" of media representations and perhaps subverting femininity's perceived naturalness. But such possibilities are curtailed when female contestants are disciplined and shamed upon failing to produce the "right" images. We witness a policing of what counts as desirable femininity, as well as a hierarchical work structure marked by authoritative and sometimes abusive supervisory relationships. Far from showing a collective bargaining situation, however, this glimpse into the normally expunged labor of modeling is bound to an implied reward system in which the "boot camp" survivors earn the capacity to attract sponsors, command high fees, and market themselves in a cool (but highly competitive) industry. On *ANTM*, the labor involved in producing "model perfect" femininity is emphasized not to overcome problems of female objectification, but to encourage profiteering through self-fashioning.

Here the concept of *immaterial labor* is helpful. While early Marxists were mainly concerned with the industrial production of tangible goods (such as automobiles or cans of soup), the postindustrial economy hinges more on the commodification of feelings, images, attitudes, styles, identities, and expressions of social life. While professional intermediaries who make and sell knowledge and culture are crucial, we all perform degrees of immaterial labor. Our work is not limited to the labor we perform at the factory or the office for pay: what we do and feel outside the job can also be channeled into the profits of employers, sponsors, and capitalism at large, which autonomist Marxists call the "social factory."

The rise of fashion modeling anticipated the mainstreaming of such immaterial labor, emerging from a "post-industrial shift toward service work and consumerism, in which non-material goods such as services, ideas and images have become products of capitalist development and circulation." Modeling also served as a testing ground for collapsing boundaries between life and work. While the factory worker has a scheduled shift followed by a period of leisure, models are expected to work on their skills, connections, and appearance all the time. Similarly, *ANTM* contestants are expected to practice body maintenance, social networking, and other value-generating activities learned on the show during their "off hours," thereby participating in constructing modeling as less a contained job than a "way of life."[7] This effect is further accentuated by their appearing on reality television, where there literally are no off-hours.

Such a way of life is spreading to other parts of the workforce. As Angela McRobbie notes, aesthetic labor is on the rise, particularly in the growing retail and service industries, which now "expect its workforce to look especially attractive and stylish." The burgeoning culture of beauty treatments, fitness, and cosmetic surgery is simultaneously being marketed to provide "added values which can enhance performance in the workplace."[8] Similarly, if the job of the model is to generate "affective" consumer responses to her activities and images,[9] similar forms of affective labor are now required by most service sector jobs, from ice cream parlor barista to retail sales clerk.

Television scholars have analyzed reality productions as immaterial labor, showing how ordinary people create the images desired by producers and sponsors for free through self-commodification within a promotional framework.[10] Reality productions trade in stock personas (the troubled girl, the crazy bitch) that participants are encouraged to adopt and perform in the interests of "good" (profitable) television. On *ANTM*, the contestants, who share living quarters mired in melodramatic tensions, perform as docusoap characters as well as aspiring pitchwomen. While only a select few will win modeling contracts, all contestants perform immaterial labor by generating promotional images in the service of brands. In Cycle 14, the women are required to perform a thirty-second advertisement, broadcast live in Times Square, in which they "encapsulate the Cover Girl attitude through their actions"—the challenge is to generate a promotional text in which their unique "personality shines through" in ways that encourage "other girls find the tools to be the best they want to be" in the Cover Girl brand. This promotional image labor isn't limited to photo shoots and television commercial filming; rather, it is extended as contestants use and discuss Cover Girl cosmetics with stylists and among themselves. These scenes valorize the historically unrecognized labor of producing femininity, but only as a means to the affective ties to images and brands sought by corporations. As Tyra Banks boasted in an interview, "I see women in the mall or on the streets who look 10 times better than I do, but can they sell a product?"[11]

While Marxism helps us to see this seep of value production into social life, it cannot fully explain contemporary reality television's relationship to gender and work in the twenty-first century. Reality productions like *ANTM* also translate the "cruelty" of work in the neoliberal economy into ritualized games, suggests Nick Couldry. In this context, the term "neoliberal" refers to the concentration of wealth, the decline of job security, and the rollback of labor regulations and mandated protections such as pensions and the forty-hour work week. These changes coexist with the rising demands of aesthetic labor, emotional performance ("service with a smile"), and expectations of always being "on call" for work. Television "smuggles past" these intolerable conditions by translating the harshest realities of work into playful renditions of extended work time, declining job security, and the "deep acting of passion," so that we are more apt to accept these conditions without question.[12] In this sense, television performs "ideological work" in the lives and minds of audiences. Yet, reality games do more than this—they also play a productive role in guiding and shaping the ideal workers sought by the neoliberal economy. Shows like *ANTM* circulate the logic, practical techniques, and resources through which contestants and TV viewers alike become laboring subjects.

Here, theories of *enterprise culture* are useful. In the context of deregulation, privatization of government services, and the intensification of the free-market mentality, the role of the individual in managing his or her own well-being and future has accelerated. To assist, an expanded culture of for-profit self-help, motivational resources, DIY information, and informal schooling has emerged. Enterprise culture does not emphasize its utility to the neoliberal economy, but encourages a new "care of the self" as a personal enterprise. As an especially visible component of these trends, reality television perpetuates a culture in which "everyone is an expert on herself, responsible for managing her own human capital to maximum effect."[13] In an insecure labor market, the self becomes "a flexible commodity to be molded, packaged, managed and sold."[14] Games like *ANTM* teach contestants (and, vicariously, TV viewers) to envision themselves as human capital, so that the line between playing a role for television, navigating the conditions of work, and creating oneself as a marketable product is inextricably blurred.

Shows like *ANTM* may not be exactly what former Federal Reserve Chairman Alan Greenspan envisioned when he promoted "lifelong learning" to prepare workers for a changing economy that values innovation, flexible labor, and entrepreneurship, but reality television offers a complimentary version of vocational guidance and schooling. Cultural and lifestyle intermediaries are crucial to this schooling, offering endless instruction on entrepreneurial behavior and strategic self-fashioning.[15] *ANTM* translates the intersecting requirements of short-term labor, outsourcing, and a shift from industrial production to promotion and branding onto resources to expand people's capacities to conduct themselves as enterprising subjects. This is not to deny the exploitation of labor, but to point out that current structures of work encourage, and indeed require that we all play an active role in fashioning, managing, and promoting ourselves. Here, too, the setting is crucial. While modeling enjoys a glamorous reputation, it is ultimately freelance work done on a project basis. Models do not receive benefits, enjoy job security, or control their working conditions. Thus a television production about models has particular salience as a technology of the self through which we all fashion ourselves as workers in a neoliberal economy.

One of the things that *ANTM* teaches is that self-enterprise is similar to being female. The self-invention demanded of workers requires an entrepreneurial relationship to the self that has much in common with the desire to make and remake femininity. What has long been demanded of women—to be adaptable, flexible, desirable, presentable, and consumable—has arguably been intensified and extended to the entire postindustrial workforce.[16] *ANTM* presents skills and attributes associated with white middle-class femininity, from makeup application to exuberant personality building, as a form of self-enterprise. This reward system perpetuates social hierarchies, but also brings women traditionally excluded from capitalist production into the logic of enterprise culture. Learning to labor requires mastery of a promotional femininity rooted in normalized class privilege and whiteness, maximizing such marketable differences. Women of color are "doubly commodified for their eroticized physical attractiveness and for their marketable personal narratives of racial self-transformation," Amy Hasinoff observes. Difference is "hyper-visible" as an indication of a so-called post-racial society, as a "malleable" commodity and as a reminder that disadvantage "can be overcome."[17] When Tiffany, an African American contestant whose grandmother reportedly went without electricity to buy a swimsuit for the competition, was eliminated in Cycle 4, it was not due to racial or class discrimination or to lack of potential, but because, as an enraged Tyra Banks says in a fan-favorite clip, she failed to "take control of her destiny."

On *ANTM*, elements of internship and competition are crucial for constituting the makeover as a route to success through self-enterprise. If modeling epitomizes the idealized attributes of white Western femininity, it is also an industry built upon entrepreneurial labor that is historically coded as corporate and

FIGURE 18.1.
A contestant is
photographed
making herself a
Greek salad, in
Greece.

masculine.[18] Models (much like new media workers) can be considered the neo-liberal economy's "shock workers," required not only to work long hours, but also to accept risks previously mediated by firms, such as business cycle fluctuations and market failures.[19] On *ANTM* these risks are born by the contestants, who participate in the production for free and invest unpaid hours in the hopes of winning the competition and finding success in a precarious field in which most fail. At a time when entrepreneurial labor is spreading throughout the media, cultural, and service industries, *ANTM* stitches the most common forms of risk-bearing—the unpaid internship and investment in a flexible, attractive, and marketable self—into the requirements and promised rewards of enterprise culture.

The *ANTM* competition rewards contestants' risk-taking and self-invention, but also requires adaptability and improvisation. Aspiring Top Models are trained to create a unique personality and "look" which must be constantly adapted and modified to project the right image for different sponsors and clients, even as their creativity is guided by intermediaries who teach them how to be sexy, wholesome, sultry, bold, passionate, or glamorous.[20] Similarly, the fast-paced nature of the competition, and the range of tasks and challenges it presents, immerses contestants (and TV viewers) in what Richard Sennett calls the new culture of capitalism. Sennett's research shows that workers across industries are increasingly required to migrate from "task to task, job to job, place to place," while retraining frequently and developing new abilities to compensate for diminished returns on fixed skill sets. The ideal worker today must also be able to switch gears at a moment's notice and mobilize a "self-consuming passion" to keep themselves mobile within the labor force.[21] Television's labor games magnify these demands and reward contestants who, in addition to developing themselves as promotional images and human capital, are adept at learning new skills quickly, orienting themselves to new demands, and performing well across a moving platform of situations and challenges. On *ANTM*, this can involve improvising a performance, putting together a new look in ten minutes, projecting a feeling or affective state on command, or switching gears midstream to cater to the desires of a particular sponsor.

While it would be implausible to suggest that *ANTM* has a direct causal influence, it is worth considering reality television's role in learning to labor. After all, it is the contestant "who passes all the tests" who wins the competition, Tyra Banks claims, and this motto applies well to contemporary educational and labor conditions. Likewise, we need to bring critical theories of labor more fully into television studies. Whose interests are served when feminine subjects are constituted as aesthetic and affective laborers, and workers are recast as risk-bearing self-enterprisers? What are the stakes of training individuals to imagine themselves as commodities with uncertain shelf lives? As Banks suggests, "your product just happens to be your physical self and a little bit of your personality too. When they don't want it anymore, don't feel discarded. Just know that your product is just not hot anymore. Know that you'll have to revamp that product or go into another field."[22] As making and selling femininity has become integral to the postindustrial neoliberal economy, *ANTM* brings the process full circle by modeling these conditions for TV viewers.

FURTHER READING

Couldry, Nick. "Reality TV, or The Secret Theater of Neoliberalism." *Review of Education, Pedagogy, and Cultural Studies* 30, no. 1 (2008): 3–13.

Hasinoff, Amy Adele. "Fashioning Race for the Free Market on *America's Next Top Model*." *Critical Studies in Media Communication* 25, no. 3 (2008): 324–43.

Hearn, Alison. "Producing 'Reality': Branded Content, Branded Selves, Precarious Futures." In *A Companion to Reality Television*, edited by Laurie Ouellette, 437–55. Malden, MA: Wiley-Blackwell.

Ouellette, Laurie. *Lifestyle TV*. New York: Routledge, 2016.

Ouellette, Laurie, and James Hay. *Better Living through Reality TV: Television and Post-Welfare Citizenship*. Malden, MA: Blackwell, 2008.

NOTES

1. Margena Christian, "Tyra Banks: Says 'It's a Lot More than Just Looks' to Become 'America's Next Top Model,'" *Jet*, May 26, 2003.

2. The phrase "learning to labor" is from the influential study *Learning to Labor: How Working Class Kids Get Working Class Jobs* by Paul Willis (New York: Columbia University Press, 1977).

3. Laura Mulvey, "Some Thoughts on Theories of Fetishism in the Context of Contemporary Culture," *October* 65 (Summer 1993): 10.

4. Chad Raphael, "The Political Economic Origins of Reali-TV," in *Reality TV: Remaking Television Culture*, ed. Susan Murray and Laurie Ouellette, 2nd ed. (New York: New York University Press, 2008), 123–41.

5. For more on the strike see Richard Verrier, "Next Top Model Writers Threaten Strike," *Los Angeles Times*, July 21, 2006; and Writers Guild of America West, "Writers at CW's America's Next Top Model Strike to Secure Fair WGA Contract," press release, www.wga.org. For video testimonial from one of the strikers, see "Kai Bowe—Reality Writer," YouTube, December 12, 2007, www.youtube.com.

6. Mulvey, "Some Thoughts," 12.

7. Elizabeth Wissinger, "Modeling a Way of Life: Immaterial and Affective Labour in Fashion Modeling," *Ephemera: Theory and Politics in Organization* 7, no. 1 (2007): 250–69.

8. Angela McRobbie, "From Holloway to Hollywood: Happiness at Work in the New Cultural Economy?" in *Cultural Economy: Cultural Analysis and Commercial Life*, ed. Paul du Gay and Michael Pryke (London: Sage, 2002), 100.

9. Wissinger, "Modeling a Way of Life," 250.

10. Alison Hearn, "'John, a 20-year-old Boston Native with a Great Sense of Humour': On the Spectacularization of the 'Self' and the Incorporation of Identity in the Age of Reality Television," *International Journal of Media and Cultural Politics* 2, no. 2 (2006): 131–47; see also Alison Hearn, "Meat, Mask, Burden: Probing the Contours of the Branded Self," *Journal of Consumer Culture* 8 (2008): 197–217.

11. Tyra Banks, quoted in Christian, "Tyra Banks."

12. Nick Couldry, "Reality TV, or The Secret Theater of Neoliberalism," *Review of Education, Pedagogy, and Cultural Studies* 30, no. 1 (2008): 3–13.

13. Nancy Fraser, "From Discipline to Flexibalization? Re-reading Foucault in the Shadow of Globalization," *Constellations* 10, no. 2 (2003): 168.

14. Laurie Ouellette and James Hay, *Better Living through Reality TV: Television and Post-Welfare Citizenship* (Malden, MA: Blackwell, 2008), 6.

15. Tania Lewis, *Smart Living: Lifestyle Media and Popular Expertise* (New York: Peter Lang, 2008).

16. Valerie Walkerdine, "Reclassifying Upward Mobility: Femininity and the Neo-Liberal Subject," *Gender and Education* 15, no. 3 (September 2003): 240.

17. Amy Adele Hasinoff, "Fashioning Race for the Free Market on *America's Next Top Model*," *Critical Studies in Media Communication* 25, no. 3 (2008): 324–43.

18. Jennifer Craik, *The Face of Fashion: Cultural Studies in Fashion* (London: Routledge, 1994).

19. Gina Neff, Elizabeth Wissinger, and Sharon Zukin, "Entrepreneurial Labor among Cultural Producers: 'Cool' Jobs in 'Hot' Industries," *Social Semiotics* 15, no. 3 (2005): 307–34.

20. Elizabeth Wissinger, "Modeling Consumption: Fashion Modeling Work in Contemporary Society," *Journal of Consumer Culture* 9 (2009): 273–96.

21. Richard Sennett, *The New Culture of Capitalism* (New Haven, CT: Yale University Press, 2006), 9–10, 93.

22. Tyra Banks, quoted in Christian, "Tyra Banks."

19

East Los High
Televised Empowerment

MARY BELTRÁN

Abstract: While most U.S. television series aim to entertain rather than to educate us, Hulu's series *East Los High* managed to do both. Featuring life lessons and factual information about birth control, domestic violence, the Dream Act, and other issues within its melodramatic storyline, the Latina teen drama proved that empowerment can be a goal of television programming that is also entertaining.

When we think about watching television, very likely we seek out programming that we imagine will be a fun diversion from our daily lives as opposed to an experience that is educational or empowering in other ways. Anticipating this, U.S. television series typically offer fictional or real-life narratives and storyworlds to which we can pleasurably escape as viewers. The majority of television programming consists of scripted and unscripted series that aim to entertain, with social impact a secondary concern, if it is considered at all. However, there has always been a subset of television programming with a different objective: to educate, enlighten, or empower viewers. Teen drama *East Los High*, which streamed on Hulu starting in 2013, is a contemporary example of this important but marginalized subset of programs.

The early development of television as a national medium in the United States included heated battles over whether educational and public service programming would be granted a major presence among other viewing choices. Had these battles ended differently, educational television might not be such a rarity today. As had been the case in the development of radio a few decades prior, debates in the late 1940s and 1950s centered on how the new technology of television should be used and over how national broadcasting would be funded. As Michele Hilmes, Allison Perlman, and other radio and television scholars have documented, educational and public service programming was a major point of contention in these negotiations.[1] Among the entities interested in using television for very different ends were commercial radio networks, the government, educational institutions, religious and civic organizations, and advertisers. Universities and other educational institutions saw television as ideally suited to augment their efforts to educate the American public, particularly in rural areas where citizens might not easily access traditional classes, while civic groups similarly envisioned it as a tool for informing and empowering citizens. In contrast, radio networks and advertisers wanted to harness television's potential as a profit-driven entertainment medium. When ultimately it was decided in their favor that U.S. television would primarily operate as a for-profit, advertising-funded industry, programming meant to educate or empower the public was relegated for the most part to the margins, aside from news broadcasts and the occasional documentary, and educational programming became the domain of public television, local television stations, and children's television producers.

As a result, series that aim to educate and improve the lives of viewers are rare in U.S. television today. Meanwhile, global health advocacy organizations—such as Population Media Center (PMC), the funder of *East Los High*'s first season— have effectively used television and radio dramas as conduits for educational campaigns. PMC dramas, for instance, have been shown to increase knowledge and empower citizens in more than fifty countries around the world with respect to health and civic issues relevant to their communities. This has included a focus on birth control methods and reproductive health in Nigeria and El Salvador, on the importance of education of girls in Ethiopia and Mali, and on water purification in the Democratic Republic of Congo and Senegal.[2] These successful "edutainment" interventions have demonstrated the potential of television that simultaneously educates and entertains. *East Los High*, while set in East Los Angeles and targeting U.S. Latina teens, had a parallel genesis in its focus on imparting relevant health knowledge.

As a Latina teen drama, *East Los High* arguably is empowering in another way as well. To consider again what motivates us to watch a particular television series, we also often instinctively seek out programs with which we can closely identify—those that feature experiences that we've also had, or portray perspectives on life similar to our own. In this regard, we often gravitate toward series that feature lead characters that are "like us" with respect to race, ethnicity, gender, age, political affiliation, or other elements of identity. But what if we don't see anyone like ourselves on television? The research and advocacy group Children Now found in 1998 that the vast majority of tweens and teens that they interviewed believed that every viewer has a right to see characters like themselves on television.[3] However, of the study participants, Latina/o, African American, and Asian American youth indicated that they seldom saw characters on TV that looked like them. While almost two decades have passed since that study was conducted and television has witnessed some progress with respect to diverse representation, Latina/os are still dramatically underrepresented, both on and behind the screen. While Latina/os are now more than 17 percent of American citizens, various studies have found that they comprise no more than 4 to 6 percent of characters on English-language, primetime television in the millennial era.[4]

Why this disparity in terms of the presence of Latina/os in U.S. television? Scholars and journalists who focus on the evolution of diverse representation on television have noted that progress in this regard has often entailed the addition of African American characters, as if diversity were only "black and white" in the United States. Confusion about whether Latina/o viewers watch television in English (despite studies that have shown that most do) has also played a role in Latina/o invisibility.[5] Latina and Latino lead characters are few and far between, as are Latina/o television writers, producers, and directors.[6] Considering the importance of seeing oneself reflected in programming, we can presume that this invisibility is detrimental to the self-esteem of (and respect conferred to) young Latinas and Latinos today. With this in mind, a series such as *East Los High* is a potentially empowering intervention. The series was created for a target audience of English-speaking and bilingual Latina and Latino teens, had an all-Latina/o cast, and was written and produced by an all-Latina/o team of media professionals.

This underscores the anomalous nature of *East Los High* among American teen dramas today. To better understand its unique blend of hip entertainment and educational mission, it's helpful to go back to the series' origin. As noted earlier, its first season was funded and produced by Population Media Center. To date, PMC has produced more than thirty-five serial dramas disseminated via radio, television, and the Internet to improve women's rights, reproductive health, and other health outcomes around the world.[7] The nonprofit organization produces media narratives using a model that includes extensive preproduction research, community feedback during the writing of scripts, and rigorous assessment of outcomes. The organization has relied heavily on the soap opera—or as it would be called in Latin American contexts, the *telenovela*—as a genre that lends itself well to its mission, given that long-running storylines allow characters to model various health-related choices and experience the consequences that these choices have on their lives. *East Los High*, however, is the organization's first U.S.-focused series. Katie Elmore Mota, executive producer of *East Los High* and former vice president of communications and programs at Population Media Center, launched the series in response to pressing U.S. Latina health issues such as a high incidence of teen pregnancy and less knowledge about birth control and

FIGURE 19.1.
Scenes like Maya's discussion with a health clinic worker about birth control and STDs provide both dramatic realism and useful information to *East Los High* viewers.

preventing STDs than reported by other American teens.[8] She noted in an interview that Wise Entertainment, her production company, chose to take the series to Hulu rather than a broadcast or cable network because Hulu was willing to air the episodes without asking for any control over the content, which was not the message they received from the broadcast and cable networks.[9]

In its attempt to empower and educate viewers, *East Los High* follows PMC's proven formula. The melodrama follows an evolving group of Latina and Latino teens through their last years at the fictional East Los Angeles High School. In its first season, the series focuses on two ordinary and earnest Latina teens, Jessie and her best friend Soli, and Jessie's cousin Maya. Things heat up for Jessie when she finds herself pitted against Vanessa and Ceci, the two not-so-nice leaders of the Bomb Squad, the school's popular hip-hop dance team, after she begins dating Jacob, Vanessa's former boyfriend, and is chosen to be a part of the team. She also finds herself at odds with Maya when her cousin shows up out of the blue, with many secrets, at the apartment Jessie shares with her mom. Throughout the series, Jessie, Soli, Maya, and other characters have to make choices about and cope with real-life issues that run the gamut from whether to have sex to dealing with past abuse to owning their academic abilities and pursuing college and careers. Notably, Vanessa and Ceci make some careless choices for which they both ultimately pay a life-changing price. As Ceci finds herself pregnant and Vanessa discovers that she has contracted HIV, the series follows their lives alongside those of other teens who have been both more careful and luckier.

While the primary emphasis of the narrative is on the main characters' romantic relationships, friendships, and emotional lives, they (and viewers, by extension) learn valuable lessons along the way, such as about convincing their partners to wear condoms, about options available in the case of an abusive partner, and about DACA (Deferred Action for Childhood Arrivals), which allows some undocumented young adults to remain in and attend college in the United States. Through relating health and social issue information as secondary to a dramatic storyline that comes across as authentic, compelling, and of-the-moment, *East Los High* arguably has multiple appeals via its mixture of gripping, soapy drama with informative content aimed at informing its viewers.

The series is above all about empowerment. Latina pride and confidence are conveyed strongly throughout the series, beginning with the opening credits. The words of the series' energetic theme song, "So What!" by musical artist San-chia, drive home this message. The song begins in Spanish with a driving chorus, backed by a strong, catchy beat:

> Soy Fabulosa, Hermosa, Glamorosa, Gran Cosa
> (*I'm fabulous, beautiful, glamorous, a big deal!*)

The lyrics continue in English:

> I'm so sick and tired of the things you say about me
> always thinking 'bout me
> why can't you just let me be
> trying to find out info, I don't really see the need
> so just back up off me, give me space so I can breathe
>
> I don't think you need to know if I'm single or taken
> I don't think you need to know if I like you
> So What!
> I don't think you need to know what I'm doing or makin'
> I don't think you need to know if I hate you
> *So What!*

While seemingly written as an ode between jealous rival girls, the bilingual message of the confident Latina who refuses to be put in anyone's box or to be exploited for another's purpose can also be seen as a powerful response to the past invisibility and hypersexualization of Latinas in past decades in film and television.[10] Brief musical sound bites of the song are repeated during narrative transitions, reinforcing the theme of Latina empowerment. In addition, the credits feature a snapshot introduction to each of the main characters, with their names appearing prominently. The characters of Jessie, Soli, Vanessa, and Jacob are among those given this promotional treatment, similar to how the film *The Breakfast Club* portrayed white American teens as unique individuals. For Latina and Latino teens, this is a television first.

The theme of empowerment by being educated, informed, and assertive extends to *East Los High*'s website, www.eastloshigh.com. It includes "Take Action," a page devoted to links to information on a wide variety of health and social issues with portals to partner advocacy organizations, including Planned Parenthood, Advocates for Youth, It Gets Better Project, and Voto Latino. Other pages of the website are dedicated to *East Los High*'s transmedia storyworld, such as vlogs (video blogs) by popular characters, often on health-related issues, including Ceci's postings about life as a pregnant teen and *Ask Paulie*, a blog by a comedic male character who attempts to answer guys' questions about sex.

The second and subsequent seasons of the series are illustrative as well of how the series differs from other teen dramas. Rather than continuing the focus on Jessie and Soli, the de facto "good girls" of season 1, the writers brought in several new characters—and thus new topics on which to educate the audience. Among the few characters that carried over was Ceci, now a young single mother, who begins coaching the Bomb Squad at her former high school. In choosing to develop Ceci as a sympathetic lead character, the *East Los High* writers used a common narrative strategy of Population Media Center melodramas: building narratives around what theater scholar Eric Bentley called transitional characters.[11] Such characters are not simply heroines or villains; in fact, they may have initially made poor choices but ultimately turn their lives around. As PMC notes on its website, such characters are especially relatable to their target audiences by having made mistakes and learned from them.

In the case of *East Los High*, the sympathetic, education-oriented focus on Ceci begins earlier in the narrative. While season 1 focuses especially on the travails of Jessie and Maya, it also sets the stage for the audience to become curious about Ceci. "Did You Just Became My Boss?," the seventh episode, is one of the first episodes focused on her life choices. The episode opens on the Bomb Squad dancers, dressed in street-wise, relaxed dance gear, rehearsing a number that combines hip-hop and African dance moves with a driving percussive beat. Some have long hair, others short hair; some are tan while others are fair skinned—each has her own unique look and arguably is confident and beautiful in her own way. Jessie is among them, hyper-focused as if she's trying to remember the moves, but otherwise dancing smoothly amid the group. Ceci, on the other hand, looks at ease and happy; she is one of the best dancers. We see her suddenly becoming disturbed, however, as she clearly feels nauseous. She lurches away, presumably to the bathroom, as the scene ends. In an earlier episode, Ceci was seen having sex with a casual boyfriend, Abe, even through he refused to introduce her to his mother and had refused to wear a condom. Ceci had yelled at him for "not pulling out in time," as he had promised to do. Based on this previous scene, viewers are primed to assume that Ceci is now pregnant.

After the rehearsal, Ceci and Vanessa talk privately about the mistakes she had made about birth control (she may have forgotten to take the pill some days) and

FIGURE 19.2. Ceci, pictured in the middle with a school staff ID, finds a job in season 2 as the coach of the high school dance squad. Otherwise she faces difficult times as a young single mother, which may spur reflection on the part of viewers on the consequences of their own decisions.

the morning-after pill (she didn't keep it with her and didn't know she had to take it within three days of having sex). They discuss the option of abortion. To Ceci's claim that she can't consider it because she's Catholic, Vanessa responds, "Well, all of the drugging, shoplifting, and sleeping around isn't very Catholic either." Vanessa corrects Ceci's assumption that choosing to have the baby will involve just a few months off—rather, eighteen years off—and argues that she can't be sure whether the baby's father will provide any help to her. Such an extended discussion would often be cut from a teen series as too adult or as pulling attention away from the emotional drama; its inclusion here provides realism and vitally useful information to viewers watching.

Ceci's life as a pregnant teen is just one story within the overall season narrative, however. Like a typical soap opera, *East Los High* shifts continually between the stories of its large ensemble of characters. Also in this season, Jessie falls for Jacob after he's dumped Vanessa for cheating on him, but also gets a crush on her choreographer, Christian. This is after Christian is blackmailed by Vanessa to seduce Jessie, so that Vanessa can get her revenge. Ceci, meanwhile, unbeknownst to Vanessa, is actually responsible for breaking up Vanessa and Jacob. And then there's Jacob, who initially likes Jessie but inadvertently falls for her cousin, Maya. These story arcs are just a small fraction of the dramatic narratives that converge and crescendo in the twenty-four episodes of the season. Ceci's story, for instance, reveals the sad banality of life for many teenagers who have a baby. Having to move in with an unsupportive baby daddy and later a shelter for homeless pregnant teens, Ceci finds herself isolated from her friends and wistfully thinking of the days when she had few cares other than teen-girl rivalries. Additional aspects of her life as a pregnant teen and teen parent are expanded on in "Ceci's Vlog," realistically addressing such topics as the expense of maternity and baby gear and the difficulties of raising a newborn baby as a teenager with little support.

Another episode in the season, "One Month Later," focuses on Jessie, who also finds herself pregnant. While most of the narrative is devoted to the many dramatic complications that arise in relation to this pregnancy—Jessie doesn't want to admit that she had sex with both Christian and Jacob, and later entraps her ex-boyfriend Jacob to marry her even though he is in love with her cousin—it also manages to slip in useful information about the options available to a pregnant teen in California, including being able to have an abortion without having to inform one's parents. While Jessie initially lets her mother make her choice for her, ultimately, in "Build a Future Worthy of You," she makes what she feels is the most empowering decision: choosing to have an abortion. In a mock documentary segment, the former students are interviewed about their lives postgraduation. We learn that Ceci is still working on her GED and has to work as a nanny for someone else's child in order to make ends meet as a single mother, while Vanessa has also faced a more limited life because of her HIV-positive status. Jessie, Soli, Maya, Jacob, and Paulie, on the other hand, are busily pursuing their college education, vocational training, and working toward their life and career goals. In this coda to season 1, viewers can see characters' wise choices rewarded, which very well might spur viewer reflection on the consequences of their own life decisions.

The straddling of education and entertainment isn't always seamless, however. One of the weak elements of *East Los High*'s season 1 is its portrayal of the local, unnamed Planned Parenthood clinic as if it has only one worker, who just happens to be available to talk to every teen that walks in. While such education-oriented moments in the series can be clumsy at times, it more often pulls off its dual purpose through its authentic-feeling depiction of East LA teens' daily lives. It also succeeds as a drama that feels timely and vibrant and is populated with appealing young Latina and Latino actors. Its viewership has proven its success as well. The series was among the top five shows viewed on Hulu in its first month streaming and was consistently among the top Latino-focused series watched on the streaming site through 2017.[12]

As one of the few U.S. television series that have been assessed by outside researchers and its production team with respect to its impact, *East Los High* was also able to offer evidence that it left its viewers more informed about various issues after watching its episodes. For instance, twenty-seven thousand people engaged on *East Los High*'s website with Planned Parenthood's links and widgets (which include extensive information and videos, as well as quizzes, games, and polls, on birth control, pregnancy, dating relationships, sexual health, and STDs) the month after the series debuted. Public health scholars Hua Wang and Arvind Singhal also found Latina viewers in particular engaged the program's transmedia experience with intensity.[13] They expressed a strong affinity for the show, closely followed its various characters' stories, explored the series website, and regularly talked with friends about episodes. They also reported greater knowledge of birth control methods and expressed greater willingness to be examined for STDs or pregnancy after viewing the series. Finally, they also expressed a desire for more series that spoke to their lives as directly as this one. *East Los High* in fact was so successful for Hulu that the streaming site funded its second through fourth seasons and used it as the central series among its Latino programming. The series' success on these multiple fronts confirms the continued gaps for Latinas, in U.S. television and on other fronts, that *East Los High* attempts to fill, as well as the potential for educational television to be appealing, empowering, and also profitable within the commercially driven television market.

FURTHER READING

Beltrán, Mary. "Latina/os on TV! A Proud (and Ongoing) Struggle over Representation and Authorship." In *The Latino Pop Cultural Studies Reader*, edited by Frederick Aldama, 23–33. New York: Routledge, 2015.

McAnany, Emile G. *Saving the World: A Brief History of Communication for Development and Social Change*. Champaign: University of Illinois Press, 2012.

Molina-Guzmán, Isabel. *Dangerous Curves: Latina Bodies in the Media*. New York: New York University Press, 2010.

NOTES

1. Michele Hilmes, *Only Connect: A Cultural History of Broadcasting in the United States*, 4th ed. (Boston: Wadsworth Cengage, 2014); Allison Perlman, *Public Interests: Media Advocacy and Struggles over U.S. Television* (New Brunswick, NJ: Rutgers University Press, 2016).

2. See Population Media Center's website at populationmedia.org. For more information about the use of radio and television dramas for global health campaigns, see Emile G. McAnany, *Saving the World: A Brief History of Communication for Development and Social Change* (Champaign: University of Illinois Press, 2012).

3. Children Now, *A Different World: Children's Perceptions of Race and Class in Media* (Oakland, CA: Children Now, 1998).

4. Dana E. Mastro and Elizabeth Behm-Morawitz, "Latino Representation on Primetime Television," *Journalism and Mass Communication Quarterly* 82, no. 1 (Spring 2005): 110–30; Alison R. Hoffman and Chon Noriega, *Looking for Latino Regulars on Prime-Time Television: The 2004 Season*, CSRC Research Report 4 (Los Angeles: UCLA Chicano Studies Research Center, 2004).

5. PwC (formerly PricewaterhouseCoopers), *Always Connected: U.S. Based Hispanic Consumers Dominate Mobile, Entertainment, and Beyond*, Consumer Intelligence Series report (New York: PwC, 2016).

6. Frances Negrón Mutaner et al. *The Latino Media Gap: A Report on the State of Latinos in U.S. Media* (New York: Center for the Study of Ethnicity and Race, Columbia University, 2014).

7. Population Media Center, www.populationmedia.org.

8. Katie Elmore Mota, personal interview with the author via Skype, December 20, 2016.

9. Ibid.

10. For more on these patterns of representation, see Isabel Molina-Guzmán, *Dangerous Curves: Latina Bodies in the Media* (New York: New York University Press, 2010); and Mary Beltrán, *Latina/o Stars in U.S. Eyes: The Making and Meanings of Film and TV Stardom* (Champaign: University of Illinois Press, 2009).

11. Eric Bentley, *The Life of the Drama*, rev. ed. (New York: Atheneum Press, 1964). This aspect of Population Media Center serial dramas and other aspects of PMC methodology are described in "Serial Dramas" on the PMC website, www.populationmedia.org.

12. "East Los High," Population Media Center, www.populationmedia.org.

13. Hua Wang and Arvind Singhal, "East Los High: Transmedia Entertainment to Promote the Sexual and Reproductive Health of Young Latina/o Americans," *American Journal of Public Health* 106, no. 6 (June 2016): 1002–10.

20

The Eurovision Song Contest
Queer Nationalism

ANIKÓ IMRE

Abstract: The televised annual pan-European music competition *Eurovision* started out in 1956 as an aspirational cultural forum to encourage a sense of European belonging among postwar nations. As the size and spectacle of the competition grew over the decades, *Eurovision* has increasingly provided a campy, ironic, queer commentary on the gap between the utopian principle of "unity and diversity" and the increasing national fragmentation and regional divisions of a post–Cold War Europe.

Cuéntame cómo pasó ("Remember When"), broadcast on channel La 1 of Television Española since 2001, is the longest-running primetime series in Spain. Perhaps best compared to the American coming-of-age dramedy *The Wonder Years*, the series is about the experiences of the Alcántara family set against the backdrop of Spain's transition to democracy beginning in the last years of the Franco dictatorship. The episodes are framed by the first-person narration of the youngest child, Carlos, who recollects those crucial years as an adult in the undefined present. The first episode, set in the spring of 1968, starts out with the family's acquisition of their first television set, which fulfills young Carlos's dream of watching *The Eurovision Song Contest* (hereafter *Eurovision*) with his family in his own living room, a massive improvement from having to sneak peaks at the neighbor's set through the window.

The episode ends with the family huddled together on the couch watching Spanish singer Massiel cruise to victory in the competition final with her song "La, la la," securing Spain's first *Eurovision* win. Perhaps there is no single televisual moment that better captures how broadcast television integrated the domestic lives of nuclear families with the public rituals that organized the life of the national family. Structuring the opening episode of the historical series around the iconic televised music competition *Eurovision* visualizes television's special transnational history in Europe. From the beginning, *Eurovision* has provided a literal stage for performing and affirming national belonging in a friendly competition that demarcates European nations and binds them together in an aspirational regional identity at the same time.

The original impetus for creating *Eurovision* was to provide a venue for promoting multinational coexistence within postwar Europe. Modeled after the Italian Sanremo Song Festival, the competition was explicitly designed in 1956 as a means of fostering European culture through the emerging mass medium of television, and it has been described as "perhaps the largest and best-organized institution promoting a cultural kind of pan-European identity."[1] *Eurovision* was created by and for the member states of the European Broadcasting Union (EBU), an association of public broadcasters. Early *Eurovision* competitions were the first experiments in live television in postwar Europe, created by the EBU's Eurovision network (after which the competition was named), whose member stations were initially connected via terrestrial microwave. Over the decades, the EBU's membership has grown beyond the borders of Europe to include participating countries from North Africa and the Middle East.

The first competition, named "Eurovision Grand Prix," was held in Lugano, Switzerland, in 1956. A jury of experts awarded Switzerland the win without any audience involvement. Since then, audiences have played an increasingly active role in selecting their national representatives and choosing the ultimate winner. Each participating country sends to the event an original song of up to three minutes in length, selected through national, televised competitions, to be performed live by no more than six people at the annual final on a Saturday each May. Each country votes on submissions different from its own through a complex and periodically updated process that combines televoting by individual viewers in each country and the votes of a jury of experts. Televoting was first tried in 1996 to give viewers more power and is now supplemented by voting via SMS and a mobile app. A single broadcaster carries the competition in each participating country and is mandated to broadcast the entire show, with the exception of commercial breaks. Songs and performers are considered representatives and, increasingly, branding devices, for their countries.[2] The host country is customarily determined by the country of the previous year's winner, rather than by bidding.

Unlike in other musical talent competitions, however, talent is not the most important ingredient and professional success does not necessarily follow from participation. In fact, artists whose careers were launched by *Eurovision*, such as ABBA (1974 winner for Sweden) and Celine Dion (1988 for Switzerland) are notable for being scarce exceptions. Rather than providing a springboard to international fame, *Eurovision* has attracted a self-reflexive, campy, popular, even trashy aesthetics of spectacle that is markedly different from the high-cultural venues of branding European nations, such as film festivals.[3]

Rather than enhancing unity among a loose federation of nations, as its original remit intended, *Eurovision* has always held up an ironic mirror to postwar Europe as an aspirational place of "unity in diversity," to evoke the European Union's slogan. Thanks to the international simultaneity of the competition enabled by networked broadcasting, *Eurovision* has always foregrounded how nations redefine themselves each year in relation to other nations, around changing figures, songs, and other elements of culture that weave the fabric of nationalism over time. Since the end of the Cold War, in particular, *Eurovision* has increasingly become a barometer of political contestation in a European Union struggling with its eastward expansion, recurrent economic crises, and rising right-wing nationalisms. The televised music competition has registered these conflicts in over-the-top performances and set designs that have regularly linked European and national politics to the politics of sexuality, gender, ethnicity, and race.

As a unique formation, an international live reality TV competition based on music's deep connection to national identity, *Eurovision* has also fascinated critics, scholars, and intellectuals across disciplines.[4] It has provided a perfect cross-section of television as a medium in which politics, economy, affect, aesthetics, and identity intersect. Accordingly, *Eurovision* has been examined from the perspectives of nation-branding, international diplomacy, broadcasting policy, audience practices, citizenship participation, music production, television trade, queer politics and human rights, transnational fan cultures, camp aesthetics, security practices, and national and European belonging.

Eurovision has come a long way from *Cuéntame*'s nostalgic commemoration of the original spirit of engendering regional cohesion among patriotic national audiences in a handful of Western European countries. In the past two decades, it has grown into a televised mega-event comparable to the Olympics, attracting between one hundred million and six hundred million viewers internationally, and a major example of television's central role in the culturalization of politics on a national and international scale.[5] Compared to its first installment in 1956, when it involved only seven nations, the competition now takes place over three days of semifinals and a grand finale, preceded by national televised music contests to determine each country's representatives and documented by lively Internet coverage.[6]

Thanks to its central function in the cultural performance of European politics, especially following the European Union's expansion in the mid-2000s to incorporate formerly socialist states and the increasing role of online audience participation, *Eurovision* has experienced a tremendous reinvigoration over the past twenty years. While *Eurovision* has always been associated with a trash and camp aesthetic and had a sizable queer (especially gay male) fan base within and beyond Europe, contests of recent years have been a carnival of politicized performances that foregrounded nonnormative ethnic and sexual identities. The gendered and sexualized excesses of these performances have taken on additional ideological charges: to define the borders of the "normal" nation, to demonstrate new EU member states' tolerant attitudes toward sexual minorities (typically to offset existing sexual or ethno-racial discrimination against minorities), and to mark out emerging regional alliances that tend to map onto Cold War divides.

The breakthrough event in politicizing sexualized performances was the victory of Israeli transgender singer Dana International in 1998 with her song "Diva." What Israeli state diplomacy subsequently touted as a proof of inclusion was aimed to distract from its restriction on Palestinian mobility following the 1993 Oslo Accords and has been criticized as "pink-washing" by many international commentators. At the same time, however, Dana International's identity as an Israeli, Arab, Mizrahi, and queer performer may have simultaneously opened up space for conversation in the Middle East about the interweaving histories and identities that Israeli nationalism aimed to suppress and homogenize.[7]

The expansion of *Eurovision*'s roster to include some postsocialist countries in 1993 and the rest of them following the European Union's major enlargement in 2004 added further political charge to queer performances, channeling the competition along post–Cold War tensions in an increasingly polarized Europe.[8] In 2007, the runner-up Ukrainian entry by Verka Serduchka, the transvestite persona of popular male comedian Andriy Danilko, performed the nonsensically titled number "Lasha Tumbai," a multilingual, delightfully excessive romp over iconic events of Ukrainian and Soviet history. While the performance appeared perfectly suited for the queer *Eurovision* stage and could simply be read by Western audiences as drag and camp entertainment, or even as a Ukrainian statement in favor of queer politics, it was replete with visual, verbal, and musical references only available to Ukrainian and post-Soviet viewers. Verka's/Danilko's mode of address was rooted in a specific late-Soviet and post-Soviet mode of irony. This mode of address allowed for a variety of readings that ranged from homophobic to pro-queer. "Lasha Tumbai" thus registered, variously, as a self-exoticizing nation-branding phenomenon to represent Ukraine for a Western European public, as an expression of national superiority for a Ukrainian and post-Soviet public, and a target of homophobia to reject nonnormative sexualities along with the "gay-loving" West.[9]

In the same 2007 competition, Serbian Marija Šerifović's winning performance of the ballad "Molitva" ("Prayer"), sung in Serbian, abounded in both nationalistic and queer imagery: an unmistakably butch-looking Šerifović, wearing a tuxedo,

FIGURE 20.1.
Serbian Marija
Šerifović's winning
performance in
2007 overflowed
with both nation-
alistic and queer
imagery.

flanked by a group of tuxedoed women moving in slow ritualistic fashion, belched out her passionate prayer for Serbia in front of a large national flag. Similar to Verka Serduchka's performance, the scene calls to mind the oxymoronic phrase "queer nationalism."[10] On the one hand, Šerifović had been subjected to virulent attacks in the Serbian press in the months leading up to her *Eurovision* victory. The attackers claimed that she was an inappropriate representative of the Serbian nation, due to her Roma ethnicity, her alleged lesbianism (she came out years later in 2013), and her alleged "ugliness." Her candidacy was even linked to conspiracy theories involving the West and Kosovo, which fed on xenophobia, anti-Semitism, and anti-Roma sentiment. On the other hand, similar to other minority musical performers from Eastern Europe, Šerifović was intensely promoted in the service of national and party politics, to give Serbia a liberal facelift following the bloody post-Yugoslav wars that made the country synonymous with war crimes. Šerifović's victory launched ecstatic national celebrations in Serbia in triumph over the West and at least culturally united the succession states of Yugoslavia, torn apart by ethnic war just a few years before, to such an extent that post-Yugoslav countries were accused of "block voting" in order to help Šerifović to victory.

Adding another twist to the "queer nationalism" that has come to characterize Eastern European contributions to *Eurovision*, Šerifović sang *Molitva* at a campaign rally for the Serbian Radical Party in December of 2007 and expressed support for the country's radical right-wing candidate for the presidential elections, commenting that her song is a prayer for a new, different Serbia. In response, the European Commission voiced concern about her status as one of fifteen European ambassadors for intercultural dialogue, a position she had just been awarded.[11]

To sum up, while *Eurovision*'s queer performances have historically been called upon to reflect on and mediate between national and European affiliations, in recent postsocialist entries, queerness has tended to highlight conflict between the two: The same prayer that earned the 2007 *Eurovision* winner the status of ambassador for fostering European intercultural integration was also deployed as an instrument of Serbian nationalistic separatism, in which the Roma, lesbian performer herself willingly participated. And she was ultimately deemed inappropriate as the representative of both.[12]

Following *Eurovision* rules, the year after Šerifović's win, Serbia's broadcaster Radio-Televizija Serbia (RTS) was slated to host the competition. This put television diplomacy to the test given the hostility toward LGBTQ rights and identities in a country where far-right groups attacked the first Pride march in 2001, leaving marches suspended. On the other hand, having Belgrade host a large number of European LGBTQ tourists in 2008 offered an opportunity to demonstrate the nation's embrace of the European Union's liberal values.

In Belgrade, Russian singer Dima Bilan won the 2008 competition, providing yet another prominent venue for television diplomacy to navigate the international tensions between the antiminority policies of repressive nationalism and the promotion of inclusivity required by (neo)liberal nation-branding. In Moscow, where the 2009 contest was held, Pride marches had been banned since 2006. State broadcaster Pervyi Kanal (First Channel), much like Serbian RTS the year before, seized on the opportunity provided by *Eurovision* to market the notion of a democratic, tolerant post-Soviet Russia, while Russian police violently repressed a Pride march organized by local activists on the day of the final.[13]

Clearly, since the early 2000s, *Eurovision* has been under mounting pressure as a cultural bridge stretching between East and West, parts of Europe that have been generally seen as drifting farther and farther from each other. Drawing on the legacy of *Eurovision* as a queer televisual forum, the status of LGBTQ minorities has emerged as the flashpoint onto which broader ideological differences have been projected. While the EU's 1997 Treaty of Amsterdam prevented discrimination on the grounds of sexual orientation and was followed by several directives in the 2000s to confirm this position, Vladimir Putin's right-wing, populist Russian government issued its infamous "anti-homopropaganda" laws in 2013, which banned the "promotion" of "non-traditional sexual relations" to minors.[14]

It was in this polarized landscape routinely characterized in the media as divided between an essentially open-minded and inclusive West and an inherently backward, homophobic Russia that Austrian drag artist Conchita Wurst (Thomas Neuwirth) rose like a Phoenix in 2014, in a stunning dress and with a closely cropped, spectacular beard. Conchita's winning song, "Rise Like a Phoenix," was explicitly meant to send a message of tolerance and inclusivity in the face of Putin's repressive measures.

FIGURE 20.2.
Austrian drag artist Conchita Wurst (Thomas Neuwirth) sent a message of tolerance and inclusivity in the face of Russia's "antihomopropaganda" laws issued in 2013.

The message was received. Post-Soviet national juries slammed the performance. Russia's Deputy Prime Minister Dmitry Rogozin posted a sarcastic tweet about the "bearded girl" signifying future of European integration. Putin's adviser Vladislav Surkov tweeted that "if Conchita is a woman, then Ukraine is a country."[15] Politician Vitaly Milonov, who had proposed the anti-LGBTQ law, called for Russia to withdraw from *Eurovision* permanently because the competition promoted "propaganda for homosexuality and moral decay" as evidenced by "the participation of the obvious transvestite and hermaphrodite Conchita Wurst on the same stage as Russian performers."[16] Meanwhile, Conchita's performance and message earned high scores from European expert juries of music professionals, who award 50 percent of the total votes. In Western Europe, journalists and activists pointed to Conchita's performance as an expression of European values of human rights and democracy, and to *Eurovision* as the central venue for embracing LGBTQ rights, which, in turn, had come to stand for shared, universal European values. Notably, popular televoting actually belied the simplistic binary opposition between East and West: Russian viewers voted Conchita to be the third most popular contender.[17]

To further entrench what has become an eerily familiar Cold War binary divide, effectively simplifying much more complex political and economic relations in terms of homophobia versus LGBTQ rights, 2014's Polish entry "We Are Slavic" by the group Donatan and Cleo featured blonde women in revealing folk-inspired dresses dancing provocatively to a mixture of hip-hop and folk tunes, and singing in English: "We're Slavic girls, we know how to use our charming beauty, now shake what your mama gave ya, clap your hands to this music, this is our nature, this is our call, this is our hot Slavic blood." Conchita appropriated the traditionally queer, campy aesthetic of the contest to mobilize a large transnational fandom around *Eurovision* and confirmed the role of the contest as a popular cultural vehicle of democratic access to the European public sphere. By contrast, "We Are Slavic" aligned with an opposite trend in the contest, which has been described as a "return to ethnicity."[18] It deployed *Eurovision* kitsch to mobilize the essentialist gendered reserves of traditional, nativist nationalism infused with a global consumerist aesthetic to produce self-orientalizing, patriotic porn.

Conchita's fate as the uncontested European spokesperson for queer rights contrasts with the much messier political career of Marija Šerifović. The former's position as a brand for Austria has been toned down in favor of standing for "universal" European values of inclusion and democracy, in response to the repressive thrust of Putin's postsocialist homo-nationalism. In comparison, Šerifović has remained firmly and willingly tied to her Serbian national brand and proved to be an inadequate representative of universal European values. This is clearly not simply an individual inadequacy on her part, that of a subject trapped by her false consciousness, unable to transcend her regressive nationalism. Rather, there is a differential, regional pattern at work here that predisposes how different nationalisms are evaluated at *Eurovision*.

There is a different relationship between nation and queerness in *Eurovision*'s Eastern/postsocialist and Western performances. Conchita's "queer" is rendered more expansive, more able to transcend nationalistic normalization by virtue of the performer's location in the West. It is less burdened by the anxious and ambivalent duty of nation-branding that attends postsocialist entries. Eastern performances are less free to transcend their nationalisms, which are seen as primal and primitive from what remains the dominant, universal European perspective. They fail to be universal and are therefore bound to fail to convert their queer aesthetic into queer politics.

As Carl Stychin argues, particularly since the end of the Cold War, *Eurovision* has become a cultural extension of the EU's antidiscrimination law on the basis of "sexual orientation," which has further helped to define the rights of LGBTQ people as human rights.[19] *Eurovision* has helped move LGBTQ rights from being seen as a matter for national determination toward a benchmark of respect for universal norms that provide a litmus test of European civilization. But it is also important to see how *Eurovision* has, in turn, been used as a litmus test to probe certain European nation-states' eligibility for participating in this civilization. While there is a great deal of danger in the advance of repressive nationalisms that deprive LGBTQ people of human rights, there is also a danger in reconstructing the familiar, false division between good and bad nationalisms in contemporary Europe: One kind can be strategically downplayed and ignored, because its power has been assumed to be offset by significant achievements in minority politics, in a cosmopolitan transcendence where universal values triumph; another, provincial kind is forever stuck in its homophobic, xenophobic, exclusionary practices. This division has been instrumental to sustaining a hierarchical division within

Europe, which allows universal ideas to be attached permanently to the core of Europe, conditioned on their positive distinction and ideological distance from places permanently unable to attain and transplant these ideas.

Political statements such as Conchita's, which explicitly deploy queer politics, automatically activate *Eurovision*'s capacity to connect the cultural and the political in confirming the hierarchy of nationalisms. In comparison, Eastern statements about nonnormative sexualities appear cynical, offering queer spectacle only to win favors and to mask antidemocratic policies, without any reverberating effects on the structure of compulsory heterosexuality embedded in "bad" nationalism.

I want to end by suggesting that we read *Eurovision* not just for fun (which is abundant) but also for its capacity to display *and critique* attitudes toward nationalism. This more subtle reading of the performances will allow for mutual and multidirectional critique, resisting the West-to-East thrust of judgment that dominates public discourses around queer performances. *Eurovision* is a unique television program by virtue of its regional scope and its history of registering political transformation in Europe. We should also deploy *Eurovision* as a rich resource for analyzing television's function as a medium for converting and calculating values among different kinds of identity, from individual viewers, nuclear families, national communities, and international/transnational belonging. The product of an era of public-broadcasting monopoly in Europe, *Eurovision* has grown from a West European venue of postwar international television diplomacy into a cultural Olympics involving countries outside of Europe and hundreds of millions of viewers worldwide. While its contestants are still mostly European, its queer visions of nationhood and nationalism are readily adaptable in a tightly networked global media universe.

FURTHER READING

Bolin, Goran. "Visions of Europe." *International Journal of Cultural Studies* 9, no. 2 (2006): 189–206.

Raykoff, Ivan, and Robert Deam Tobin, eds. *A Song for Europe: Popular Music and Politics in the Eurovision Song Contest*. Aldershot, UK: Ashgate, 2007.

Stychin, Carl F. "Queer/Euro Visions." In *What's Queer About Europe? Productive Encounters and Re-enchanting Paradigms*, edited by Sudeep Dasgupta and Mireille Rosello, 171–88. New York: Fordham University Press, 2013.

NOTES

1. Robert Deam Tobin, "Eurovision at 50: Post-Wall and Post-Stonewall," In *A Song for Europe: Popular Music and Politics in the Eurovision Song Contest*, ed. Ivan Raykoff and Robert Deam Tobin (Aldershot, UK: Ashgate, 2007), 28.

2. Galina Miazhevich, "Ukrainian Nation Branding Off-line and Online: Verka Serduchka at the *Eurovision Song Contest*," *Europe-Asia Studies* 64, no. 8 (2012): 1505–23.

3. Paul Allatson, "'Antes Cursi Que Sencilla': Eurovision Song Contests and the Kitsch-Drive to Euro-Unity," *Culture, Theory and Critique* 48, no. 1 (2007): 87.

4. Carl F. Stychin, "Queer/Euro Visions," in *What's Queer About Europe? Productive Encounters and Re-enchanting Paradigms*, ed. Sudeep Dasgupta and Mireille Rosello (New York: Fordham University Press, 2013), 176.

5. Catherine Baker, "The 'Gay Olympics'? *The Eurovision Song Contest* and the Politics of LGBT/European Belonging," *European Journal of International Relations* 23, no. 1 (2017): 97–121.

6. Katrin Sieg, "Cosmopolitan Empire: Central and Eastern Europeans at the Eurovision Song Contest," *European Journal of Cultural Studies* 16, no. 2 (2013): 244–63.

7. Baker, "The 'Gay Olympics'?"

8. *Eurovision* allowed Yugoslavia, a nonaligned socialist country, to participate from as early as 1961.

9. Miazhevich, "Ukrainian Nation Branding."

10. Lisa Downing and Robert Gillett, "Introduction," in *Queer in Europe: Contemporary Case Studies*, ed. Lisa Downing and Robert Gillett (New York: Ashgate, 2011).

11. Elitsa Vucheva, "Eurovision Winner's Links to Serb Radical Worries," *EUobserver*, January 24, 2008, https://euobserver.com.

12. Stychin, "Queer/Euro Visions," 179.

13. Baker, "The 'Gay Olympics'?"

14. Ibid.

15. Baker, "The 'Gay Olympics'?," 109.

16. Ibid.

17. Baker, "The 'Gay Olympics'?"

18. Sieg, "Cosmopolitan Empire," 246.

19. Stychin, "Queer/Euro Visions."

21

Fox & Friends
Political Talk

JEFFREY P. JONES

Note for the Second Edition: This essay was written in 2012, before Gretchen Carlson left Fox News in the wake of a sexual harassment settlement against Fox founder Roger Ailes. Additionally, since Donald Trump was elected president, numerous press reports have detailed the intimate relationship President Trump has with the program—not just as a regular viewer and guest on the program but also by routinely allowing conversations and opinions on the program to influence or direct presidential communications and administration policy edicts.

Abstract: That Fox News is slanted conservative has passed from criticism into truism and branding strategy. However, there is danger in simply accepting this view and neglecting critical analysis of what continues to be the most highly rated cable news network. Jeffrey P. Jones shows how the long-running *Fox & Friends* turns the morning talk format on its head, performing an "ideological, often hysterical view of the world" that, he argues, impacts and transforms our world in the process.

It just feels like high school all over again. There's the intellectually challenged and dim-witted jock wannabe, the guy who still refers to women as "babes" and "skirts," yet who is clearly outclassed by all the women around him.[1] Then there's the popular and attractive mean-girl who thinks she needs to show her legs first and her smarts second, whose viciousness and bitchiness are exceeded only by her ambition.[2] And then there's the gay guy, always exhibiting a smirk wrapped in smarm, the go-to guy for the group's requisite mean-spirited put-down or latest innuendo and salacious rumor. Brian Kilmeade, Gretchen Carlson, and Steve

Doocy form the trio of hosts for the Fox News Channel's morning talk show, *Fox & Friends*.[3] And whereas the broadcast networks' morning talk shows—*The Today Show, Good Morning America, The Early Show*—have historically offered an ensemble of hosts designed to invoke the feeling of a happy family (the trustworthy brother, the cute sister, the wacky uncle, etc.), *Fox & Friends* is more akin to a trip back to the high school homeroom. Fox has staged the show in this way not just to stand out from the competition through a different look and feel, but also to create the necessary discursive setting for furthering the channel's ideological goals and agenda.

While this formulation is overly reductive and dismissive—much like the discourse on the show itself—these pejorative descriptions only begin to capture what Fox is crafting in its popular morning talk vehicle. Fox has assembled a group of distinct personality types whose job is to ruminate collectively over the previous day's events, including political ones. Yet unlike Fox News's primetime hosts, who assemble a group of yes-people to confirm and reify what the stars such as Bill O'Reilly and Sean Hannity proclaim, the morning crew has no standout star talent around which to build a show. But then that isn't the objective. Instead, the show is designed to thrust the viewer into the world of common-sense groupthink, complete with all the rumors, smears, innuendo, fear-mongering, thinly veiled ad hominem attacks, and lack of rational discourse they can muster—you know, just like high school. Indeed, the function of the program is to begin the broadcast day with cavalier discussions of political matters—to trot out all manner of conspiracy theories, catchphrases, and buzz words that can prime the audience, both cognitively and semiotically, for similar narratives derived from contemporary right-wing conservative ideology which they will encounter throughout Fox's schedule.[4]

In general, narratives play an important role in shaping public opinion about national politics. Most citizens may not understand the intricacies of or competing ideas and debates about issues of governance such as economic policy, regulatory structures, or international diplomacy, but they certainly understand stories. And stories are what media are in the business of providing—tales that continuously contribute to and often shape what politics *mean*. Trade imbalances, national security policies, Supreme Court rulings, Medicare solvency—none of these things make any *sense* unless they are explained, contextualized, and judged as good, bad, or indifferent to the daily lives of citizens. Competing political narratives thus abound and, indeed, are part of the battleground in currying favor with voters and viewers. But competing news narratives are especially powerful in the cable era, and nowhere more starkly asserted than on Fox News. Fox has proven itself a strong rhetorical force in crafting political narratives that oppose whatever political "reality" liberals or Democratic politicians might construct on a given day. This is true as well on *Fox & Friends*, where such narratives are performed through a genre and program perfectly cast to achieve such political and ideological ends.

That Fox News is conservative in its programming is an undeniable point, despite the channel's own denials. Scholars and media watchdog groups have provided detailed and copious evidence of Fox's overtly ideological narratives in both its news and opinion programs.[5] Audiences also recognize Fox as conservative, as demonstrated in both their opinions of the channel and their viewing behaviors: notably, self-defined conservative viewers overwhelmingly flock to Fox News over any other television news source.[6] Arguments over whether Fox is or isn't conservative, or that its ideology is noticeable only because all other media are liberal, are diversionary, at best—a rhetorical move that allows Fox and its supporters to shift the focus from its questionable rhetorical practices that hide behind the veil of "news" to the chimera of supposed bias in traditional journalism outlets and established reporting practices.

Political intentionality aside, conservative ideology is how the channel has branded itself, making it distinctive from its competition as a commercial product that consumers can depend on to deliver predictable or reliable results. With three competing cable news channels needing to fill twenty-four programming hours each day (as opposed to the thirty minutes of national news in the broadcast network era), markers of distinction are significant in attracting and retaining niche audiences. But as with all brands, that distinct image has to be constructed through a consistent set of practices or offerings that reiterate the brand's identity. That is to say, it must be *performed* regularly.

It is here, in the realm of performance, that we should look to understand how and why *Fox & Friends* not only differs so much from its morning talk show competition, but also serves a particular role in branding Fox News as conservative. There are two distinct aspects of "performance" at play here: performance as *aesthetic expression*, or the stylistics or poetics that dramatize, in this instance, ideological thinking; and what theorists of language describe as *performativity*, or how speech acts or utterances don't just report or describe something, but actually bring that thing into *being* through the act of speaking.[7] A classic example of a performative speech act is a wedding official pronouncing a man and woman "husband and wife," changing material reality through speech. Accordingly, this analysis will examine both how *Fox & Friends* routinely brings ideology to life through its dramatic performances and how it crafts reality—literally making things performatively "real"—through its repeated rhetorical assertions.

Let's first look at the broadcast networks' morning talk shows, though, for a rough sketch of how the genre has traditionally operated, using NBC's *Today* show, the historical standard bearer and ratings leader, as the genre definer. The

Today show's cast is designed to mesh with the waking family having breakfast or preparing for work and school, offering friendly faces that can easily blend with the family unit. Thus, its content steers clear of the politically controversial, offering instead light fare comprised of a smattering of news headlines, weather updates, and interviews with newsmakers, typically foregrounding the human-interest side of news. Primarily, though, the show is geared toward women viewers who are fashioned as mothers/homemakers and treated as the primary household consumer, with a majority of content focused largely on entertainment, cooking and food, parenting, fashion and beauty, relationships, travel, money, and health. These aspects of the show are performed when experts discuss child rearing, for instance, or the latest fashion trends are highlighted, chefs offer cooking demonstrations, or guest musical performances are put on. In the digital era, the show has also attempted to foster a feeling of community among fellow female viewers and the show, its hosts, its online content, and other offerings in the NBC television family.[8]

Fox & Friends also attempts to craft a feeling of community, but not in terms of gender or consumption interests. Rather, conservative ideology serves as the crucial mechanism linking Fox viewers to each other and to the channel. As with much of Fox's programming, the narratives on the morning show are comprised of a discourse that embraces what has become standard ideological tenets of contemporary conservatism—militaristic patriotism, patriarchal gender norms, conservative cultural "values," Christian religiosity, Second Amendment rights, and free-market capitalism, while also castigating and villainizing government, immigrants, liberals, labor unions, and non-Christian religions (especially Islam). Importantly, this discourse is repeatedly wrapped in expressions of celebration and triumph or, more typically, fear and anxiety as manifested through a tone of anger and disgust, a rhetoric of victimization, and a posture of defiance.[9]

Take, for example, *Fox & Friends'* soft-news program segments. The show welcomes the winter holiday season not just with features on food or shopping trends, but also with a barrage of stories they have manufactured called the "War on Christmas." This made-up war arises from the belief that secular society is removing the Christ from Christmas, and then becomes the occasion to demonstrate this "fundamental attack on American values" through repeated anecdotal evidence.[10] In 2011, for instance, *F&F* repeatedly ran stories under the "War on Christmas" segment graphic with such topics as "Are Christians the Only Ones Being Forced to be Tolerant?" and "FL City Bans Christmas Trees and Menorahs," as well as several stories attacking Rhode Island Governor Lincoln Chafee for calling the Christmas tree in the capitol a "holiday tree" (even posting the governor's phone number on screen while encouraging viewers to call him to express their outrage). That *F&F* manufactures this supposed "war" is seen in this last instance, in which the hosts castigate the governor for his invitation to a "holiday tree lighting" ceremony, even though the previous Republican governor had produced exactly the same invitation two years earlier.

Yet nothing riles up the hosts' hatred and full-throated high school smears quite like President Barack Obama. *F&F* has become a favored location on Fox to entertain an array of right-wing conspiracy theories, from claims that Obama was "educated in a madrassa" and "raised as a Muslim," to his not being a natural born citizen of the United States to the accusation that Obama's first book was written by former 1960s radical Bill Ayers.[11] But the high school-ishness of it all is perhaps best seen in two petty attacks, the first being a segment that debated whether it was appropriate for President Obama to wear flip-flops while he was on vacation.[12] The other occurred when, during a period of persistent U.S. unemployment hovering above 9 percent, Obama introduced a jobs bill in a White House ceremony. Steve Doocy felt it proper to attack the choice of paper clip that Obama used in holding up the proposed legislation to the public! Graphically highlighting the supposedly unseemly nature of the offending clip, Doocy exclaimed, "President Obama's jobs bill, hot off the presses—at Kinko's? Hundreds of billions in tax hikes and new spending bound together with a chintzy clip. Look at that thing."[13]

Another technique for attacking its villains while supporting its ideological performances involves attributing a critique or counterclaim to unnamed sources by simply saying, "some would say." For instance, in attempting to blame a poor economy on labor unions, Gretchen Carlson offered, "Some would say that it's the unions that have crippled the U.S. economy and led to the United States' debt." As Media Matters notes, the "some" referred to in the formulation are often simply other Fox News hosts, as opposed to experts such as, in this instance, economists.[14] In other instances, the show's anchors use the saying as a rhetorical set-up to introduce guests, yet in the process establish the key attack as an unproblematic reality. "So is this a continuation of the president's plan to promote class warfare, [as] some are suggesting? Joining us now is Fox News legal analyst Peter Johnson," went one analysis of an Obama speech. A similar rhetorical move occurs in guest introductions where the host makes an extreme assertion, yet poses it as an "innocent" question. For instance, Steve Doocy introduced one guest by asking, "Could President Obama be running the most destructive administration in our history?" Such loaded phrases are simply not found in the language of other morning shows or newscasts. The fact that these instances happen repeatedly and with such venom and vigor marks the program as both ideologically and generically distinctive.

What is also noteworthy in these two examples is how *F&F* features guests to perform the argument the hosts want to make, while arranging for the guests

FIGURE 21.1. Hosts Doocy and Carlson express their daily dose of outrage and emotional intensity over the latest news.

to be directly responsible for making the claim, in such a way that the hosts' comments are effectively insulated from charges of bias. As we will see below, guests are also used to demonstrate villainy in their "us versus them" formulation, thereby establishing "the Other" while supposedly demonstrating that Fox is "fair and balanced" by giving the other side an opportunity to be heard.

We must look not just at the ways ideology is encoded in their performances, but also at the ways in which the language employed may bring certain "realities" into being. As noted above, understanding language as *performative* involves a recognition that language often produces, not just reflects upon, that which it names.[15] Performativity theory highlights how words can be "actions in themselves"—they bring into being that which is spoken.[16] The "War on Christmas" is one example, for no "war" exists outside that which Fox has constructed and brought into being. Similarly, Fox News's speech acts may name something—for instance, labeling a proposed Islamic community center in the lower Manhattan neighborhood near the former World Trade Center a "Ground Zero Mosque"—but the utterance also warns citizens of a supposed threat to American values and honor, perhaps even mobilizing people to vote in the midterm congressional elections for candidates voicing opposition to such a "mosque." Thus the repeated iteration of such utterances not only creates realities—"mosque," not community center, becomes the standard usage on other news channels—but now has the potential to mobilize concrete political actions through their performative power.

Fox & Friends was at the forefront of the "Ground Zero Mosque" event, repeatedly running segments on the Park 51 project (as it was officially called) that stoked the flames of fear, paranoia, revenge, hatred, racism, and whatever else could be mustered three months before the midterm congressional elections.[17] Not only did the hosts pick sides, but through repeated invocation, they literally brought a proposed "mosque" into being—as a religious center, as a "command center" for terrorists, as a slap in the face of Americans, as a threat, as evil, as a *controversy* that did not exist in the early stages of the project.[18] Despite the facts that an actual mosque existed in the former World Trade Center prior to 9/11, and that one still exists today in the Pentagon, Fox saw an opportunity to link the 9/11 terrorist attacks to the project, transforming a place of community gathering and worship into an imagined terrorist threat with alleged ties to radical Islamic terrorist groups worldwide.

Here again, guests on *F&F* played a crucial role. In one segment, the program hosted Imam Feisal Abdul Rauf, the project's organizer. But instead of interviewing him directly, the hosts literally pitted him against a 9/11 firefighter who was opposed to the project, featuring the firefighter as the lead guest. Despite the fact that the Imam and firefighter sat together on the same couch, *F&F* chose to frame the two men in picture boxes—allowing viewers to see them not just as rhetorically opposed, but visually as well, thus crafting a cognitive tool to posit key dichotomies to further its rhetorical ends: good versus bad, white person versus person of color, Christian versus Muslim, 9/11 victim versus 9/11 perpetrator.[19] Given the way this visual framing routinely occurs on the show, we might refer to the technique as "Boxes of Discord and Empathy." In a different episode, the show featured another 9/11 firefighter who was suing the "mosque's" developers for $350 million. As the firefighter and his lawyer discussed their reasons for entering the suit, the firefighter was framed in a picture box, but this time counterpoised with images of the attack on the World Trade Center and its smoky aftermath.[20] In both instances, the guests help perform the ideological function—visually and representationally, as much as anything they have to say—of constructing clear heroes and villains, threats and sacred objects.

In sum, *Fox & Friends* has played a central role in constructing a specific "reality," a threat made tangible and real through its ability to mobilize emotion. That reality is brought into existence through its repeated performance, as well as being brought to life through the dramatic presentations that the format of the talk show encourages and allows. What repeated viewing of the program also demonstrates is how emotion and drama feed off each other, as the program's repeated installments of a "War on Christmas" or "Ground Zero Mosque" become, in essence, hysterical. And as with all hysterical performances in American history—Puritan witch hunts, early twentieth-century temperance movements, hearings seeking postwar Communists in the military, claims of secret Muslims in the White House—those who participate in them generally come to believe they have "found" what they have created through their performances. In short, *Fox & Friends* performs an ideological, often hysterical view of the world, and in the process, transforms that world through its dramatic rendering.

By branding itself conservative, and performing that ideology twenty-four hours daily within an array of programming types, Fox has now become a central rhetorical force in articulating and asserting a conservative ideological worldview. But *Fox & Friends* is more than just another programming venue for the channel's ideological appeals. The program has radically altered the morning talk genre in significant ways, in particular the important role the genre has traditionally played in offering viewers some degree of what Roger Silverstone calls "ontological security," or the feeling of trust—often achieved through habits and rituals such as watching television—that the chaotic world is not a direct threat to one's self-identity or to one's family.[21] Morning talk shows typically offer a relief of anxieties by integrating the family unit into the broader world of politics and consumption through its soft-news features, and vice versa, by taking the threats of the world and domesticating them through nonthreatening and noncontroversial performances of normality.

Fox & Friends offers ontological security, but not through normalizing the chaotic world. Quite the opposite, *F&F* destabilizes the world by presenting most of it as a threat to the viewers' values and ways of life. The show then provides the security found in an ideological worldview that aggressively and defiantly challenges those threats—all of which is normalized through the banter and groupthink of the trio of hosts. Trust is achieved and equilibrium restored by speaking a language that everyone understands—not the elitist language of the learned, but the base level of smears, innuendo, and aggressive attacks on that which seems threatening. You know, just like in high school.

FURTHER READING

Auletta, Ken. "The Dawn Patrol: The Curious Rise of Morning Television, and the Future of Network News." *New Yorker*, August 8, 2005.

Bell, Elizabeth. *Theories of Performance*. Los Angeles: Sage, 2008.

Dickinson, Tim. "How Roger Ailes Built the Fox News Fear Factory." *Rolling Stone*, May 25, 2011.

Greenwald, Robert, and Alexandra Kitty. *Outfoxed: Rupert Murdoch's War on Journalism*. New York: Disinformation Company, 2005.

Jamieson, Kathleen Hall, and Joseph N . Cappella. *Echo Chamber: Rush Limbaugh and the Conservative Media Establishment*. New York: Oxford University Press, 2008.

Swint, Kerwin. *Dark Genius: The Influential Career of Legendary Political Operative and Fox News Founder Roger Ailes*. New York: Union Square Press, 2008.

NOTES

1. See media watchdog Media Matters for an extensive history of Kilmead's sexism: www
.mediamatters.org/brian-kilmeade.

2. Carlson is a former Miss America pageant winner whom *The Daily Show with Jon Stewart* has critiqued for intentionally dumbing-down her on-screen persona to appease Fox
viewers. See "Gretchen Carlson Dumbs Down," *Daily Show with Jon Stewart*, December 8,
2009, www.thedailyshow.com.

3. These are the hosts for the weekday versions of the program, with alternate hosts serving
weekend duties.

4. As one investigative journalist reported, "According to insiders, the morning show's anchors, who appear to be chatting ad-lib, are actually working from daily, structured talking points that come straight from the top. 'Prior to broadcast, Steve Doocy, Gretchen
Carlson—that gang—they meet with [Fox President] Roger [Ailes],' says a former Fox
deputy. 'And Roger gives them the spin.'" See Tim Dickinson, "How Roger Ailes Built the
Fox News Fear Factory," *Rolling Stone*, May 25, 2011.

5. See Kathleen Hall Jamieson and Joseph N. Cappella, *Echo Chamber: Rush Limbaugh and
the Conservative Media Establishment* (New York: Oxford University Press, 2008). See
also Media Matters for America (http://mediamatters.org), a watchdog group dedicated to
monitoring and reporting on right-wing media (in particular Fox).

6. "Fox News Viewed as Most Ideological Network," Pew Research Center for the People and
the Press, October 29, 2009, www.people-press.org.

7. James Loxley, *Performativity* (London: Routledge, 2007).

8. Jeffrey P. Jones, "I Want My Talk TV: Network Talk Shows in the Digital Universe," in *Beyond Prime Time: Television Programming in the Post-Network Era*, ed. Amanda Lotz (New
York: Routledge, 2009), 14–35.

9. For an account of the correlation between the rhetoric of fear in Fox's programming to
that being sold by Fox's advertisers, see Mark Andrejevic, "Fox News: 'Don't Worry, Be
Anxious,'" *In Media Res* (blog), April 2, 2007, http://mediacommons.org/imr.

10. Media Matters dates Fox's creation of this "War on Christmas" to 2004 and notes that the
organization has accumulated nearly 250 instances in Fox's programming. Eric Boehlert,
"How Fox News' War on Christmas Is Like The Nutcracker," Media Matters, December 9,
2011, www.mediamatters.org.

11. Eric Schroeck, "New Low? Fox & Friends Hosts Conspiracy Theorist Cashill to Peddle
Claim That Ayers Wrote Obama's Memoir," Media Matters, March 29, 2011, www.media
matters.org.

12. Simon Maloy, "Fox News Goes After Obama's Sandals," Media Matters, January 5, 2011,
www.mediamatters.org.

13. "Doocy Mocks Obama for Using Binder Clip to Hold Paper Together," Media Matters,
September 13, 2011, www.mediamatters.org.

14. Melody Johnson, "Fox Puts the 'Some' in 'Some Would Say,'" Media Matters, December 2,
2011, www.mediamatters.org.

15. For the original formulation of the theory, see J. L. Austin, *How to Do Things with Words*,
ed. J. O. Urmson and Marina Sbisa, 2nd ed. (Cambridge, MA: Harvard University Press,
1975). For a summary of performativity theory, including its relationship to other theories
of performance, see Elizabeth Bell, *Theories of Performance* (Los Angeles: Sage, 2008).

16. Loxley, *Performativity*, 2.

17. The issue mysteriously and suddenly disappeared from Fox News after the election.

18. Less than a year earlier, a Fox News host publicly supported the project. See "Extremist Makeover: Homeland Edition," *Daily Show with Jon Stewart*, August 19, 2010, www.thedailyshow.com.

19. "9-11 Firefighter Tim Brown Debates $100M Mosque at Ground Zero," KeepAmericaSafe.com, YouTube, May 11, 2010, www.youtube.com.

20. "First Responder Suing 'Ground Zero Mosque' Developers," Freedom Watch, YouTube, September 14, 2010, www.youtube.com. For similar visual framing using picture boxes to create visual cues of identification and discord, see "Fox and Friends: Pamela Geller vs Nicole Neroulias on Ground Zero Mosque and Bus Campaign," YouTube, August 11, 2010, www.youtube.com.

21. Roger Silverstone, *Why Study the Media?* (Los Angeles: Sage, 1999), 118–19.

22

Full Frontal with Samantha Bee
Feminist Comedy

AMBER DAY

Abstract: *Full Frontal with Samantha Bee* is a rare example of unabashed feminist conviction on television. Amber Day describes how the program invites audience members into a community wherein a feminist perspective is common sense, striking back at the trolls who would shout down outspoken women, and reclaiming feminist anger as both empowering and fun.

In the teaser introduction for the first episode of *Full Frontal with Samantha Bee*, we see the title comedian at a faux press conference. The crowd of reporters in front of her shout questions, all of which revolve around her femaleness in increasingly absurd terms, including, "How can I watch your show as a man?" and "What is it like to be a female woman?" Over the din of overlapping questions, one reporter yells, "Do you have a problem with your ovaries falling out, or anything?" Finally, in answer to a question about what it took to make the show a reality, Bee responds, "hard work, a great team, maybe just a little bit of magic." She winks exaggeratedly as a cutaway shot shows her engaged in frenzied occult rituals. Back at the press conference, she facetiously confirms, "It's true; we're all witches." The introduction allowed Bee to acknowledge the buzz around her uniqueness, as she was breaking a long-standing glass ceiling in American television by becoming the only female host of a late-night comedy program, while also humorously thumbing her nose at the sexism still clearly pervasive both in the industry and in the culture at large.

Beyond simply being female, from the first episode of *Full Frontal*, Bee distinguished herself by developing a style of delivery dripping with colorful curses, hilariously embellished insults, and undisguised irritation at public folly, often aiming her barbs at sexist policymaking and patriarchal norms. In other

FIGURE 22.1. "It's true; we're all witches." In her first episode, Bee thumbs her nose at the sexism still pervasive in the industry and the culture at large.

words, she introduced something previously almost unheard of on television: feminist anger (indignation over instances of discrimination and sexism). Bee's incorporation of enthusiastic insult comedy, combined with the show's attentiveness to issues related to gender equality, has opened up a mainstream space for unapologetic feminist humor that blows away the stereotype of feminists as unfunny prudes. The show has attracted both ardent fans and angry anti-fans, both likely influenced by the fact that it positions feminism—the pursuit of equal rights for the sexes—as mainstream, common sense, and far more fun than its opposition.

In that first episode, after covering the then ongoing presidential primary races, Bee debuts a segment she calls "Elected Paperweight of the Month," zeroing in on a Kansas state senator named Mitch Holmes. Holmes, we learn, has written up a dress code for the capitol building, but only for women, because he believes that "men already know how to look professional." Bee quickly reviews the many problems the people of Kansas face due to a dire lack of funds and then turns her attention to what Holmes's legislative priorities have been. Addressing Holmes, she explains, "Before appointing yourself host of Project Runway: Horny Senators Edition, you spent your time sponsoring desperately important legislation: commending the pastors, priests, and rabbis of Kansas, restricting abortion, recognizing the Boy Scouts of America for being awesome, restricting abortion, and high-fiving the Wichita basketball team—basically an entire legislative career spent controlling women and celebrating the groups that exclude them." After a further unflattering recap of Holmes's statements on the dress code, Bee concludes, "You don't get to regulate what other people wear to work. I mean, I wouldn't try to regulate your finger-painted tie, or your skeevy facial hair. And if

I get distracted wondering whether that yellow stain around your mouth is whiskers or just the lingering impression of a glory hole, that's my problem, not yours. You do you." At this, Bee's audience erupts into guffaws and cheers.

Bee's femaleness in the notorious boy's club of comedy, combined with her stridency and self-confidence, makes her both remarkable and upsetting for some. *Full Frontal* debuted at a culturally contradictory moment. It is one in which there is an expanding number of outspoken female performers granted public platforms within television and film, often to critical acclaim. Some of the more recent include Tiffany Haddish, Leslie Jones, Kate McKinnon, Jessica Williams, Michelle Wolf, and Ali Wong. At the same time, however, the backlash that has been brewing has suddenly become increasingly visible as the online vitriol directed at confident women in the public eye has tipped into nearly ubiquitous rape and death threats and even harassment in the offline world.

Women in positions of power have long pointed to the difficult double bind they experience. If they appear too soft, they are dismissed as weak and ineffectual, while if they are too strident, they are criticized for being shrill, frigid, or bitchy. Women in comedy, in particular, have historically had to navigate an especially challenging balancing act. As Linda Mizejewski points out, there has long been an implicit binary set up for women that puts "funny" and "pretty" in opposition to one another. The assumption goes that for real (i.e., heterosexually desirable) women, looks are most important. It is only the otherwise unattractive ones who cultivate the male attribute of being funny, meaning that their femininity is itself suspect.[1] Indeed, journalist and cultural commentator Christopher Hitchens published an essay in 2007 dedicated to the continued endorsement of this line of thinking titled "Why Women Aren't Funny," wherein he expounded on the supposed biological basis for women's lack of humor, wildly distorting the scientific studies he used to make his point.[2] As Jennifer Foy explains, comedy has always been particularly fraught for women who tell dirty jokes or use gross-out humor. While female comedians have historically been interpreted as sexually loose, this judgment becomes all the more heightened when the material is a little risqué. She argues that in telling a joke, especially a dirty joke, a woman has to shift into the aggressive position traditionally reserved for men, which often has negative consequences, as it is read as promiscuity rather than seduction and thus "invokes the social alienation commonly associated with promiscuity."[3] In other words, being a female comedian has historically come with a host of social challenges and restrictive expectations.

Of course, there have been female performers at various points of time who have challenged or played with these expectations, to varying degrees of success. And in recent years, as television has moved further into a niche broadcasting model (rather than one premised on appealing to a wide cross-section of the population), and Internet virality has encouraged edgier material, network and studio executives are awakening to the idea of granting more outspoken women their own platforms. While Bee is the lone host in the world of late-night and parodic news programs, a number of other female comedians are heading up situation comedies and sketch programs or are transitioning into producing, including Tina Fey, Amy Poehler, Amy Schumer, Ilana Glazer, Abbi Jacobson, and more. And not incidentally, as Samantha Bee was debuting her program, Hillary Clinton was believed by many to be the presumptive next president of the United States, holding out the possibility that another milestone for female empowerment was about to be reached.

At a glance, it all might look like a simple story of social progress and equality achieved, but it is of course not quite so simple. At the same moment, the uncivil tone of discourse on YouTube comment pages has, in many ways, become a dominant form of communication on the Internet, from Twitter feeds to Reddit discussion boards. In such forums, outspoken or otherwise visible women, and especially women of color, are routinely targeted with vicious critique, insults, and threats. This kind of abuse certainly existed under the radar of mainstream popular culture for some time, but it more visibly bubbled to the surface beginning with the #Gamergate controversy in 2014, when several female videogame developers and a feminist videogame journalist were targeted for abuse (including rape and death threats), some of whom were driven from their homes out of safety concerns after their addresses were distributed online.[4] Another high-profile example of organized misogynist harassment occurred in 2016 around the release of a new *Ghostbusters* movie. Some fans of the original films were angry at the idea of an all-female *Ghostbusters* team and, after a belittling review by right-wing provocateur Milo Yiannopoulos, in which he referred to the black female cast member, Leslie Jones, as "spectacularly unappealing," legions of his fans took to Twitter to harass Jones in brutally racist terms, referring to her as a "big lipped coon" and implying that she was a gorilla.[5] One might wonder why audience members who dislike a particular performer/writer/developer, and so forth might react with such intense anger, rather than simply deciding to change the channel or choosing something else with which to engage. *Guardian* journalist Matt Lees answers that question by arguing that many white, male self-described nerds see women in these roles as "the culture they considered theirs being ripped away from them. In their zero-sum mindset, they read growing artistic equality as a threat."[6] It is against this background that *Full Frontal* debuted.

What is particularly interesting about Samantha Bee's approach on the program is that she calls attention to this type of abuse, particularly the strain of it that might be leveled at her, and rather than feeling intimidated, she gleefully makes it a major target of her humor. She takes it as a given that her very

FIGURE 22.2. Bee mocks the trolls who plague outspoken women.

presence will be offensive to some and makes clear that she is not going to attempt to soften her image. As she explained in an interview, "There are plenty of people who won't tune in because a woman's voice bothers their eardrums. Their ear canals can't handle the sound of my shrill voice talking at them about a subject. I guess I just don't really care about those people."[7] Instead, she makes it a regular habit to shine a spotlight on the insults and rage both she and many other women in the public eye receive. In the lead-up to the show's first episode, when *Full Frontal* existed only in promo materials, the trolls had already started to pile on, prompting her to set up a hotline for rape threats. Though the intent was clearly tongue-in-cheek, the hotline did in fact exist. After dialing in, callers would hear "Hello, you have reached the Samantha Bee Rape Threatline. Nobody's here to answer your call, but your offer of nonconsensual sex is important to us, so please select from the following menu." Options included "to tell me I'm a dumb bitch that needs to be raped, press 1," and "to tell me you wouldn't even rape me because of how old and disgusting I am, press 4."[8]

On the program itself, she has drawn attention to similar invective leveled at women in other fields, including an extended segment on five Seattle city councilwomen who, in a vote that split along gender lines, sided against funding a new sports stadium for the Seattle Seahawks and were then subject to tirades of abuse online. Bee begins the segment by explaining that "being a woman on the internet means receiving frequent bouquets of chivalrous offers to tear you in half cunt first. Especially if you have the nerve to run for president, or talk about politics on TV, or criticize literally any video game" (May 16, 2016). As she speaks, we see pictures for each type of woman in the list (such as Hillary Clinton, Carly Fiorina, herself, and Megyn Kelly), annotated to include some of the more colorful insults each has received online (like "porky bitch twat waffle" and "bimbo megacunt"), as well as article headlines about incidents like Gamergate.

Bee goes on to offer viewers some background on the Seattle story, including the statistics on stadium projects consistently draining city coffers. Declaring "looks like those 'fucking bitches' on the city council aren't so stupid after all," she affects an exaggerated sportscaster voice to introduce each of the individual women, listing their qualifications, the reason they voted against the stadium, and a choice quote from an Internet troll, finally shouting, "Let's all give it up for the Seattle Sea-wards!" At the end of the episode, she screens footage of each of the councilwomen reading some of their insults and laughing, figuratively robbing the words of their demeaning power. Bee concludes by stating, "As a fellow stupid bitch, I salute you," as her audience applauds.

It is important to note that when the show does draw attention to Internet trolling, threats, or other put-downs, it always does so with laughter, defanging the insults by ridiculing them. For instance, one of the online extras for fans of the program is a recurring segment called "Real or Fake" in which Bee tries to distinguish real hate mail from fake versions made up by her staff. She appears to find all of the comments hilarious, though her staff has a hard time producing material that competes with the real commentary. After reading a tweet that begins "dam you liberal women are so ugly!! Yes you look like a turd" followed by some incomprehensible and ungrammatical insults, she remarks that she would like someone to needlepoint the tweet on a pillow so that she can sleep with it. In another installment, she muses of the commentators, "Maybe we could throw you a party. Maybe we could all go to brunch. Everyone likes brunch. Even fucking weirdos." Indeed, when read for a sympathetic audience, the collective laughter acts as an antidote to the hateful rhetoric and creates the feeling of strength in numbers. Such segments bring the language of the trolls into the light of day, clearly showing them to be both mean-spirited and crazy—the ramblings of "fucking weirdos" who the audience agrees are laughable. Here the laughter is itself a form of feminism, used as a weapon to dismantle the type of intimidation aimed at keeping women out of the public sphere.

Bee's strategy lies partially in turning the language of the trolls back on the trolls themselves (and at others with whom she has a bone to pick). Without using terms that are rooted in sexism, racism, or other forms of social discrimination, she has adopted the florid insults of the Internet for her own purposes, as fodder for comedy, and as an assertion of power. She uses the hateful troll form so often wielded to silence women and transforms it into her own noisy art form. On her first episode, she refers to the presidential candidates as "Hermione Clinton" (Hillary Clinton), "human Che Guevara t-shirt" (Bernie Sanders), "sentient caps-lock button" (Donald Trump), and "fist-faced horse-shit salesman" (Ted Cruz). But the insults definitely get more pointed in proportion to her anger. As Donald Trump (in many ways the ultimate Internet troll) secured the Republican nomination and was later heard casually discussing sexual assault, she referred to him as a "crotch-fondling slab of rancid meatloaf," a "dick-waving Berlusconi knockoff," and (after he won the presidency) a "leaky whoopee cushion full of expired cottage cheese who threatens to erode the very foundations of our liberal democracy." It is fitting that so many of her more biting insults are aimed at Trump. As Emily Nussbaum of the *New Yorker* observes, the fight between Trump and Clinton was directly related to the explosion of female-centered comedy and culture, as "Trump's call to Make America Great Again was a plea to go back in time, to when people knew how to take a joke. It was an election about who owned the mike."[9] In other words, Trump is the most visible symbol of the backlash against female empowerment.

Of course, we know who won that election (though not the popular vote), but, perhaps consequentially, the culture war continues to be waged more fiercely than ever, particularly as far as feminism and women's rights are concerned. What is striking about *Full Frontal* is that it unapologetically interpolates its audience as feminist, as well as anti-racist. Although much of the show focuses on the same current events as other parodic news programs, it more frequently tackles issues of inequality, from sexual discrimination to the plight of refugees. These segments are always premised on the assumption that audience members will be as outraged as Bee is when legislators attempt to infringe on human rights, or when other media outlets cover female public figures with sexist condescension. And in addition to expressing outrage, she often provides suggestions for action, frequently reminding viewers that they can have an impact in local political battles in particular. Clearly staking their turf in the aforementioned culture war, the show has also raised money for organizations like Planned Parenthood, by selling T-shirts that read "Nasty Woman" (after the epithet Donald Trump directed at Hillary Clinton in a presidential debate), or "Thundercunt" (after an insult Bee received online). The show offers the opportunity for audience members to identify with Bee and with each other, turning what might otherwise feel like intimidation into collective laughter and strength.

On *Full Frontal*, Samantha Bee performs important work that goes beyond providing a comedic take on the week's news and current events: She invites audience members into a community wherein a feminist perspective is simply common sense (despite that not being the reality in most of the world). Further, she nakedly reclaims female anger from those who would like to dismiss and malign its existence through terms like "feminazi," instead offering up feminist anger as both empowering and fun. The combination of foul-mouthed comedy, witty disgust, and nakedly passionate female conviction sets the program apart from its male-dominated counterparts and allows Samantha Bee to situate feminism as mainstream despite the cultural forces pushing against it.

FURTHER READING

Day, Amber. *Satire and Dissent: Interventions in Contemporary Political Debate*. Bloomington: Indiana University Press, 2011.

Gray, Jonathan, Jeffrey Jones, and Ethan Thompson. *Satire TV: Politics and Comedy in the Post-Network Era*. New York: New York University Press, 2009.

Mantilla, Karla. *Gendertrolling: How Misogyny Went Viral*. Santa Barbara, CA: Praeger, 2015.

Mizejewski, Linda. *Pretty/Funny: Women Comedians and Body Politics*. Austin: University of Texas Press, 2014.

NOTES

1. Linda Mizejewski, *Pretty/Funny: Women Comedians and Body Politics* (Austin: University of Texas Press, 2014).
2. Rebecca Krefting, *All Joking Aside: American Humor and Its Discontents* (Baltimore: Johns Hopkins University Press, 2014), 106.
3. Jennifer Foy, "Fooling Around: Female Stand-Ups and Sexual Joking," *Journal of Popular Culture* 48, no. 4 (2015): 703–13.
4. Jay Hathaway, "What Is Gamergate, and Why? An Explainer for Non-Geeks," *Gawker*, October 10, 2014, http://gawker.com.
5. Kristen Brown, "How a Racist, Sexist Hate Mob Forced Leslie Jones Off Twitter," Fusion.net, July 19, 2016, http://fusion.net.
6. Matt Lees, "What Gamergate Should Have Taught Us about the 'Alt-Right,'" *Guardian*, December 1, 2016, www.theguardian.com.
7. Rebecca Traister, "Smirking in the Boys' Room," *New York Magazine*, January 25, 2016, http://nymag.com.
8. Sarah Burton, "Samantha Bee Created a Rape Threatline for Trolls and It's Genius," *Buzzfeed*, December 11, 2015, www.buzzfeed.com.
9. Emily Nussbaum, "How Jokes Won the Election," *New Yorker*, January 23, 2017, www.newyorker.com.

23

The Hunt with John Walsh
True Crime Storytelling

AMANDA KEELER

Abstract: In her analysis of *The Hunt with John Walsh*, Amanda Keeler explores the public service function of true crime television programs that feature unsolved or unresolved cases. Through an investigation of visual style and narrative elements, Keeler examines the multiple intentions of television programs that seek to entertain audiences and simultaneously help solve crimes.

True crime storytelling is a popular, nonfiction genre that spans a broad range of programs with different subjects, purposes, and outcomes. It encompasses "closed-case" television programs, such as *Forensic Files* and *Homicide Hunter: Lt. Joe Kenda*, which re-create previously solved cases to communicate that even the most difficult investigations can be resolved through cooperation among police, district attorneys, and forensic scientists. Another type of true crime program instead interrogates already-prosecuted criminal cases. These "reinvestigation" programs, such as the podcast *Serial* and *Making a Murderer*, frame their individual case studies as flawed and, in doing so, invite viewers to reexamine the validity of the original evidence and subsequent criminal trials. The popularity of these programs has brought attention to what many viewers see as fissures in the criminal justice system, although critics of these programs acknowledge the difficulty of revisiting criminal cases through an alleged selective presentation of evidence. True crime reinvestigation programs share some commonalities with what Richard Kilborn calls "collaborational" programs, which typically showcase unsolved or open cases.[1] These programs, such as *America's Most Wanted* and *Disappeared* crowdsource detective work, explicitly asking the audience to divulge any pertinent information that might help solve the crime or locate missing persons. Such programs recognize that in certain cases, the

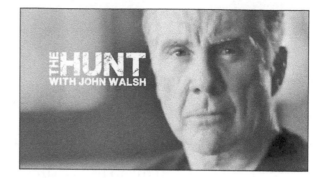

FIGURE 23.1.
True crime TV veteran John Walsh appeals directly to audiences to help police resolve cases.

audience's assistance can help to solve open cases, situating the audience as a "televisual member" of the police.[2]

While the form and purpose of true crime programs varies, in their own way each attempts to perform a public service. The public service of a closed-case program such as *Forensic Files* demonstrates the effectiveness of social institutions—particularly the police and the courts—that have successfully investigated cases and prosecuted the perpetrators. Conversely, reinvestigation programs like *Making a Murderer* attempt to perform a public service by focusing a critical lens on these same institutions. These programs serve the public by locating and analyzing perceived flaws in the criminal justice system in order to remedy miscarriages of justice. Finally, collaborational true crime programs seek to provide a public service by eliciting tips from the audience in an attempt to identify and capture perpetrators who have evaded law enforcement. This essay focuses on the collaborational CNN program *The Hunt with John Walsh*, which reconstructs unresolved crimes and their investigations to fuse television entertainment with a public service mission.

While each different type of true crime storytelling seeks to serve the public differently, the notion of using radio and television as a public service has shifted over time. According to media historian Paddy Scannell, this concept emerged in the 1920s from the BBC director-general John Reith's vision for broadcasting. Reith defined the BBC's mandate to create programming not merely "for entertainment purposes alone."[3] In both the United States and the UK, public service broadcasting was later tied to the "uplift" of audiences through "high culture" programs designed primarily to educate, and secondarily to entertain.[4] More recently, Peter Lunt writes that reality and "lifestyle" programs challenge traditional notions of public service broadcasting because they "aim to help people improve their lives rather than raising them to the higher plane of knowledge, experience, and consciousness."[5] Lunt suggests that the reconceived notion of public service broadcasting has created "shifts in the nature of expertise" whereby the audience becomes a participant in, rather than a mere viewer of, the information presented.[6] Within the context of true crime programs, many reinvestigation and collaborational programs offer a mechanism to help people who feel left behind by the police and/or the criminal justice system, implicitly shifting the onus of solving difficult cases onto the viewer. Concurrently, these programs demonstrate the power and possibilities of participatory, amateur detective work as they attempt—sometimes successfully—to bring closure to seemingly unsolvable cases.

As a collaborational true crime program, *The Hunt with John Walsh* presents cases in which the individual allegedly responsible for the crime is known yet remains free in unknown whereabouts; less frequently it features cases that do not have a clear suspect. *The Hunt*'s first season highlights the breadth of the program's cases, from a father on the run after the murder of his family to the abduction of a young boy by an unknown perpetrator. Using reenactments, archival news footage, home video, and interviews with the victims' friends, family members, and law enforcement, *The Hunt* appeals directly to audiences, suggesting that only with the cooperation of the viewer-as-amateur-detective can the police resolve these cases. It seeks to ameliorate the perceived failures or loss of trust in public institutions that citizens turn to for safety and justice. Within this public service, however, are basic expectations for garnering an audience and sufficient television ratings. In this regard, *The Hunt* must attract viewers in order to compel them to participate in the collaborational, public service process. Furthermore, with an abundance of true crime programs currently available across television and streaming services, *The Hunt* must set itself apart from its competitors. To do this the program experiments stylistically with its reenactments and its slow, methodical presentation of the facts of each featured case. Its experimental form seeks to bring an audience to fulfill its public service mission.

The Hunt is not the first television program that seeks to simultaneously entertain audiences and provide a public service. It owes its format and purpose to programs such as *America's Most Wanted* (*AMW*), which was originally conceived as an "interactive," "participatory" television forum to present open and unsolved criminal cases to audiences.[7] In the late 1980s *AMW* producers worked closely with the FBI and other law enforcement officials to create a program that would inform audiences and solicit their help in capturing criminals, asking viewers to call a toll-free number with tips or information. While law enforcement officials had some reservations about the program, they were nonetheless enticed by the idea that a television program might help to capture known criminals—which it accomplished after its first airing. In his promotional tour for the debut of *The Hunt*, John Walsh remarked that throughout its run *AMW* was responsible for "the capture of 1,231 fugitives and the recovery of 61 missing children."[8] It proved the possibility of providing a public service through the presentation of unsolved cases, while also entertaining millions of viewers each week.

The Hunt represents John Walsh's successful return to hosting a true crime television program. Perhaps the best-known and most trusted public figure in true crime storytelling, John Walsh's initial connection to the genre came as a result of his own personal history dealing with the long-unsolved abduction and murder of his son Adam in 1981. In the aftermath of his son's murder, Walsh worked to change the way that local police and the FBI investigate missing persons cases and has continued to advocate for victims' rights. Executive Producer Michael Linder notes that when he was seeking a host for *America's Most Wanted*, he and several other producers felt that Walsh was ideal because he was "an everyman, an ordinary guy who had been hit hard by crime."[9] On *The Hunt*, John Walsh explicitly invokes his own personal narrative as the defining purpose of his involvement in the program. In the opening sequence Walsh looks directly at the camera and tells the audience,

> Back in 1981, I had the American dream—the beautiful wife, the house in the suburbs, and a beautiful six-year-old son. And one day I went to work, kissed my son goodbye, and never saw him again. In two weeks, I became the parent of a murdered child, and I'll always be the parent of a murdered child. I still have the heartache. I still have the rage. I waited years for justice. I know what it is like to be there waiting for some answers. And over those years I learned how to do one thing really well, and that's how to catch these bastards and bring them back to justice. I've become a man hunter. I'm out there looking for bad guys.

As his opening statement suggests, Walsh puts himself at the center of *The Hunt's* public service mission, which is deeply rooted in his own personal mission to fight crime. He employs his experiences as a victim of crime to address the powerlessness of other families who find themselves in similar situations. His status as a "parent of a murdered child" invokes his qualifications in this quasi-law enforcement position. As Walsh looks directly into the camera, he implies that anyone in the audience who is faced with a similar life-altering crime can rely on him to be "out there looking for bad guys." As Brian Lowry notes in his review of *The Hunt*, Walsh is "once again acting as the audience's surrogate avenger."[10]

As noted earlier, to be successfully collaborational, a public service television program must find ways to stand out from similar programs in order to attract an audience. In its dual mission to draw an audience and to elicit clues by revisiting unresolved cases, *The Hunt* relies on storytelling elements found in many true crime programs. Much like *America's Most Wanted*, *The Hunt* continually chooses to refocus attention on the suspect, reminding the audience of their role in apprehending fugitives and solving these open cases. At every commercial break the program displays the information about the known or unknown perpetrator, with a photograph and details regarding any known information about the suspect's hair color, age, and height. At the end of each sequence, Walsh implores viewers to share any pertinent information: "If you have any information relating to this crime, please go online at cnn.com/TheHunt. You can remain anonymous. We'll pass your tip along to the proper authorities and, if requested, will not reveal your name." At the CNN website, viewers can electronically send a tip or find a toll-free number to contact the proper law enforcement officials.

While *The Hunt*'s storytelling parallels some true crime programs, it diverges from many of its contemporaries in important stylistic ways. Each episode focuses on only one or two cases, providing time for each crime and its investigation to unfold methodically, noting the leads, clues, and dead ends that have stumped the police. This slow pacing seeks to correct a perceived problem with *America's Most Wanted*, as Walsh notes that in an effort to include as many cases (and therefore captures) as possible, *AMW*'s reenactments became rushed: "We would have recreations that were two minutes long. You never got a sense of the victims. You never got a sense of what was going on."[11] *The Hunt*'s use of narrative slowness allows it to elaborate on the intricate details of the crime, its aftermath, and the complex web of clues unearthed in the subsequent investigation—clues that might lead viewers to realize they have information to share with law enforcement. This slowness connects to the program's public service mission, as concentrating on one case for a longer period of time reveals the case's minute details gradually in a way that could more effectively trigger a viewer's memory. This deliberate pacing also metaphorically parallels the slow and lengthy investigations connected to these featured cases, representing years of waiting for justice.

The Hunt also employs a significant amount of reenactment footage. Though re-created scenes are a staple of true crime storytelling, the program uses several deliberate aesthetic choices to differentiate its reenactments. Rather than distracting from the program's public service, the reenactments incorporate stylistic flourishes in an attempt to attract an audience to participate in its collaborational objective. For instance, the program does not overtly label its reenactment sequences. In other true crime programs, such as *Deadly Women*, reenactments are prominently marked on screen as "Dramatization." Instead, *The Hunt* uses its own unique style to demarcate when and where these re-created scenes appear between interviews and other footage, including speed manipulation. This effect occurs throughout "Justice Denied," which presents the missing person case of Jacob Wetterling, who was abducted on October 22, 1989, in St. Joseph, Minnesota. The re-creation of Wetterling's abduction plays out in slow motion, with images of three boys riding bikes on a dark rural road as a masked man with a gun approaches them. The chronological manipulation of this depiction draws out the gravity of the situation, mimicking how it might have felt in the midst of this crime unfolding—like a moment in which time nearly stops. "Justice Denied" also uses time-lapse cinematography to represent the complicated passage of time as Jacob's mother Patty Wetterling deals with the aftermath of her son's abduction. Time-lapse cinematography depicts the actress playing Patty as she sits in a chair in her living room, remaining motionless while dozens of people approach her, talk to her, and interview her. As the mass of people slowly thins, the emptiness around her visually conveys the often-discussed aftermath of media attention in the weeks after a child is abducted in the United States. Walsh tells the viewer,

> In the beginning, there's this initial surge. The media's fascinated. People try to help you, strangers you never met try to help you in some way, police are really on top of the case. But then that reality sets in that, if your child is missing for a certain period of time, a couple weeks, sometimes a month, now your child drops from being the hottest case, the top of the news, to just another poster of a missing child.

This time-lapse reenactment uses conventions of fictional, dramatic storytelling to evoke the emotional intensity of the crime, in turn further engendering audience sympathy for this family's loss.

The Hunt's reenactments also manipulate color saturation, making some colors more vivid while desaturating others. In the episode "Trafficking in Death," the police are investigating the mass murder of eleven individuals who sought to immigrate to the United States illegally, facilitated by human trafficker "coyote" Guillermo Madrigal Ballesteros. One of the reenactments in this episode portrays the victims as they succumb to high temperatures and dehydration while locked in a train car, as the footage visually shifts. The images begin in muted red colors, suggesting the unbearable heat of the train car, and slowly fades to black and white, signifying the deaths of the eleven victims.

The Hunt's use of reenactments that visually manipulate the color and speed of the footage challenges Richard Kilborn's dichotomy that suggests that crime program reenactments can or should only function as "factually enlightening" or "dramatically entertaining."[12] The reenactments discussed here break from this schema in their attempt to innovate the genre in subtle ways. Despite the stylistic choices depicted in these reenactments, they nonetheless strive for authenticity rooted in the remaining fragments of information about a crime committed decades in the past. As the program's host, John Walsh forgoes the voiceover narration that frequently accompanies reenactments on true crime programs. He appears only briefly, breaking away from the current crime case study to interject a comment or an opinion about the case. Instead, the program frames the reenactments with commentary by firsthand accounts, when possible. For example, in "Justice Denied," as the reenactment of Jacob Wetterling's abduction unfolds on

FIGURE 23.2.
The Hunt uses stylistic conventions of dramatic storytelling to evoke emotional
intensity.

screen, the only sound heard is one of the original 911 calls. Accompanied by the
on-screen notation, "911 Recording," the viewer hears Trevor, Jacob Wetterling's
brother who was present at the time of the abduction, detail the perpetrator's appearance. This slow-motion reenactment, combined with Trevor's description of
the man who abducted his brother, creates a powerful moment in which the program most reflects John Grierson's infamous description of documentary as "the
creative treatment of actuality."[13]

As one of the objectives of *The Hunt* is to seek the audience's collaboration in
solving these open cases, we need to contemplate how, or if, the public service they
attempt to provide can be measured. The two episodes of *The Hunt* discussed here
present two possible outcomes that occurred in the wake of their airdates. Despite
the program's intervention, the families affected by the murders in "Trafficking in
Death" continue to wait for Guillermo Madrigal Ballesteros's capture. However,
other episodes have demonstrated that the public can be served by crowdsourced,
amateur detective work. Following the airing of "Justice Denied," the FBI decided
to reopen Jacob Wetterling's abduction case.[14] This episode prominently features
Joy Baker, a freelance writer and blogger, who in 2010 began reinvestigating the
Wetterling case. In a long segment, Baker traces a number of crimes that occurred
in neighboring towns in the years before Wetterling's abduction, uncovering several related cases that the police had never connected. Using DNA from the case
of Jared Scheierl, a young man who had been kidnapped and sexually assaulted in
a nearby town several months before Wetterling's abduction, authorities arrested
Danny Heinrich, who later confessed to Wetterling's abduction and murder, and
led police to his body. While Heinrich will not be tried for this crime per a plea
deal, he is now serving a twenty-four-year sentence for possession of child pornography. However, the credit here cannot entirely be bestowed upon *The Hunt*.
While "Justice Denied" prompted the FBI to reopen the case, it was partially Baker's research and the reinvestigation of Scheierl's assault, not tips or information
received from viewers, that led to the resolution of Wetterling's abduction case.

The Hunt frames its overall purpose as providing a public service when the police and the FBI have not been able to solve certain crimes. Although it has demonstrated its value in this regard, some questions remain, particularly in the complex intersection of true crime storytelling that seeks to pursue justice and entertain audiences simultaneously. Does the series need to solve crimes as a service to the public, or does it merely need to entertain viewers? Should its delivery of cautionary tales of an unsafe world be considered part of its public service to viewers, or is this perhaps a disservice by stoking fears and distrust? Although no television program must necessarily accomplish anything other than drawing an audience and advertisers, the ongoing fascination with true crime programming and the proliferation of these programs across television networks, cable channels, and streaming services suggests that questioning the responsibilities, expectations, and methods of these programs remains an important endeavor.

FURTHER READING

Duvall, Spring-Serenity, and Leigh Moscowitz. *Snatched: Child Abductions in U.S. News Media.* New York: Peter Lang, 2016.
Jermyn, Deborah. *Crime Watching: Investigating Real Crime TV.* London: I. B. Tauris, 2007.
Standiford, Les, with Joe Matthews. *Bringing Adam Home: The Abduction that Changed America.* New York: HarperCollins, 2011.

FURTHER LISTENING

In the Dark. APM Reports podcast season 1 featuring the Jacob Wetterling case. 2016.

NOTES

1. Richard Kilborn, *Staging the Real: Factual TV Programming in the Age of* Big Brother (Manchester, UK: Manchester University Press, 2003), 68.
2. Gray Cavender, "In Search of Community on Reality TV: *America's Most Wanted* and *Survivor,*" in *Understanding Reality Television,* ed. Su Holmes and Deborah Jermyn (New York: Routledge, 2004), 159.
3. Paddy Scannell, "Public Service Broadcasting: The History of a Concept," in *Television: Critical Concepts in Media and Cultural Studies,* ed. Toby Miller, vol. 4 (London: Routledge, 2003), 214.
4. Michele Hilmes, "Who We Are, Who We Are Not: Battle of the Global Paradigms," in *Planet TV: A Global Television Reader,* ed. Lisa Parks and Shanti Kumar (New York: New York University Press, 2003), 56, 63.
5. Peter Lunt, "Television, Public Participation, and Public Service: From Value Consensus to the Politics of Identity," *Annals of the American Academy of Political and Social Science* 625 (September 2009): 131.
6. Ibid., 132.

7. Jack Breslin, *America's Most Wanted: How Television Catches Crooks* (New York: HarperCollins, 1990), 139; Kevin Glynn, *Tabloid Culture: Trash Taste, Popular Power, and the Transformation of American Television* (Durham, NC: Duke University Press, 2000), 5.

8. David Bauder, "John Walsh Back on TV Hunting Fugitives in New CNN Show," *Canadian Press*, November 7, 2014.

9. Michael Linder, quoted in Breslin, *America's Most Wanted*, 83.

10. Brian Lowry, "TV Review: *The Hunt with John Walsh*," *Variety*, July 11, 2014.

11. Bauder, "John Walsh Back."

12. Kilborn, *Staging the Real*, 72.

13. Ibid.

14. Esme Murphy, "'It Got Frustrating': Blogger, Survivor Pushed Investigators to Re-examine Wetterling Case," *CBS Minnesota*, September 13, 2016.

24

Parks and Recreation
The Cultural Forum

HEATHER HENDERSHOT

Abstract: Throughout its history as a mass medium, network television strove for wide appeal, while also occasionally courting controversy. In this look at the recent sitcom *Parks and Recreation*, Heather Hendershot considers how television might still function as a site for negotiating controversial topics and modeling civic engagement, even in an era of niche programming when there seems to be less and less shared culture.

In their landmark 1983 essay "Television as a Cultural Forum," Horace Newcomb and Paul M. Hirsch argue that television provides a space to express collective cultural concerns. To put it simply, TV's stories gravitate to issues in which we are all interested. This "we" might at first sound a bit fishy to someone reading the essay today. After all, in a fragmented, post-network environment, most TV targets rather specific, narrow interests: cooking, travel, pets, home improvement, classic films, and so on. But in the pre-cable days, programs did generally seek out large groups of viewers, not atomized constituencies. The American audience had a sense of collectivity insofar as "we" all saw the same shows. Whether or not you liked the 1977 miniseries *Roots*, it was a major phenomenon, and you might watch it just to be in the loop. And if the president made a speech, it was on all three channels; you could only escape it if you turned off the tube. Watching TV by no means guaranteed that we were better citizens, but it did make us feel like we were, to some extent, all on the same page, even if we disagreed about what belonged on that page or what the page meant.

Newcomb and Hirsch explain that a single program might be of interest to viewers holding a wide range of political perspectives. Feminists watching *Charlie's Angels* upon its initial 1970s release might have disparaged the show's display of jiggle and its silly sexual banter, while more conservative viewers might have reacted negatively to exactly the same factors, albeit for different reasons. Rather than imperiously declaring the program "really" to be liberal, conservative, or simply exploitative, the authors find it more interesting to observe that different viewers made their own meanings of a text that tapped into an issue of general interest—namely, the rise of the working woman.

In discussing an episode of 1950s sitcom *Father Knows Best* that seems to support the notion that women should work in traditionally male professions (daughter Betty wants to be an engineer), only to backtrack with a disappointing heteronormative conclusion (Betty decides to date an engineer instead), Newcomb and Hirsch wonder to what extent the cursory ending actually cancels out the preceding twenty-five minutes. (In fact, years later the author of the script for that episode, Roz Rogers, said that the ending, which had been tacked on in order to reach a quick resolution, "did not ring true" for him.[1]) Certainly, individual viewers will make what they will of the episode's conservative conclusion. The truly interesting thing, then, is not whether the show is actually pro- or anti-feminist, but, rather, the fact that a putatively "innocuous" show even debates the issue of gender roles.

Newcomb and Hirsch's essay still contains much of value for contemporary readers, especially for the historically minded. Particularly interesting is the authors' turn to discussing activists: "In forming special interest groups, or in using such groups to speak about television, citizens actually enter the [cultural] forum. Television shoves them toward action, toward expression of ideas and values."[2] The very idea of reformers seeking to improve television is one of the most dated aspects of the essay, and it is precisely this datedness that is fascinating. A wide range of citizen-reformers—African Americans, gays and lesbians, anti-abortion advocates, pro-choice advocates, fundamentalist Christians—sought to influence network programming throughout the 1960s, 1970s, and 1980s.[3] While one should not romanticize or overvalue such activism—it was hardly "typical" viewer behavior—it is important to remind ourselves, in this age of obsessive presentism and futurism, that very different approaches to interacting with media existed in the past, and that in the days of only three networks it was easy to spot controversy and to feel personally invested in the outcome. Was your favorite show in danger of cancellation because of pressure group activism? Was that show really immoral, racist, sexist, homophobic, or whatever was being claimed by irate protestors?

Today, with hundreds of channels on offer, it is difficult for a program to generate high-profile controversy, and viewers may find that politically challenging series are easy to ignore.[4] Previously, as Newcomb put it in an interview in 2007, TV made you "confront your beliefs." Such confrontation was central to the cultural forum model and, thus, specific to the network era; in a niche-viewing environment, however, viewers tend to gravitate to content that matches their preexisting interests. Narrowly targeted niche TV thus provides "self-confirmation," leaving little room for the old cultural forum ideal of ideas in conflict.[5]

What place, then, might programs with potentially "controversial" political aspirations have in today's televisual environment? Can programs hope to address—or even confront, challenge, or offend—a "mass" rather than a "niche" audience, or does our narrowcasting environment ensure that politically ambitious programs preach to the choir? If the old cultural forum idea truly fizzled out with the decline of the dominance of the Big Three networks, would any series dare to speak to a heterogeneous audience? There is at least one program that strives to do exactly this: NBC's *Parks and Recreation*. Celebrating the virtues of local government and staking a claim for the value of civic engagement and the possibility of collaboration—or at least peaceful coexistence—between different political camps, *Parks and Recreation* offers a liberal pluralist response to the fragmented post–cultural forum environment.

Appearing at a moment of right-wing resurgence amid the Obama presidency—with Tea Partiers calling for the elimination of social welfare programs, extolling the virtues of gun ownership, and opposing gay marriage—*Parks and Recreation* offers a retort to the Right by insisting that government is a positive force that provides necessary, basic services. In advancing its argument, the show makes a few interesting maneuvers. First, it avoids direct confrontation with highly polarizing issues like abortion and focuses instead on municipal rather than state or federal government issues. Second, it insists that local government should be politically neutral; providing services does not count as "liberalism," per se, the show insists. Third, through its characters of varying political stripes, the program conveys the basic goodness of public servants. Fourth, it celebrates the virtues of the public sphere, a utopian space where even irrational debate can produce social harmony, or at least the kinds of *truces* that enable society to function. Two episodes in particular, "Pawnee Zoo" and "Time Capsule," illustrate how *Parks and Recreation* gently conveys a liberal perspective without ever naming it as such.

Before turning to these episodes, it will be helpful to discuss the two characters at the political heart of the program, Leslie Knope and Ron Swanson. Leslie, the deputy director of the Parks and Recreation Department in Pawnee, Indiana, does not overtly identify herself as a liberal, claiming that Pawnee's public servants are expected to be neutral (a local garbage collector, she notes, was suspended for wearing an anticancer Livestrong bracelet). Her office is decorated with photos of powerful women, from left, right, and center—Bella Abzug, Madeleine Albright, Condoleezza Rice, Hillary Clinton, and Nancy Pelosi.

Leslie's love for her job and bottomless optimism are virtually unmatched on TV; only Sponge-Bob SquarePants out-enthuses Leslie Knope. Leslie's work ethic, I would argue, is a crucial "conservative" aspect of her character; liberals don't devalue hard work, but the celebration of individual achievement and meritocratic rewards is certainly a cornerstone of contemporary conservative values. Today's televisual landscape is littered with cynical characters who hate their jobs, with housewives (real, desperate, or otherwise) lacking career objectives, and with drunken, fornicating twenty-somethings with no visible source of income. In Leslie, by contrast, we find a character who earnestly embraces a can-do work ethic and keeps her sex life relatively private. So, on the one hand, Leslie resonates with certain conservative values, and *Parks and Recreation* as a whole is distinctive for its emphasis on the civic virtue of hard work. On the other hand, Leslie's cheerful understanding of government as a public good can only be construed as liberal in the current political climate. Conservatives will find in Leslie someone who sees hard work as the cornerstone of happiness, yet who works for "the enemy," the government.

While it would be reductive to construe *Parks and Recreation* only as a response to the current surge in right-wing anti-government sentiment, this clearly must be understood as one key aspect of the program, and Ron Swanson, Leslie's boss, is the linchpin of that response. Director of Pawnee's Parks and Recreation Department, Ron works for the government but is explicitly anti-government. In fact, he favors privatizing parks and having corporations run them, citing Chuck E. Cheese's as a business model. His drive for privatization is portrayed as flawed, yet the series works hard to keep the character likeable; Ron is not vilified for his beliefs. Indeed, while Ron is consistently "masculine" (sexy, if you will), he is never misogynist; drawn to powerful women, he goes to "an inordinate number of WNBA games." He and Leslie disagree about many things, but he is more often her ally than her foil.

Ron can be understood as a Tea Partier—though he is never named as such—insofar as he echoes and satirizes many of their positions ("child labor laws are ruining this country"), but one must also bear in mind that the Tea Party is a disjointed movement, not a centralized organization with a strictly coherent platform. Movement participants range from libertarians on one end to evangelical Christians on the other. While these two contingents likely agree about taxation and gun control, they may strongly disagree about abortion and gay marriage. *Parks and Recreation* pulls its punches, clearly, by establishing Ron as a libertarian, not a social/religious conservative, and by allowing him to attack taxation and celebrate gun-ownership without ever mentioning issues such as reproductive rights. However, though such issues remain unspoken, it is hard to imagine Ron meddling in the personal decisions of others, as he is strictly concerned with individual liberties. Pawnee is the fourth most obese city in America, but for the local government to encourage good health, he contends, would be wrong: "The whole point of this country is if you want to eat garbage, balloon up to six hundred pounds and die of a heart attack at forty-three, you can. You are free to do so. To me, that's beautiful."

Thus, Ron and Leslie offer something to both conservative and liberal viewers, even if the show ultimately lampoons the conservative-libertarian perspective and privileges a liberal one. It is important to stress that what we find here is not the "balanced" approach that was typical of the network era, when a conservative character would be countered by the presence of a liberal character. Nor do we find the common post-network "something for everyone" approach in which shows assemble a heterogeneous crew of characters to attempt to appeal to a wide range of viewers. One reason that programs such as *Heroes* and *Lost* use highly diverse ensemble casts is to lure a post-network version of the "mass" audience. As *Heroes* writer Jesse Alexander puts it, "if you don't like the cheerleader, you'll like someone else."[6] The hope is that a diverse cast will appeal to numerous demographics, with one "mass" show theoretically providing "niche"-like self-confirmation. *Parks and Recreation*, by contrast, does not simply use Leslie to appeal to the Left and Ron to appeal to the Right. Rather, it shows how opposing factions can communicate and collaborate.

If Ron and Leslie embody the program's dialectical political aspirations, season 2's "Pawnee Zoo" is perhaps the episode that most specifically encapsulates the show's political perspective. The episode opens with Leslie choreographing a "cute" event to create publicity for the zoo: she officiates at the wedding of two penguins, Tux and Flipper. The birds consummate their marriage *immediately* upon being pronounced "husband and wife," and one of the children in the crowd of onlookers asks the zookeeper if they are making a baby. He responds that, no, these are two *male* penguins, so they really should have been pronounced "husband and husband." Having accidentally performed Pawnee's first gay marriage, Leslie is celebrated by the local gay community, while the local conservative evangelicals from the Society for Family Stability Foundation attack her, explaining that "when gay people get married, it ruins it for the rest of us." Leslie had not intended to do anything controversial, having assumed that the penguins were male and female, and she tries to decline the celebration held for her at a gay bar, but she finds herself swept away by the drinking and dancing. Meanwhile, the pro-family activists demand that she both annul the penguin marriage and resign from her job. Leslie stands up for herself on the local talk show, *Pawnee Today*, and the episode ends with Leslie delivering Flipper and Tux to a zoo in Iowa, where gay marriage is legal.

"Pawnee Zoo" is clearly a product of the post-network era insofar as the program raises a "controversial issue" without neatly resolving it. When overtly addressing controversial issues, network era programs tended to insist that each side (there were generally only *two* sides) had to "learn a valuable lesson" from the other. Leslie and the anti-gay marriage activists don't exchange ideas in order to become better people, as per the formula of earlier shows. Notably, though, Leslie does learn a lesson from Flipper and Tux that she can apply to her own life: her would-be lover Mark is not her "gay penguin" (penguins mate for life), but maybe Mark is destined to be her friend Ann's "gay penguin," so Leslie realizes she must relax about her friends dating each other. It's all a bit silly—this is a comedy after all—but it's also quite smart. Rather than jumping up on a soapbox and speechifying in favor of gay marriage, Leslie simply respects the right of two penguins to be in love, and she extends this respect to others. This sort of character improvement evokes the old days of network TV, reminding us that *Parks and Recreation* may not actually reach a huge mass audience, but it *is* on NBC, where advertising stakes are higher than they would be elsewhere and where even a rather unusual show like *Parks and Recreation* is unlikely to be too "edgy."

Notably, the protest that might have arisen in the network era is worked into "Pawnee Zoo" itself, with the Society for Family Stability Foundation's humorless spokesperson Marcia Langman standing in for the angry activist groups that used to come out of the woodwork when a program dared to address gay issues. "Pawnee Zoo" doesn't expect the Moral Majority to rise from the grave to attack it; but by representing right-wing protest within its fictional world, it conveys the notion that if the Christian Right would actually *notice* this gutsy show, they might reasonably be provoked.

Sadly, although both the Gay and Lesbian Alliance Against Defamation and TV critics praised "Pawnee Zoo," almost no one else noticed the Flipper and Tux affair. In fact, the ratings for *Parks and Recreation* have been consistently poor. "Pawnee Zoo" would seem to raise issues of wide interest—the old cultural forum idea—and years ago the Religious Right would have jumped on it, just as they jumped on *Soap*'s gay character in 1977 and, later, on the lesbian kiss on *Roseanne* in 1994. But why attack "Pawnee Zoo," an episode that appears to have made so little impact? We end up with the old "if a tree falls in the woods . . ." koan: if a program raises important issues, but no one is watching, does it matter? Provisionally, I would argue that in a multichannel and multiplatform age of widely dispersed content, programs often find their audiences gradually over time. Given that many people now watch programs whenever and wherever they want, ratings are simply no longer a very useful gauge (if they ever truly were) for determining the impact of a program. Viewers looking

FIGURE 24.1. Leslie visits the penguins at the zoo, where anti-gay activists have proclaimed, "It's Flipper and Eve, not Flipper and Steve!"

for smart, funny TV will make their way to *Parks and Recreation* eventually—if not soon enough to guarantee the show a long life on NBC. Setting aside such speculation, it is worth marveling at the episode's efforts to humorously portray the collision of liberals and conservatives around the gay marriage issue, and to do so without bitterness. Though siding with gay rights, the program does not hate "the other side." Rather, it contends that some differences are probably irreconcilable; we simply have to find a way to get along, even if we cannot change each other's minds.

"Time Capsule" is a more didactic episode. Leslie is gathering items for a time capsule representing the Pawnee of 2011, and a local citizen suggests that she include a copy of Stephanie Meyer's *Twilight*. Leslie counters that *Twilight* is not really about Pawnee, but the insistent citizen will not give up. To resolve the question of what belongs in the capsule, Leslie calls a public forum—or, as Ron describes it, a "crackpot convention"—to debate the issue. In the process, the episode presents a comic version of the public sphere as conceptualized by social theorist Jürgen Habermas, who proposed that rational discussion and debate enables democracy to function. Critics of the Habermasian ideal have noted its limits: members of "the public" who speak from a position of privilege are more likely to be heard than those who speak from a disempowered position. In other words, the public sphere should be a level playing field, but it rarely is.[7]

In the would-be utopia of Pawnee, though, everyone's voice is heard. Indeed, Leslie considers listening to her constituents' complaints to be a highlight of her job. Predictably enough, sourpuss Marcia Langman reappears and complains that *Twilight* is anti-Christian and contains "strong sexual overtones" and a "tremendous amount of quivering." A ticked-off member of the National Civil Liberties Association, conversely, complains about the book's "overt Christian themes." Leslie's first solution to the time capsule crisis—acquiesce to everyone's demands and create multiple capsules to hold the Bible, urns containing ashes of beloved pets, the Bill of Rights, baseball cards, and *Crazy from the Heat* (the David Lee Roth story)—is not practical. A colleague tells Leslie that he finds the whole discussion "kind of impressive. I've been to a lot of towns, and usually people don't care about anything. I mean, don't get me wrong, these people are weirdoes, but they're weirdoes who care." This inspires Leslie to put only one item in the time capsule, a video recording of the public forum. In a speech addressed to those opening the capsule in the future, Leslie explains that "This is truly what life was like. A lot of people, with a lot of opinions, arguing passionately for what they believed in." She thus acknowledges that it is *conversation* (rational or not, loud or soft) that keeps democracy alive. Ultimately, the episode offers a humorous civics lesson in what a public sphere could look like.[8]

The televisual cultural forum that Newcomb and Hirsch identified so long ago may not exist today, but *Parks and Recreation* suggests that we *should* respond to the issues it raises. In effect, the show models how controversy and debate can function in a democracy. The message is a decidedly centrist one: extremes of both left and right can coexist, but only a moderate approach can resolve our problems. While one might argue that *Parks and Recreation* lessens its political efficacy by advocating "middle of the road" solutions, it is precisely its insistence upon keeping its politics understated, coupled with its insistence upon the humorousness of extremism (and the humorlessness of extremists), that makes *Parks and Recreation* work particularly well as a retort to the rising tide of right-wing, anti-government sentiment. The lesson offered, as Leslie might declare with naive optimism, is that liberals and conservatives can work together within local government—perhaps even sharing a plate of waffles—in order to make the world a better place.

Thirty years ago, Newcomb and Hirsch sought to transcend conventional left-right debates over TV, where one side argued that the medium was one of indoctrination into hegemonic beliefs, and the other argued that TV undercut traditional values. They shifted the discussion to claim that TV's emphasis was on "process rather than product, on discussion rather than indoctrination, on contradiction and confusion rather than coherence."[9] This was the essence of their conception of television as a cultural forum. And this is the essence of *Parks and Recreation*'s vision of a healthy democratic society.

FURTHER READING

Cowan, Geoffrey. *See No Evil: The Backstage Battle over Sex and Violence in Television.* New York: Touchstone, 1980.

Gitlin, Todd. "Prime Time Ideology: The Hegemonic Process in Television Entertainment." In *Television: The Critical View*, edited by Horace Newcomb. 6th ed. New York: Oxford University Press, 2000.

Levine, Elana. *Wallowing in Sex: The New Sexual Culture of 1970s American Television.* Durham, NC: Duke University Press, 2006.

NOTES

1. Rogers cited in Nina C. Leibman, *Living Room Lectures: The Fifties Family in Film and Television* (Austin: University of Texas Press, 1995), 49.

2. Horace Newcomb and Paul M. Hirsch, "TV as a Cultural Forum," in *Television: The Critical View*, ed. Horace Newcomb, 6th ed. (New York: Oxford University Press, 2000), 570.

3. Kathryn C. Montgomery, *Target: Prime Time: Advocacy Groups and the Struggle over Entertainment Television* (New York: Oxford University Press, 1990).

4. Heather Hendershot, "'You Know How It Is with Nuns': Religion and Television's Sacred/Secular Fetuses," in *Small Screen, Big Picture: Television and Lived Religion*, ed. Diane Winston (Baylor, TX: Baylor University Press, 2009). The Parents Television Council (PTC) and the Gay and Lesbian Alliance against Defamation (GLAAD) are the only high-profile advocacy groups currently stoking audience protest. PTC encourages citizens to submit complaints about explicit sexual material to the FCC, while GLAAD protests negative images of gays, but also strives for a noncensorious image by honoring programs that offer positive gay/lesbian stories and characters.

5. "Horace Newcomb in Conversation with Tara McPherson," *e-media studies* 1, no. 1 (2007), http://journals.dartmouth.edu.

6. Jesse Alexander, "Cult Media" panel, Futures of Entertainment 2, MIT conference, November 16–17, 2007.

7. Craig Calhoun, ed., *Habermas and the Public Sphere* (Cambridge, MA: MIT Press, 1993).

8. One might argue that this episode problematically implies that the civically engaged are kooks who must be kept in line by officials. I read the community meeting more as a send-up of how difficult it is for opinionated people to get things done. Anyone who has ever attended a contentious faculty meeting should be able to able to identify with Leslie's frustration. Further, season 4's campaign manager, Jennifer Barkley, drives home a key theme: passionate people may be nutty, but it is the dispassionate we should most fear when it comes to politics. Leslie runs for office because she believes in something; for Barkley, politics is just a job.

9. Newcomb and Hirsch, "TV as a Cultural Forum," 564.

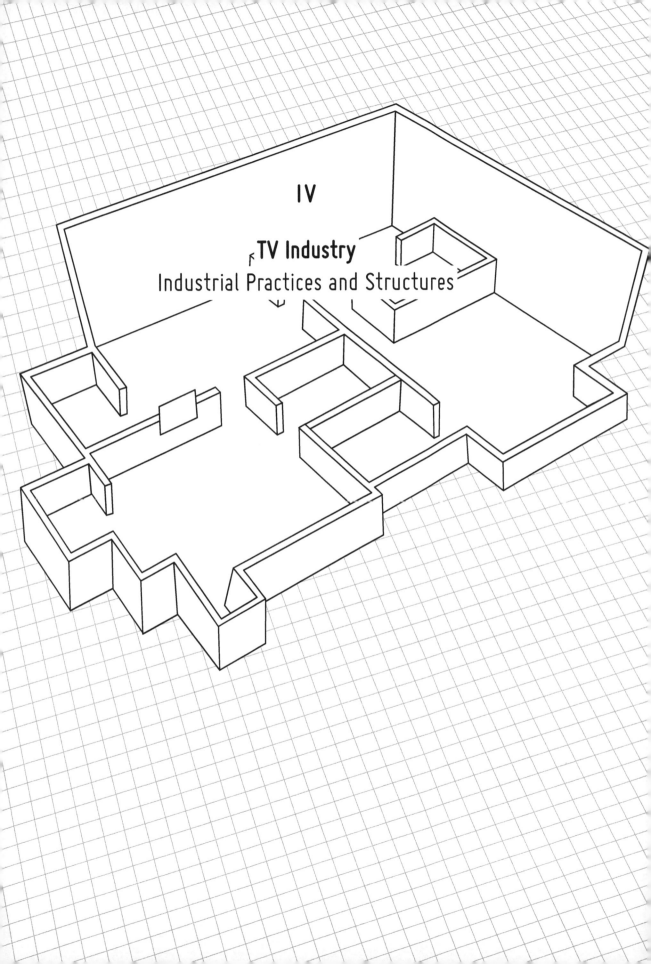

IV

TV Industry

Industrial Practices and Structures

25

The Ernie Kovacs Show
Historicizing Comedy

ETHAN THOMPSON

Abstract: Ernie Kovacs was a one-of-a-kind television comedian who enjoys cult status today, though he died at the height of his popularity in the early 1960s. In this essay, Ethan Thompson models how to historicize television, drawing upon articles in the press, as well as archival production materials and fan letters, to make sense of how Kovacs made comedy and how viewers made sense of him.

A single television comedy can elicit significantly different reactions from audiences, ranging from uncontrollable guffaws to puzzled silence, disdain, and even physical discomfort. Depending on who's watching, the same comic narrative, sketch, or monologue may be a brilliant success or a dismal failure. When we watch comedy made decades ago, this "hit or miss" tendency gets amplified. Maybe this is why the laugh track is so maligned: No one wants to be told when they should laugh. But how do we move beyond our own personal reactions to better hear, and understand, the laughter of audiences in the past?

Take the work of Ernie Kovacs, a cult figure in the history of comedy who has also been heralded as TV's original "video artist." From the early 1950s up to his sudden death in 1962, Kovacs appeared in local and national programs, as guest host and as host of his own shows, in regular series and in specials, on live and taped programs, and as a panelist on game shows. Though Kovacs never found a long-term home on a particular network (or even format), he was widely known and written about in his day. Kovacs was famous not just for being funny but also for making comedy that looked unlike anything else on TV. As Susan Murray has argued, early television "vaudeo" comedians like Milton Berle and Jack Benny brought vaudeville-style theatrical performance to television.[1] But Kovacs built elaborate sets and toyed with technology to produce comedy that could only be made with—and seen on—television, treating it as a distinctive artistic medium and drawing attention to its form. Critics have described how Kovacs used the same sort of "defamiliarizing" strategies in his TV shows that video artists would be lauded for decades later.[2] But when we watch clips of Kovacs today, the techniques of his comedy are not necessarily self-evident—it isn't always clear what is supposed to be funny, or why. Should we be laughing? Why were audiences in the 1950s or 1960s?

This essay examines Kovacs's unique comic aesthetic historically, recognizing his individual genius and comic innovations yet showing how his work emerged within the production logic of the era's television industry. In order to do this, we can start with an example from one of his TV "texts," then look outside that text to "historicize" it, placing it in historical context. Our example is a segment from a special that aired on ABC in 1962 and was included in a *Best of Ernie Kovacs* series broadcast on U.S. public television in 1977, and later released on VHS and DVD. As of this writing, you can find the segment on YouTube and the academic video source CriticalCommons.org.[3]

Kovacs begins the segment in front of a group of television monitors, smoking his trademark cigar and making this assessment of the television industry: "There's a standard formula for success in the entertainment medium, and that is, beat it to death, if it succeeds." He then proposes changes to be made to the "New Western" to regain the attention of audiences bored by the genre's saturation of the airwaves. After audiences became used to the climactic shoot-out, Kovacs shows more interesting camera angles to shoot such duels. He claims that a hat company even sponsored a shot of a camera filming through a hole in a hat, above which "Yucca Hats" is written. "The only thing we hadn't seen," says Kovacs, "was a gunfight from the perspective of the bullet." Then Kovacs shows exactly what that would look like: A man fires a pistol and a bullet slowly hovers toward an actor, then passes through his body, leaving a video "hole" through which we see the opposing gunfighter celebrate.

The "New Western" isn't all camera angles and trick photography though. Kovacs introduces a new show titled "Rancid the Devil Horse," where the evil gunfighter doesn't ride a horse but *is* a horse, and we see someone in a cheap horse costume with a toy pistol tied to its hoof. The segment also produces comedy through parody, hybridizing the western with other cultural texts. In a reference to Rod Serling, writer-producer of *The Twilight Zone*, Kovacs says that a western is being produced "in the Serling-manner" as a cowboy walks through a surreal landscape filled with smoke as a Theremin (an early electronic instrument) plays eerily. Trees are filled with cattle skulls, and women with vampire teeth and grotesque fingernails taunt him. The cowboy fires his pistol, but a bouquet of flowers comes out the barrel and then turns into a bunch of bananas. Next Kovacs

FIGURE 25.1.
In contrast to sophisticated camera angles and special effects, the segment also features silly gags such as this horse with a pistol tied to its "hoof."

borrows from B-movie science fiction: A cowboy rushes into a ranch house to warn that a spaceship has landed nearby, "and there's a mighty big cowboy got out of it." Sure enough, a boot crushes a model town underfoot, and the gigantic eye of "The Colossal Cowboy" peers inside the house.

The combination of technically advanced video techniques such as the chroma-keying Kovacs used to create the bullet hole and the less sophisticated gags such as the horse costume and the boot crushing the model town characterizes the comic strategies of the segment. But how typical is this combination in Kovacs's comedy across the various programs, formats, and years? Critics and fans rave about Kovacs as a unique artist and comedian, but some of these jokes look rather cheesy. What might audiences have thought about the "New Western"—and found funny—back when it first aired?

Whether we start with a random clip found on YouTube, an episode streamed online, or a program viewed at a media archive such as the Paley Center in New York or the Peabody Collection at the University of Georgia, an important step in historicizing television is to determine how representative a particular example is. The "Best of" packages from which this segment came were assembled by taking sketches and comic bits out of their original programs and rearranging them into thematic thirty-minute episodes, disproportionately culling from his later specials. As of this writing in 2019, searching YouTube for "Ernie Kovacs" yields several volumes of the "Best of" programs, an A&E Biography, lots of individual short sketches, an episode of *What's My Line?* featuring Kovacs and wife Edie Adams, a couple of his Dutchmaster cigar ads, and two videos that purport to be full episodes of *The Ernie Kovacs Show*. One of these last two is dated September

3, 1956, and says it is from NBC, and the other says it is from ABC in 1962.[4] All of these are worthy of our attention, but we might watch to get a sense of whether the juxtaposition of video effects and slapstick gags in the "New Western" is representative of Kovacs's work—watching reveals that they are typical, suggesting that Kovacs was as much a parody auteur and prop comic as he was a video artist.

We then turn to another type of historical source: popular press articles contemporaneous to Kovacs's programs, written for "popular" audiences, usually in advertising-supported newspapers and magazines.[5] Precisely because they lack the historical perspective of scholarly research or biographies written years later, popular press stories help us understand how a comedian was made sense of at the time. What was suggested to be different about him from other comedians? What might readers learn about Kovacs that would turn them into viewers, which was the goal of such promotion?

One example is a *Newsweek* article about Kovacs appearing opposite Milton Berle and Bishop Fulton J. Sheen on *Uncle Ernie* in 1953. Though that program doesn't show up on YouTube or anywhere else to watch, the article notes "Kovacs at night is very much like Kovacs in the morning" and says the main difference is that his primetime show had an orchestra "with cymbalon and Theremin."[6] This reviewer has done the work of watching a lot of Kovacs, noting, "As before, the most successful part of the show is his spoofing of TV programs and commercials," before ending with, "Kovacs came up with a lot of laughs for very little money last week." When we read more reviews, we begin to see that although his video manipulations may be what he is known for now, during his career he received as much attention for his parodies of television. *Time* in 1957, for instance, called Kovacs "the one television comedian who finds most of his tee-hee in TV itself," though it also praised how he used "cameras, sets, sound effects to make rowdy electronic fun."[7] *Time* also confirms that the hodge-podge of programs available on YouTube reflects the variety of programs on which Kovacs appeared: "His cultivated madness . . . has been delighting and annoying audiences only irregularly and at odd hours since he first leered onscreen seven years ago. Neither Kovacs nor his employer, NBC, seems able to explain why there is still no niche for his comparatively languid, low-pressure talent in a business that constantly turns lesser comics into living-room idols."[8] A *Saturday Evening Post* article asked him why he hadn't had a more regular network gig: "I was offered a couple of regular shows, but in each case the below-the-line budget—that's the part which includes the sets—was so small I knew that I couldn't build the things I wanted to build."[9]

Other articles include insights into production limitations, some focus on his family life, and some give Kovacs a chance to show off his comedy theories. Kovacs made the cover of *Life* in April 1957, and inside he explained some of his

FIGURE 25.2.
A *Life* cover story in 1957 featured Kovacs explaining some of his "electronic tricks."

"electronic tricks," such as superimposing shots in order to peer through costar Barbra Loden's head, and making himself and singer Tony Bennett disappear from the waist up. Through the use of multiple panels, he also explained how to appropriately stage a gag in which a housewife shoots a TV pitchman, warning against "too much camera" or "too much slapstick."[10]

These examples illustrate how the popular press didn't just promote Kovacs but also speculated on the reasons for his inability to keep a steady network gig, and even detailed the processes by which he produced his inventive visual comedy. The repeated attention to these topics suggests they were of interest to the general public, not just insider industry types or hardcore comedy fans. They also evidence a curiosity on the part of the audience with the technology of video and its manipulation. Still, they present a public-facing version of how Kovacs produced his comedy. If he's been dead well over fifty years, how can we find out more about how he made his comedy? What did he think about what he was doing and how he did it?

That's where another kind of primary source comes in: documents housed in archives donated for preservation and study. An archive is a treasure trove for the media historian who wants to research where TV came from, as it may contain production notes, scripts, and all sorts of business and personal correspondence.[11] However, working with archives requires some legwork, as their materials are rarely accessible online, and we also need to set some reasonable expectations about what we hope to find there.[12] Historiography—the work of researching and "writing history"—is not about looking things up but about reconstructing the past by discovering traces of evidence, making connections and inferences, and then drawing conclusions. In this way, historiography is an evidence-based creative process. In our case, we are unlikely to find a single document in which Kovacs expounds upon his reasons for combining high-tech video tricks and low-tech gags in the "New Western." We need to cast a wide net and hope that through spending a significant number of hours looking through boxes and boxes of documents, we will find a few pieces of evidence that shed light on his approach to television comedy.

The Ernie Kovacs Papers are housed at the University of California at Los Angeles and consist of seventy-one boxes and thirty-three oversize boxes.[13] This definitely qualifies as a treasure trove, and just like YouTube, we can easily get lost in the archive, digging ourselves further and further down a rabbit hole. It helps to refine our research questions to guide our search through boxes of materials, since we are no longer just browsing an index. Kovacs's early shows were broadcast live with very low budgets, but his later specials were sponsored by Dutchmaster Cigars, providing more time, more money, and better tools to produce them. A reasonable question might be, why did Kovacs continue to combine both high-tech video effects and low-tech prop-based gags in his comedy, even as video technology increased in availability and he had more resources to spend on them? Why did he continue to have low-budget gags like "Rancid the Devil Horse"? How conscious was Kovacs of his own techniques for engaging his audience? What did he think he was up to with his electronic tricks and slapstick gags? How did he view his own content, and what guided how he put together his shows?

A few of the documents I found in the Kovacs papers can help answer these research questions. Because Kovacs was not just the star but also the producer of many of his programs, some correspondence with cast members and executives overtly discusses the commercial imperatives shaping his content. Kovacs describes strategies to attract and maintain the attention of viewers, mentioning strategies that will lend to "habitual viewing" as well as the need for added effort during "sweeps." In one memo, he writes that in the past, it proved less important to have well-developed scripts than a "family set-up" that viewers would want to tune into. Daytime slots, he says, needed a "generalized honest" address to the viewers: "both in presentation and in personal feeling. . . . In other words, a kind of happy family."[14]

In an outline for a new morning show, *Kovacs Unlimited*, he refers to the production of earlier live shows, saying that "the ostensible lack of a rigid format was the solution" for filling large segments of programming every day.[15] Kovacs outlines the daily segments, including the "Nevada Saga," presumably a western spoof, as well as "Ignorance Unlimited," a parody of panel shows. We can see, then, that parodic sketches or spoofs weren't freeform improvisations that simply materialized on the spot, or even secondary considerations. Rather, parody provided a reliable formula for producing comedy that could be flexed with improvisation as necessary to fill programming time. True to those who would later call him a video artist, this same memo proposes "experimental camera work using full facilities of electronic matting amplifier, prisms, etc." But the memo also calls for "at least in hypothesis, a baby elephant as a regular cast member weighed daily, etc." This combination of parody, experimental camerawork, and a hypothetical baby elephant highlights that Kovacs was, in this morning show especially, creating a show for a mixed audience of adults and children. "I don't think there is any question as to who govern the station selection at that hour," reasons Kovacs in the memo. "Any youngster would fore-go an 'all-news' program."[16]

These memos not only outline plans for a new Kovacs program in the early 1950s but also reinforce what we have seen and read about his work. He is describing his own comic aesthetic that we see repeated over the years: a structural mix of parody (lightly scripted, improvisational, and cheap) and electronic camerawork (meticulously planned and often expensive). The archival documents confirm that the "New Western" sketch from a primetime special exhibits the same comic aesthetic prescribed by Kovacs for a morning show ten years earlier, and this aesthetic was shaped by budget limitations as well as the logic of creating a daily show that would appeal to a mixed audience of adults and children.

In Kovacs's era before social media, viewers wrote their favorite performers letters. Because archival collections often contain fan mail, they can provide insights about viewing practices as well. We can read through such letters and try to draw conclusions about how (at least some) fans made sense of Kovacs's comedy. In his short-but-influential paean to Kovacs, archivist and author Robert Rosen wrote that Kovacs created a "dynamic interactive relationship with the home audience."[17] Letters from fans in the Kovacs papers provide evidence of interaction, not just because they exist, but because of what they say. Many comment upon what the writers believe to be unique about his work and suggest targets for future parodic sketches. One fan, Mrs. A. Maddaloni, sent Kovacs a prioritized list of what she believed to be the key contributions to his success. Sight gags, electronic effects, or anything that might have meant his "electronic tricks" is nowhere on the list. Instead, she praises the show as "informal," "unconventional," and "diversified." In terms of specific program content, she mentions his guest interviews and her belief that his treatment of advertisements is "not too frequent or aggressive." She also cites "skits," especially those in which Kovacs "pokes fun" at other programs. Her final reason for her fandom is that she believes the show ends too soon, and this leads viewers to "wait for the next installment like a comic strip."[18]

Another fan's letter from 1956 goes beyond suggesting targets for parody and seems to be performing parody itself. It praises Kovacs's stint as guest host on

NBC's *Tonight*, as well as his earlier work on daytime television. When his show was on in the daytime, she says she had trouble getting things done because the kids wouldn't leave the house. Now, however, Kovacs actually improves her ability to get her work done. "Seriously, since you are on 'Tonight' I get all my ironing done. With you to watch my friend, a starched shirt becomes a breeze, my iron floats on wings of laughter."[19] She mocks the language of advertising that suggests household drudgery could be so easily transformed or disguised. In repurposing this language, she applies parody, one of the comic strategies used by Kovacs himself, to address commercial culture. This last letter is a good reminder that it is not just the TV shows themselves but also the documents we look to for historical context that may require informed interpretation.

Although he would become best known posthumously for work featured in network specials produced on videotape, Kovacs's comic aesthetic was shaped by the logic of low-budget, live TV production, and remained consistent throughout his too-short career. By historicizing one example of his comedy, we get a better understanding of why much of his work looked and sounded the way it did. We also find evidence of what his viewers valued in that comedy. That is, we get a better sense of why they laughed—even if, as in the "New Western," there's no laugh track to hear them.

FURTHER READING

Horton, Andrew. *Ernie Kovacs and Early TV Comedy: Nothing in Moderation*. Austin: University of Texas Press, 2010.

Murray, Susan. *Hitch Your Antenna to the Stars: Early Television and Broadcast Stardom*. New York: Routledge, 2005.

Spigel, Lynn. *TV by Design: Modern Art and the Rise of Network Television*. Chicago: University of Chicago Press, 2008.

Thompson, Ethan. *Parody and Taste in Postwar American Television Culture*. New York: Routledge, 2011.

NOTES

1. Susan Murray, *Hitch Your Antenna to the Stars: Early Television and Broadcast Stardom* (New York: Routledge, 2005).

2. See Robert Rosen, "Ernie Kovacs: Video Artist," *Transmission: Theory and Practice for a New Television Aesthetics*, ed. Peter A'Gostino (New York: Tanam Press, 1985); and Bruce Ferguson, "The Importance of Being Ernie: Taking a Close Look (and Listen)," *Illuminating Video: An Essential Guide to Video Art*, ed. Doug Hall and Sally Jo Fifer (New York: Aperture, 1990).

3. "The Ernie Kovacs Show: New Western Segment," 1962, Critical Commons, www.critical commons.org.

4. "Ernie Kovacs Show" (NBC), September 3, 1956, YouTube, www.youtube.com; "The Ernie Kovacs Show" (ABC), 1962, YouTube, www.youtube.com.

5. These stand in contrast to the "industry press" (*Hollywood Reporter*, *Variety*) that covers entertainment for an industry audience.

6. "'Uncle Ernie' Kovacs," *Newsweek*, January 12, 1953, 70.

7. "Utility Expert," *Time*, January 28, 1957, 66.

8. Ibid.

9. Peter Martin, "I Call on Edie Adams and Ernie Kovacs," *Saturday Evening Post*, December 28, 1957.

10. "An Electronic Comic and His TV Tricks," *Life*, April 15, 1957, 167–79.

11. Few archives have materials available online for reasons mostly to do with the vast amount of materials that would need to be made available, and the deficit of institutional support (money and labor) to put them there.

12. Ernie Kovacs Papers, 1940–1962 (Collection 1105), Department of Special Collections, Charles E. Young Research Library, University of California, Los Angeles.

13. Finding aid: "Ernie Kovac Papers, 1940–1962," OAC: Online Archive of California, Collection 1105, https://oac.cdlib.org.

14. Ernie Kovacs, memo, April 29, 1953, box 55, folder 7, Ernie Kovacs Papers.

15. Ernie Kovacs, letter to Dr. Frank Stanton, CBS, October 19, 1953, box 63, folder 16, Ernie Kovacs Papers.

16. Ernie Kovacs, letter to Lawrence, Hough, et al., October 19, 1953, box 63, folder 16, Ernie Kovacs Papers.

17. Rosen, "Ernie Kovacs," 144.

18. Mrs. A. Maddaloni, letter to Ernie Kovacs, April 24, 1954, box 58, folder 4, Ernie Kovacs Papers.

19. Unknown letter writer to Ernie Kovacs, October 16, 1956, box 61, folder 5, Ernie Kovacs Papers.

26

Gilmore Girls: A Year in the Life
TV Revivals

MYLES MCNUTT

Abstract: While the 2016 return of Amy Sherman-Palladino's series is part of a long lineage of development patterns (sequels, prequels, and reboots) built on existing properties, its choice to "revive" the show's unfinished story signals a new era of reiteration. Myles McNutt explores how the creative choices in the *Gilmore Girls* revival speak to how contemporary shifts in television distribution are changing how TV stories are told and how audiences engage with those stories.

In October 2016, hundreds of coffee shops around the United States and Canada were transformed into "Luke's Diner," the fictional Stars Hollow haunt of Lorelai Gilmore and her daughter Rory on *Gilmore Girls*, a family dramedy that ran for seven seasons between 2000 and 2007 on The WB and then The CW.

This type of "pop-up" promotion is not uncommon surrounding contemporary television series—for example, HBO set up food trucks with *Game of Thrones*–themed dishes ahead of the fantasy series' 2011 premiere. But what sets *Gilmore Girls* apart is that this is a promotional campaign based on a show that ended in 2007, more than nine years before hundreds of fans stood in line for hours to get their cup of "Luke's" coffee. And this campaign was being organized not by The WB or The CW but rather by Netflix, who revived the series with four ninety-minute episodes in November 2016, dubbed *Gilmore Girls: A Year in the Life*. Those who visited "Luke's" locations were not just indicating their fandom for a canceled TV series; they were also registering their excitement that this series would live on, with a "revival" that would continue the story left off when The CW canceled the series in 2007.

Gilmore Girls: A Year in the Life (*AYITL*) is part of a long lineage of television development patterns built on existing properties in order to minimize risk.

FIGURE 26.1. Signage sent to local retailers for the "Luke's" pop-up event in October 2016, seen here at Borjo Coffeehouse in Norfolk, Virginia.

However, while television "reboots"—in which existing series or films are reimagined with a new cast for a new audience—are long-standing practice, "revivals" like *AYITL* are relatively new, built on contemporary shifts in how television stories are told and how audiences engage with those stories. These revivals—including but not limited to *Arrested Development* (seasons 4 and 5 on Netflix), *24* (*24: Live Another Day* in 2015), *The X-Files* (2016–2018), *Heroes* (2016's *Heroes: Reborn*), *Prison Break* (2017), *Twin Peaks: The Return* (2017), and *Roseanne* (2018)—carry a greater burden for both the producers and the distributor, who must cultivate enthusiasm and manage expectations in equal measure. By exploring the process of bringing *Gilmore Girls* back to (streaming) television, this essay considers how revivals are strongly motivated by industrial logic but carry distinct narrative burdens shaped by public discourse and fan reception, and result in mixed reactions that highlight the double-edged sword of returning to these worlds in a contemporary context.

The logic supporting the trend of television revivals depends on three key factors. The first, and simplest, is that television development remains driven by existing media properties: Movies, past television series, books, videogames, and even podcasts are developed into new series based on the idea that an existing fanbase and cultural awareness will create a built-in audience for that series. It's a general logic that also supports reboots—in 2016, CBS developed a new version of *MacGyver* and picked it up to series despite throwing out the entirety of the series' pilot outside of two actors. The "idea" of rebooting *MacGyver* was valuable enough to CBS that they were willing to start from scratch, and similar logic led Fox to order series based on both *Lethal Weapon* and *The Exorcist* during the same development season. None of these series share any direct connection to the original series beyond the title—they were sold purely on the perceived industrial value of name recognition.

Revivals, however, are dependent on more than brand recognition. The second key factor to a revival is ongoing success in aftermarkets: The trend is built on shows that have had significant afterlife beyond their initial broadcast, whether through traditional syndication, DVD sales, or—increasingly—through streaming platforms like Netflix. A series' presence in these aftermarkets provides continued visibility, such that new viewers can become invested in the series and existing viewers can have their interest in the series refreshed. In a contemporary marketplace, a show's fanbase is not just those who watched a show when it aired but also those who have been exposed to it through the increasingly large number of spaces where that television series lives.

In the case of *Gilmore Girls*, for example, the series became a staple on multiple cable channels—including ABC Family/Freeform and Up—through syndication, was released in both single-season and complete series DVD box sets, and in 2014 was made available streaming on Netflix for the first time. Although discussions about continuing the series in some capacity had been active in the years since the show's cancellation, interest grew in the wake of the series' streaming availability, which expanded viewers' ability to watch or rewatch the series in its entirety and reentered the show into cultural conversation for both existing fans and a younger generation who were now the age of the show's target audience when it first aired.

Third, and most intangibly, there needs to be evidence that people are taking advantage of this opportunity, and that viewers are still invested in these characters. This can come from data: *Prison Break*, for example, was revived based on data showing new viewers were binging the show on Netflix, both in the United States and abroad.[1] It can also come through fan conventions, where panels for *The X-Files* and its stars, Gillian Anderson and David Duchovny, thrived in the years since its cancellation and supported a revival in 2016. While development logic supports bringing a series back for more episodes, and streaming platforms make these shows and their narratives more accessible, these projects still depend on audiences who care about seeing these stories continued, rather than simply revisiting old episodes or seeing the premise refreshed.

For *Gilmore Girls*, there were two significant developments that spoke to the series' continued resonance with its audience. The most prominent was a cast reunion staged at the Austin Television Festival in June 2015, where creator Amy Sherman-Palladino joined the series' ensemble cast to reflect on its journey. In addition to drawing a theater full of fans, the reunion also generated significant media coverage, including a lengthy interview with the cast on NBC's *Today*.[2] But among fans, a more grassroots effort had similarly reignited interest in the series: Late in 2014, Kevin Porter and Demi Adejuyigbe started the *Gilmore Guys* podcast, which used the series' debut on Netflix as a launching pad to revisit the show episode by episode. They combined close analysis with interviews with cast and crew, creating a gathering place for tens of thousands of fans of the series—dubbed "Gillies"—and showcasing those fans' investment in returning to Stars Hollow.

Some combination of this logic led Netflix and Warner Bros., the studio that produced *Gilmore Girls*, to determine that there was a market for a revival, but that is only the beginning of any development process. A revival also requires a story to tell, and Sherman-Palladino said at the Austin reunion that "it would have to be the right everything—the right format, the right timing . . . it would have to be honored in a certain way."[3] While the financial value of "more *Gilmore Girls*" is self-evident, the narrative value of revivals is more complicated. While some revivals focus primarily on creating more stories with characters the audience enjoys (*Arrested Development*), *Gilmore Girls* is among the revivals that carries the narrative burden of resolving an unfinished story.

This is a potential function of a revival, allowing shows that were canceled unexpectedly or failed to resolve in a satisfactory fashion to get a "do-over." *Gilmore Girls* qualifies in this case: When The CW made the decision to end the series in May 2007, it was after the show had already filmed its season 7 finale, "Bon Voyage." Although the episode was designed in a way that could serve as a series finale if The CW were to not order an additional season, it meant that the actors and crew were unsure if it would be their final episode. As dramas are increasingly allowed to end on their own terms—for example, *Lost*, *Mad Men*, and *Breaking Bad*—these types of "accidental" finales for long-running series are becoming less common and serve as a motivation for a revival to "right this wrong."

However, in the case of *Gilmore Girls* this injustice goes one step deeper, as the entire final season has been the subject of significant criticism. At the end of the sixth season, contract negotiations between The CW and creator Amy Sherman-Palladino and her fellow executive producer and husband Daniel Palladino broke down, resulting in them leaving the show and a new showrunner—David S. Rosenthal, a writer on the series—being installed in their place. The result was a final season that alienated many fans, drawing criticism for failing to capture the series' distinctive rhythms and making story choices that some believed were in opposition to what Sherman-Palladino would have done. Accordingly, a revival was not simply perceived by fans as a chance to give the show a proper farewell—it was perceived as a chance to give Sherman-Palladino the opportunity to write the farewell she envisioned and that fans had been denied thanks to behind-the-scenes conflicts.

This authorship over *Gilmore Girls* was not something that simply emerged from the facts of the situation but rather something that Sherman-Palladino actively cultivated in an interview following her exit. Sherman-Palladino had previously revealed to journalists that she had always known how she intended to conclude the series, and in an interview with *TV Guide* after negotiations broke down she revealed that she knew the "final four words" of the show.[4] But Sherman-Palladino did not pass these words onto Rosenthal, meaning that fans never got to see the original ending that the creator intended for the series.

The mythology of the "Final Four Words" became a significant part of the *Gilmore Girls* fandom: It was one of the questions brought up at the reunion event at the Austin Television Festival, and the *Gilmore Guys* podcast featured an ongoing segment entitled "What Are the Final Four Words?" asking their listeners to send in their guesses. When the *Gilmore Girls* revival was officially announced in October 2015, Michael Ausiello—the journalist who interviewed Sherman-Palladino back in 2006—reinforced the importance of this unsolved mystery by opening his report with a simple exclamation: "We're getting those final four words!"[5]

In Austin, Sherman-Palladino promised fans that "if [a revival] ever happened, I promise you I'd do it correctly."[6] However, the complexities of reviving an existing series mean that one's understanding of "correctly" is highly variable. Revivals as a genre are in a fight with time: Their existence is built on returning to the past, but their narratives must also acknowledge the temporal gap in the narrative, which in the case of *Gilmore Girls* was roughly eight years. This interest in temporality is compounded in the case of *AYITL*, as it had considerably less time to tell its story: While the original series was a traditional hour-long drama, with twenty-two episodes each season, the revival came as four ninety-minute installments, each covering a particular season beginning with "Winter" and concluding

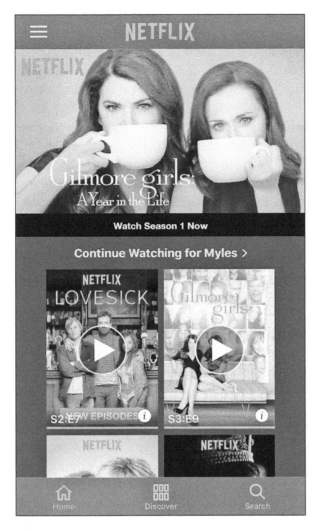

FIGURE 26.2.
A screenshot of the Netflix home page on the day of *Gilmore Girls: A Year in the Life*'s release, displaying its separation from the original series.

with "Fall." This shift in structure was reflected in the fact that the revival was also branded and promoted separately from the series itself: While Netflix's *Arrested Development* revival was positioned as "season 4" of that series, *AYITL* debuted as its own entry on the service, acknowledging its distinct storytelling approach.

The choice to only do four episodes offers limited real estate and drew criticism for its inability to serve all of the show's characters. While Rory's friend Lane Kim was a considerable narrative focus in the show's later seasons, she has a very limited role in the revival, to the point that the *Gilmore Guys* podcast developed a recurring feature tracking her screen-time to point out the disservice being done. With limited space, the choices made by Sherman-Palladino and Palladino regarding their focus create greater scrutiny: For instance, the ten-minute-long musical sequence in "Summer" was heavily criticized online not just by people who failed to find it funny but also by those who thought about what else could have been done with that time.[7] Fans had spent years imagining what the various residents of Stars Hollow might have been up to, and any time the revival spent elsewhere worked against some fans' understanding of how to "correctly" revive the series.

That being said, the central focus of the revival is directly invested in fan expectations and in resolving the storylines left dangling by the series' abrupt and authorially complicated conclusion. This focus is most apparent in Lorelai's storyline, which centers on her relationship with diner-owner Luke Danes. The two characters' romantic tension early in the series eventually led to a relationship beginning in season 4, but Sherman-Palladino's final episode in season 6 dissolved that relationship, and they only reconciled in the final moments of the series finale. Although "Bon Voyage" makes it clear that the two have reconnected, it does not feature a significant reunion and offers only glimpses of their "happy ending" before leaving the story behind for good.

Accordingly, Lorelai's storyline in *AYITL* is designed to offer more significant closure to their relationship. Although roughly eight years has passed when the revival begins, Luke and Lorelai have not married during this period, a decision that the revival explores over the course of its four episodes. This eight-year gap is a narrative challenge, but in this case the Palladinos make the argument that Lorelai and Luke's relationship was frozen in time, with each fearing that disrupting the status quo could threaten the relationship. This allows the writers to give viewers storylines—like Luke and Lorelai considering having children—that they were denied by the series' cancellation, even if the idea of those conversations not happening for eight years stretches credulity. Although the revival creates tension around their relationship, it eventually concludes with clear resolution, providing viewers with the romantic and whimsical wedding that the original series might have built to if it had been given an additional season. Lorelai's storyline offers the clearest case of the revival serving as a corrective to the original series—although Sherman-Palladino was the one who actually set Lorelai and Luke's breakup in motion, Rosenthal was the one who kept them apart and who failed to give audiences the type of reunion they might have wanted.

This focus on resolution is echoed in the storyline for Emily, Lorelai's mother and the matriarch of the Gilmore family. In this case, however, the series was responding to a real-life tragedy. Emily's storyline revolves around the death of her husband Richard, who had been played by Edward Herrmann in the original series—Herrmann died in late 2014, before discussion about a revival had emerged. His death created questions about how Richard's absence would affect the family, and the revival answers them by using it as the cornerstone of Emily's storyline. Midway through "Winter," the first installment, the series flashes back to Richard's funeral several months earlier, providing the audience with a chance to grieve while also laying the foundation for tensions between Emily and Lorelai following Richard's death. While not a direct continuation of a storyline from the original series, Emily's narrative nonetheless showcases the ability for revivals to reflect on how the passage of time has affected the series' legacy, and in this case how Herrmann's death resonated with those involved in the production. "Fall" heavily features Richard's memory: Lorelai's moment of self-discovery is tied to a memory of her father, visual effects bring Rory's memories to life as she tours her grandparents' house, and the final montage features Emily tenderly bidding Richard's portrait good night.

While fans broadly supported the "temporal flux" of these storylines, the same cannot be said for Rory's narrative in the revival, which drew the most criticism online following its premiere despite featuring the most prominent closure—the "final four words"—promised by *AYITL*. Rory's storyline focuses on her stalled journalism career, as she struggles to build on a piece in the *New Yorker* and ends up back in Stars Hollow running the local paper in "Summer." Her storyline offers elements of closure: Her solution to her aimless career is to write her life story as a book, which Lorelai suggests she call *Gilmore Girls* in a self-reflective nod to the series' legacy, and points to the passage of time since the original series effectively.

However, the storyline runs into two central pitfalls of revivals. First, Sherman-Palladino largely ignores where Rory's storyline actually left off in season 7, which she reportedly never watched after leaving the series. Rory's final storyline in the original series saw her leaving Stars Hollow to follow Barack Obama on the campaign trail, but the revival never mentions what came of this story, or what Rory's journalism career evolved into in the eight years that followed. This problem is also echoed in the character of Rory's ex-boyfriend Logan, whom she is having an affair with in the revival; while the seventh season notably softened the character and gave him independence from his dynastic upbringing, the revival returns him to the family business and seems much less sympathetic to the character. For fans who may not have dismissed season 7 based on Sherman-Palladino's absence, the revival's disinterest in acknowledging the events of that season risks alienation.

In addition, Rory's storyline points to the double-edged sword of the "final four words," and Sherman-Palladino's insistence on ending the revival the same way she had intended to end the series originally:

Rory: Mom.
Lorelai: Yeah?
Rory: I'm pregnant.

The narrative relevance of these words is clear: Lorelai's teenage pregnancy is central to the show, and Sherman-Palladino emphasized in interviews that she was interested in bringing the story "full circle."[8] However, the storyline appears in a very different context than she originally intended: If Rory had been twenty-three or twenty-four when this happened, the storyline would have more closely evoked Lorelai's past, as she gave birth to Rory at age sixteen. But Rory is thirty-two in *AYITL*, and the notion of pregnancy carries far different weight that the revival does not acknowledge. In general, Rory's storyline—aimless career prospects, returning home, and pregnancy scares—reads as a leftover storyline from the original series that Sherman-Palladino decided to tell in the revival, although the passage of time makes the context of those storylines very different.

The "Final Four Words" are also compromising for the revival because they offer none of the closure they promised: Although audiences finally knew the "final four words," the choice to feature a cliffhanger means that unanswered questions remain, including a definitive answer on the father of Rory's child, Rory's intentions for the pregnancy, and how this affects her relationships with both Logan, the most likely father, and her ex-boyfriend Jess, who is seen in "Fall" looking longingly at Rory and remembering their past connection. While the revival is designed to find closure for Lorelai and Emily, it actively resists closure for Rory and arguably replicates the lack of resolution that created interest in the revival to begin with.

The decision to leave on a cliffhanger was allegedly Sherman-Palladino's intention for the original series as well, but it also raises questions about whether *AYITL* is really intended as "closure": while all parties indicated there had been no discussions about additional episodes at the time of the revival's premiere, and the Palladinos moved on to producing the Emmy-winning *Marvelous Mrs. Maisel* for Amazon with no signs of a return to Stars Hollow in the near future, the cliffhanger notably leaves the door open for additional episodes. The same logic that supports the existence of television revivals supports those revivals continuing—*Gilmore Girls: A Year in the Life* generated huge amounts of media coverage and social media conversation, all valuable brand recognition for Netflix.

However, while revivals like *The X-Files* and the 2017 return of NBC's *Will & Grace* were renewed for additional episodes, the same cannot be said for *Gilmore Girls: A Year in the Life* and many other revivals, which some might argue is a good thing. Revivals are made because both industrial logic and fan narratives support their existence as a way to leverage continued interest in the series while also providing characters with the conclusion or continuation they deserved: If these series were to continue, however, the fan narratives shift dramatically, and "Another Year in the Life" risks reading as a cynical iteration of an existing franchise rather than a necessary revival of a story fans are invested in. Revivals sit at the complicated crossroads of industrial logic and creative imperative, and *Gilmore Girls* is neither the first nor the last program to explore the challenges of bringing a series back to life in an age where revisiting your favorite show is as easy as loading up Netflix or Hulu.

FURTHER READING

Johnson, Derek. "Party Like It's 1999: Another Wave of Network Nostalgia." *Flow Journal*, April 21, 2015. https://www.flowjournal.org.

Lizardi, Ryan. "Mourning and Melancholia: Conflicting Approaches to Reviving *Gilmore Girls* One Season at a Time." *Television and New Media* 19, no. 4 (2018): 379–95.

Loock, Kathleen. "American TV Series Revivals: Introduction." *Television and New Media* 19, no. 4 (2018): 299–309.

NOTES

1. Christopher Hooton, "Prison Break Is Coming Back with a New Season Thanks to People Binging the Old Ones on Netflix," *Independent*, August 7, 2015, www.independent.co.uk/

2. "Gilmore Girls Cast Reunion (Full Interview)," *Today*, YouTube, June 11, 2015, www.youtube.com.

3. Christopher Rosen, "Gilmore Girls Movie Not Happening Yet, Says Creator," *Entertainment Weekly*, June 7, 2015, http://ew.com.

4. Michael Ausiello, "Team Palladino: The Interview," *TV Guide*, April 24, 2006, www.tvguide.com.

5. Michael Ausiello, "Gilmore Girls Limited-Series Revival Set at Netflix—This Is *Not* a Drill," *TV Line*, October 19, 2015, http://tvline.com.

6. Rosen, "Gilmore Girls Movie."

7. In a poll of nearly five thousand of their Twitter followers, the Gilmore Guys found 55 percent believed the musical was "okay, just too long"; 31 percent "hated it."

8. Jen Chaney, "Gilmore Girls' Amy Sherman-Palladino and Daniel Palladino Discuss Those Final 4 Words and Whether Stars Hollow Would Vote for Trump," *Vulture*, December 1, 2016, www.vulture.com.

27

I Love Lucy
The Writer-Producer

Abstract: Often hailed as a landmark series for a range of innovations, *I Love Lucy* can also be seen as groundbreaking for how it assembled its production staff and established the vital role of television's writer-producer. Miranda Banks explores the history of *Lucy*'s production and creative personnel, connecting it with key moments in establishing labor practices and production norms in the early days of television.

In 1953, Lucille Ball made history by giving birth to two boys in one night, 3,000 miles apart. One, Desiderio Arnaz, arrived by Caesarean section in Los Angeles; the other, Little Ricky Ricardo, was the first child to arrive via television airwaves into homes across the country from a fictional New York. By celebrating rather than shying away from showing the first pregnant woman on television, *I Love Lucy* and the arrival of little Ricky secured the Ricardos as a television family.[1] The series was globally adored for its comedy and its star—although *I Love Lucy* was not just a hit, but also a TV milestone. *Lucy* was a major force for ushering in certain changes that would ultimately define American commercial television. In the annals of television history, *I Love Lucy* is most often celebrated for five things: 1. Lucy and Ricky's position as the first interracial couple on television; 2. cinematographer Karl Freund's use of a multicamera system to record the series on film in front of a live audience; 3. the announced arrival of Little Ricky; 4. making its stars, Lucille Ball and Desi Arnaz, the first television millionaires; and 5. being one of the series that convinced networks and studios that telefilm production in Hollywood would become the future of the industry. Less well-known is how *I Love Lucy* also, in a manner of speaking, gave birth to a role in television production that, while commonplace in Hollywood today, was surprisingly controversial at the time: the "hyphenate" writer-producer.

I Love Lucy was technically, culturally, industrially, and aesthetically ground-breaking; its significance as a single series within the history of the medium is virtually without rival. If *Lucy* was a contemporary series, it is quite likely we would be ascribing its success to a particular person: the series showrunner, heralding this person (or in some instances, persons) as a brilliant leader, technician, author, and, perhaps, creator. "Showrunner," a relatively new term that began appearing only in 1990 in the trade press, provides an easy road map to assigning credit that heretofore had been somewhat less decipherable.

"Showrunner" is not an official credit, per se. Without some knowledge beyond the credits listed on-screen or on IMDB.com, deciphering who is "in charge" of a television series is often a difficult task. Rather than the screen credit of "executive producer" or the older trade term of "head writer," the showrunner is someone who gives a series—and just as importantly, those who work for the series—a sense of structure and direction. The showrunner is in charge of the production and the creative content of a television show. The job demands the skills of a visionary: someone who can hold the entire narrative of the series in their head; who is the gatekeeper of language, tone, and aesthetics on the set and behind the scenes; who knows where the series has been and a sense, if not a plan, for its future. So, then, how did a television series that was such an overwhelming success "run" without a showrunner? Or was there a showrunner who was never celebrated as such? And if there was, who then deserves credit for *I Love Lucy*?

The easy answer would be to point to star Lucille Ball. From the show's first run in the 1950s to the present day, in the United States and around the globe, audiences have been enchanted with the unruly housewife who attempts to escape the confines of her apartment, only to find herself in the most outrageous of situations each week: stomping on grapes for an Italian film shoot ("Lucy's Italian Movie"), shoving chocolates into her mouth trying to keep up with her job on a conveyor belt at a candy factory ("Job Switching"), peddling Ricky's sponsor Vitameatavegamin on his TV show ("Lucy Does a Commercial"). These scenes are regularly celebrated as some of the finest performances in television comedy. It was Ball and her signature character that made the series the most popular show on television for four of its six seasons. However, while the show was entirely centered on its heroine, and she was one of the owners of Desilu Studio that produced the series, Lucille Ball was neither a manager nor was she responsible for running the series.

On further reflection, the answer to who is responsible for *Lucy* is not as easy as one might think. Desi Arnaz, as the head of Desilu, was like the best of studio moguls of the Hollywood era, assembling the most talented workers available. In this way, Arnaz himself could arguably be seen as the man in charge, especially since television corporations at the time were regularly considered more powerful—and more like media authors—than any individual.[2] Arnaz loved the

FIGURE 27.1.
In this famous "Vitameatavegamin" scene, audiences are treated to a brilliant comic performance by Lucille Ball. Today, we would say the "show-runner" responsible for the episode was Jess Oppenheimer.

attention pointed toward him as the series shot up in the ratings, and he gave himself an executive producer credit even though his role—at least in the early years of the series—was much more in line with actor and studio head.

Ball was the centerpiece of the series, and Arnaz was a young mogul who had a gift for locating the best person for each job on the Desilu set. The talent collected to make *I Love Lucy* run was some of the best TV would ever see. In many ways the series highlighted how collaborative the new medium could be. The crew that assembled was new to television—but each of them arrived with years of experience working in other media. Every one of these craftspeople brought with them knowledge and experience in entertainment, but arguably it was the mix of knowledge that led to the genius of the production. Writer Madeline Pugh Davis explained how the makers themselves were delighted by the diversity of the cast's and crew's talents, skills, and experiences: "Danny Cahn, who edited the first show . . . said the writers were from radio, Karl Freund was from the movies, Desi was from the theater and the stage, Lucy was from the movies, and everybody got together and put in their two cents and made it work . . . It was like inventing the wheel, as it all turned out rather well."[3]

The success of *Lucy* was a rare story, but it did mirror the general success of television: audiences craved great storytelling, and these makers of all different forms of popular entertainment—radio, film, and theater—who had been so talented in their original medium, turned their attention to television and together developed content that appealed to the new, and rapidly increasing, television audience. With all of this talent behind the scenes and in the front office, one moves on to ask who first "created" *I Love Lucy*.

Nowadays when we think about the author of a narrative television series, we assign a privileged role to its creator. The creator provides the original story, building a storyworld that an ensemble cast inhabits, and often has a continuing role as head writer-producer. The head writer is—at best—a benevolent dictator who provides a consistency of voice from episode to episode, runs the writers' room, works on set with the director, actors, cinematographer, and designers ensuring that the words on the page translate to the screen, and often sits in the editing room helping the editor craft a story. One could easily assume that it was Lucille Ball and Desi Arnaz who were the show's creators, but they were not. *Lucy*'s creator was a man whose name is barely remembered and rarely mentioned: Jess Oppenheimer.

Oppenheimer was a young radio writer, director, and producer on a number of hit series including Fanny Brice's *The Baby Snooks Show*. This hyphenate role that Oppenheimer played in the series, in fact, had its roots in radio soaps and later in other celebrated popular series. He was brought in to run Lucille Ball's radio series *My Favorite Husband*. When CBS and Desilu began conversations about creating a television series, Oppenheimer worked with stars Ball and Arnaz, his two co-writers on *My Favorite Husband*, Madeline Pugh and Bob Carroll, Jr., and the Milton Biow advertising agency. Out of this emerged a one-page treatment outlining the basic plot idea.

> He is a Latin-American orchestra leader and singer. She is his wife. They're happily married and in love. The only bone of contention between them is her desire to get into show business, and his equally strong desire to keep her out of it. To Lucy, who was brought up in the humdrum sphere of a moderate, well-to-do middle western, mercantile family, show business is the most glamorous field in the world. But Ricky, who was raised in show business, sees none of its glamour, only its deficiencies, and yearns to be an ordinary citizen, keeping regular hours and living a normal life.[4]

Then Desilu created a pilot episode. Somewhere along the way, Oppenheimer realized he needed to protect his idea, and with a single dollar bill and one slip of paper, he registered his premise for *I Love Lucy* with the Screen Writers Guild.

The hyphenated role of both writer and producer that Oppenheimer played on the set was something new. His interest and focus on storytelling provided consistency of narrative and voice that was helpful to the writers and guided the direction of the series. To Ball, Oppenheimer was known as "the brains" behind the show. Director William Asher called him "the field general." While the title had yet to be invented, this language of managerial control and creative authority is echoed in the descriptions used for today's showrunner. In an interview, writers

Bob Schiller and Bob Weiskopf described Oppenheimer as a "stern taskmaster" and the best producer they ever worked for. He was the only producer they had ever written under who turned the radio off, who cut the phone to the writers' room, who refused to be distracted by concerns about casting, costumes, and make-up. The writers' room was broken into two writing partnerships: Pugh and Carroll, and Schiller and Weiskopf. After a day spent working as a team of five, Schiller and Weiskopf would take a first pass at writing a draft. Oppenheimer would make comments and then Pugh and Carroll would do a second draft. Finally, Oppenheimer came in to do a final draft. No script would ever reach the set without Oppenheimer's final pass. As he said:

> I made it a point, no matter how good their draft was, to re-dictate the entire thing from beginning to end, because that way each of the characters consistently spoke the same way each week. It didn't have to be *me*, necessarily, as long as it was filtered through one person's sense. But I felt that I knew best the mood and feel of our previous shows, and that I could bring it all into line so that nothing sounded too different or out of character. . . . The more consistency there is, the more comfortable [the audience is], and the more you can enjoy everything that happens. So, rightly or wrongly, the show sounded the same each time because it funneled through me.[5]

This language is quite common now, as staff writers on television series often talk about the need for consistency of voice from episode to episode. Writers even talk about needing the skill of a mimic, as they learn to write like the head writer. As both a writer and a producer, Oppenheimer had the vision, the skill, and the authority to create regularity in the series from episode to episode, season to season. This skill was unnecessary for film writers, as aside from serial shorts or the occasional film series, film writers need only be concerned with consistency of narrative within a single 75–160 minute window.

So was this successful and talented writer, rising to the top of this newly formed industry, venerated in Hollywood as the first of a new breed of writer? One might assume that though his name might not be known by audiences, people within the industry would know him as one of the brains behind bringing Hollywood writers new business in the form of the telefilm. The answer, though, is quite the opposite: Oppenheimer's role as both a writer and a producer proved extremely threatening to a community of writers who saw producers as management, and therefore their adversaries in contract and labor negotiations. Although Oppenheimer was a dues-paying member of the Screen Writers Guild as well as the newly formed Television Writers of America, his position as a producer overshadowed his work as a writer. Hollywood writers' agitation regarding Oppenheimer's hyphenated role ultimately played itself out in a National Labor Relations Board hearing.

In May 1953, two years after the premiere of *Lucy*, and its second year at the top of the television ratings, Oppenheimer—creator, head writer, and producer of *I Love Lucy*—was called in front of the board that was placed in the middle of a battle between the Television Writers of America (TWA) and the Screen Writers Guild (SWG) regarding jurisdiction over television.[6] Testimony that day related to Oppenheimer's disparate roles: as a producer working for Desilu, as Vice President of the Television Writers of America, and as head writer of *Lucy*. The attorney for the SWG insisted that as a prestigious producer and a potential employer of writers, Oppenheimer was exercising an undue amount of influence recruiting writers to join the Television Writers Guild.[7] The Screen Writers Guild could not see how Oppenheimer, as both a producer and a writer—and thus, both as management and employee—should have any power to decide which trade organization would represent him, let alone have the potential to strong-arm his fellow writers to follow suit with whichever organization he preferred. Oppenheimer in his role as a writer-producer was a shocking new force in the history of relations between writers and producers. The Screen Writers Guild was in the business of representing writers in negotiations and disputes against management. And as of late, relations between the two were difficult at best. Just five years before the premiere of *I Love Lucy*, the Hollywood Ten (eight of them writers) were sent to jail for refusing to testify about accused Communist sympathies. Dozens of screenwriters had been blacklisted and lost their contracts with the studios. On this stage arrived Oppenheimer, and thus the Screen Writers Guild could see only the danger in this new role of writer-producer. Little could they foresee the power that hyphenates would soon carry in this new medium—power that ultimately would help not just television writers, but screenwriters as well.

Nowadays it seems absurd that a showrunner would be seen as a threat to his or her own series in negotiations between labor and management. The names of showrunners are venerated within the television community as powerful voices on series as well as for the rights of writers: Matt Weiner (*Mad Men*), Joss Whedon (*Buffy the Vampire Slayer, Angel,* and *Firefly*), and Norman Lear (*All in the Family, Maude,* and *The Jeffersons*) have all walked picket lines as Writers Guild members. But in the 1950s, the landscape of Hollywood looked quite different. After twenty years of battling against management, the Screen Writers Guild could not fathom the idea that a writer could balance his own interests as a producer and as a writer. Thus, they viewed the hyphenate role of a writer-producer as a powerful new threat and a potential infiltrator into the union.

There were at the time a number of other hyphenate writer-producers who were blazing a trail for a new role for writers in this new medium. One of them, in particular, was far more powerful than Oppenheimer ever could be. The role (if not the term) of the hyphenate writer-producer stems back to the earliest days of episodic television, even before *I Love Lucy*. Gertrude Berg, star of the early radio-cum-television series *The Goldbergs*, is arguably the first and foremost example of what a television showrunner would become in the contemporary era. Berg embodied the hyphenate as a television pioneer: she was a writer, producer, and actor, and true show-woman. She was, unquestionably, a showrunner forty years before the term was ever conceived.

While there were examples of television writers beyond Oppenheimer and Berg who served as producers, the hyphenate truly emerged in the mid-1950s, when television production moved primarily to Los Angeles. Ultimately, the TWA dissolved in 1954, and all writers of scripted entertainment for film, television, and radio gathered under the umbrella of the Writers Guild of America. But it was on account of writers for shows like *Lucy*, who first claimed credit as writers and as producers, that conflicting notions of authorship and ownership came to a head for the guilds that represented these media workers. With the ascension of the hyphenate, a significant number of writers were placed in a position of power and authority previously unseen within the industry. Hyphenates had significantly more creative control of their series than screenwriters ever held on film sets. While screenwriters often had more cultural and financial capital, their loss of rights of authorship weighed heavily on many of them and gave television writers good reason to appreciate their lot.

In 1960, film and television writers walked the picket line together as the Writers Guild of America, demanding radical shifts in payment and benefits structures. With the rise of the Hollywood telefilm, as well as the airing of motion pictures on television networks, writers argued that compensation should be extended to cross-media exhibition and the rerun. Negotiations finally established a system of royalties, and years later the residual system, which has since ensured writers would see a profit from each replay of films and television series, as well as required payment by the studios and networks into member's pension and health benefits. Though at first the WGA was an uncomfortable marriage of film, television, and radio writers who had literally taken each other to court, by 1960 its members had realized that this alliance could emerge as a powerful labor force and as a strong voice for creative workers within the American media industries.

So the question of who deserves credit for *I Love Lucy* is partly only rhetorical: there was no singular showrunner, in name at least, and yet without someone leading a brilliant cast and crew of dozens through the rigorous filming schedule demanded in the early days of television, the series could have easily fallen apart. Nowadays, the person in charge of a television series is always listed as a producer—as was Jess Oppenheimer even in those early days—and rarely is the role of producer his or her only title. Sometimes the hyphenated role the person carries is that of director, as with Bruce Paltrow in *St. Elsewhere*. Sometimes that person has multiple roles in front of and behind the camera, as does *30 Rock* star, actor, writer, and producer Tina Fey.

Lucy taught television about its potential as a medium. When we flip our way around the dial and find a show that is truly exceptional, we have a natural inclination to assign credit to creative genius. We see something funny, thoughtful, wise, beautiful, or compelling, and we want to believe that such brilliance can emerge out of hard work and ingenuity. Creativity is often defined as a singular vision: so how can such singularity of mind come from a collection of, arguably, dozens of people? And yet, sometimes if it's the right collection of media makers, the results can turn into the best television has, and perhaps ever will, offer.

FURTHER READING

Banks, Miranda. *The Writers: A History of American Screenwriters and Their Guild*. New Brunswick, NJ: Rutgers University Press, 2016.

Henderson, Felicia D. "The Culture Behind Closed Doors: Issues of Gender and Race in the Writers' Room." *Cinema Journal* 50, no. 20 (Winter 2011): 145–52.

Landay, Lori. *I Love Lucy*. Detroit, MI: Wayne State University Press, 2010.

Newman, Michael Z., and Elana Levine. *Legitimating Television: Media Convergence and Cultural Status*. New York: Routledge, 2011.

Perren, Alisa, and Ian Peters. "Showrunners." In *The Sage Handbook of Television Studies*, edited by Manuel Alvarado, Milly Buonanno, Herman Gray, and Toby Miller. Thousand Oaks, CA: Sage, 2015.

NOTES

1. See Mary Desjardins, "Lucy and Desi: Sexuality, Ethnicity, and TV's First Family," in *Television, History, and American Culture: Feminist Critical Essays*, ed. Mary Beth Harolovich and Lauren Rabinovitz (Durham, NC: Duke University Press, 2001), 56–74.

2. See Alisa Perren and Ian Peters, "Showrunners," in *The Sage Handbook of Television Studies*, ed. Manuel Alvarado, Milly Buonanno, Herman Gray, and Toby Miller (Thousand Oaks, CA: Sage, 2015).

3. Interview, Archive of American Television, November 24, 1997, Academy of Television Arts and Sciences Foundation, www.emmytvlegends.org.

4. Jess Oppenheimer with Greg Oppenheimer, *Laughs, Luck and Lucy: How I Came to Create the Most Popular Sitcom of All Time* (Syracuse, NY: Syracuse University Press, 1996), 139.

5. Ibid., 189.

6. In 1952, thirty-five television writers gathered together to form the Television Writers of America (TWA), a branch of the Authors League of America. The TWA had two primary concerns: that they were receiving low pay and that they had no benefits. They turned to the National Labor Relations Board for certification and to be officially named bargaining agents for television writers. Jess Oppenheimer was named vice president. Almost immediately, the Screen Writers Guild filed a complaint with the NLRB and demanded a hearing against the TWA.

7. "New Desilu Hearing Completed," *Television Writer* 2, no. 2 (May 1953): 2.

28

Modern Family
Product Placement

KEVIN SANDLER

Abstract: Although television is overwhelmingly a commercial medium, audiences still expect boundaries between commercials and program content, particularly in narrative programming. Kevin Sandler examines an interesting case of product integration: the controversy that surrounded an episode of the hit sitcom *Modern Family*, the narrative of which conspicuously centered on Apple's iPad just days before that device became available for purchase.

"Game Changer," a first season episode of ABC's *Modern Family*, begins with Phil Dunphy all set to wake up early the next day—his birthday—and get in line at 6 a.m. at the Apple Store to buy an iPad. "It's like Steve Jobs and God got together to make this the best birthday ever!" he says. His wife Claire, thrilled to have a handle on what her husband Phil actually wants for his birthday (her previous idea was light-up barbecue tongs), offers to camp out at the Apple store to get him the iPad. Alas, she falls asleep on the couch, and the iPad is sold out before she arrives. Claire subsequently enlists her two daughters, Haley and Alex, to "Facebook, chat, buzz, bling" their way to an "iPad thingy." In the meantime, Claire hears about a new shipment of iPads at the Apple Store, only to get thrown out of line with her brother Mitchell (who retrieved her wallet from home) for fighting with a man who cut in front of them. Ultimately, though, Phil's son Luke obtains an iPad by emailing all of his father's "geek friends," claiming that Phil is dying and his final wish is to get an iPad. The episode concludes with Phil getting his iPad and celebrating his birthday with his family. Happy ending achieved, narrative equilibrium restored.

Prior to the airing of "Game Changer," *Modern Family* had received nearly universal acclaim from critics and fans since its debut in September 2009. The show was the highest-rated new comedy of the broadcast season, and eventually won the Emmy Award for Best Comedy Series later that August. By its second season, *Modern Family* had become the most watched scripted broadcast series in the 18–49 demographic.[1] In fact, "Game Changer" drew the series' biggest number in that key demo in almost two months—a 3.8 rating (with each point translating into 1.3 million viewers).[2]

In what proved to be merely a temporary setback to the series' reputation, a heated debate ensued in the news media and blogosphere regarding the episode's iPad-centric nature. Two distinct camps emerged: one side considered the iPad integration to be unforgiveable and shameless, a profit-driven partnership of *Modern Family*'s production company, Twentieth Century Fox Television, the ABC network, and Apple. Another faction found it realistic and convincing, a savvy creator-fueled storyline that made sense within the show's fictional world. Characterizing these divergent positions was a widely circulated pair of posts appearing on the "The Live Feed" blog of the *Hollywood Reporter* that involved television editor James Hibberd and *Modern Family* co-creator (with Steve Levitan) Christopher Lloyd. Hibberd suggested that "the iPad scenes felt like an advertisement," the end result being that ABC "water[ed] down a brand with the perception of selling out . . . especially if it didn't sell out."[3] In response, Lloyd claimed, "there was no product placement," though *Modern Family* "ha[d] made those agreements with other companies." In this case, he said, no financial transaction was guiding the iPad's representation, as "it was all story-driven."[4]

The "agreement" that Lloyd refers to here was the season-long product-placement deal for *Modern Family* that ABC had previously struck with Toyota for its Sienna and Prius vehicles. Unlike the iPad, these Toyota product integrations, which had totaled over eight minutes of airtime up to this point, drew virtually no media response.[5] "Game Changer," however, was a different story. Questions arose akin to Hibberd's and Lloyd's contrasting assessments over the motives behind the iPad integration. For instance, had ABC crossed the line in corporate synergy under the influence of Apple CEO Steve Jobs, who, at the time, was the largest shareholder and sat on the board of ABC parent corporation, The Walt Disney Company? Did *Modern Family* violate its trust with the viewing public, as the series had received a Peabody Award for its "distinguished achievement and meritorious public service" on the exact morning that "Game Changer" aired? Did the iPad qualify as product placement, since the device's actual debut was April 3, three days after the episode's airdate?

This brief controversy surrounding the iPad's presence in *Modern Family* highlights the increasingly blurred line between entertainment and marketing that characterizes the contemporary U.S. television landscape. With more viewers making use of ad-skipping digital video recorders, watching TV on DVD, or streaming (or stealing) content off the Internet, marketers have begun to push for more ways to intertwine their products within network programming itself. Product placement, product integration, and branded entertainment—three common terms to describe a form of advertising in which a product, corporate logo, or brand name is positioned as a "prop" in a program or is used as an integral part of the storyline—is one of those strategies. All have become a staple of broadcast and cable television, particularly with the influx of "nonscripted" or reality television since the success of *Survivor* in its debut season. *American Idol, The Amazing Race*, and *Top Chef* all continually weave advertisers' products within their storylines and gameplay. Integration has also found its way into scripted television with such notable examples as NBC's *The Office* and Staples, *30 Rock* and Snapple, and *Chuck*'s season-long Subway integrated sponsorship. *Modern Family*'s integration of the iPad, therefore, is more the rule than the exception in today's media landscape.

Timothy Havens and Amanda D. Lotz provide a model that helps to explain how the iPad integration in "Game Changer" underscores the ongoing tensions between art and commerce in the media industries.[6] They propose an "Industrialization of Culture" framework to take into account the wide range of cultural, economic, institutional, professional, and personal forces that lead media practitioners to shape the aesthetic content and ideological meaning of texts on three different levels of influence: mandates, conditions, and practices. A mandate is the primary purpose of an industry organization, its reason for operating, such as profit-seeking or public service. Conditions refer to the broader behavior of the media sectors—the various technologies, regulations, and economics that affect how media industries operate. And practices encompass the myriad of professional roles and activities that make up the day-to-day operations of the media industries. Together with various social trends, tastes, and traditions that media producers might draw on when creating programming, this framework can account for how media industries bring a show into being. Media workers, particularly those in commercial media organizations, have only some degree of individual autonomy, or, as Havens and Lotz call it, "circumscribed agency." Cultures, mandates, conditions, and industry practices invariably all work to impinge on the agency of media professionals. Yet, "the drive for popularity," they argue, "and the conflicting and competing interests of a wide range of decision makers involved in creating an individual media text provide opportunities for agency and self-expression."[7]

When viewed through this framework of circumscribed agency, the iPad integration and ensuing debate over "Game Changer" exposes the myriad pressures faced by *Modern Family*'s creators in constructing an episode of commercial television. ABC's primary mandate, as one division within a massive publicly traded company, is to make money for its parent company's shareholders. It does this primarily through selling the audiences gathered by its content to advertisers. For instance, the cost of a thirty-second spot for *Modern Family* began at $130,388 in fall 2009 before the show's ratings were proven.[8] However, not all audiences that comprise the value of this spot are created equal. The most coveted demographic for the television industry is 18–49-year-old white, college-educated males with above-average incomes. Advertisers consider such audience members to have more discretionary income and be more susceptible to changing brands than other demographic segments. Networks thus create programs, first and foremost, to serve these specific demographic and advertiser needs.

Since *Modern Family* was designed to attract this demographic, and subsequently has drawn a large portion of it, it is not surprising that ABC would enter into a brand partnership with Apple. While the demographics for a typical Apple user skew differently across product lines, the computer company also pays attention to the psychographic market segment of the "early adopter"—a person who embraces an advantageous new product or technology before others do. A 2007 report conducted by Solutions Research Group on the potential first-generation "early adopters" of the iPhone concluded they were educated men in their thirties, living in New York or California, with household incomes of $75,600 a year.[9] The late thirtysomething, affluent, Californian Phil Dunphy—the self-identified "early adopter" himself—makes "Game Changer" a textbook description of this psychographic. A preliminary market research report shortly before the airing of "Game Changer" lends further support to this argument, revealing that 27% in the 18–34 age range (compared to 18% of all consumers) expressed an interest in buying the iPad.[10] Five months after the device's release, iPad users, according to Nielsen, were 65% male and 63% under the age of thirty-five. Additionally, 25% of iPad users had incomes of $100K or more, while 51% had a bachelor's degree or higher.[11] This demographic and psychographic compatibility suggests that integrating the iPad into *Modern Family* was a no-brainer: a high-profile show integrating a highly desired device just days before its launch made perfect sense.

Demographic alliances between brands like ABC and Apple have greatly increased due to profound technological and economic changes in the media industries during the last ten years. These partnerships reflect a volatile historical moment in which networks, advertisers, and viewers are reevaluating the terms of their relationships with one another. Media clutter, audience fragmentation, and digital convergence have increasingly made it more difficult for media companies to reach the younger end of the 18–49 demographic. The increase in the number of media, media outlets, and media technologies has given audiences more choices for consuming entertainment where they want, when they want, and how they want. For instance, almost 36% of TV households (up from 13.5% three years earlier) were equipped with digital video recorders (DVRs) when "Game Changer" aired, while the average American was watching more than ten hours of time-shifted TV per month.[12] Together with viewer erosion, greater competition, and rampant piracy, social and cultural shifts such as these have dramatically reshaped the way the media industries do business with one another.

Increased product placement deals have become one solution to this crisis; integration spending in television, movies, Internet, videogames, and other media totaled $3.61 billion in 2009 and is poised to double by 2014.[13] Certainly, the hostility directed at the iPad integration in "Game Changer" partly had to do with the overwhelming pervasiveness of product placement in contemporary U.S. media. From the standpoint of Apple, the ABC network, and the program's production studio, Twentieth Century Fox Television, *Modern Family* represented a timely marketing opportunity that could attract widespread media publicity for both the iPad and the series while also combating DVR ad-skipping in the home. Many viewers, however, felt that these companies had violated a social contract they had with the series by seemingly joining forces to impose a sales pitch into the narrative fabric of a beloved show purely for profit and marketing purposes. In their mind, the timing of the episode—three days before the release of the iPad—reeked of opportunism at the hands of corporate executives. The iPad integration seemed to be coordinated no differently than the well-timed, multiplatform product placements ever present in reality shows. In cases like *The Amazing Race* or *Survivor*, product integration is to be expected. Not so with scripted comedies and dramas, particularly those series like *Modern Family* that are defined as "quality television" by various interpretive communities.[14] It is assumed that "quality television" series are not inhibited by the same financial constraints, popular trends, and advertising demands that plague most other television productions. *Modern Family* was believed to be above such base commerce for these critics and viewers. Or so they thought.

Even if ABC adhered to its commercial mandate and demanded that Levitan and Lloyd integrate the iPad into *Modern Family* at the behest of Steve Jobs, such an explanation does not fully account for the positive response about the product placement from many fans and critics, for whom Phil Dunphy's excitement over the new device seemed to be a logical extension of his character rather than an advertisement for Apple. Longtime television journalist Josef Adalian of The Wrap personally took Hibberd and CNET's Chris Matyszczyk to task for claiming product integration without proof and for being TV storytelling purists. "If you're trying to tell a story about a character irrationally lusting over a tech product circa spring 2010, spoofing the iPad was the obvious (and reasonable) choice. If it had been spring 2009, Phil would no doubt be praying for a Kindle. And if it were 2011, he'd probably be begging for a 3-D TV set."[15] In fact, Levitan remarked that Phil's frenzy over getting an iPad for his birthday would better tap into the zeitgeist rather than the original choice—a videogame.[16]

The writers of *Modern Family* had made Phil's obsession with technology and gadgets clear earlier that year in "Fifteen Percent." That plotline concerns Claire's inability to work Phil's universal remote for their new theater system. After Claire breaks the remote out of frustration, Phil informs her, "The experts at CNET.com rated it the best remote. They gave it three-and-a-half mice." Following this setup, the iPad in "Game Changer" can appear then to be story-driven and a natural fit for techno-geek Phil. When Phil tells Claire, "Next week! That's like the worst thing you can say to an early adopter," after she fails to get him the iPad on its release day, his words likely rang true for many audience members. Thus, Phil's stroking of his iPad at the end of the episode while whispering "I love you" to it, can easily be perceived as true to character and a satisfying ending to the episode's narrative arc, rather than an awkward product placement.

When viewed as creative synergy between art and commerce rather than corporate synergy among Fox, ABC, and Apple, the general success of the iPad integration can partially be attributed to a certain amount of agency that Levitan, Lloyd, and their writing team had in the decision-making process. Even though the specific nature of their negotiations with executives over the aesthetic and narrative use of the iPad is unknown, the writers' creative agency over the depiction could not have been completely unfettered or unregulated. Thus, when viewed within Havens and Lotz's Industrialization of Culture framework, it becomes apparent that various industrial forces and practices circumscribed their autonomy, shaping how the device would be narrativized in the episode. These concessions—fueled largely by the profit motive of ABC and Apple—may have compromised *Modern Family*'s free creative reign and might give validity to viewer claims that the show "sold out." "Organic"—a marketing term that suggests seamless, subtle, or inconspicuous product integration—disguises the notion that the iPad, like any product, must always be presented in a positive, consumer-friendly light. In this vein, one could view Phil's description of the device as "a movie theater, library, and music store all rolled into one awesome pad" as a virtual commercial about the iPad's selling points preapproved by Apple executives.

Or consider the dramatic pause on the exterior of the Apple Store in "Game Changer" as Claire rushes to the back of the line to pick up an iPad from a new shipment. Panning her movement screen right to left in wide shot, the camera momentarily freezes when the Apple logo hits the center of the frame in an aesthetic decision unmotivated by narrative concerns. And one can construe another scene as explicitly promoting Apple, as when Claire presents Phil his virtual birthday cake (after Luke ate the material one) in the form of an iPad app.

FIGURE 28.1.
Phil blows out the
birthday candles
on his brand new
iPad.

As Phil professes his love to his iPad at episode's end, celebratory music kicks in on the soundtrack as family members gather behind him in a picturesque tableau, all equally mesmerized by the iPad. These lines of dialogue and aesthetic choices appear market-driven rather than character-driven, designed to celebrate the device's functionality and splendor. Such a reading is reinforced by the absence of any criticism of the iPad in "Game Changer," though a number of limitations of the device's first version were in fact well known before it became available for purchase. No camera or video recorder, no multitasking capability, no Flash support (the latter a particular complaint since the introduction of the iPhone)—any of these deficiencies could have been addressed in the episode. That they are not suggests the creative limitations placed on the creators of *Modern Family*. Had there been no such limitations surrounding product integration, one might have expected to see an episode in which the Dunphys were terrified of driving their Toyota Sienna after unintended acceleration problems caused the automaker to recall over nine million vehicles in November 2009 and January 2010.

When viewed through this framework of circumscribed agency, it is arguable that whether Apple paid for the placement of the iPad in "Game Changer" does not really matter. The episode exposed the internalized logic of American commercial television, one that supports a broader consumerist mindset regardless of actual sponsorship. In fact, "Game Changer" was a textbook example of scripted brand integration of products into a primetime television program, as James Grant Hay, the founder and CEO of Australian brand integration agency InShot, has observed. For Hay, *Modern Family* told the iPad story in a compelling, innovative, and *organic* way: the iPad was strongly integrated into the story narrative, the device was positively mentioned in several different contexts, and the actors emotionally engaged with the product while using it on screen.[17] Apple need not have paid for the iPad placement because the internalized logic of commercial television is to promote consumerism, turn audiences into commodities, and celebrate a product as a vital component of "realism." In the end, a light comedy like *Modern Family* could never critique a real product, questioning the functionality of the iPad or the safety of Toyota cars, as doing so would bristle against the norms of general consumer culture.

Two months after the airing of "Game Changer," Jeff Morton, a producer on *Modern Family*, told attendees at the Produced By Conference that the episode "may have gone a little too far in hindsight." While he confirmed that Apple compensated no one at Twentieth Century Fox Television or ABC for the brand integration, he did acknowledge that "the public thought it was a giant sellout" and that it "sort of backfired on us."[18] Since "Game Changer's" airing, *Modern Family* has not entered into any conspicuously overt product placement like that of the iPad. Or perhaps they have not found any prominent advertiser with whom to strike an iPad-like integration. Then again, there goes Phil, in the season 2 episode, "The Musical Man," hurrying daughter Haley outside the side door of his Toyota van, exclaiming, "The doors slide, the seats slide. What can't the Sienna do?"

FURTHER READING

NOTES

1. Nellie Andreeva, "Full 2010–2011 TV Series Season Rankings," *Deadline Hollywood*, May 27, 2011, www.deadline.com.
2. Joe Flint, "'Modern Family' Gives Some Free Love to the iPad," *Los Angeles Times, Company Town* (blog), April 1, 2010, http://latimesblogs.latimes.com/entertainmentnews-buzz/2010/04/modern-family-gives-some-free-love-for-the-ipad.html.
3. James Hibberd, "Release the iPad! Products Disrupt Wednesday Hits," *Hollywood Reporter's The Live Feed* (blog), April 1, 2010, www.hollywoodreporter.com/blogs/live-feed/release-ipad-products-disrupt-wednesday-53365.
4. James Hibberd, "Modern Family Co-Creator Explains iPad Use," *Hollywood Reporter's The Live Feed* (blog), April 1, 2010, www.thrfeed.com/2010/04/modern-family-cocreator-explains-ipad-use.html.
5. Brian Steinberg, "Why Modern Family Still Drives Toyota," *Advertising Age*, March 8, 2010, http://adage.com.
6. See chapter 1 of Timothy Havens and Amanda D. Lotz, *Understanding Media Industries* (Oxford: Oxford University Press, 2012), 1–26.
7. Ibid., 23.

8. Brian Steinberg, "'Modern Family' Featured an iPad but ABC Didn't Collect," *Advertising Age*, April 1, 2010, http://adage.com.

9. Solutions Research Group, 2007, www.srgnet.com.

10. "Apple Owners Nearly 40 Percent More Interested in the iPad than Non-Apple Owners, according to NPD," NPD Group, March 26, 2010, www.npd.com.

11. "State of the Media: The Increasingly Connected Consumer; Connected Devices: A Look Behind the Growing Popularity of iPads, Kindles and Other Devices," Nielsen Media Research, October 2010.

12. Robert Seidman, "DVR Penetration Grows to 39.7% of Households, 42% of Viewers," *TV by the Numbers*, March 23, 2011, http://tvbythenumbers.zap2it.com; "State of the Media: TV Usage Trends: Q3 and Q4 2010," Nielsen Media Research, 2011.

13. Andrew Hampp, "Product Placement Dipped Last Year for the First Time," *Advertising Age*, June 29, 2010, http://adage.com.

14. For the debates about the term "quality" in relation to television, see Jane Feuer, Paul Kerr, and Tise Vahimagi, *MTM: "Quality Television"* (London: BFI, 1984); Janet McCabe and Kim Akass, eds., *Quality TV: Contemporary American Television and Beyond* (London: Tauris, 2007); and Mark Jancovich and James Lyons, eds., *Quality Popular Television: Cult TV, the Industry, and Fans* (London: BFI, 2008).

15. Josef Adalian, "The iPad-'Modern Family' Non-troversy: Enough!" *The Wrap*, April 2, 2010, www.thewrap.com. Adalian was referring to Chris Matyszczyk's online column in which he called the iPad integration on *Modern Family* "less of a product placement and more of product kidnapping a show and holding it by the neck very tightly indeed until it handed over a pile of money." See "30-Minute iPad Ad on 'Modern Family,'" CNET, April 1, 2010, http://news.cnet.com.

16. Quoted in Sam Schneider and Suzanne Vranica, "iPad Gets Star Turn in Television Comedy," *Wall Street Journal*, April 2, 2010.

17. James Grant Hay, "The Genesis of Apple's 'Modern Family' iPad Story," InShot: Your Brand in Film, Television, and Multimedia, http://inshot.com.au.

18. Joe Flint, "'Modern Family' Producer Says iPad Episode 'Went Too Far in Hindsight,'" *Los Angeles Times, Company Town* (blog), June 5, 2010, http://latimesblogs.latimes.com/entertainmentnewsbuzz/2010/06/modern-family-producer-says-ipad-episode-went-too-far-inhindsight.html.

29

The Real Housewives of Beverly Hills
Franchising Femininity

SUZANNE LEONARD

Abstract: Bravo's popular reality franchise *The Real Housewives* participates in a larger zeitgeist where the term "housewife" no longer refers to a woman who labors primarily inside the home. In this new paradigm, argues Suzanne Leonard, the housewife's job is to be a professional woman. The 2011 season finale of *The Real Housewives of Beverly Hills* illustrates that housewives commercialize wifedom at the same time that they are commodified by it, as they work for a network that has staked its fortunes on cultivating an affluent consumer base.

In a franchise already famous for its revelry in conspicuous consumption, privileged and pampered excess, and self-interest bordering on solipsism, Bravo's sixth installment in its housewives juggernaut, *The Real Housewives of Beverly Hills*, sits at the epicenter. Hallmarked by bodies augmented by plastic surgery; featuring a cast favored with jaw-dropping fortunes (many of whom have a foot in the door of the entertainment industry); and peppered with plotlines involving alcohol abuse, domestic violence, assisted reproduction, and even suicide, *The Real Housewives of Beverly Hills* formalizes the themes and intensifies the currents that comprise *The Real Housewives* franchise writ large. In addition, it participates in a larger zeitgeist where the term "housewife" no longer refers to a woman who labors primarily inside the home. Instead, Bravo's housewives relish acts of pampered leisure, engaging in aesthetic rituals and regimes of self-care including shopping, dining out, and hiring others to assist them with their clothing, hair, makeup, fashion, and jewelry. In this new paradigm, the housewife's job is, in essence, to be a professional woman. Whereas one might expect the housewife's family to comprise her most central or prized affective bond, the relationships the housewives have with each other more often hold this designation. Housewives commercialize wifedom at the same time that they are commodified by it, and their work is defined by a network that has staked its fortunes on cultivating an affluent consumer base.

In 2006, the first installment of what would become the franchise, *The Real Housewives of Orange County* presented itself as a docu-soap take on ABC's then popular, fictional *Desperate Housewives*. Bravo initially promised that its show would depict "real-life 'desperate housewives' with an authentic look at their day-to-day drama."[1] Despite this ethnographic claim, *The Real Housewives* programs quickly became known as career makers for their stars. The crashing of a White House state dinner in 2009 by the status-seeking couple Michaele and Tareq Salahi, who were at the time being filmed for the short-lived *The Real Housewives of Washington DC*, stands as perhaps the most preposterous example of how the show has historically rewarded the quest for exposure with more exposure. For numerous women, in fact, appearing on *The Real Housewives* is tantamount to the start of a new career, and their appearances testify to an impulse to use an already wealthy lifestyle in service of both profit and exposure. In addition to earning money by allowing cameras to follow them as they dine out, shop, and attend high-end soirees, the housewives' public perch grants them the access and legitimacy to turn their professionalization of wifedom into a profitable business enterprise.

Bravo has also ushered careers whereby housewives serve as entrepreneurs purveying luxury high-status goods. These commodities run the gamut to include clothing, makeup, shoes, handbags, beauty products, advice books (particularly in the realm of diet and exercise), memoirs, cookbooks, wines and spirits, food, workout accessories, and beyond. As June Deery observes, "If the participants don't have a business to publicize when a series starts, most eventually do. Hence, the show in part creates the wealthy lifestyle it portrays . . . some participants afford their lifestyle in part by selling its props (clothing, cosmetics, alcohol) to others."[2] Though varied, housewives' products nevertheless remain tethered in some way to the concept of aspirational femininity, connecting the sort of appearance or activity that a well-heeled woman might enjoy to a marketable item that allows purchasers to indulge in the fantasy of a high-end life.

In addition to marketing actual goods, participants on *The Real Housewives of Beverly Hills* also sell their fame, and this effort to ensure access to celebrity culture has taken a number of telling turns. Camille Grammer, for example, appeared on the first two seasons of the show, encouraged by her then husband Kelsey Grammer, famous for his work on the sitcoms *Cheers* and *Frasier*. Though the couple at the time worked together at the production company founded by Kelsey, he advised his wife to join *The Real Housewives of Beverly Hills* as a way to pursue a career trajectory separate from his. This advice soon looked like his own cynical calculation, a move designed to divert her attention while he moved to New York, pursued an extramarital affair, and eventually acquired a new wife. Former child star Kim Richards and her sister Kyle, both half sisters to Kathy Hilton and aunts to socialites Paris and Nicky Hilton, have been on the Beverly Hills series since its inception. Kim Richards's erratic behaviors, recurring struggles with drug and alcohol addiction, and mental illness (including a conviction for shoplifting) resulted in her dismissal in 2015, though she continues to appear on a guest basis. As if to further shore up its investment in offering viewers an insider perspective on Hollywood, in 2014 *The Real Housewives of Beverly Hills* began casting actors from soap operas and nighttime serials looking to expand their performative registers, including *Melrose Place* star Lisa Rinna and soap opera doyen Eileen Davidson. In 2017, Teddi Mellencamp, daughter of rock musician John Cougar Mellencamp, joined the cast. The show was augmented again in 2018 by Denise Richards, actress, model, and ex-wife of Charlie Sheen.

The Real Housewives of Beverly Hills offers viewers seemingly unfettered access to the lives of stars and their relatives, plotlines presented in sensationalist styles. In keeping with the generic requirements of the docu-soap, dramas tend to revolve around marital and familial disruptions, misunderstandings between castmates, and frequently, intentional or unintentional deceptions. The show's ethos is therefore congruent with larger trends in celebrity culture whereby celebrity status is not merely tied to but ameliorated by familiarity with fans and what seems to be open access to a star's wants, desires, disappointments, and triumphs.[3]

This access to celebrity affluence (and its backstage drama) distinguishes Bravo's network brand. Beginning initially as an arts channel, most famous for *Inside the Actor's Studio*, Bravo was purchased by NBC in 2002 and network executives quickly attempted to find Bravo's footing in this larger roster of programming.[4] Known for semi-highbrow content that called to older audiences, Bravo signaled a shift in tone with its introduction of *Queer Eye for the Straight Guy*, a makeover show where five gay men gave grooming, manners, houseware, and fashion advice to a hapless straight man, often at the behest of his long-suffering wife or girlfriend.[5] With this program, Bravo indicated an evolution in its network identity, one that would eventually crystalize into a distinctive brand focusing primarily on upscale lifestyle content meant to appeal to men and women alike. That said, depictions of gay men tend to appeal specifically to women viewers, argues Katherine Sender, thanks to "their historical association with taste and fashion, their status as straight women's best friends, and their availability as objects of desire (however unattainable)."[6] Sender calls this "dualcasting" and asserts that gay men's appearances on Bravo were used to attract young, female audiences to this heretofore somewhat stodgy network. Gay men served well in this capacity because, in Sender's rendering, they are "trend-setting, affluent, female-friendly, and newsworthy,"[7] an ascription that serves as an apt encapsulation of Bravo's program content and brand appeal.

In 2007, Bravo commissioned a self-study to more fully map the contours of its audiences and to better comprehend how its turn toward glossy, reality television programs was attracting advertiser-coveted demographics. Subsequent to this study, Bravo coined the phrase "affluencer" to suggest the sort of audience member that it most actively sought to court. The term connotes the union of "influence" and "affluence" and underscores the equal significance of the two. Affluencers enjoy displaying the objects and experiences to which their wealth grants them access, and they simultaneously exist as influential brand ambassadors, acting as tastemakers and trendsetters. By codifying its intended market appeal to be both descriptive of what it *actually* did and prescriptive in the sense of what it *should* do, Bravo extended and expanded what was already a recognizable niche. *The Real Housewives* franchise was in turn instrumental in this effort, concretizing the Bravo brand by clarifying its values, aesthetic, and appeal.

Importantly, *The Real Housewives* franchise is closely aligned with executive producer Andy Cohen, the no-holds-barred creator and host of *Watch What Happens Live with Andy Cohen* as well as moderator of the always-incendiary *Real Housewives* reunion specials. As Martina Baldwin rightly points out, "As a middle-aged, openly gay, urban, tech savvy, educated, pop culture-obsessed man, Cohen is essentially the consummate affluencer."[8] Cohen's seminal role in having both created and set the tone for the franchise—specifically his encouragement of confessional exchanges between housewives that paradoxically privilege competition and vulnerability at the same time—shore up affective parameters that demand that housewives engage in relational efforts while also curating performances of femininity.

In its own rendering, Bravo is a premiere lifestyle destination for "food, fashion, beauty, design, digital and pop culture,"[9] and the women appearing on *The Real Housewives* present audiences with precisely such a vision of femininity. Their lives and lifestyles valorize consumerism, celebrate body modification, and revel in conspicuous consumption, according to Nicole Cox and Jennifer Proffitt.[10] A sense of competition over material goods, as well as the status and visibility that such access affords, organizes the lives of housewives, and Bravo cultivates a demand for perfection vis-à-vis the operationalized existence of success. Bravo's housewives, as well as its ideal audiences, are affluent, educated, social connectors, ambitious about their lives, their looks, and their social capital. *The Real Housewives of Beverly Hills* long-standing cast member Lisa Vanderpump, owner and operator of a number of exclusive eateries and bars, exemplifies this affective and economic register. The inspiration for the spinoff *Vanderpump Rules*, which takes viewers behind the scenes of the "it" restaurant SUR in West Hollywood, Vanderpump is defined by her staggering wealth, British accent, scathing dismissals of the other housewives, and seemingly unshakeable confidence in her righteousness and unassailable taste.

Wealth clearly provides both the mise-en-scène and the narrative impetus for the panoply of shows that fall under the moniker of *The Real Housewives*—they all offer viewers the pleasure of being granted access to upscale public spaces, gala events, high-profile charity auctions, and vacations in exotic locales. Public forays are in turn matched with private confessionals wherein heavily-made-up, lavishly accessorized, and elegantly dressed housewives appear in palatial homes, offering reflections and comments, and specifically dishing on their feelings about the other housewives. Thanks to this focus on fashion, femininity, and female groups, the shows also share an aesthetic sensibility with HBO's *Sex and the City*, another series that was heralded for having provided an enviable vision of a feminized high life and drew female viewers on this basis. Although *Desperate Housewives* was often claimed as *Sex and the City*'s progeny, due in large part to its concentration on female friendship and a premier date just months after *Sex and the City*'s final episode, the nonfiction *Real Housewives* more aptly deserves this attribution. Both *Sex and the City* and *The Real Housewives* stress female scrappiness and self-assurance, tales told against the backdrop of high-end locations, particularly restaurants and bars. Similarly, *Sex and the City* was instrumental in helping lend HBO its "quality television" designation, much as *The Real Housewives* assisted in concretizing Bravo's appeal to the affluencer demographic.

At the same time, and in a manner very unlike the tone found in *Sex and the City*, the housewives' friendships are often superficial and transactional, if not downright acrimonious. Often, the production transparently criticizes this untoward behavior, specifically through editing techniques such as reaction shots that showcase the housewives as vain, catty, materialistic, and mean. Bravo, explains Jorie Lagerwey, "simultaneously promotes its performers, their products, and the luxurious lives they appear to lead, while conspiring with middle- and upper-middle-class consumers to mock and discipline their out-of-reach consumption and out-of-bounds behavior."[11] This strategy also dovetails with the presentation of the housewives' now-notorious fights by granting viewers a chance to stand back and take an ironic view of the women's foibles. "The show's mockery and prosecution of tremendously wealthy women may also let the merely affluent viewers off the hook," speculate Michael Lee and Leigh Moscowitz.[12] "In their role as viewer-judge, they may conclude that some rich people do their class comically wrong."[13] A distanced perspective also allows viewers to better position themselves as savvy observers who are in on the joke. This collective sense of audience remove is a hallmark of the postfeminist mediascape, which tends to sell women's insignificance and narcissism back to them under the mantle of irony.[14] All the same, the show allows viewers to witness women suffering from affective disappointments and gain insight into the vagaries of female groups, a viewpoint that has proved attractive to female audiences.

The franchise's prioritization of intimate bonds, lifestyle drama, and evocative mise-en-scène also confirms its melodramatic tendencies; according to Pier Dominguez, it "publicizes and spectacularizes the private and the everyday."[15] This designation need not, however, be an indictment, insofar as melodramas, as a historical media category, often display a remarkable ability to unearth emotional truths. In the case of *The Real Housewives* franchise, Bravo's shows routinely testify to a willingness to acknowledge the secrets that lie beneath the surface of manicured lives. Despite the appearance that such fractures are spurred solely by petty slights, invented injuries, and salacious gossip, in truth, these fissures may be instigated by deeply personal traumas.

One particularly telling example of the way that *The Real Housewives of Beverly Hills* traffics in melodramatic conventions can be found in the first season finale "Unforgivable" from 2011. The episode serves as a climax of the season's myriad domestic tensions, including the crumbling marriages of the Grammers and Armstrongs; bickering disagreements that would later be the undoing of the union between Adrienne Maloof and Paul Nassif; the antics of a mooching houseguest of indistinguishable sexual predilection named Cedric Martinez, who glommed onto Lisa Vanderpump; and an increasingly strained relationship between sisters Kyle and Kim Richards. Things come to a head in a terribly awkward birthday party thrown for Taylor Armstrong by her husband Russell, a conflict that would eventually culminate in accusations that Russell abused Taylor, her filing for divorce, and finally in his suicide in August 2011. Armstrong took his own life in the midst of rumored financial ruin, and on the same day that Bravo disseminated a press release stating that the second season of *The Real Housewives of Beverly Hills* would feature Taylor's continuing struggles with "a loveless marriage."

"Unforgivable" is in fact bookended by disintegrating pairs. The opening sequence offers a glimpse into the behind-the-scenes misery of a seemingly glamorous life, as Camille Grammer heads to New York to accompany her now-estranged husband Kelsey at the Tony Awards. The sequence films the couple as they dress, toast the nomination, ride in the limousine together, and pose on the red carpet,

FIGURE 29.1.
The crumbling marriage of Taylor and Russell Armstrong played out over the course of the first season of *The Real Housewives of Beverly Hills*, with tragic results.

yet is interspersed with Camille Grammer's talking head sequences, where she admits that her husband told her before the event that he wanted to dissolve their marriage. Her attempts to make him outwardly acknowledge or praise her are met with silence or evasion and, post facto, Camille divulges that she was not recognized when she tried to enter the couple's New York apartment. Apparently, another woman had been residing there, whom the doorman naturally assumed was the actual Mrs. Grammer. It is plausible, of course, that Camille Grammer's narrative was more than a bit self-serving, given the large sums of money that were soon to be at stake in the couple's lengthy and contentious divorce. Yet her pain over the breakup of her marriage is still palpable, as is the fact that her position on the cast is contingent on revealing such acutely painful details. Such dramatic confessionals are indeed a requisite job requirement for continued employment as a Bravo housewife. (As a noteworthy follow-up, Grammer left the cast after two seasons but returned as a regular cast member in 2019, in the midst of planning her Hawaiian beach wedding to attorney David C. Meyer.)

The centerpiece of the episode is Taylor's rooftop birthday party where the redolent tension between her husband and her is made manifest in a lackluster toast where he stands next to her and vacuously claims, "It's a been a wonderful year. I really look forward to the next year. Happy Birthday," as the other housewives avoid eye contact and stare purposelessly into their drinks. In fact, earlier in the episode, Taylor talked openly of the couple's plans to take an extended holiday in Mexico following the party to repair their estrangement, and admitted to her own speculation over whether the marriage would survive. This awkward exchange is eclipsed only by the fight that follows, wherein, after whispering to Lisa Vanderpump that her sister is acting drunk, Kyle Richards proceeds to join the rest of the housewives in accusing Kim of not speaking up for her in a fight that

FIGURE 29.2.
The first season's myriad tensions climaxed with Kyle Richards's outbursts and revelations in a cramped limo.

Kyle had previously with Camille. In a typical melodramatic eruption, Kim tells a group, which includes Taylor, Lisa, Kyle, and Adrienne, "I don't even really enjoy any of your company," after she is fingered as stirring up drama in the group. The episode ends with a fiery, painful exchange between the sisters inside a cramped limo, where they each accuse the other of not recognizing their sacrifices on behalf of the other. Ultimately, a distraught and provoked Kyle blurts out that Kim is an alcoholic, an admission that, at the time, served as a revelation to audiences. The extent to which long-buried family secrets emerge in this episode—and specifically the symbolism whereby the enclosed quarters of the limo speak to the sisters' entrapment in this sordid family drama—point out the emotional undertaking that is public wifedom in the sphere of reality television.

The women featured on Bravo's *Real Housewives* franchise often become "housewives" to further their exposure, monetize their daily lives, and commodify classically feminine pastimes. All the same, they earn this moniker by living out the sort of familial, melodramatic storylines that comprise much female-centered reality television, allowing cameras to record their fractured friendships, marriage meltdowns, financial crises, and intergenerational conflicts. Though the unsightly realities of their personal lives may be obscured by glitz and glamour, the show unveils secrets that are vile and even violent, contrasting pleasant surface and ugly reality. While trafficking in and profiting from heavily stylized versions of femininity, *The Real Housewives* franchise is quick to reveal the housewives as ordinary in their problems and yet extraordinary in their privileges. In this way, their housewifery exists as both aspirational and cautionary. Such meaty contradictions have also proven to substantially benefit the Bravo network, helping to achieve the goal of market and channel segmentation by attracting upscale audiences eager to pry into the oftentimes paradoxically unbecoming particularities of wealthy women's lives.

FURTHER READING

Dominguez, Pier. "'I'm Very Rich, Bitch!': The Melodramatic Money Shot and the Excess of Racialized Gendered Affect in the *Real Housewives* Docusoaps," *Camera Obscura* 30, no. 1 (88) (2015): 155–83.

Lee, Michael J., and Leigh Moscowitz. "The 'Rich Bitch': Class and Gender on *The Real Housewives of New York City*," *Feminist Media Studies* 13, no. 1 (2013): 64–82.

Smith, Erin Copple. "'Affluencers' by Bravo: Defining an Audience through Cross-Promotion." *Popular Communication* 10 (2012): 286–301.

NOTES

1. Quoted in John Kenneth Muir, *TV Year*, vol. 1, *The Prime Time 2005–2006 Season* (New York: Applause Books, 2007), 112.
2. June Deery, "Mapping Commercialization in Reality Television," in *A Companion to Reality Television*, ed. Laurie Ouellette (Malden, MA: Wiley Blackwell, 2014), 19.
3. Suzanne Leonard and Diane Negra, "Celebrity," in *Keywords for Media Studies*, ed. Laurie Ouellette and Jonathan Gray (New York: New York University Press, 2017), 28–31.
4. Ironically, Bravo became so successful that it eventually eclipsed its parent company. By 2010, Bravo was worth five times more than NBC. Peter Lauria, "The 25 Most Valuable Cable Channels," *Daily Beast*, September 20, 2010.
5. Daisy Whitney, "Bravo Stretches, Adds Viewers and Advertisers," *Advertising Age*, June 9, 2003. The show *Queer Eye* was rebooted by Netflix in 2018, though that network cunningly annexed the "for the Straight Guy" moniker.
6. Katherine Sender, "Dualcasting: Bravo's Gay Programming and the Quest for Women Audiences," in *Cable Visions: Television Beyond Broadcasting*, ed. Sarah Banet-Weiser, Cynthia Chris, and Anthony Freitas (New York: New York University Press, 2007), 310.
7. Ibid., 313.
8. Martina Baldwin, "Buzz by Bravo: A Trendsetting Niche Network's Place within Contemporary Television" (PhD diss., University of Illinois at Urbana-Champaign, 2016), 40.
9. "About Bravo Media," NBC, www.nbcuniversal.com.
10. Nicole Cox and Jennifer Proffitt, "The Housewives' Guide to Better Living: Promoting Consumption on Bravo's *The Real Housewives*," *Communication, Culture and Critique* 5, no. 2 (2012): 295–312.
11. Jorie Lagerwey, *Postfeminist Celebrity and Motherhood: Brand Mom* (New York: Routledge, 2016), 53.
12. Michael J. Lee and Leigh Moscowitz, "The 'Rich Bitch': Class and Gender on *The Real Housewives of New York City*," *Feminist Media Studies* 13, no. 1 (2013): 79.
13. Ibid.
14. Suzanne Leonard, "The Americanization of Emma Bovary: From Feminist Icon to Desperate Housewife," *Signs: Journal of Women in Culture and Society* 38, no. 3 (Spring 2013): 647–69.
15. Pier Dominguez, "'I'm Very Rich, Bitch!': The Melodramatic Money Shot and the Excess of Racialized Gendered Affect in the *Real Housewives* Docusoaps," *Camera Obscura* 30, no. 1 (88) (2015): 158.

30

Roseanne
Programming Flow

TAYLOR COLE MILLER

Abstract: For decades, media scholars have theorized television programming not just as individual shows but as a flow, a carefully curated sequence of shows mingling with commercials, bumpers, teasers, hashtags, promos, scheduling, and so forth, any part of which might affect how we understand what we are watching. Using one episode of *Roseanne* that played on multiple different channels over the course of two decades as his case study, Taylor Cole Miller demonstrates one way of watching TV critically—dissecting the whole to grapple with the flow of its parts.

On March 1, 1994, ABC's *Roseanne* began with a warning: "Tonight's episode deals with mature sexual themes and may not be appropriate for young viewers. Parental discretion is advised." Known informally as the "Lesbian Kiss Episode," from spring sweeps week of the show's sixth season, "Don't Ask, Don't Tell" features a gay bar called Lips that Roseanne (Barr) and sister Jackie (Laurie Metcalf) visit to prove their hipness to newly out friend and business partner Nancy (Sandra Bernhard). But all goes awry when Nancy's girlfriend Sharon (Mariel Hemingway), an erotic dancer, unexpectedly kisses Roseanne, piercing her veil of heterosexual nonchalance and revealing a dark underbelly of gay anxiety and homophobia.

With increasing press attention ahead of the possible smooch, sponsors pulled their ads, and conservative/parent watchdog groups protested its representation of homosexuality, transforming "Don't Ask, Don't Tell" into something of a cultural event as ABC viewers sat through two full segments and a commercial break, anxiously awaiting the kiss. More than thirty million people tuned in, besting that year's Grammy Awards in head-to-head competition at the time of its airing, 9 p.m.[1] Twenty-three years later, at 9 a.m., CMT (Country Music Channel) played the episode—gay kiss intact—with no fanfare, no announcement, and no watchdog outcry. But it wasn't just sensitivity to the content of the episode that changed in the cultural context of the intervening years—the content itself changed. The station bumpers, teases, commercials, interstitials, logos, viewer warnings, TV ratings, time of day, and even some of the final edits differ between the two versions of "Don't Ask, Don't Tell" that aired on ABC and CMT. Added up, the experience of watching two versions of one episode of a television program can vary enough to alter a reader's interpretation, illustrating how context is an essential facet of television. Indeed, if the changes between two versions are significant, there is utility in considering each as distinct, comparable texts, the latter having been *retextualized* by reconfiguring pieces from the former with new pieces that together create a text with new possible meanings, sort of like a ransom note made from ripped magazine letters.[2] The most direct way of analyzing differences between two versions of one broadcast episode is through Raymond Williams's foundational concept of *flow*.

At the height of network television in the 1970s, Williams's theory of flow helped crystalize TV studies around a medium-specific theoretical idea. Instead of just reading the content of a program as meaningful, Williams highlighted the bridges and gaps between shows on a schedule, with programming blocks and commercial breaks flowing around and between segments as part of the "text" itself. His concept of flow as "the defining characteristic of broadcasting simultaneously as a technology and as a cultural form" articulates the centrality of a show's taken-for-granted periphery.[3] Flow is a sequence of sequences: There's the sequence of program content, the sequence of trailers for the network, the sequence of shows before and after, and the sequence of other commercial "interruptions." Nick Browne further frames a network as "a relay in a process of textualizing the interaction of audience and advertiser."[4] In other words, in the medium of television, shows are not surrounded by commercials, but commercials are surrounded by shows, with program segments as the connective tissue of the "flow" of advertisements. Browne coined the term "super-text" to clarify this combination of segments and breaks as his object of study.

Analyzing flow allows us to see a text in its natural environment, studying how all the different contexts and sequences surrounding program content might affect viewer interpretation, especially because, despite DVD and streaming technologies, live viewing is still the dominant way America watches television. Even in a world with fast-forward buttons, we miss the forest for the trees if we only approach textual analyses of shows without considering the contexts and channels on which they air. American television offers viewers more than individual programs with random commercial interruptions; rather, it offers "a planned flow, in which the true series is not the published sequence of program items but this sequence transformed by the inclusion of another kind of sequence."[5] Building upon the sequences of program content, network trailers, and commercial "inter-ruptions" that Williams argues comprise flow, I add intertextual sequences (the infinite connections and allusions between texts) and cultural sequences (the "real world" context and perspective that may frame a viewer's reading), as with Barr's racist tweets that led to the cancellation of the reunion series in 2018 that, for some, reframes the original series entirely. Through flow, all these sequences co-alesce to form a new, more comprehensive understanding of the text. What do the additions of or changes to commercials, teasers, bumpers, promos, syndica-tion cuts, and cultural discourses all tell us about a text, a channel's interest in that text, the targeted audience, and the different meanings a viewer may take away from different viewing experiences? To address these questions, I use mul-tiple versions of *Roseanne* to consider three important aspects of flow: content, context of airing, and the commercials that "interrupt."

The content of *Roseanne* featured female-driven, taboo topics like masturba-tion, domestic violence, birth control, and menstruation long before it premiered "Don't Ask, Don't Tell" in 1994. ABC initially rejected "Don't Ask, Don't Tell" be-cause of the kiss between two women; as then senior vice-president and ABC general counsel Steve Weiswasser said, the kissing scene "is not the lifestyle that most people lead."[6] Executive producers Barr and then husband Tom Arnold went public with the rejection, inciting a wave of press coverage and pressure by groups like GLAAD. Network executives strongly encouraged Barr either to edit the kiss or to cancel the episode, but she retorted "the real cause for con-cern should be centered around the endless depictions of women being raped, mutilated, and killed, every day on prime-time TV."[7] While the heretical kiss was its most spectacularized aspect, the episode as a whole represented a "radical de-parture in its cogent and sustained attack on homophobia and exploration of the shifting parameters of sexual desire."[8] Because Barr had a progressive reputation for supporting gay rights at the time, because Bernhard was once rumored to be Madonna's lover, and because Hemingway starred in the lesbian-themed film *Per-sonal Best*, cultural contexts and intertextual knowledge also colored the episode's story with meaning, although those "sequences" of information—as with the po-litical meaning behind its title "Don't Ask, Don't Tell"—may be lost on newer audiences whose first contact with the episode is in reruns.

The kiss occurs at the end of the second scene of the episode's second seg-ment. Its preceding scene, which I call the "Standalone Scene," is a three-minute tangent at the Conner home featuring only Roseanne's daughters and their boy-friends who are not part of the rest of the episode; in syndication, that irrel-evance will become meaningful. Afterward, the narrative focus shifts back to the gay club Lips for the remainder of the segment. Nancy and Sharon enter the club first, the music of Evelyn Champagne King pulsing as gay couples dance,

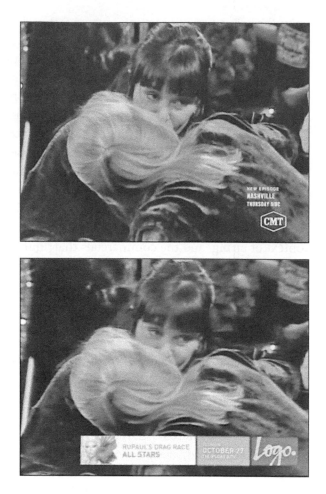

FIGURES 30.1 AND 30.2.
Same kiss, different flow:
"Don't Ask, Don't Tell" aired
multiple times on different
channels owned by Viacom
in 2017.

hug, and hold hands in the background. Entering a few moments later, arm in arm, Roseanne and Jackie are immediately mistaken for a lesbian couple by a woman that Jackie stammers is her "mailman . . . woman . . . lesbian," the fumbling of which embarrasses Jackie but delights Roseanne who plays along to tease her younger sister. "Now I know why there's never any mail for your husband," the mail-lesbian says. "No, no, you don't understand," an obviously pregnant Jackie protests, attempting to clarify how she's "traditional." "Oh, now, you don't have to hide our love, Pookie," Roseanne says, caressing Jackie's face. "Hi, I'm Roseanne. I'm the father." This "mail-lesbian scene" represents Roseanne as comfortable around queer people (and with her own sexuality), a foil to Jackie's immediate anxiety and hetero-defensiveness. It also sets up the humorous reversal later in the episode when Roseanne panics after being kissed by Sharon, as Roseanne has to reconcile her pro-gay politics with her newfound homophobic feelings, which later manifests as an obsessive cleaning binge. The sequence of LGBTQ characters interacting with one another also helps establish the club's queer identity and the show's own comfort representing such a space.

Notably on CMT's 2017 airing, the mail-lesbian scene is cut three minutes shorter, while the narratively irrelevant standalone scene remains intact. It is an industry standard that to increase profits in rerun syndication, two to three minutes of commercial time will be added to each thirty-minute episode, meaning two to three minutes will need to be cut from the original content. Writers know and prepare for these edits, especially when, like *Roseanne*, a show enters reruns before ending its original run. At the exact length of time needed to be regained, the standalone scene, which offers neither plot development nor any connection to the rest of the episode, is clearly the writers' sacrificial offering to syndication, and its placement at the beginning of the segment makes it even easier to kill. Instead, three minutes are removed from the mail-lesbian scene that introduces the audience to Lips, portrays a community of background LGBTQ characters, and texturizes Roseanne's hip gay politics; its removal thus has important ramifications for many of the episode's jokes and a cultural understanding of the episode overall.

Cable channels like CMT or Logo acquire reruns and movies to build brand identities for increasingly narrow target audiences. As demand for original programming increases, however, they quilt together lineups of older shows already popular with targeted viewers, which will also contextualize new programming for an affordable price. As a media conglomerate, Viacom bargained for a package of *Roseanne* episodes to air on its cable channels Logo (targeted to LGBTQ viewers) and CMT (right-leaning, country-western viewers), as well as TV Land (for nostalgic audiences).[9] All three channels aired "Don't Ask, Don't Tell" no fewer than three times each during a two-month span in 2017, and except for on-screen graphics, all featured the same cuts of the episode. In that same timeframe, Laff, a digital multicast network, also aired the episode with similar but fewer cuts to the mail-lesbian scene, showing a background of normalized "everyday" queerness in the nightclub you wouldn't see on CMT. Consequently, while Viacom rated the episode TV-PG (parental guidance suggested), Laff rated its version TV-14 (parents strongly cautioned), suggesting that a depiction of a gay club and potentially pregnant lesbian demand more parental discretion than a same-sex kiss shared with a straight woman.

CMT played the episode as part of a marathon of sixth season episodes that regularly feature the show's recurring gay characters, Nancy and Leon (Martin Mull). CMT's other acquired programs include *Raising Hope*, *Reba*, and *Mama's Family*, mirroring its target audience: working-class audiences in the "flyover" states. These programs stabilize the channel's brand identity for its originals such as *My Big Redneck Wedding, Guntucky,* and *Country Fried Home Videos.* Like characters on many of these shows, Roseanne and Jackie are blue-collar, midwestern, self-identified "white trash" women. Vintage wood paneling adorned with country art and rural oddities, chicken decor, and an "American Gothic" print texturize the background of the diner they own where the majority of the episode occurs. The heartland tastes represented by the diner frame the presumption of their matching rustic, old-fashioned political and cultural ideals. By going to Lips, they aim to prove to Nancy their straight lifestyle is not in opposition to hers, but as is the nature of the sitcom, conflict arises instead.

Roseanne successfully introduced pro-gay politics to a mass audience on ABC in the 1990s, and the show's frequent use of recurring queer characters in a non-urban setting helped destigmatize gay-themed storylines elsewhere on the network, which in turn led to an increase in *Roseanne*'s gay content. Similarly, CMT airs the reruns to help contextualize and destigmatize a gay musician character on its own original series *Nashville* (an ABC castoff); the channel stamped every episode of *Roseanne* with graphics for *Nashville.* By juxtaposing these two shows, it's easy to read CMT's version of "Don't Ask, Don't Tell" from the straight perspective of Roseanne and Jackie. They might struggle as allies of gay people in the same way CMT's audience might struggle as allies for the character on *Nashville*—blue-collar "country folk" trying to navigate political and cultural attitudes about sexual identities that are new or confusing to them.

Like CMT, Logo primarily airs *Roseanne* episodes starting halfway through the series' run, after it began regularly featuring Nancy, Leon, his husband Scott (Fred Willard), and Roseanne's out-late-in-life mother, Bev (Estelle Parsons). Logo airs *Roseanne* alongside other queer-favorites such as *The Golden Girls* and *Bewitched* in themed blocks with names like "Sitcom Therapy" or "Day Camp." Punctuating these blocks are channel bumpers and interstitials showing gay couples watching television, PSAs for HIV/AIDS prevention, spots for other themed blocks (including one for Halloween with Leon dressed as Hillary Rodham Clinton), and teasers for the channel's original programming such as *RuPaul's Drag Race* (a reality competition for drag queens) and *Finding Prince Charming* (Logo's gay version of *The Bachelor*). In addition to the narrative sequence of the episode, the commercial breaks and segments overlaid by audience tweets, hashtags, and pop-up queer trivia all coalesce to create a "second-sequence" flow of narrative information that together form the "super-text" on Logo.

Because Viacom's edit strips out much of the mail-lesbian scene, the ratio of time Roseanne is represented as pro-LGBTQ is reduced while her uneasiness and homophobia post-kiss are proportionally extended. While that cut makes the episode more palatable for CMT's typically right-leaning viewers, when filtered through Logo's queer flow, viewers like me are encouraged to identify more with Nancy and Leon than Roseanne, as we delight in watching Roseanne cautiously tiptoe into the queer space of *our* world like our own well-meaning mothers and be horrified by what they find there. "So, Friday Night, I'll get my chance to see Roseanne out with my people. That should prove quite entertaining!" Leon says. "How can I put this delicately? A gay bar is sort of like a size 12 dress. You just won't fit in!" The queer flow of non-content sequences surrounding *Roseanne* on Logo allows for the reading of a show that centralizes its gay characters and speaks to the perspective of targeted queer viewers, a stark difference from the show's original ABC airing warning parents to protect the sensitivities of their children, while the network protected the sensitivities of its advertisers.

The word "parental" in the warning that played before the original airing of "Don't Ask, Don't Tell" evokes an image of parents sheltering the vulnerable, impressionable minds of their children from flagrant acts of homosexuality or "mature sexual themes." Despite initially rejecting the episode, its phenomenal ratings prompted ABC to select it (without the warning) for summer re-airing in 1994. It has played on television multiple times every year since that original broadcast without the warning, often during daytime hours that reach signifi- cant child audiences. Given ABC's immediate re-airing, was that original "think of the children!" parental warning really about protecting younger audiences? Maybe not, especially because there's evidence of the network being overly cau- tious for the sake of advertisers. Kraft General Foods, for example, publicly pulled ads from the episode by "mistakenly" faxing an internal memorandum to reporters, which stated that "no KGF commercials can run in the episode . . . it deals with homosexuality."[10] But the publicity surrounding the Kraft cancellation had an unexpected benefit for other advertisers wanting to market themselves as progressive and gay-friendly, leading to an interesting example of niche broad- cast marketing.

Companies like Ultra Slim Fast, the marquee sponsor of the original air- ing, recognized the consumer value of marketing to what Ron Becker calls the SLUMPY demographic: socially liberal, urban-minded professionals.[11] In the nineties, SLUMPYs consumed gay programming as "a convenient way to affirm their open-mindedness" for similar reasons that Roseanne and Jackie visit Lips, and for similar reasons that some advertisers sponsored the episode to begin with—to publicly perform progressiveness. Because the warning appears only at the beginning of the episode and not just before the gay kiss segment, viewers weren't sure when the lip-lock would actually happen. Tuning in to see which other companies would be "brave" enough to join Ultra Slim Fast was thus a huge draw for "Don't Ask, Don't Tell," because advertisers weaved their way into the cultural message, self-branding as progressive so viewers would patronize their businesses. Alongside Isuzu, *People Magazine*, and several PG-13-or-higher movies, one notable sponsor was the early online service Prodigy, which bought the commercial spot immediately following the kiss.

In 1994, Prodigy was the first dial-up service to offer full web access. Its commercial for the episode emphasized the electric liveness of the web and its service as the fastest way to connect to other users, such as other *Roseanne* viewers. The commercial starts with a countdown before a narrator begins, "Hi, we're live on Prodigy at 9:14 [p.m.] Eastern!" She uses a computer to navigate to Prodigy's "Communications" page and Bulletin Boards (user forums), which conveniently feature a board devoted to "topics for parenting." Prodigy thus subtly suggests viewers use the service to discuss what they've just seen in real time, offering an early form of social media integration. It was no coincidence that the kiss came right before a commercial break, nor that this subsequent commercial spot would be its most profitable. Indeed, the moment still works as a powerful cliffhanger in airings today for brands using the same technique.

Like Prodigy, advertisers on Logo take advantage of the channel's narrowcast audience to garner the "pink dollars" of the queer community and its allies. Brands like Orbitz or JG Wentworth buy time in bulk on Logo for a variety of different spots, paying to air several commercials during a block of programming or over a set period of hours in a day, as opposed to a single ad on a single (but more watched overall) network program. For this reason, channels like Logo need a fairly consistent branding presence and established audiences to demonstrate strong ratings performance to advertisers with targeted viewers. Because Nielsen doesn't figure sexuality into its ratings demographics, Logo relies instead on the reputations of shows popular within the gay community to reach and establish this intended audience. Given that some viewers' first contact with *Roseanne* was in Logo's syndicated reruns, the channel thus had a vested financial interest in continuing to brand the show as queer-friendly through a variety of flow sequences and graphics so that the show could return the favor for Logo's brand. Advertisers on CMT, meanwhile, had a different kind of audience in mind, as evidenced by a commercial for Discovery's *Diesel Brothers*, a show in which a crew builds and restores mega-diesel monster trucks. The commercial played during *Roseanne* shows a monster truck crushing a small Toyota Yaris to destroy a "think small" mentality through hyper-masculinity and heterosexual dominance, a marked difference from the Groupon commercial on Logo featuring an assortment of "fabulous" women, diverse groups, and interracial couples doing activities like acrobatics, yoga, and visiting the salon.

Studying the sequence of these commercial "interruptions" as part of a greater analysis of flow in syndicated programming can be especially insightful because of cable's narrowcasting practices. They offer excellent clues about a channel, a brand, and the cultural value and textual meaning behind some of history's most prominent television shows. Such a flow-based approach to television criticism, as with my exploration of various versions of "Don't Ask, Don't Tell," reveals more than textual analysis alone can provide. Additionally, the study of such contexts becomes important cultural history, as *Roseanne* reruns were temporarily pulled from Viacom's channels following the controversy around Barr's racist tweets in 2018, returning months later to CMT but not Logo—only by documenting such ephemeral airings through analyzing flow can we understand how many viewers experienced the program before it was removed from television schedules. When studied in conjunction with the sequences of content and context—all three coalescing to become *flow*—a new, retextualized object of study is rendered to illustrate the importance of flow on how we watch television.

FURTHER READING

Gray, Jonathan. *Show Sold Separately: Promos, Spoilers, and Other Media Paratexts*. New York: New York University Press, 2010.

Harrington, C. Lee, and Denise Bielby. "Flow, Home, and Media Pleasures." *Journal of Popular Culture* 32, no. 5 (August 2005): 834–54.

Williams, Raymond. *Television: Technology and Cultural Form*. Hanover, NH: Wesleyan University Press, 1992.

NOTES

1. David Zurawik, "Homosexual Characters Blossom in May: Networks Open the Closet after Roseanne's Kiss Episode Earned Top Ratings of the Year," *Edmonton Journal*, May 3, 1994, B6.
2. While it's not the focus of this chapter, different versions were made for streaming and DVD. Ahead of the 2018 reunion series, the distribution company FilmRise remastered, tilt-and-scanned, cut down, and inserted its logo into each episode for streaming on Amazon Prime.
3. Raymond Williams, "Programming as Sequence or Flow," in *Media Studies: A Reader*, ed. Paul Marris and Sue Thornham (New York: New York University Press, 2000), 79.
4. Indeed, Nielsen measures what it calls "audience flow." Nick Browne, "Political Economy of the Television (Super) Text," in *American Television: New Directions in History and Theory* (New York: Routledge, 2013), 74.
5. Williams, "Programming," 83.
6. "ABC Kisses Off Roseanne Episode," *Vancouver Sun*, February 7, 1994, C1.
7. Suzanna Danuta Walters, *All the Rage: The Story of Gay Visibility in America* (Chicago: University of Chicago Press, 2003), 69.
8. Ibid.

9. Viacom would lose money (or collect insurance) from canceling reruns still under contract after Barr's racist tweets went viral in 2018.

10. E. Stuart, "Big Marketers Are Divided on Issue of Homosexuality," *New York Times*, February 23, 1994, 2.

11. Ronald Becker, *Gay TV and Straight America* (New Brunswick, NJ: Rutgers University Press, 2006).

31

Tales from the Crypt
Content Regulation

LUKE STADEL

Abstract: From its commercial inception, American television has been subject to careful regulation by the federal government, regulation that has shaped the content of television as well as its economic and technical infrastructures. This essay explores the shifting discourse of television regulation in the 1980s in relation to *Tales from the Crypt*, HBO's first successful venture into scripted programming. As a show that infused the prestigious anthology format with graphic violence, explicit sexuality, and profane language, *Tales from the Crypt* both emulated and transgressed the aesthetic conventions of older regulatory paradigms, offering a model for content production that would be taken up by numerous subsequent HBO series, especially shows of the "quality" tradition, helping to cultivate niche address as a feature of post-network television.

According to late comedian George Carlin, there are seven words you can "never say on television." When Carlin, who first reached a mass audience in the 1960s with straight-laced turns alongside Johnny Carson on *The Tonight Show*, recorded this joke in 1972, the three broadcast networks had recently completed an overhaul of their respective primetime lineups, undergoing a "turn to relevance" meant to attract precisely the younger viewers who comprised the audience for Carlin's edgy brand of comedy. Yet if television's content during the 1970s, as epitomized by hit shows like *M*A*S*H, All in the Family*, and *The Mary Tyler Moore Show*, attempted to cater to the tastes and politics of younger audiences, it did so under the same self-imposed restrictions on content under which the networks had operated since the 1950s. American New Wave cinema of the 1960s and 1970s invigorated the box office as youth audiences flocked to films that showcased profane language, graphic violence, and explicit sexuality, yet television broadcasters continued to fastidiously censor all three.

While the 1970s sustained long-standing structures of content regulation in television, in which controversial subject matter was contained more by narrative structures than outright censorship, the medium would soon experience sweeping changes. The same year Carlin drew widespread attention to censorship on broadcast television, Time Warner would launch the channel Home Box Office (HBO) in lower Manhattan, and over the next four-plus decades, HBO would wage a relentless assault on the boundaries of content regulation, a process seen clearly in the network's breakout scripted series, *Tales from the Crypt*.[1] In 1978, the Supreme Court ruled in the case of *FCC v. Pacifica Foundation* to allow the FCC to regulate the broadcast of offensive content on television between the hours of 6 a.m. and 10 p.m., a ruling that assumed "television" to be a singular phenomenon.[2] The next decade, though, would see a significant shift in the sort of content allowed on TV, as definitions of the medium began to change with the emergence of cable and satellite system. The history of content regulation offers a useful lens through which to view major changes in the structure and cultural function of American television, especially the emergence of "narrowcasting" or niche address as a counterpoint to television's long-standing function as a medium for "broadcasting," a transformation to which the production and reception of *Tales from the Crypt* was essential.

Produced by Hollywood luminaries Richard Donner, David Giler, Walter Hill, Joel Silver and Robert Zemeckis, *Tales from the Crypt* was HBO's first significant foray into competing with the broadcast networks in the market for scripted original programming, marrying Hollywood-style production values with historically forbidden television content. The show was a clear success, with new episodes appearing on HBO for seven seasons, becoming the network's first show to have a syndicated run on broadcast stations, while spawning two Saturday morning spinoffs (*Tales from the Cryptkeeper* and *Secrets of the Cryptkeeper's House*) and two feature films (*Demon Knight* and *Bordello of Blood*). Although the FCC could regulate content on broadcast channels, cable operators like HBO were exempt from this restriction, creating a lucrative commercial niche. Given the relatively small and self-selecting audience of paying customers for pay-per-view vendors, cable system operators, and satellite providers in the early 1980s, American courts ruled that subscribers to such services could avoid (or indulge in) offensive content at their own discretion. In serving up nearly a hundred primetime episodes chock full of mutilated bodies, philandering husbands, bare-fleshed temptresses, and buckets of verbal filth, *Tales from the Crypt* offered a master course in indulgence, setting HBO's programming apart from the comparatively inoffensive fare available on broadcast television.

This essay outlines the context of the changing environment for content regulation in relation to the industrial and cultural norms surrounding television during the 1980s and 1990s. Viewers today who encounter Carlin's "seven dirty words" on television are likely to do so while watching the most critically lauded and culturally revered programs, a seemingly contradictory development that can be traced back to the mode of address cultivated by *Tales from the Crypt*.[3] Although now it's a largely forgotten piece of 1990s kitsch, *Tales from the Crypt* was a lynchpin program in the history of content regulation on television, bridging the inversion of moral hierarchies that would see forms of television content long considered culturally lowbrow elevated via twin processes of deregulation and industrial fragmentation during the 1980s and 1990s, processes with significant implications for the cultural function of contemporary American television.

The early years of American television broadcasting were fraught with debates over content regulation. Contrary to nostalgic conceptions of the 1950s, in which blandly inoffensive suburban sitcoms stand in for the entirety of the decade's programming in popular memory, television often pushed the boundaries of decency and taste in its early years, forcing the industry to self-regulate to avoid official government intervention, much in the way the film industry had done two decades earlier with the implementation of the Hays Code. Specifically, these debates reflected a tension between the kind of content popular in the metropolitan areas, where television was both produced and first adopted, and rural and suburban localities, whose audiences were crucial to the interests of advertisers but frequently did not share the mores and values of their urban counterparts. The earliest framework for content regulation was the Code of Practices for Television Broadcasters of the early 1950s, frequently referred to simply as the Television Code, a doctrine that would remain in use for more than thirty years.

Development of the Television Code was driven by two imperatives: protecting the medium's commercial structure and satisfying conservative moral critics. The commercial structure television inherited from radio gave sponsors significant power over content, as television shows were conceived first and foremost as a way of delivering audiences to advertisers. Television networks had a vested interest in adhering to the expectations of sponsors, who did not want to risk negative connotations from offensive material, an especially tricky task given the medium's early reliance on live transmission and the single-sponsor model. Furthermore, conservative critics bristled at the popularity of "immoral" programs, such as the allegedly lurid and violent crime anthologies *Lights Out*, *Suspense*, and *Danger*, which comprised as much as half of the primetime slate by 1950; these critics wielded significant political influence, forcing the networks to confront the threat of government censorship.[4] With congressional hearings scheduled to address public concerns over television content, the National Association of Broadcasters passed the Code of Practices for Television Broadcasters in 1951. The lengthy doctrine spelled out the moral responsibilities of broadcasters to their audiences and forbade subject matter including profanity, representations of "illicit sex relations," gambling and drunkenness, and even "horror for its own sake." Programs adhering to the code would feature the Seal of Good Practice.

Although use of the seal began to decline in the 1970s, as the FCC attempted to scale back network influence over television content, the code offered a largely effective solution to the problem of content regulation for the broadcast era. As a medium of cultural consensus, television was compelled to make mass appeal one of its central features, ensuring that mainstream programming would always have to be partially reconciled with conservative tastes and traditional moral values. The introduction of HBO in 1972, however, signaled the impending decline of traditional television economics, and with the reach of cable and satellite systems growing year by year, the Television Code was dissolved in 1983. Although earliest debates over the introduction of pay television argued that it would provide space on the airwaves for higher-brow content to proliferate, pay-based TV systems were just as likely do the opposite, serving up content too low, vulgar, or offensive for a mass audience.[5]

Regulatory and legal developments of the 1980s, especially those surrounding the various failed challenges to pornographic programming in the post-*Pacifica* era, opened up the possibility of content formerly forbidden under the Television Code appearing on television.[6] The era of network decline that began in the 1980s saw broadcasters competing not only against one another for the growing audience they enjoyed during the "Baby Boom" era but also with cable and satellite operators that were fragmenting that mass audience at a rapid pace. This more relaxed attitude toward content regulation can be seen in late-1980s sitcoms like *The Simpsons*, *Married . . . with Children*, and *Roseanne*, all of which introduced degrees of sexual frankness, violence, and vulgarity that were unprecedented in the genre. Yet if the working-class setting of these programs was a vehicle for cruder content to appear on broadcast networks, the scandals that accompanied their reception would demonstrate the persistence of the same kind of conservative taste structures that had long dominated television. For example, the raunchy comedy of *Married . . . with Children*, the Fox network's first breakout hit, was tempered in the wake of a boycott spearheaded by conservative activist Terry Rakolta, founder of Americans for Responsible Television (ART). ART's campaign against the show would see Fox move it to a later time slot, with network censors going so far as to ban a completed episode from airing.[7] As such, the boundaries of television content would primarily be explored on cable and satellite channels by funneling such content through television-specific rhetorics of distinction, a process that can be clearly seen in the textual structure of *Tales from the Crypt*.

At a narrative level, *Tales from the Crypt* evoked the quality aesthetic of the 1950s and 1960s while also presenting material that would have never passed network censors, wrapping formerly off-limits subject matter in a nostalgic package that baby boomers would simultaneously associate with distinguished programs of the pre-cable era and the subversive content of the EC Comics series from which the show borrowed its title and storylines. The show's appeal to quality involved three interrelated aesthetic choices: the anthology format, the use of a recurring narrator, and reliance on Hollywood talent. While the highest critical accolades of the 1980s went to ongoing series like *Hill Street Blues*, *Cagney and Lacey*, and *L.A. Law*, the most prestigious format of television's original "Golden Age" was the anthology, specifically the live anthology drama.[8] In contrast to ongoing episodic series, which presented characters and settings that recurred from episode to episode and season to season, anthology dramas would instead present a self-contained story and characters limited to a single episode, typically spanning a whole hour in length. While both formats had their origins in radio, the television anthology drama attempted to borrow the cultural prestige of theater, with programs like *Kraft Television Theater* and *The Philco Television Playhouse* putting the medium's crass commercial imperatives, implied by the presence of the sponsors in the title of the programs, in the service of a presumably legitimate and culturally valuable form of artistic expression.

By the late 1950s and early 1960s, anthology dramas began to be replaced in network lineups by episodic programs in genres like the sitcom, the Western, and science fiction, much to the chagrin of critics who decried the shift from programming aimed at sophisticated urban adults to programs that catered more to suburban and rural viewers, as well as the rapidly exploding youthful baby boomer audience. In 1958, the Emmy awards would institute separate categories for anthology series and series with continuing characters, with only one anthology series claiming the medium's top prize after 1961. That same year, FCC chairman Newton Minow's designation of television as a "vast wasteland" cordoned off television's earliest era of distinctive and valuable programming from subsequent aesthetic developments in the medium, a sentiment that would largely persist until the late 1990s. In reviving the anthology format for a primetime series, *Tales from the Crypt* hailed prospective viewers with a mode of televisual address that would seem distinctive from the episodic fare that remained the primary focus of network programming, an aesthetic difference that reinforced the inherently upscale appeal of consuming a subscription-based rather than ad-supported service.

The framing device of the recurring narrator also evoked the experience of critically acclaimed anthology series, specifically *The Twilight Zone* and *Alfred Hitchcock Presents*, both of which bridged the transition from anthology drama to genre programming as the television's dominant form. Following an

FIGURE 31.1.
The Cryptkeeper collapsed highbrow and lowbrow in a single figure, as seen in the conclusion of *Demon Knight*.

elaborate introductory sequence punctuated by a splashy videographic title, episodes of *Tales from the Crypt* were bookended by segments featuring the eponymous Cryptkeeper, a grotesque puppet voiced by John Kassir. At the level of voice performance and textual positioning, the Cryptkeeper was presented to evoke earlier anthology hosts by combining Rod Serling's dry New York tenor with the droll London affect of Alfred Hitchcock, with the character's penchant for chaining bad puns, further drawing on Hitchcock's auditory repertoire.[9] The function of the Cryptkeeper as simultaneously a figure of distinction and a figure of abjection, both a marker of a certain highbrow mode of television address and a literally grotesque and horrifying figure, typifies the way that *Tales from the Crypt* would establish a tight connection between cultural prestige and forbidden televisual pleasures, both of which served as appeals to prospective HBO subscribers.

The higher-brow address of the anthology format was reinforced by the imprimatur of Hollywood talent, with names ranging from the series' A-list executive producers (like Zemeckis and Hill) to more than two dozen current or future Academy Award-nominated actors, not to mention the lavish sets and stylized presentation that pushed production costs to unprecedented levels at the time, nearing $1 million per episode. For example, in season 3, Joe Pesci starred in the episode "Split Personality," playing sleazy con artist Vic, just eighteen months removed from his win for Best Supporting Actor for his performance in *Goodfellas*. After ripping off a fellow card player (played by fellow Academy Award winner Burt Young) at the beginning of the episode, Vic lounges in his motel bed with a prostitute, relaying a perverse fantasy of "making it" with twins, a wish he'll soon find granted. In a somewhat obvious twist of fate, the next scene finds Vic stranded at a mansion inhabited by a pair of wealthy recluses, who just so happened to be identical twins. When Vic first approaches their bizarre modernist mansion, he exclaims, "what the *fuck* is this *shit*?!" combining two of Carlin's seven words in a single turn of phrase. Over the remainder of the episode, Vic attempts to con the twin spinsters with a fictitious twin of his own, scheming to inherit their entire fortune rather than just the half he'd get from choosing

FIGURE 31.2.
Tales from the Crypt
frequently engaged in
stylistic flourishes cop-
ied from Hollywood
auteurs.

one or the other. Although Vic is ultimately punished for his bad behavior, his comeuppance comes in the form of a gruesome murder by chainsaw, with the episode concluding a De Palma-esque split-screen shot of each sister cuddling in bloody-soaked silk sheets with a dismembered half of Vic's corpse. The episode typifies the dual address of the series, cramming in every form of offensive content possible—even risking narrative coherence to do so, seemingly only because it can—while at the same time presenting itself as culturally superior to broadcast television by virtue of its pay-based model, as reflected by the flashy production values and presence of name-brand, award-winning Hollywood talent.

The episode "Television Terror," from the show's second season, offers perhaps the best example of this contradictory pairing of lowbrow content and highbrow address, in service of an allegorical narrative that emphasizes the divide between cable and broadcast television, framing the ad-supported nature of "free" television as an inherent moral shortcoming of traditional broadcasting. Despite the episode's often gratuitous foregrounding of sleazy sex, foul language, and graphic violence, these strategies are marshaled in service of a narrative that presents cable as inherently superior to the scandalous, lowest common denominator imperative of the quest for rating on broadcast television, as typified by the tabloid genre. In this episode, tabloid talk show host Horton Rivers (played by actual tabloid TV personality Morton Downey Jr.) stages a live investigative report at an abandoned mansion that was the alleged sight of a series of gruesome murders. For Rivers, the exposé is nothing more than a cheap ratings ploy, likened to an upcoming episode of his show featuring stripper nuns with breast implants. Of his audience, Rivers declares, "They'll believe what I tell 'em to believe," evoking long-standing concerns over the trustworthiness of broadcasters allowed to use public airwaves in a for-profit fashion. In typical *Tales* fashion, Rivers's various moral shortcomings, including having an affair with a production assistant, are punished when he and his cameraman are brutally murdered by a horde of ghosts, with Rivers's production team unwilling to intervene due to the soaring ratings his plight has drawn. The narrative concludes with Rivers doing a bumper promo about women who will discuss on his show "what it's like to have sex with Satan" overlaid on an image of his bloody corpse hanging from a window.

As an allegory of industrial crisis, the episode offers a critical perspective on the political economy of broadcast television that suggests ratings and advertiser support fundamentally compel networks to engage in a zero-sum game, leading to a perversion of American television's mandate to preserve the public trust. In casting Morton Downey Jr. to essentially reenact his real-life television persona, this episode offers a clever inversion of traditional moral hierarchies imposed on television content. This perspective was starkly at odds with contemporary critical sensibilities, as reviews of *Tales from the Crypt* generally framed the show as a fulfillment of television's lowest impulses, the medium's quintessential bad object. For example, the *Washington Post*'s Tom Shales, America's best-known television critic of the period, accused the show of targeting children, likening the eventual profits from syndication to "blood money."[10] Even as "Television Terror" offered a crude rebuttal to such critiques of the series, it also predicted the eventual reversal of traditional moral hierarchies associated with television content regulation. The growth of cable and satellite systems driven by the success of HBO and other networks would lead to a whole-scale shift in earlier broadcast paradigms with the passage of the Telecommunications Act in 1996, a development that paved the way for unregulated television content to rise to the top of televisual aesthetic hierarchies. The on-screen TV ratings introduced in 1997 by the Telecommunications Act would see the label of TV-MA, "for mature audiences only," become a marker of distinction for quality TV shows, which deployed the term "mature" to connote a degree of sophistication, rather than crudeness or indecency.

Although widely disdained by critics of the time, the success of *Tales from the Crypt* helped to naturalize HBO's subscription-based model and focus on niche audiences that would increasingly dominate television from the 1990s onward. This trajectory saw content regulation reduced to a quaint anachronism, something that only applied to the worst of television programming, not the best. This trend can be seen in the critical success of the show that would succeed *Tales from the Crypt* as arguably HBO's signature program, *The Sopranos*. A critical darling from day 1, *The Sopranos* was the first cable program to be nominated for a Primetime Emmy for Best Drama, finally claiming the top prize for its fifth season. While its critical reception differed sharply from *Tales*, its content was, in many ways, nearly identical: The show highlights the life of a mob family in New Jersey, a setting awash with graphic violence, substance abuse, and profane language, as well as a strip club setting to ensure plenty of gratuitous nudity. The most significant difference between the two series was the substitution of an anthology format for serial narratives, a process that involved elevating a formerly undistinguished narrative structure that was previously identified primarily with the daytime genre of the soap opera. Even if critics found the show to make more "artistic" use of such content, as a commercial and aesthetic strategy, *The Sopranos* followed a template for cultural distinction established by *Tales from the Crypt*, as would subsequent critically acclaimed HBO hits like *Six Feet Under*, *Deadwood*, *True Blood*, *Boardwalk Empire*, and *Game of Thrones*.

Within a decade, subscription-based channels would come to dominate the Primetime Best Drama category, with only two network shows since 2010 receiving nominations in the category. Joining HBO, pay-cable channels like Showtime (*Homeland*); basic cable networks like AMC (*Mad Men*, *Breaking Bad*, and *Better Call Saul*), FX (*The Americans*), and USA (*Mr. Robot*); and streaming platforms like Hulu (*The Handmaid's Tale*) and Netflix (*The Crown*, *House of Cards*, and *Stranger Things*) have convinced audiences of three mutually dependent conditions: The best programs on television are not free to watch, they do not need to have mass appeal, and they challenge the boundaries of television content norms. At a deeper level, these are notions that are reflective of larger changes in the political economy of American television. While contemporary critical discourses have seen television elevated to previous uncharted cultural heights, leading to a seemingly endless string of "great" TV programs, it is important to understand the historical path of distinction that has been interwoven with the cultural values expressed by shifting hierarchies of content regulation.

FURTHER READING

McMurria, John. *Republic on the Wire: Cable Television, Pluralism, and the Politics of New Technologies, 1948–1984*. New Brunswick, NJ: Rutgers University Press, 2016.

Newman, Michael, and Elana Levine. *Legitimating Television*. New York: Routledge, 2011.

Stadel, Luke. "Cable, Pornography, and the Reinvention of Television, 1982–1989." *Cinema Journal* 53, no. 3 (2014): 52–75.

NOTES

1. *Tales from the Crypt* was preceded by three short-lived satirical comedy series produced in-house at HBO, but *Tales* heralded what television historians Bambi Haggins and Amanda Lotz identify as the "emergent" period of HBO programming, spanning from the early 1990s to the premiere of *The Sopranos* in 1999. "At Home on the Cutting Edge," in

The Essential HBO Reader, ed. Gary R. Edgerton and Jeffrey P. Jones (Lexington: University of Kentucky Press, 2008), 162.

2. FCC v. Pacifica Foundation, 438 U.S. 726 (1978). Ironically, Carlin's "seven dirty words" routine was the key exhibit in this case.

3. While television historian Christopher Anderson argues that HBO situates itself "against the profane flow of everyday television," I would instead suggest that *Tales from the Crypt* demonstrates the deep indebtedness of quality programming to the "profanity" of mainstream TV. Christopher Anderson, "Producing an Aristocracy of Culture in American Television," in *The Essential HBO Reader*, 23–41.

4. William Boddy, *Fifties Television: The Industry and Its Critics* (Urbana: University of Illinois Press, 1990), 94–110.

5. On early class-centered debates over pay television systems of the 1950s and 1960s, see John McMurria, *Republic on the Wire: Cable Television, Pluralism, and the Politics of New Technologies, 1948–1984* (New Brunswick, NJ: Rutgers University Press, 2016), 87–110.

6. For a summary of debates over TV content restrictions in light of *Pacifica*, see Luke Stadel, "Cable, Pornography, and the Reinvention of Television, 1982–1989," *Cinema Journal* 53, no. 3 (2014): 52–75.

7. This episode, "I'll See You in Court," was eventually broadcast in syndication in 2002 in an edited form.

8. On the relationship between seriality and discourses of "quality," see Michael Newman and Elana Levine, *Legitimating Television* (New York: Routledge, 2011). On the anthology drama and television's first "golden age," see Boddy, *Fifties Television*.

9. Keen listeners will also note the influence of Margaret Hamilton's performance as the Wicked Witch of the West from *The Wizard of Oz* (Victor Fleming, 1939) on the Cryptkeeper's vocal inflection.

10. Tom Shales, "Hauntingly Familiar: HBO's New Crypt," *Washington Post*, June 10, 1989.

32

The Toy Box
Transmedia and Transgenerational Marketing

DEREK JOHNSON

Abstract: As a competition reality series, *The Toy Box* offers a productive site for analyzing the commercial partnerships between the toy and television businesses, as well as industry strategies relying on the transgression of boundaries between childhood and adulthood to determine the value of work. Exploring the partnerships among ABC, Mattel, and Toys "R" Us that drove the series, this essay reveals how reality television supports "transmedia" industry strategies based in licensing, cross-promotion, and intellectual property management, making these strategies legible through the "transgenerational" articulation of adulthood, childhood, and creative labor.

"Kids!" exclaims aspiring toy inventor Marguerite Spagnuolo. "My favorite people!" In the hopes of seeing her toy concept—the Grandmas2Share doll—manufactured by industry giant Mattel, Spagnuolo is one of thirty-five contestants on the first season of *The Toy Box*, a reality competition series launched on U.S. broadcast network ABC in 2017. Having just entered the eponymous space of the "Toy Box," she confronts a panel of children who will ask questions about, play with, and evaluate the merits of her prototype. The pleasure she performs in meeting these children, however, contrasts with her reported feelings in crosscut interview footage: "These kids are holding the key to my success," she says. Contestant Rick Aguila shares this assessment in a separate episode. "The tables have flipped here," the Party Cannon inventor notes, juxtaposing the situation to his day job as a middle school teacher with authority to determine student grades. Yet here in the television world of *The Toy Box*, children evaluate the creative efforts of adults and serve as gatekeepers for the culture industries. The pleasures of the series thus turn on the conceit of inverting typical power relationships between children and adults, while imagining the knowledge, expertise, and evaluative perspectives of children as productive participants in real industry decision-making processes.

These representations of industry creativity make *The Toy Box* a productive site for analyzing the commercial partnerships between the toy and television businesses, as well as for considering how such industry strategies can rely upon the transgression of boundaries between childhood and adulthood in determining the value of work. In this sense, *The Toy Box* is ultimately about the ways in which industry power might extend from the management of the boundaries between adults and kids. By looking first at the industrial function of the series for ABC, toymaker Mattel, and retailer Toys "R" Us, this essay reveals how reality television can support "transmedia" industry strategies based in licensing, cross-promotion, and intellectual property management, making these strategies legible through the "transgenerational" articulation of adulthood, childhood, and creative labor. While child judges are presented as authorities, adult contestants perform identities and professional ways of being that establish their connections to childhood and suit their aspirations to work in this child-centric industry. Ultimately, *The Toy Box* not only unites television and toy marketing but also frames those convergences as a negotiation of the unequal power relations between adults and kids, producing transgenerational media industry from creative work positioned across those boundaries.

Although not as highly rated in terms of viewership, *The Toy Box* most closely resembles ABC's reality competition *Shark Tank*, in that each aspiring inventor presents an entrepreneurial concept to a panel of business experts. In the first season, competitors faced not only the kid judges who held dominion over the segments set in the Toy Box but also adult "mentors" who served as industry gatekeepers in the first half of each episode. These adult professionals included Pixar toys creative director Jen Tan, candy bar creator Dylan Lauren, and toy reviewer Jim Silver. For the second season, ABC eliminated this mentor layer to focus solely on the evaluations of child judges. The series' promotional Facebook page framed this change as one of handing even more power over to children: "Who run [*sic*] #TheToyBox? KIDS! We're having a lot more fun for Season 2." This effort to center the decision-making agency of its kid judges followed ABC's broader interest in child-focused reality series, as it simultaneously developed a "kid-centered" *Dancing with the Stars* spinoff.[1] Extending established franchises like *Dancing* and premises like *Shark Tank*, this interest in kid-centric reality programming builds upon and reinforces ABC's existing network lineup. The selection of Eric Stonestreet—best known for his role as Cameron on ABC's *Modern Family*—as *Toy Box* host strengthened this network branding.

Yet while the series offers valuable industrial intertextuality for ABC, greater significance comes in building strategic partnerships between television and the toy industry. *Toy Box* is the first major television project developed by Mattel Creations, the content arm of the major toy manufacturer (in partnership with Hudsun Media, which handles practical production).[2] In promising to manufacture the winning toy concept, Mattel treats the series as both an extended marketing opportunity and a means of acquiring new intellectual property. *The Toy Box* serves as a "program length commercial"—or perhaps more accurately, a season-length commercial—building up to the announcement and release of new Mattel product, consistent with strategies of toy marketing through programming that have long been a concern of parents and regulators. The buildup to reveal a new Mattel product over multiple episodes also recalls the "total merchandising" strategies employed by Disney in its 1955 *Disneyland* series, the first season of which chronicled the construction and opening of the theme park.[3] Additionally, the reality competition of *The Toy Box* also afforded Mattel a significant source of research and development. Although the winning contestant is promised $100,000 for the rights to their toy concept, the submissions agreement casting form MysticArt Pictures requires all *Toy Box* contestants to sign explains that any concept submitted for the television program becomes freely exploitable by Mattel, whether they win the contest or not.[4]

The partnership between television and toy industries extends to the retail sphere as well, with the series promising viewers that the winning toy would be available at major U.S. toy retailer Toys "R" Us at the conclusion of the first season. In the finale on May 19, 2017, the series' panel of judges selected Ryan Stewart's Artsplash (a device for creating three-dimensional liquid art) as the winner; by store opening the next day, shoppers could find the product on their local Toys "R" Us shelves. With the retailer participating in this transmedia promotion, subscribers to its online marketing lists received weekly reminders to watch the television series in anticipation of the retail experience to come, even encouraged to reserve the winning toy in advance in order "to be part of this moment in toy history!" Other weekly emails from ToysRUs.com encouraged customers to enter a contest to meet the winner and tour Mattel headquarters. Throughout the serial unfolding of the reality competition, retail spaces served to connect consumers with these television and toy industries. The fact that Toys "R" Us soon after declared bankruptcy and started liquidating its U.S. stores in 2018 speaks to both the struggles facing toy retail that would motivate promotional partnerships with television and the dependence of this kind of television programming on the participation of toy retailers. Having lost the retail support of Toys "R" Us, Hasbro and ABC elected not to invest in any more episodes beyond the first two 2017 seasons.

Indeed, when considered as a television series alone, *The Toy Box* hardly set the world afire. Industry reports suggest that the series was only "quietly renewed" for its second season in 2017, without any fanfare or special attention. Its Nielsen ratings were neither impressive nor catastrophic, with 2.4 million viewers total for the first season finale.[5] Nevertheless, the series' industrial significance sits beyond its status as a television series in its attempts to forge ongoing development and marketing partnerships across the commercial worlds of television and toys. Moreover, the series' reality competition format also serves to render the labor of the toy industry visible. While *The Toy Box* builds television entertainment out of a strategic crossing of industry boundaries, its reality competition thrives on crossing cultural boundaries between adulthood and childhood, defining creative professionalism at this transgenerational intersection.

The ongoing development of the *Toy Box* format suggests producers and marketers see the spectacle of precocious children wielding power over adults' professional fortunes as its primary narrative appeal. Facebook promotions, for example, consistently focused on the panel of kids judges to emphasize how "these kids are in the driver's seat when it comes to their toys" and how "kids are taking control of their toys." Promotions focused on the power kids held over the adults working in that creative space: "If you want to see children crush the dreams of adults . . . ," one update read, "#TheToyBox is new at Friday 8/7c on ABC."[6] The series promises to give to child judges an industrial power over adults, determining who will and will not be allowed to move from the amateur sphere of reality television competition to professional relations with Mattel. In this way, the series positions children as cultural gatekeepers and arbiters of adults' professional dreams. By examining how the series centers its child judges as industry participants charged with evaluating adult contestants' worthiness (or lack thereof) to serve as professional creators in that kid-centric space, we can see how television renders the transmedia work of *The Toy Box* as a transgenerational enterprise. In this intersection of transmedia and transgenerational creativity, narratives of industrial aspiration, belonging, and legitimacy undermine adulthood and childhood as hierarchical categories.

The Toy Box uses the power of television to bring meaningful visibility to the toy manufacturing industry. Marketing analyst Jason Lynch noted that some toy industry professionals saw the series as an opportunity to bring new notoriety to their typically anonymous work. While the series made the Mattel brand central to its representation of the industry, it also shone its spotlight at the level of creative labor, telling stories about the perspectives and agency of industry aspirants. One consultant interviewed by Lynch compared the toy industry negatively to other creative industries at a level of authorship: Unlike literature or songwriting, "very rarely do you know the names of people who invented some of the most important games and toys we have." By comparison, *The Toy Box* made it possible for you "to care about the person who created the product."[7] However, while *The Toy Box* invites us to see toy designers as authorial creators, its simultaneous emphasis on product evaluation also invites recognition of managerial labor as a crucial and compelling part of the creative process.

In other words, the series frames the creative labor of the toy industry not only in terms of adult designers but also in terms of work its kid judges do to identify and validate creativity. The toy industry has long relied upon children as market research subjects in playtesting and focus groups, but *The Toy Box* both presents kid feedback as a novelty and repositions child users as an executive authority. To be clear: *The Toy Box* does not show the toy industry as it actually functions; within its reality competition narrative, the positioning of children as central participants in creative labor relations performs important cultural work. Mattel's chief content officer Catherine Balsam-Schwaber claimed that being "able to see our business from a kid's perspective is a great opportunity."[8] However, what *The Toy Box* adds to basic market research—through its emphasis on the power of kid evaluators over aspiring adult professionals—is a meaningful framework for reading the industry and the creative labor of adults in tune with and actually governed by the perspectives of children.

Within this framework, the child judges work less as end users and more as executive and managerial agents driving the industry. While each judge exudes adorable child cuteness, reality television conventions simultaneously position them as titans of industry, inhabiting an otherwise adult mode of professionalism and status. In the package that introduces each season 1 judge, Aalyrah is shown in line at a coffee shop alongside busy business people, presumed peers from whom she is only differentiated by her choice of hot chocolate. The dialogue used to establish the judges' characters similarly establishes them as forces of industry professionalism. Another judge, Toby, wants "to give constructive criticism when I crush someone's dream," while Sophia Grace claims to be "the serious judge. Like, I don't mess around." The series thus presents its child judges not as end users but as a performance of tough professional class with knowledge, expertise, and social standing that puts them atop industry hierarchies (despite, of course, the lack of child executives in any creative industry in the real world). At the same time, the cuteness of that performance can often offer a parody of these typical business clichés.

Most exemplary of this narrative strategy is seven-year-old judge Noah, consistently costumed in ties and blazers to affect an adult executive habitus. In his introductory package, he sits in a barber's chair, asking for "a little off the top." His precociousness underwrites claims to professional expertise, where "I know toys like the back of my hand, just like I know where I got this scar: treadmill accident." Like all the judges, Noah is a child actor, with numerous prior ap-pearances on *The Ellen DeGeneres Show*, and here he performs his character by inviting us to imagine him cramming some exercise into a busy work schedule. His popular culture references also seem too adult for his age; he quotes *Scarface* while testing a projectile parachute toy in a later episode: "Say hello to my little friend!" While Eric Stonestreet remarks, "That's a highly inappropriate movie for children!" this transgression of childhood boundaries nevertheless reinforces Noah's claim to belonging in the otherwise adult space of industry. Notably, of the four original judges, Noah alone retained his role for season 2—suggesting his brand of executive performativity fit best with the overall series vision. At the same time, however, Noah's performance might also be read as critical par-ody of adult executive habitus (as well as reality television representations of the business world on *The Apprentice* and *Shark Tank*). His frequent combination of nonsensical remarks with strong claims to expertise, as well as combative and insensitive attitude, highlight the possibility that executive authorities might ac-tually lack the knowledge to arbitrate the creative labor of others. Noah exag-gerates his experiences building forts out of pillows and blankets, for example, as having had a prior career as an architect. In response to a line of multicul-tural dolls with specialized hairbrushes, Noah remarks "that will be really good for kids that live in the world of disco!" He also refuses to pronounce the doll's name, Niya, correctly ("potato, potato" he offers when corrected). In a later epi-sode, he constructs a crude implement out of TubeLox construction toys and asks his fellow judges "who needs a back massage?" to which an uncomfortable Sophia Grace responds, "Um, not me." While embodying executive power, Noah allows that adult executive authority to be ascribed to childishness and even the white, male privilege behind his performances of power. Whether such a critical parody of industry hierarchies is intended, *Toy Box* deploys Noah and the other judges to articulate childhood to executive professionalism.

Meanwhile, program contestants blur categories of age and generation in other ways, defining their status as aspiring creative industry professionals in relation to nostalgic ideologies of childhood dreams, parental identities defined in rela-tion to childhood, and transgressions of adult boundaries. As showrunner Susan House notes, the series' combination of adults' creative ambitions with childhood themes supports broad audience appeal across generational lines: "It's celebrat-ing invention, creativity, childhood and nostalgia," she explains, "and everyone can relate to that."[9] More specifically, however, the series links successful creative invention and professional potential to greater proximity to childhood. The most common narrative framework imposed on contestants in the first season framed creative work as the culmination of childhood fantasies. Inventor Rick Aguila, in the first episode, describes his aim of working with Mattel as something that

FIGURE 32.1. On *The Toy Box*, kid judge Noah parodies adult executive professionalism.

would "fulfill a childhood dream." This theme stretches throughout the first season, with press releases announcing Ryan Stewart's victory in the competition as the fruition of childhood desire: "Ever since I was young, inventing was my dream and I created Artsplash to give kids a new way to create their own masterpieces. . . . To be able see something I created on-shelf at Toys "R" Us is a childhood dream come true."[10] Significantly, the transmedia industry partnerships driven by the series become meaningful through the destabilization of distinctions between adult creativity and childhood imagination.

Simultaneously, contestants personalize their creative labor by situating it within the bounds of family and child rearing. In the first episode, all five contestants situate their creative labor as some kind of extension of their relationship with their kids. Rick Aguila hopes his Party Cannon will provide his family "a better quality of life" and make them proud. The package for Greg Spigel, inventor of the Snap N Roll car, shows him with his family—his "ultimate priority"—and stresses how, after marrying his childhood sweetheart, he wants to share "the American Dream of inventing" with that family. TubeLox designers Rachel and Steve McMurtney tell of adopting two children after having difficulty conceiving, crediting those sons as "the driving motivation for what we do." Rachel reinforces this suggestion of professional credibility through proximity to children when mentioning that their home state, Utah, has the most children per capita in the United States. This connection between creative labor and child rearing frequently involves both risk to children and collaboration with them. The series foregrounds contestant stories about pulling kids of school, diverting college savings, and losing quality time with children to the inventing process. Meanwhile, contestant Troy Orsburne calls his appearance a "big moment" for his family because he devised his concept "with my children." Indeed, as presented in the series, inventor-child dynamics can often compensate for other missing markers of creative professionalism. In the fourth episode, Larry and Steven Huetteman utterly lack polish or presentational style when sharing their Chromotag concept. They exude amateur mediocrity in their plain white tees and khakis; yet the packaging of the Huettemans as a father-son team throughout the episode helps to underwrite the selection of Chromotag at the end of the episode over competing concepts like Parashoot that equally excited the judges: The Huettemans occupy a transgenerational ideal that other contestants (such as the fresh-out-of-college inventor of Parashoot) did not.

Within this transgenerational crossing of boundaries, some contestants perform childishness and hip youthfulness themselves. When his AryaBall wins approval of the kid judges, Babak Forutanpour gushes, "You guys have given me the best birthday present!" Other aspiring professionals shrug off "adult" composure, instead allowing their enthusiasm to bubble to the surface against the industrial authority of the judges. While Melissa Rivera, inventor of the Lightbox Terrier, claims no explicit connections to children, her own success in the fourth episode appears to extend from her "cool" factor and youthful ability to connect with kid judges. Considering her spiky hair and orange pants, Sophia Grace asks her, "Are you really as cool as you look on the outside?"

In the end, *The Toy Box* reality series turns on the troubling of boundaries. On the one hand, the industry strategies driving the series create partnerships across television distribution, toy manufacturing, and retail marketing, carving out a cross-promotional relationship among ABC, Mattel, and Toys "R" Us to merchandise new products via season-long journeys to a narrative conclusion upon launch. On the other hand, looking beyond marketing to the content of the series itself and its attempts to render creative labor behind that product more meaningful and visible, *The Toy Box* tells a story about an industry culture in which power derives from the ability to destabilize—but also work within—notions of adulthood and childhood. The kid judges on the series perform, and even critique, an executive managerial agency that inverts typical power relationships between adulthood and childhood. At the same time, the presentation and evaluation of contestants often measure adult creative labor in some relation to the dreams, identities, and relationships of childhood and child rearing. *The Toy Box* establishes a transmedia marketing strategy between industries and makes creative labor relations within that industry structure meaningful by articulating professional status and authority to the transgenerational. Of course, this is all reality television and no indication of how the toy industry actually works. Yet as a reality competition television series, *The Toy Box* markets not only products but also ideologies of industrial value and authority.

FURTHER READING

Banet-Weiser, Sarah. *Kids Rule! Nickelodeon and Consumer Citizenship*. Durham, NC: Duke University Press, 2007.

Johnson, Derek. *Media Franchising: Creativity and Collaboration in the Culture Industries*. New York: New York University Press, 2013.

Ouellette, Laurie, and James Hay. *Better Living through Reality TV: Television and Post-Welfare Citizenship*. Malden, MA: Wiley-Blackwell, 2008.

NOTES

1. Kate Stanhope, "ABC's 'The Toy Box' Renewed for Season 2," *Hollywood Reporter*, June 16, 2017, www.hollywoodreporter.com.
2. Ibid.
3. Christopher Anderson, *Hollywood TV: The Studio System in the Fifties* (Austin: University of Texas Press, 1994).
4. "Toy Box 2017," MysticArt Pictures, 2017, www.mysticartpictures.com.
5. Patrick Hipes, "'The Toy Box' Headed for Season 2 On ABC," *Deadline Hollywood*, June 15, 2017, http://deadline.com.
6. "The Toy Box," Facebook, 2017, www.facebook.com.
7. Jason Lynch, "Mattel Is Teaming Up with ABC for a New Competition Series to Find Its Next Big Toy," Adweek, March 26, 2017, www.adweek.com.
8. Ibid.
9. Ibid.
10. "Artsplash Is the Winner of ABC's Hit Series, 'The Toy Box.'" *PR Newswire*, May 19, 2017, www.prnewswire.com.

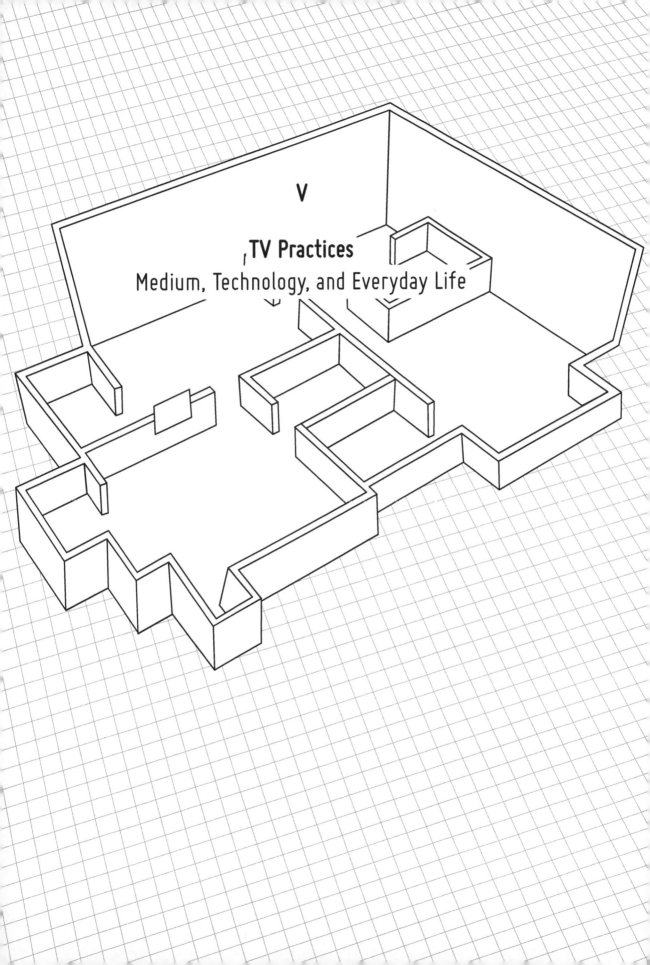

V

TV Practices
Medium, Technology, and Everyday Life

33

Battlestar Galactica

Fans and Ancillary Content

SUZANNE SCOTT

Abstract: Being a fan of a TV program in the convergence era increasingly means engaging "official" ancillary content such as podcasts and webisodes produced in conjunction with the series itself. Suzanne Scott's examination of such "textual expansions" of *Battlestar Galactica* shows how ancillary content enriches fan experience while also channeling participation in ways that best suit the industry's financial and ideological interests.

Most weeks, the opening credits sequence of the Sci-Fi (now SyFy) Channel's cult hit *Battlestar Galactica* featured title cards that read: "The Cylons were created by man. They evolved. They rebelled. There are many copies . . . and they have a plan." These lines were designed to summarize the premise of the show for audiences, but they also provide a useful allegory to explore the shifting relationship between the television industry and fans within media convergence. When the first studies of television fans emerged in the early 1990s, scholars focused on the transformative works (fan fiction, fan vids, and fan art) created and circulated within female fan communities.[1] These early studies framed fans as "textual poachers," producing texts that queered, critiqued, or expanded on the source material. Fans weren't passive consumers who were content to follow producers' textual "plan," but rebels waging a tactical resistance on both dominant representations and the intended meanings of the media industry. Alongside the massive growth of online fan culture in the past decade, the television industry's business model evolved to respond to technology's destabilizing effect on the relationships both between producers and consumers and between networks and advertisers. One way the television industry has tried to appeal to fans and acknowledge their growing promotional importance in a post-network business plan has been through ancillary content models.

Located on a television series' official website, ancillary content models consist of webisodes, webcomics, episodic podcasts, blogs/vlogs, alternate reality games (ARGs), and a range of other content aimed at fans. While these textual expansions and supplements are free, ancillary content develops alternate revenue streams for the industry via banner ads and embedded commercials, as well as being designed to reinforce the narrative value of the "primary" television text. It is easy to see how ancillary content enriches fans' experience of consuming a television series, but we must also consider how ancillary content channels fan participation in ways that best suit the industry's financial and ideological interests. Positioning a television series within a web of ancillary content that impacts the unfolding serial narrative offers the audience incentives to watch episodes as they air and eradicate time-shifting (streaming shows online or watching them through a DVR). Ancillary content also uses place-shifting (viewing television on mobile devices such as laptops) to the industry's advantage, encouraging fans to consume online content to achieve a comprehensive understanding of the series' master "plan."[2]

Using *Battlestar Galactica* (*BSG*) as a test case, this essay examines how the television industry's recent attempt to reach out to fans through a continuous flow of ancillary content might have a counterintuitive effect, alienating preexisting fan communities and negatively impacting fan creativity. Henry Jenkins argues that the transformative works that fans create thrive on textual ambiguities and routinely "work to resolve gaps, to explore excess details and underdeveloped potentials" in the text.[3] As television series begin to strategically fill the narrative and temporal "gaps" between episodes and seasons with ancillary content, certain modes of fan engagement are privileged over others. Through an analysis of the ancillary content surrounding *BSG*'s season 3 premiere episode, "Occupation," we can address broader concerns about the temporal and ideological strictures that ancillary content models place on fans, and consider the affirmational forms of fandom they endorse. Unlike transformative fandom, which values "appropriation over documentation, and multiple interpretations over hierarchical authority," affirmational fandom is characterized by a deep investment in both authorial intent and the "rules" that govern a fictional universe, along with a desire to comprehensively understand that universe.[4] As the television industry begins to reach out to fans, recognizing them as a powerful promotional force, it is important to consider which types of fans, fan practices, and fannish modes of textual engagement the industry is attempting to attract and encourage through ancillary content.

Creator and Executive Producer Ronald D. Moore ("RDM" to fans) launched his reimagining of ABC's 1978 cult series *Battlestar Galactica* as a three-hour miniseries in 2003, and quickly became a visible and vocal proponent of digital ancillary content.[5] In particular, Moore's weekly podcast commentaries and his avid defense of the narrative value of webisodes during the 2007 Writers Guild of America strike helped to position him not only as *BSG*'s primary gatekeeper of information and guardian of narrative continuity, but also as an advocate for integrating ancillary content into viewers' television experience.[6] The webisode series "*Battlestar Galactica*: The Resistance," and Moore's podcast commentary for "Occupation" confirm that the bulk of *BSG*'s ancillary content is concerned with executing and justifying Moore's "plan" for the series; at the same time, they also suggest a broader industrial plan to encourage affirmational modes of fan engagement.

Though Moore's *BSG* had always taken its inspiration from post-9/11 culture, the popular press immediately honed in on the season 3 premiere's clear parallels to the U.S. occupation of Iraq, and its sympathetic framing of the show's human characters as insurgents (thereby aligning their once-genocidal Cylon adversaries with American occupying forces). "Occupation" concluded with one of the series' minor human characters, Duck, infiltrating a graduation ceremony for the newly formed "New Caprica Police" (human patrolmen working for the Cylons) as a suicide bomber. Moments before Duck detonates the bomb, he murmurs, "I'll see you soon, Nora." Without further context, fans might have watched the credits roll with questions flooding their brain: What past "mistakes" is Duck referring to as he prays before the bombing? Who is Nora and how did she die? In the past, fans would have immediately begun to pick away at these ambiguities, debating potential answers and scribbling in the textual gaps and margins to create and circulate answers of their own.

Instead, many of these questions were preemptively answered over ten installments of the webisode series "*Battlestar Galactica*: The Resistance," released on Scifi.com in the month prior to "Occupation." Because the webisodes collectively had the same running time as an episode of the television series, were produced by the same creative team, and featured the same cast, many fans viewed them as the first "episode" of season 3. Accordingly, in addition to promoting the season 3 premiere, the webisodes laid the narrative groundwork for the season's first story arc, detailing the early stages of the Cylon resistance movement. Focusing on a pair of minor characters from the *BSG* universe, former Viper pilot Duck and former Galactica deckhand Jammer, each of the two- to four-minute webisodes detailed their motivations to join and betray the resistance movement, respectively.

The content of the webisodes informed the audience's understanding of a number of key narrative developments in season 3. Most prominently, the murder of Duck's wife, Nora, by Cylon Centurians in webisode 4 directly motivated Duck's suicide bombing in "Occupation," as well as dictating the episode's closing line. Duck's prayers in the temple in "Occupation" resonated more deeply with fans who knew of his conflicted faith from the webisodes. Likewise, Jammer's recruitment to join the New Caprica Police and serve as a Cylon informant in webisodes 7 and 8 enhanced fans' understanding of the death order carried out by Jammer and foreshadowed Jammer's eventual execution later in season 3. Because the webisodes were conceived and shot after filming for season 3 had begun, they ironically replicated fans' own production process, beginning by identifying elusive or ambiguous facets of television episodes and retroactively providing context. Some of these moments of ambiguity in "Occupation" are expressed verbally (e.g., Duck's statement that "Since they killed her, I don't have anything to live for") while others are created aesthetically (e.g., the slow motion shots of Duck during the Pyramid game, signaling his significance, or the pointed close-up of Jammer as Roslin's diary/voiceover notes that those serving the Cylons might be people they "least expect"). Because the webisodes aired prior to "Occupation," they functioned to answer fans' questions before they were given the opportunity to ask, settling debates before they were allowed to grow lively, and exploring the minor character backstories and relationships that were once the domain of fan texts.

If the *BSG* webisodes sought to preemptively resolve narrative ambiguities, Moore's weekly podcast commentaries functioned to retroactively contextualize and justify narrative decisions. Thus, the rise of producer/creator podcasts as a popular component of ancillary content models over the last several years might be viewed as an overt attempt by the industry to maintain interpretive power, while simultaneously providing a space for creators to articulate their "plan" for the series to fans. Jonathan Gray argues that commentaries have always functioned to "add an authorial voice that instructs readers on how to make sense of scenes and themes . . . thus constructing a clear 'proper interpretation'" of the text.[7] Moore's weekly *BSG* podcast commentaries routinely suggest proper interpretations, but they also suggest that the author himself is a key ancillary text for fans to consume.

Recorded in Moore's home, often with his wife Terry Dresbach (or "Mrs. Ron," as she was known on the SciFi.com message boards) present, the podcasts' amateurish aesthetic and their blend of intimacy and authority make them fascinating texts to decode in their own right. For example, the "Occupation" podcast opens with the couple debating whether to hold a fan contest to name their newly adopted kittens (a suggestion from Mrs. Ron that Moore quickly rejects). If Moore generally plays the paternalistic role of the all-knowing auteur in the podcasts, laboriously detailing and justifying every editing decision and plot point, Mrs. Ron's role might be seen as lending a "fannish" presence: we hear her complain that she can't hear the episode, gasp at plot twists, and make intertextual references, quipping that Starbuck being held in her domestic prison by Leoben is

FIGURE 33.1. Ancillary content on the official *Battlestar Galactica* website.

like "a dark *Groundhog Day*," and humming the theme to *The Patty Duke Show* as Moore discusses the technical logistics of shooting multiple "copies" of Cylon characters. At one point, Mrs. Ron openly privileges her fan identity, noting to her husband, "I'm not listening to you, I'm reading my thread on the SciFi [message] board." Yet, despite these displays of fan participation and Mrs. Ron's complaints that "everyone gets so literal" when interpreting the show, the podcasts work to reinforce the value of Moore's voice and interpretations, and affirmative sites of fan engagement, such as the show's official message board.

Derek Kompare has argued that it is "difficult to conceive of a more direct assertion of authorship" than a commentary, and that weekly creator podcasts make "such authorial exegesis . . . a normal part of the cult television viewing experience."[8] Moore's podcast commentary for "Occupation," which was available for download the day after the episode aired, clearly positions itself both as a central component of fans' viewing experience and a direct assertion of Moore's authorship over the television text as a whole, encompassing both the series and the ancillary content that surrounds it. When Moore presents alternative narratives, in this case reading directly from an early (and ultimately abandoned) draft of "Occupation" that opened with a Cylon propaganda film, he is less concerned with opening up new narrative avenues for fans to explore in their own transformative works than with exhaustively explaining why those roads lead to dead

FIGURE 33.2.
Fan art of
series creator
Ron Moore
by Arne
Ratermanis.

ends. In the case of the propaganda film, Moore simply states that "it just felt like the wrong tone," but there are many other more detailed examples of narrative justification, such as Moore's explanation of the placement of Laura Roslin's "diary" exposition sequence within the episode, or the rationale behind moving Starbuck's captivity plotline from season 2 to season 3.

Even when Moore's exertions of authority are playful (such as when he jokes about killing off a popular character), they ultimately reinforce the power of that authority (the claim is that such a joke would create "300 threads [on fan message boards] in about four minutes."). Moore also uses the "Occupation" podcast to stress the significance of ancillary content, and his role as an authorial overseer of that content. When Moore emphatically states that he's "sure all of you [fans] listening to this have watched [the webisodes] several times," discusses their development and intersection with the series, and emphasizes the need to view them "several times," he accentuates the narrative significance of ancillary content. By framing fans as narrative collectors rather than creators, Moore appears to be equating fan "participation" with consuming ancillary content.

Such ancillary content models could be viewed as a more covert form of cease and desist letters, temporally and ideologically (rather than legally) discouraging fans from certain interpretations of or elaborations on the text. First, there are the intensified consumption patterns that ancillary content models encourage. Because ancillary content is released between seasons or episodes of a show, fans who wish to explore narrative gaps and ambiguities through the creation of their own fan texts increasingly find those gaps either already filled in by the show's creators, or difficult to develop before another piece of ancillary content overwrites or negates it. Thus, while a narrative nugget of information dispatched in ancillary content might inspire fans, the creative window of opportunity for fans to play with it has shrunken considerably. We can read this shrinking window of time for fans to textually engage with an unfolding television series narrative as an exacerbated form of what Matt Hills calls "just-in-time fandom," in which fan productivity "become[s] increasingly enmeshed within the rhythms and temporalities of broadcasting."[9] Ancillary content creates a compounded form of "just-in-time fandom" that encourages an increased rate of consumption and the collection of narrative data, rather than fannish speculation and textual production.

Conversely, being unable to access and consume ancillary content poses a different form of temporal control. Australian media scholar Tama Leaver, writing about his inability to access "The Resistance" webisodes prior to season 3, has expressed concerns about the "tyranny of digital distance" that occurs when the economics that underpin digital distribution are exposed. Leaver argues that because the "expectation of near-synchronous global distribution [was] not fulfilled," fans outside the United States were forced to avoid participating in broader online fan communities for fear of being "spoiled," or to acquire these texts illegally via peer-to-peer file sharing. In deciding to limit the reach of the webisodes, NBC-Universal not only privileged American fans, but also displaced global fans from the intricate rhythms and temporalities their ancillary content created.[10]

Second, ancillary content could be viewed as a mode of ideological control, suggesting "intended" or "preferred" interpretations of the text. Ancillary content not only scribbles in the margins that used to belong to fans; it also encourages them not to color outside of the (often heteronormative) lines. A prime example is *BSG*'s second webisode series, "The Face of the Enemy," released online between December 12, 2008, and January 12, 2009. The first webisode in this series featured a fleeting kiss between Felix Gaeta and Louis Hoshi, alluding to a romantic relationship that Gaeta ultimately breaks off in the final webisode. The lack of prior evidence of Gaeta's bisexuality or his relationship with Hoshi on the television series and (a few knowing glances aside) no subsequent acknowledgement of their relationship for the remainder of the series are telling. Ancillary content models present a less commercially charged space to explore homoerotic storylines and frequently push queer readings or queer characters to the periphery of the narrative. This allows for a concurrent acknowledgment of the latent homoerotic subtext that inspires slash fiction (transformative works that construct a romantic relationship between two characters of the same sex) and a containment of such readings that neatly isolate them from the primary commercial television text.[11] *BSG* writer Jane Espenson claims that Gaeta's sexuality was never mentioned on the television series because sexual orientation was "simply not an issue in their world," but this utopianism doesn't sufficiently explain why some narrative connections between the television show and ancillary content are emphasized, while others remain invisible on the show's margins.[12]

Inevitably, some fans embrace this influx of ancillary content; others argue that interpretive power should belong to the audience for whom exploring ambiguities makes fan participation pleasurable. We shouldn't devalue affirmational forms of participation or presume that this binary between affirmational and transformative modes of fan participation adequately captures the diversity of fan identities or types of engagement. That said, it is worth noting that the affirmational fandom that ancillary content "sanctions" is characterized by more monologic than dialogic relationship with the text and its producers, facilitating the fan's industrial incorporation as a promotional tool. Though ancillary content presents itself as a more participatory model of consumption and appears to be facilitating more points of contact between audiences and creators, it remains firmly rooted in the "old media" broadcast ethos of television. Audiences within the era of ancillary content may have more sanctioned and visible modes of talking back to their television screen online, but these "conversations" are typically one-sided and privilege creators' voices and viewpoints.

The media industry's growing reliance on ancillary content and the corresponding creation of "official" fan sites online privilege affirmational modes of engagement, and reward hegemonic textual interpretations that neatly align with the creator's (or network's or corporation's) preferred understanding of the text. Ultimately, the concern is that ancillary contents' emphasis on affirmational modes of fan engagement may reinforce a hierarchy, legitimating some fan practices and marginalizing others.[13] Because the process of "watching television" now commonly includes consuming ancillary content, fans are presented with the Cylonian options of rebelling (continuing to pry open the text to construct new narratives of their own) or "evolving" (moving along sanctioned narrative paths and accepting the author's "plan"). Whether fans are "affirmational" or "transformative" in their engagement, the industry's "plan" for mobilizing and monetizing fandom and how fans respond to and potentially undermine that plan deserve further study.

FURTHER READING

Jenkins, Henry. "*Star Trek* Rerun, Reread, Rewritten: Fan Writing as Textual Poaching." In *Fans, Bloggers, and Gamers: Exploring Participatory Culture*. New York: New York University Press, 2007.

Kompare, Derek. "More 'Moments of Television': Online Cult Television Authorship." In *Flow TV: Television in the Age of Media Convergence*, edited by Michael Kackman, Marnie Binfield, Matthew Thomas Payne, Allison Perlman, and Bryan Sebok. New York: Routledge, 2011.

Leaver, Tama. "Watching *Battlestar Galactica* in Australia and the Tyranny of Digital Distance." Media International Australia 126:1 (2008): 145–154.

Pearson, Roberta. "Fandom in the Digital Era." *Popular Communication* 8, no. 1 (January 2010): 84–95.

Russo, Julie Levin Russo. "User-Penetrated Content: Fan Video in the Age of Convergence." *Cinema Journal* 48, no. 4 (Summer 2009): 125–30.

NOTES

1. See Camille Bacon-Smith, *Enterprising Women: Television Fandom and the Creation of Popular Myth* (Philadelphia: University of Pennsylvania Press, 1991); and Henry Jenkins, *Textual Poachers: Television Fans and Participatory Culture* (New York: Routledge, 1992).
2. See Cynthia B. Meyers, "From Sponsorship to Spots: Advertising and the Development of Electronic Media," in *Media Industries: History, Theory, and Method*, ed. Jennifer Holt and Alisa Perren (Oxford, UK: Wiley-Blackwell, 2009), 77.
3. Jenkins, *Textual Poachers*, 278.
4. Julie Levin Russo, "Twansformative? The Future of Fandom on Twitter," paper presented at the Flow Conference, Austin, TX, October 1, 2010, http://j-l-r.org; "Affirmational fandom vs. Transformational fandom," Obsession_inc, June 1, 2009, http://obsession-inc.dreamwidth.org.
5. Created by Glen A. Larson, the original *Battlestar Galactica* ran for only one season on ABC in 1978–1979. It was resurrected as *Galactica 80*, a spinoff that ran for only half a season in 1980.
6. Jenny Hontz, "Webisodes: A Battle against the Empire," *Newsweek*, October 23, 2006.
7. Jonathan Gray, *Show Sold Separately: Promos, Spoilers, and Other Media Paratexts* (New York: New York University Press, 2010), 89.
8. Derek Kompare, "More 'Moments of Television': Online Cult Television Authorship," in *FlowTV: Television in the Age of Media Convergence*, ed. Michael Kackman, Marnie Binfield, Matthew Thomas Payne, Allison Perlman, and Bryan Sebok (New York: Routledge, 2011), 107.
9. Matt Hills, *Fan Cultures* (New York: Routledge, 2002), 178–79.

10. Tama Leaver, "Watching *Battlestar Galactica* in Australia and the Tyranny of Digital Distance." *Media International Australia* 126:1 (2008): 145–154.

11. See Sara Gwenllian Jones, "The Sex Lives of Cult Television Characters," *Screen* 43 (2002): 79–90; and Catherine Tosenberger, "'The Epic Love Story of Sam and Dean': *Supernatural*, Queer Readings, and the Romance of Incestuous Fan Fiction," *Transformative Works and Cultures* 1 (2008), http://journal.transformativeworks.org.

12. Michael Jensen, "Live Chat with Jane Espensen," *AfterElton.com* (blog), March 19, 2009, www.afterelton.com/blog/michaeljensen/live-chat-with-jane-espenson. For a discussion of the "persistence of heteronormative containment" on *BSG*, see Julie Levin Russo, "Hera Has Six Mommies (A Transmedia Love Story)," *Flow*, December 19, 2007, http://flowtv.org.

13. Kristina Busse, "Podcasts and the Fan Experience of Disseminated Media Commentary," paper presented at the Flow Conference, Austin, TX, October 2006, www.kristinabusse.com.

34

Everyday Italian
Cultivating Taste

MICHAEL Z. NEWMAN

Abstract: While all commercial television has an investment in promoting consumerism in its audiences, few genres are as focused on the various dimensions of consumption as cooking shows. Michael Z. Newman analyzes Food Network's *Everyday Italian* with Giada De Laurentiis as an instance of lifestyle television, perpetuating cultural norms of gender, class, and taste.

American television is, with some exceptions, a commercial medium supported by advertising that pays for the programs. A TV show's audience is not only a collection of a large number of persons (a million viewers may not be that many, depending on the network and time of day), but also a commodity whose attention is sold by the TV station or network to the advertisers who want to reach those persons with commercial messages. Making meaningful and entertaining television content may be the agenda of those who create it, but to succeed commercially, TV shows need to attract audiences who are desirable to advertisers in terms of age, gender, and income, among other traits. One central purpose of television in American society is thus to promote consumption of the goods and services advertised during the commercial breaks. Seen this way, television is a consumerist medium, encouraging us to spend our money on burgers and sodas, movie tickets and jeans, smartphones and videogames, vacations and cars.

Everyday Italian with Giada De Laurentiis has aired in the United States on the Food Network since 2003 (original episodes were produced through 2008), and has more recently been airing on its spinoff cable outlet, the Cooking Channel. Each episode shows the host in a home kitchen preparing several dishes connected by a theme such as "Italian street food" or "Sicilian summer," as well as brief scenes away from Giada's kitchen discussing the episode's theme, shopping, and dining, often with others. Most of the show is concerned with demonstrating recipes, leading the audience through a series of steps toward serving an impressive and delicious meal. At the same time, cooking shows like *Everyday Italian* epitomize the commercial function of TV, serving as especially sharp examples of television's consumerist mandate.

Everyday Italian explicitly and implicitly promotes consumption in several ways. The thirty-second commercial spots that run in between segments of course do what commercials always do: they address messages to audiences to get them to buy items typically advertised during cooking shows, such as yogurt and paper towels, which often appeal to a household's "grocery decision makers."[1] But the show itself, the content, is also thoroughly commercial and consumerist, exemplifying a growing trend in recent media in which content is itself in some ways like a commercial. For instance, reality shows like *Extreme Makeover: Home Edition* promote Sears home improvement products and services, while *American Idol* features its contestants in ads for Ford cars. *Everyday Italian* is a food show, so episodes implicitly encourage the audience to shop for groceries to use following Giada's recipes. The setting is a kitchen where the host prepares dishes using a variety of tools, and so the show likewise invites us to acquire similar knives and appliances. Indeed, many cooking show stars, including Giada, endorse lines of kitchenware and prepared food. The Giada De Laurentiis Collection of products for sale at Target department stores includes cookware and bakeware, gadgets and cutlery, and DVDs of her television shows.

We might also think of *Everyday Italian* as an elaborate promotion for Giada herself, a Food TV star whose image and identity sell those cookbooks, knives, casseroles, pans, and jars of pesto that feed her status as a celebrity chef and extend her personal brand beyond TV. This star persona, promoted on her television series as well as in her cookbooks and in magazine interviews, combines a relatable and cheerful guide to cooking Italian food with a young, sexy, even seductive physical presence. For instance, in 2007 Giada appeared in *Esquire* magazine photographed in a skin-tight, low-cut white dress, the top of which resembles a push-up bra, with her hands and lower body drenched in bright red tomatoes, making clear the overlap of food and sex in her public identity. Giada's hyper-feminine and sexualized appearance and performance on *Everyday Italian* makes the show more than mere instruction in culinary technique. By offering up a fantasy of sensuality, *Everyday Italian* promotes not only the consumption of food and other products, but also of Giada herself as an image of sexualized desire and pleasure.[2]

For decades, televised cooking shows have had a strong pedagogical dimension, addressing audiences as students of culinary practice. For instance, in the 1960s Julia Child's *The French Chef* assured a generation of middle-class American home cooks that they could prepare impressive food themselves with the ingredients and tools available to them, and find satisfaction in the pleasures of cooking and eating.[3] Pedagogical food TV since Child has offered instruction to home cooks not only in efficient and practical skills of the kitchen, but also in appreciation of food and its effective preparation as an essential component of the good life. "Dump-and-stir" shows on the Food Network and the Cooking Channel like *Everyday Italian* continue in this tradition, offering lessons in various aspects of cooking as a practice requiring knowledge and skill. Giada De Laurentiis guides us as a peppy teacher instilling good habits and special knowledge about ingredients and techniques. She takes care to describe her ingredients (cinnamon is "warm," parmesan cheese is "nutty," olives are "rich and fruity") and to explain her techniques (shocking vegetables in ice water prevents overcooking, mustard helps bind a vinaigrette). She takes care to introduce unfamiliar viewers to the ingredients and practices of Italian cookery, translating the literal meaning of *biscotti* ("twice cooked" cookies) and explaining the uses of Italian pantry staples like hazelnut chocolate spread and *vin santo*, a dessert wine.

The audience of *Everyday Italian* is addressed in a number of overlapping but distinct ways: as consumers of food and other goods, as subjects submitting to fantasies of sensual experience, and most explicitly as students of kitchen technique. But in addition to the details of this culinary pedagogy, shows like *Everyday Italian* instruct audiences in a more general way of thinking and living. These shows open up viewers to a vision of good taste, presenting a model of how to live that we might attain, but more likely merely aspire to. Cooking shows are one type of "Lifestyle TV," a category of consumerist media including home decorating and personal makeover programs on channels such as HGTV and TLC. These shows are about the consumption of products (like food on cooking shows, furniture on decorating shows, and apparel on makeover shows) that are supposed to realize the viewer's desire for fashioning an identity particularly in terms of social class—or at least to offer an ideal of how this identity might be fashioned. Seen this way, a show like *Everyday Italian* is instructing us not only how to grill shrimp or bake a cake. It is also showing us how to exploit this knowledge as a form of *cultural capital*, a term the French sociologist Pierre Bourdieu coined to describe the way knowledge and skill function as tools for realizing and maintaining distinctions of social power and status. Taste can be very personal, and often seems deceptively simple and natural, as we tend to think of taste as being just good or bad. But it also has a social power to elevate those who assert their good taste and its superiority over those who lack it. Cooking shows cultivate their audience's competence in cooking and eating as part of a wider constellation of consumer choices.

Even as they offer us various kinds of practical knowledge and skill, however, such shows also function as an escape from social realities into a fantasy realm of sensual pleasures. The everyday routines of hurried schedules—of foods chosen more for availability and ease of preparation than nutrition or taste, of banal pre-packaged and hastily assembled, good-enough meals—may be cast aside. Turning to a show like *Everyday Italian* at a time of leisure allows for a vicarious indulgence in a seemingly more authentic and dignified, and more satisfying, experience of food preparation and consumption. The fantasy is not merely of having Giada's knowledge and skill, but the time, freedom, counter space, equipment, and grocery budget to indulge in the kind of gustatory pleasures represented in *Everyday Italian*. The idea that the recipes prepared are for "everyday" consumption is evidently more hopeful than practical. While the dishes do not usually involve the elaborate or fancy preparations we might find in another kind of Food Network show hosted by a restaurant chef (e.g., *Emeril Live*), it is also not the "everyday" food typical of American quotidian life.

Giada assures us that her pork chops are "never dry," as she dresses them up in ingredients that are uncommon to American home cooking, such as capers. Her rice (actually *risotto*) is served with porcini mushrooms and Gorgonzola. Rather than pulling the lid off a pint of supermarket ice cream, she churns her own, made from ricotta cheese. This is a marked contrast to the types of food advertised in the show's commercial breaks. During the episodes airing daily in the summer of 2011 on Cooking Channel, for instance, the products advertised repeatedly included DiGiorno frozen pizzas, Hillshire Farms sliced turkey, Honey Nut Cheerios, Hamburger Helper, Keebler cookies, The Laughing Cow cheese, and Hidden Valley ranch dressing. These are convenience or snack foods, often processed and requiring little if any preparation and appealing to a broad mainstream of American consumers. To the extent that any might be considered ethnic, they are among the most commonplace ethnic foods in the American diet. Such items as frozen dinners and bottled dressings are not at all the kinds of ingredients one finds in Giada's dishes, which are presented as authentic, from-scratch preparations, and products of her unique skill and personal touch. This contrast between the food in the episode and the food in the commercials reveals the appeal of shows like *Everyday Italian* as one of escape from the ordinary and into a realm of deeper—if vicarious—pleasure.

Sometimes such vicarious experience of pleasure in cooking shows (as well as in magazines like *Saveur* and *Bon Appetit* and blogs and other websites about cooking and eating) leads to the use of "food porn" as a description of these texts and their appeal.[4] The charged metaphor of porn suggests a number of features of the visual style of food media, and of the reception of shows like *Everyday Italian*. One aspect of food porn is the fetishized emphasis on the desirable object, the food, often depicted in adoring and vivid close-up photography. This is a food equivalent of pornography's graphic depictions of isolated body parts and sexual acts. The *Everyday Italian* episode "Roasting Show" shows us such fetishized views of ingredients in the forms of ripe pears held in the host's bare hands, fresh green stalks of rosemary and grains of salt pinched by her fingers, pale yellow olive oil glistening as it is drizzled over a loin of pork, with Giada's hands working an herb rub into the surface of the meat. The pleasure of this kind of television viewing is highly visual, and it arouses a sensory desire, a wish to feel or taste, which it cannot directly satisfy. Perhaps also like conventional pornography, food porn offers an idealized and unattainable representation, manipulated and stylized by media production techniques in ways that are aimed at maximizing the audience's desire.

But in addition to the appeal of the food, and closely connected to it, the representation of Giada De Laurentiis herself is also in some ways designed to arouse sensual desire and vicarious pleasure. She is obviously represented to have sex appeal, modeling an image of female sexual desirability. We may assume that heterosexual female viewers are expected to idealize this image and that heterosexual male viewers are invited to desire it sexually. This makes shows like *Everday Italian* appeal to several audience segments, including those straight men who may not be most likely to take her instruction in cooking but still might enjoy the spectacle of her performance in the kitchen. Giada is thin but curvy, in some ways a voluptuous kitchen goddess like Nigella Lawson; though as self-consciously sexualized as Nigella, Giada's Italian ethnic identity conveys sensuality more than Nigella's Englishness could.⁵ Rather than wearing chef whites as some Food Network hosts do, Giada dresses in low-cut casual tops in the kitchen, invariably showing her cleavage. In introductory sequences shot away from the kitchen, Giada addresses the camera in more dressy feminine attire like a clingy cocktail dress, with her hair down and more elaborately coiffed, and her face made up glamorously. Her image is one of conventional female attractiveness, the kind on the covers of women's magazines like *Vogue, Redbook*, or *Cosmopolitan* more often than those in the cooking section of the magazine rack. In the kitchen, she often expresses strong feelings about her food, accentuated with bold gestures and bright wide smiles, exuding physical presence. The momentary pleasures she performs when tasting her own cooking at the end of each episode, closing her eyes and enjoying a brief private moment before opening them to describe the flavors and textures while still visibly chewing and swallowing, are voyeuristic offerings to an audience eager for its own desires to be stimulated and satisfied. Giada's image as a fit and sexy woman is also reinforced in her cookbooks. For instance, *Everyday Italian*, a bestselling companion book to the TV series, includes not only the obligatory glossy food shots, but more than fifty images of the chef herself. The pleasures of eating and of sex are of course distinct, but in combining these two forms of sensuality, cooking shows like *Everyday Italian* invite us to consider them together, to see the ways that media forms like the cooking show can create overlapping and intermingling desires and fantasies.

FIGURE 34.1.
Giada in the kitchen on
Everyday Italian.

In "Roasting Show," we find many of the characteristics of *Everyday Italian* considered so far. Giada prepares roast pork loin with fig sauce, which she introduces by comparison to pork chops and applesauce, a dish more familiar to American viewers. This positions her food as a more Italian, authentic, distinguished version of a familiar combination of pork and fruit and encourages the audience to consume the dish as a means of social distinction. As she pairs the meat with roast fennel and parmesan cheese, the pedagogical dimension of cooking shows is realized in Giada's discussion of possibly unknown ingredients in the savory main and side dishes. The fig sauce contains port wine and rosemary, which she describes as sweet and pine-like, respectively. Giada introduces fennel, "still foreign to a lot people," as her favorite vegetable, and one that is eaten throughout the year in Italy. She excitedly compares its flavor to licorice. The camera closes in for tight shots of the fennel bulbs and fronds, emphasizing its exoticism and enticing green color and soliciting our desire. Giada shows off her ethnic heritage, performing her identity as Italian American, when she articulates terms like *Parmigiano-Reggiano* (Italian parmesan cheese) in a pronounced, affected accent. This is to demonstrate the authenticity of her culinary practice and her authority as a chef. She is also represented visually as a sexually desirable woman, in a scoop-collared top with a plunging neckline and glossy red lips. She often leans forward toward the camera to reach items on the counter or to open the low oven door, revealing more cleavage.

The flow from content to advertising in *Everyday Italian* creates overlapping commercial messages, making repetitive appeals to the audience to consume both food products and the host's star persona. Introductory and interstitial portions (those between the kitchen scenes) show Giada shopping for groceries and chocolate candies, and the commercial spots as recorded during an airing in

2006 feature several advertising foods, including one for "the other white meat." Both content and advertising have redundant consumerist messages, reinforcing one another: eat pork. During the kitchen segments, though, we also find shots of Giada framed by brand-name appliances in the background, and close-ups of her hands chopping fennel give us a nice glimpse of her high-end Global chef's knife. These images also encourage our consumption.

In the episode's concluding segment, Giada sits at an outdoor bistro table covered in a tablecloth sipping from a glass of red wine before tasting the dinner she has prepared. She characteristically pauses to contemplate and savor the first bite of each dish, chewing with eyes closed before proceeding to explain the virtues of the recipes as she has prepared them: "The meat is moist, and the fig sauce is perfectly sweet." Roasting the fennel has mellowed out its licorice flavor, Giada says, and "the cheesy crust from the parmesan cheese, it's salty, buttery, and fantastic!" All of these lines are delivered with accompanying body language, broad hand gestures, and facial expressions to accentuate her satisfaction. Her pleasure in the sensual experience of eating is as important for the show's messages as the more pedagogical moments of explanation and demonstration. A cooking show like *Everyday Italian* is centrally concerned with this representation of distinguished, authentic, gustatory, and even erotic pleasure as an escape from everyday realities. Its ultimate purpose, however, is to return us to the usual experience of familiar supermarket foods that both the content and commercials urge us to consume.

Television can be many things, but our typical experience of TV in the United States is of a medium that encourages us to improve our lives and realize our dreams by exercising our agency as consumers. Such appeals typically involve more than the obvious sales pitches of thirty-second commercials; they can be woven through television's "content" as much as through its ads. Wherever we encounter them, these appeals, explicit or implicit, work by summoning our desires for social status and personal pleasure. Such desires are often aroused through sensual means, such as the audiovisual representations of food and femininity in *Everyday Italian*, in which Giada De Laurentiis's image is offered as a focus for our consumerist fantasies. As in many forms of television—not only lifestyle TV, but programs in many other genres such as game shows, reality series, and dramas—our appetite for consumption is often tempted by combinations of sex, star image, and fantasies of pleasure.

FURTHER READING

Collins, Kathleen. *Watching What We Eat: The Evolution of Cooking Shows*. New York: Continuum, 2009.

Ketchum, Cheri. "The Essence of Cooking Shows: How the Food Network Constructs Consumer Fantasies." *Journal of Communication Inquiry* 29 (2005): 217–34.

Palmer, Gareth, ed. *Exposing Lifestyle Television: The Big Reveal.* Hampshire, UK: Ashgate, 2008.

Ray, Krishnendu. "Domesticating Cuisine: Food and Aesthetics on American Television." *Gastronomica: The Journal of Food and Culture* 7 (2007): 50–64.

NOTES

1. "Advertise with Us," Food Network, www.foodnetwork.com.

2. For further considerations of gender politics and representations in recent cooking shows, see Rebecca Swenson, "Domestic Divo? Televised Treatments of Masculinity, Femininity, and Food," *Critical Studies in Media Communication* 26 (2009): 36–53; and Elizabeth Nathanson, "As Easy as Pie: Cooking Shows, Domestic Efficiency, and Postfeminist Temporality," *Television and New Media* 10 (2009): 311–30.

3. Dana Polan, *Julia Child's The French Chef* (Durham, NC: Duke University Press, 2011).

4. For a more elaborate consideration of cooking shows as pornography, see Andrew Chan, "*La grande bouffe*: Cooking Shows as Pornography," *Gastronomica: The Journal of Food and Culture* 3 (2003): 46–53.

5. Nigella Lawson's shows include *Nigella Bites* (UK Channel 4, 2000–2001; later seen in the United States on the Style network) and *Nigella Feasts* (Food Network, 2006–2008).

35

Gossip Girl
Transmedia Technologies

LOUISA STEIN

Abstract: While television is often thought of as a predigital mass medium distinct from online "new media," contemporary television programs are frequently intertwined with transmedia digital contexts and practices. Louisa Stein examines *Gossip Girl*'s representations of digital technologies, advertising tie-ins, and online extensions to highlight how digital media functions as a central theme, a style of representation, and mode of engagement for this popular teen drama.

According to my Social Climbing agenda, I have a busy few days ahead of me. I'll be attending a charity fundraiser, the Bass Industries Anniversary Party, and the launch of Eleanor Waldorf's fashion line. At these events, I'll be eavesdropping for pieces of scandalous information that I can send to the anonymous blogger, Gossip Girl, to help my pursuit of upward social mobility, and at the same time I'll be hoping to be captured in a cell phone snapshot doing something scandalous, like knocking over a champagne bottle and blaming the mess on someone else. With any luck, I'll earn "spotted points" and "scandal points" and will soon be receiving invites to more intimate events with Upper East Side socialites Blair Waldorf, Chuck Bass, and Serena van der Woodsen. And as I rack up scandal points, I'll be watching the snow fall outside the window of my Vermont home. Because of course I've been describing an online game I was playing in winter 2012—specifically the transmedia game Social Climbing, which extends the storyworld of the television series *Gossip Girl* by way of Facebook. From within Facebook, I can consult my Social Climbing agenda and virtually attend fictional gatherings in *Gossip Girl*'s version of New York City. In this way, *Gossip Girl*'s fantasy narrative extends into the everyday digital representations of self and community on Facebook.

The *Gossip Girl* television series revels in the scandals and personal dramas of wealthy teenagers in New York City. The series' characters use digital tools to gain and maintain power and status in an already elite community. With its emphasis on using digital tools to see and be seen, the Social Climbing *Gossip Girl* game, currently still in the initial testing (or "beta") phase, invites me to participate in the TV series' fantasy of digitally infused social power-play from within the frame of my own Facebook account. *Gossip Girl*'s Social Climbing game is the latest in a line of transmedia extensions that have invited viewers to partake in the series' elite social world, a world shaped by consumerist excess and privilege. In all cases, *Gossip Girl*'s online extensions have offered ways for viewers to spend real money to participate in the virtual pleasures connected to *Gossip Girl*. For example, one can purchase additional scandal or spotted points in Social Climbing in order to attain invitations to more intimate gatherings with the key players of the *Gossip Girl* fictional community.

This essay considers *Gossip Girl*'s representation of digital power in its narrative, online extensions, formal elements, and advertising. All four of these dimensions work in unison to depict a digital culture shared by *Gossip Girl* characters and viewers, in which digital tools offer the powers and pleasures of access, networking, and intervention. Transmedia extensions offer an obvious space for film and television to invite viewer participation in a narrative's fantasy world. However, in the case of *Gossip Girl*, the televisual text of the series itself indirectly invites the viewer to intervene in the program's very form, through the integration of do-it-yourself aesthetics into the series' imagery. These indirect invitations to viewer intervention offer an expansive vision of *Gossip Girl* viewers as digital authors, a vision that is also increasingly echoed in its marketing and product advertising. The premise of *Gossip Girl* suggests a double-edged vision of digital culture, where the digital equals both threat and power, but the series' larger transmedia logic mark a turning point in cultural representations of the digital, shedding long-standing fears of the dangers of cyberspace in favor of a more marketable vision of the empowered digital viewer turned cultural author.

Gossip Girl's ambivalent representation of the relationship between young adults and digital technology echoes contradictory public discourses about the new generation of millennial youth growing up in an already digital world. These discourses depict millennials as highly skilled digital "natives" and, at the same time, as potential victims navigating dangerous digital terrain.[1] William Strauss and Neil Howe popularized the vision of "millennials" as a digitally proactive generation who use the tools of the web to enact social change.[2] However, prototypical millennial TV programs like *Buffy the Vampire Slayer* and *Degrassi* tell a different story, featuring storylines about online stalkers (be they supernatural robots or adult men) posing as teen boys to ensnare naïve teen girls.[3]

Such episodes and many others like them paint a fearful picture of the dangers facing young people (and especially young women) in the unknown realm of the digital.

Like popular discourse, academic analysis of youth engagement with digital technologies also constructs a contradictory picture. On the one hand, much of academic discourse bolsters perceptions that contemporary youth are digitally savvy, arguing that digital technologies significantly shape the outlook and life experiences of children, teens, and young adults. For example, in *The Young and the Digital*, S. Craig Watkins argues that young people experience their social connections through a mix of in-person and digital interactions.[4] Likewise, the studies represented in Kazys Varnelis's collection *Networked Publics* describe a multifaceted terrain of young people using digital technologies to engage with each other, thus forming and embodying the "networked publics" of the book's title.[5] But academic studies also warn that not all teens have equal access and digital skills, and that intersecting issues of economics, race, and ethnicity shape teens' access to and use of digital networks in significant ways. Watkins has argued that race, ethnicity, geography, and class inform the way young people relate to and deploy technology, and that the resulting differences in technological access and use have in turn created "participation gaps."[6] Other scholars contend that our sense of teens' competency in technology use may be dangerously overstated; for example, all teens do not equally understand the stakes of carefully controlling privacy settings on Facebook, and these differences can have significant ramifications.[7] Thus, both academic and popular discourses acknowledge that many young peoples' lives are infused with and shaped by digital technology, while also calling attention to ways in which the spread of digital technologies have uneven and uncertain outcomes.

The premise of *Gossip Girl* seems likewise ambivalent about the role of digital technologies in millennial lives. On the one hand, it seems to feed off of and fuel anxieties about millennials' overdependence on digital media. *Gossip Girl* features young adults immersed in and dependent on digital technologies. Each episode of the series opens with narration from the pseudonymous blogger, Gossip Girl. Through her blog posts, Gossip Girl sets the social agenda for the teens of New York City's Upper East Side by releasing rumors and scandals, the threat of which cast a pall over the teenagers' lives. The series depicts its teen protagonists trapped by the digital technologies that pervade their lives. Many episodes revolve around the threat that Gossip Girl will reveal personal details that may wreak havoc on the teens' social lives, or even get them kicked out of school. The teens of *Gossip Girl* live in fear that their secrets will be posted on the Gossip Girl blog, and, as the seasons progress, many also live with the ramifications once the private has indeed been made public for the blog-reading masses.

Yet *Gossip Girl* isn't simply a horror show about the terror of digital access. The teens in *Gossip Girl* depend on and revel in their digital networks, and through various digital campaigns, the series hails viewers who are assumed to be equally digitally connected. A late second-season episode entitled "Carnal Knowledge" playfully depicts the teens at a complete loss for how to behave when their teacher demands they hand in their cell phones. The series consistently highlights how its teen characters depend on and utilize the very digital technologies that terrorize them. Indeed, the teens of *Gossip Girl* are their own digital bullies. They gain the upper hand in contested relationships by sending out carefully timed information to Gossip Girl's blog, which she in turn sends out to everyone in "blasts" of digital knowledge-as-power. The season 2 climax ("The Goodbye Gossip Girl") hinges on the teens realizing that not only could any one of them be Gossip Girl, but that in a way each one of them is Gossip Girl—that Gossip Girl is a construct of the social and digital network to which they all subscribe and which they together constitute. This ambivalent representation of Gossip Girl (both the blogger and the teens that make up the Gossip Girl network) depicts "her" as simultaneously a source of teen bullying and a source of teen power. And, through the aspirational hailing of *Gossip Girl*'s transmedia extensions, we as viewers are also included in and thus responsible for Gossip Girl's pleasurable network of terror and power.

Gossip Girl thus not only constructs an ambivalent picture of digitally connected millennials, but also goes one step further: it interpellates its viewers into this mixed position by deploying game-like transmedia extensions that allow viewers to play at being part of *Gossip Girl*'s world of digitally networked power and danger. Over its six seasons, *Gossip Girl* offered a range of immersive transmedia experiences that encourage viewers to interact with the storyworld of *Gossip Girl* using digital technologies, and more specifically to participate in the processes of digital gossip and consumerism as featured in the series. The first large-scale transmedia extension took the form of a digital version of the New York City lifestyle featured in the series, represented through the software interface of Second Life. *Gossip Girl*'s Second Life extension allowed viewers to explore a virtual Upper East Side, where they could create an avatar who could shop in digital representations of high-end department stores and attend online parties.[8] In 2008, The CW teamed with fashion retailer Bluefly.com to translate the digital shopping imagined in *Gossip Girl*'s Second Life into actual online shopping. Visitors to Bluefly.com could shop in the *Gossip Girl* "store," where they could purchase not *Gossip Girl* t-shirts and merchandise as one might imagine, but clothing and brands that the characters on the show might wear. The *Gossip Girl* store was divided into sections by character, so viewers-turned-online-consumers could purchase clothes as part of their identification with, or appreciation of, the style of a particular character in the storyworld.

In 2012, both *Gossip Girl*'s Second Life and the *Gossip Girl* Bluefly shop were defunct, but viewers could try out the *Gossip Girl* Social Climbing Facebook Game. As I described in my opening, *Gossip Girl*'s Social Climbing invites viewers to move directly from their involvement with the "real life" digital social network of Facebook to their engagement with a *Gossip Girl*–based fantasy play-space. As with the Bluefly *Gossip Girl* shop, this digital extension invites players to spend real money in order to purchase enough "scandal" and "spotted" points to have access to the virtual elite of *Gossip Girl*. In Social Climbing, participants fill their appointment books with invitations to activities such as art exhibits and exclusive parties, each of which (if one can afford to enter) becomes the opportunity to be "spotted" by *Gossip Girl* characters or to snap photos of fictional friends as fodder for *Gossip Girl*'s blog. The Facebook Social Climbing game overtly constructs digital ambivalences (of wielding power or being exposed) and offers them as purchasable pleasures that signify inclusion in the *Gossip Girl* fantasy.

But while it's easy to recognize *Gossip Girl*'s more overtly interactive transmedia extensions like the Social Climbing game as key places for immersive viewer participation, what's perhaps more remarkable is how *Gossip Girl* embeds invitations to digital interaction into the television text itself. Indeed, *Gossip Girl*'s transmedia dimensions extend participatory invitations already at work in the televisual text of the series. Sharon Ross describes how TV texts can invite viewer participation through a mix of direct and indirect address to viewer knowledge and viewer interactive practices.[9] For *Gossip Girl*, the series' emphasis on the status of televisual text as representation continually invites viewer participation. At key moments, the series' visual language calls attention to its status as televised fiction and artifice by interrupting or freezing the image, creating an aesthetic of the interrupted process of the celluloid image of film. One of the most iconic—and fan-beloved—of these moments occurs when two fan-favored characters, power-hungry teen Blair Waldorf and power-entrenched teen billionaire Chuck Bass, first become involved with each other. In "Victor/Victrola," Blair and Chuck kiss for the first time in a cab that is racing through a New York City night. As the music crescendos and they lean into a kiss, the image flickers, becomes desaturated, and skips, as if it were simultaneously an old projected silent film with accumulated dust and a skipping TV image. Finally, the image ruptures and burns away, like projected celluloid film on fire. This playful visual imagery layers various indicators of "pastness" in media, collapsing them into a collective aesthetic of nostalgia and emotion conveyed through form. At the same time, the aesthetic play interrupts the series' realism (such as it is) with highly reflexive mediation; that is, the moment calls attention to *Gossip Girl*'s status as television by layering its contemporary televisual brand of melodramatic realism with codes of previous media forms. Thus melodrama overtakes realism and offers a way in for the viewer via the *form* of the series itself, suggesting the possibility of achieving emotionally resonant imagery via invasive editing. This moment invites the viewer to consider all of *Gossip Girl*'s status as codified representation. *Gossip Girl*'s reflexive framing emerges throughout the series via self-conscious intertextual references: each episode title is modeled after the title of a well-known Hollywood film, and episodes often feature dream-like sequences that cast Blair in the role of a famous figure from classic cinema. For example, the episode "The Blair Bitch Project" opens with a dream sequence in which Blair approximates the role of Holly Golightly in *Breakfast at Tiffany's*, running through the rain in a trench coat to find her cat.

Gossip Girl's consistent play with past media, and more specifically its occasionally aggressive deployment of a nostalgic/analog film aesthetic, is tied to a larger cultural embrace of the digital evocation of celluloid. This trend can be seen recently in mobile apps Hipstamatic and Instagram, both of which simulate analog film aesthetics, approximating through digital means Polaroid and Holga-style imagery to communicate an emotional interpretation of a found moment. This and other instances of formal nostalgic style within *Gossip Girl* draw on current aesthetic vernacular to invite the viewer to enter in and rework the digital text, or at least to imagine doing so. In comparison to the invitations to viewer participation in *Gossip Girl*'s transmedia extensions (like Social Climbing and Bluefly), the series' invitation to imagine reworking the televisual text through editing encourages a more open-ended form of viewer engagement, including a marked shift from audience to author. Where the Social Climbing player must navigate the game's restrictions to achieve specifically delineated goals and rewards, *Gossip Girl*'s moments of nostalgic, do-it-yourself aesthetics invite viewers to imagine themselves as creators transforming the raw material of the series itself.

And indeed these moments of digital cinematic fissure become favorites in fan reworkings through digital remix. Many fan-made remix videos (known within fan culture as "fanvids") build to the moment described above of Chuck and Blair kissing in the cab, with its skipping image and burning up film strip, using this stylized imagery unaltered at the climax of a song or in its climactic refrain. And many of these and other vids use video-editing filters to create a similar feel of "pastness" throughout their vids, altering more realist *Gossip Girl* footage with sepia filters, or desaturating imagery to black and white, or interrupting footage with white flares that mimic an image burning up.[10] The series aligns emotionally dramatic moments with an emphasis on the TV image's status as representation, thus inviting an aesthetic intervention into televisual language; viewers turned vidders then use digital media tools such as Adobe Premiere and Final Cut Express to explore and expand upon the characters that inspire them to create more storyworld, more narrative, and more analysis.

FIGURE 35.1. This fan-produced video uses filters to add a layer of nostalgia to footage from *Gossip Girl*.

The series' product advertising in turn builds on this invitation to viewers to intervene with televisual form, for example through the promotional campaign for the "Nikon Coolpix" digital camera. In spots that ran within commercial breaks, these ads directly reworked *Gossip Girl* scenes. Serving double duty as promotional spots for both the show and the Nikon camera, the advertisements rendered *Gossip Girl* footage in a campy yet nostalgic aesthetic. Like the scene from "Victor/Victrola" analyzed above, these spots refer to a range of past media styles, employing an over-the-top male voiceover, flicker filters for an old home movie feel, a laugh track to add a classic sitcom flavor, and interrupted still images with photo frames. All of these elements reshape carefully selected clips of salacious dialogue between *Gossip Girl's* romantic pairings, making the series sound like a racy screwball comedy with 1940s pacing and twenty-first-century sexual innuendo. The camera advertised through this playful synthesis features internal editing abilities, with the campaign tagline "create in any light." Its advertising emphasizes the Nikon Coolpix's in-camera special effects tools (including what Nikon terms a "nostalgic sepia" option), framing, and other "creative" filters that could be used for exactly the type of modern/nostalgic remix intervention modeled by the advertisement itself.[11] Thus, both the aesthetics of the advertisement and the digital tool being advertised encourage the viewer to take a position of playful and creative mediation with the televisual text, a position already posited within the program itself. In this way, The CW, *Gossip Girl*, and Nikon together integrate the do-it-yourself practices and aesthetics of remix and fan culture into their joint commercial enterprise.

Gossip Girl mines our culture's deep ambivalence toward and fascination with the spread of the digital. The series' ambitious characters strive for social safety both from and through the tools of digital media. While *Gossip Girl* may depend on our innate sense of ambivalence toward the digital, if there's one takeaway from the show, it's that its millennial characters live in a world inextricably infused with digital media. At least in the upper-class fantasy world of *Gossip Girl*, there's no going back. *Gossip Girl*'s transmedia extensions echo this sentiment, especially with the Social Climbing game situated within Facebook users' everyday online experience. But what's most striking perhaps is that both audience-instigated digital productivity and *Gossip Girl*'s marketing campaign seem to leave the narrative's ambivalence behind, celebrating the power of transformation through user access to digital tools. On the one hand, it's no surprise that The CW and Nikon would take this opportunity to shed the negative weight of anxieties about the threat of digital culture, capitalizing instead on the market potential for tools of digital authorship like a Nikon camera. But all the same, the result is a celebration of viewer power, a merging of viewer emotional investment in power-hungry characters like Blair Waldorf and Chuck Bass with a sense of assumed viewer right to the power of re-representation and transformation.

From the start, *Gossip Girl* has negotiated between two narratives of the digital—between anxious warnings about the dangers of digital power and visions of digital transformation as power and play. *Gossip Girl* depicts digital technologies as tools of social policing, but also as tools of social mobility through expressive authorship. The series' play with aesthetics of mediation highlights the latter, encouraging the viewer to approach the series as representation—as raw digital material for creative intervention. As the seasons progress, *Gossip Girl*'s continued emphasis on playful aesthetic manipulation, echoing and in turn echoed in fan practice, suggests that we are at a watershed for cultural understandings of the digital, in which commercial and vernacular culture both are moving away from a fear of digital dangers and toward an embrace of the powers and pleasures of digital play.

FURTHER READING

Pattee, A. S. "Commodities in Literature, Literature as Commodity: A Close Look at the *Gossip Girl* Series." *Children's Literature Association Quarterly* 31, no. 2 (2006): 154–75.

Ross, Sharon Marie. *Beyond the Box: Television and the Internet*. Malden, MA: Blackwell, 2008.

Stein, Louisa. "Playing Dress-Up: Digital Fashion and Gamic Extensions of Televisual Experience in *Gossip Girl*'s Second Life." *Cinema Journal* 48, no. 3 (2009): 116–22.

Watkins, S. Craig. *The Young and the Digital: What the Migration to Social-Network Sites, Games, and Anytime, Anywhere Media Means for Our Future*. Boston: Beacon Press, 2009.

NOTES

1. Marc Prensky, "Digital Natives, Digital Immigrants," *On the Horizon* 9, no. 5 (2001), www .marcprensky.com.

2. Neil Howe and William Strauss, *Millennials Rising* (New York: Vintage, 2000).

3. See *Buffy the Vampire Slayer*, "I Robot, You Jane," April 28, 1997, and *Degrassi: The Next Generation*, "Mother and Child Reunion," July 1, 2002, for examples of millennial televisual narratives representing digital fears.

4. S. Craig Watkins, *The Young and the Digital: What the Migration to Social-Network Sites, Games, and Anytime, Anywhere Media Means for Our Future* (Boston: Beacon Press, 2009).

5. Kazys Varnelis, ed., *Networked Publics* (Cambridge, MA: MIT Press, 2008).

6. "The Young and the Digital: Interview with S. Craig Watkins," New Learning Institute, March 2, 2011, http://newlearninginstitute.org.

7. See Chris Jay Hoofnagle, Jennifer King, Su Li, and Joseph Turow, "How Different Are Young Adults from Older Adults When It Comes to Information Privacy Attitudes and Policies?" public comment to Federal Trade Commission roundtable on consumer privacy, April 14, 2010, www.ftc.gov.

8. Louisa Stein, "Playing Dress-Up: Digital Fashion and Gamic Extensions of Televisual Experience in *Gossip Girl*'s *Second Life*," *Cinema Journal* 48, no. 3 (2009): 116–22.

9. Sharon Marie Ross, *Beyond the Box: Television and the Internet* (Malden, MA: Blackwell, 2008).

10. For examples of such vids, see the book's website at http://howtowatchtelevision.com.

11. Coolpix US Sell Sheet, http://cdn.press.nikonusa.com.

36

High Maintenance and *The Misadventures of Awkward Black Girl*
Indie TV

AYMAR JEAN CHRISTIAN

Abstract: How has web and mobile (networked) distribution changed television production, narrative, and marketing? The influx of indie producers making television for sites like YouTube has expanded the art of television beyond a show's storytelling and visual style to include its overall development—financing, production, and marketing. Aymar Jean Christian contrasts two indie series with short episodes, distributed independently but later picked up by HBO, to demonstrate the changing art of TV.

Through the rise of online distribution, we can now access television series anytime, anywhere, from any producer, large or small, with episodes of any length. Distribution can be many-to-many and peer-to-peer, not just Hollywood-to-everyone. The influx of indie producers into television has expanded the art of television beyond a show's storytelling and visual style to include its overall development—financing, production, and marketing. So multiplicitous are the models for developing TV after the Internet that this essay uses not one but two indie series with short episodes (most well under twenty minutes), distributed independently on Vimeo and YouTube and later picked up by HBO, to demonstrate the changing art of TV.

Created by Katja Blichfeld and Ben Sinclair in 2012, *High Maintenance* follows an unnamed cannabis dealer as he delivers product to stressed-out New Yorkers. Each episode focuses on a different customer and how weed figures into their life. Told in three-episode "cycles" instead of seasons, the low-budget anthology series appealed to online users because of its decentered, spreadable narrative, sincere acting and writing, and creative social media engagement. *The Misadventures of Awkward Black Girl*, by contrast, focuses on one character's struggle to maintain social relations amidst race- and gender-based expectations. Released by writer-star Issa Rae in 2011, *Awkward Black Girl*'s sensitivity to the complexities of black women's experiences and politics eventually earned Rae a large base of fans. Yet her show's less flexible serial narrative increased production costs, and Rae soon sought development from legacy television networks. Rae's earliest efforts faltered as she lacked the clout to insist on her vision, so to maintain her fan base while in development, Rae released films and web series by other producers, developing a network and production company for minority and women writers. Both *High Maintenance* and *Awkward Black Girl* demonstrate the art of short-form storytelling and its value to producers, fans, small web TV distributors (Vimeo and YouTube's iamOTHER), and legacy TV channels (HBO). Indie producers grow their series not only through compelling narratives but also by adapting norms of production and distribution to extract the most value out of fewer resources and promoting spreadability in networked contexts where fans have more control.

By developing series as new intellectual properties without financing from corporate distributors, indie TV producers transform the market for "pilots"—the first episode of a series traditionally produced long before the rest of the season. In the indie space, an entire season of short-form episodes serves to "pilot" the show, introducing characters and, in an improvement on the legacy model, building fan bases. Indie TV producers reinvented piloting as building a community of producers and fans. Traditionally, television comedies and dramas have one or two creators who produce a pilot based on a successful pitch. After a network orders more episodes, creators establish a "show bible" with characters and plots to be executed by a writing team led by a showrunner. This hierarchical structure ensures continuity in broadcast and cable shows whose narratives run for hours each season. With fewer resources and shorter run times, many indie TV creators find tight control over the story a luxury they cannot afford, so they incorporate actors into the production process and design series to maximize fan engagement with characters.

High Maintenance best exemplifies a collaborative and flexible approach to production. Among the most critically acclaimed independent web series, the anthology series achieved notoriety first by cultivating meaningful, if undercompensated, work for above- and below-the-line producers in New York, with Blichfeld and Sinclair developing the program's tone and voice along with their collaborators. Their "series of shorts" functioned as an extended pilot with a diverse array of characters, contexts, and plots.[1] There is no overarching plot, just a series of vignettes where weed and its dealer play central roles.

FIGURE 36.1.
This *High Maintenance* episode shot in a cramped apartment typifies the series' deliberate lack of plot in favor of vignettes in which weed and its dealer play central roles.

In its "Helen" episode, we see a woman coughing as she lies next to her son in a cramped bedroom. She wants him to shave his beard, but he says he won't for another two to three weeks because his oatmeal-based shaving cream is on back order. In a montage, we see how consumption shapes the man's life. We see photos and drawings of Helen Hunt on the walls (hence the episode title). The man orders all types of goods online, and we see some delivered from delivery workers who clearly know him as a regular client. Suddenly, we see the man's next delivery worker, and he's delivering weed. At the man's apartment, he puts on a new shirt, and they engage in idle chatter before the man asks for Pink Kush for his mother. When the delivery guy leaves, the man puts the Pink Kush in a box full of unsmoked weed: He needs the company more than the weed. The episode ends, doing little to advance the plot of the series, nor does it do much to develop the central character, the weed Guy, played by Sinclair.

Originally conceived as a vehicle for Sinclair with then partner and Emmy Award–winning casting director Katja Blichfeld, *High Maintenance* started production when the creators reconceived it as a more open, flexible character study: "We just want to get inside the apartment and meet these characters. And that was it," Blichfeld told me. "It's more intriguing, I think, to just speculate what's this guy's backstory than seeing it." Vimeo eventually picked up the show for six episodes for its On Demand platform, but soon after Blichfeld and Sinclair secured a six-episode series order from HBO, rare for the premium network accustomed to producing pilots before ordering a full season. The HBO deal was concrete evidence that indie TV series can function as pilots.

Blichfeld and Sinclair's approach to episodic storytelling defies legacy TV's approach to story development, where pilots clearly introduce and explain central characters, settings, and plots. The flexibility of their production and storytelling practices allowed the *High Maintenance* creators to develop a devoted fan base via Vimeo, not because they aggressively pursued fans but because their show offered multiple points of entry beyond plot, be it identification with the characters, the city, or weed culture. Episodes can be watched in any order. As *New Yorker* critic Emily Nussbaum writes in her review of the web series, "Because *High Maintenance* has no obligation to follow any one character, or make a season-long arc pay off, it can take different risks. Gradually, the episodes build up a detailed and empathetic image of a specific demographic slice of New York, one cramped apartment at a time."[2] Rejecting the pilot requirement of introducing the characters and plot, the creative team cultivated a realistic world based on their location, the actor, and identity. The production team went off-script depending on who and what was on set. For "Helen" they shot in the apartment of one of their producers, Russell Gregory, a talent manager whose clients are in the series. Gregory's apartment was small, traditionally considered a production constraint—legacy shows seek large apartments or studio sets for added production value. But Blichfeld and Sinclair, serving as their own art directors, stuffed the space with *more* furniture to give it a cramped feel. "I think really that's where the idea came from, was having the space first," Blichfeld told *Fresh Air*'s Ann Marie Baldonado.[3] Serendipitously, the day of shooting, a street festival was rerouted to outside the apartment. Initially viewing this as a problem, they realized it provided a cinematic contrast to the hermetic protagonist, as well as a sense of unpredictability and spontaneity characteristic of living in New York.

Independent web series producers are more reliant on actors than legacy studios are, as actors' depth of participation greatly affects how the story proceeds. An actor dropping out can halt a production without a casting budget. Because they are essential on set and very often (but depending on scale, not always) needed for large blocks of shooting, indie series creators ask more of their actors' time but often compensate by giving them more control over their characters and the story. For *High Maintenance*, even though Blichfeld and Sinclair wrote all episodes of the show other than "Helen," they continually redistributed creative ownership over the narrative. As a casting director who eventually secured an Emmy Award for casting *30 Rock*, Blichfeld said they were "super fortunate that we've all been in that community for as long as we have":

> We're really performance-oriented. Like more than anything. So, we're just interested in what's going to get the best performance from our actors. Which really informs our whole process. It's why we keep our sets to a very minimal group of people. It's why we tell actors, "Ok. Here's the script. Ultimately make sure you hit that and hit that. But if this doesn't sound right coming out of your mouth, just say it in your own words." We like really try to make them feel like . . . they have some ownership over their character. And we're asking them to do very little, usually. We're usually asking them to just kind of be themselves. Because we're usually writing for actors and hoping they're going to bring themselves to the character.[4]

Blichfeld's description of their development process makes perfect sense for a series in which every episode rests on a small number of performances and whose producers all work with actors on a daily basis. With each episode consisting of just two or three scenes, actors drive the story and creators shape production to best utilize talent, which is common in other web series as well.

Blichfeld and Sinclair wrote for specific actors, revealing how indie production reshapes the legacy casting process. Rather than auditioning, the creators focused on getting to know the talent and building rapport to support sincere performances and ensure a smooth filming process. "We don't have a traditional audition process. But the thing that could be equated with that is just us hanging out with the person that we'd like to write for," said Sinclair, who cited the casting of Dan Stevens (*Downton Abbey*) in "Rachel," the episode that won them a Writers Guild Award. "We basically hung out with him a half dozen times before we realized what character would fit best for him." The first episode, "Stevie," has Bridget Moloney, Sinclair's sister-in-law, as the lead (Blichfeld met Sinclair through Moloney). "Olivia," the most popular episode on Vimeo according to view counts, features Heléne Yorke, Gregory's client, and Max Jenkins, a friend of Sinclair and Blichfeld and star of Bobby Hodgson and Karina Mangu-Ward's web series *Gay's Anatomy*. Blichfeld cast both Yorke and Jenkins in very small parts on *30 Rock*. Yet casting for *30 Rock* was a challenge because Blichfeld needed strong actors who could keep up with career comedians Tracy Morgan, Tina Fey, and Alec Baldwin, and also deliver laughs with just a couple of lines: "I started fantasizing—and strategizing—about ways that I could somehow . . . put a spotlight on some of these actors who I am obsessed with," she said.

Indie TV narratives spread on social media when characters and narratives appeal to specific types of fans, so marketing and plot are deeply intertwined. In Issa Rae's third and most popular web series, *The Misadventures of Awkward Black Girl*, the first episode is a delicate balancing act between universal and specific black women's experiences, clearly designed for spreadability, a theory of media distribution centering fans' affective connections in "going viral."[5] The show opens with the protagonist in her car in Los Angeles. "Am I the only who pretends I'm in a music video when I'm by myself?" narrates J, played by Rae. J, a twentysomething, dark-skinned black woman with shaved hair, is alone rapping loudly to an original song written for the show: "My booty shawts, booty shawts . . . Niggas wanna fuck me from behind . . . niggas wanna feel up on this booty, they ain't got a chance." Suddenly a coworker drives up next to her car, waving profusely. She waves back, as if to dismiss him politely, but they keep meeting at successive stop signs. It is a common and relatable "awkward moment," J says. In the next scene, J introduces herself: "My name is J and I'm awkward . . . and black. Someone once told me those were the two worst things anyone could be." In the

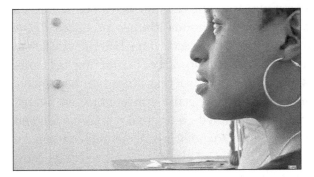

FIGURE 36.2.
From the four-minute pilot episode of *The Misadventures of Awkward Black Girl* to her series *Insecure* on HBO, Issa Rae has expanded the art and production of TV.

four-minute episode we learn that J has recently been dumped by her boyfriend, D, twice: first for vague reasons, then, after a one-week reconciliation, because her shaved natural hair freaked him out, triggering homophobia. Despondent, J copes by crying in the mirror, getting drunk at the office holiday party, and sleeping with a coworker, A. Her secret coping mechanism, though, is writing violent rap lyrics: "I'm a bad bitch. You're a pussy nigga," she says on screen. "What the fuck rhymes with 'pussy nigga'? . . . Burn in hell, nigga! Burn in hell, nigga!"

The pilot episode, which a year later had been viewed one million times, is masterful in its ability to signify black youth culture and awkward-comedy tropes of misrecognition and misinterpretation, breaking the rules of both the web and TV.[6] Rae bookends the episode with excerpts from comically offensive rap songs, a nod to the dominant, marketable black television form since the 1990s. But those lyrics are filtered through J, her individual awkwardness and her post-breakup anxieties: The rap is divorced from its masculine and corporate media context. Instead, J signals blackness by referencing its position in culture and the market (it's one of the "worst things anyone could be"). Rae integrates experiences specific to black women—most importantly, the politics of natural hair—with familiar plot devices from women's sitcoms and rom-coms such as getting dumped, crying in the mirror, cutting one's hair, and sleeping with a loser.

I recount the first episode of *Awkward Black Girl* not only because it is the series' most-watched episode—as is the case with most TV series—but also because its explicit appeal to black women worked: *Awkward Black Girl* retained over half its large opening audience. Within a year, Rae had been profiled by a diverse group of media outlets, from mainstream outlets like CNN and the Associated Press to black media like *Essence* and *The Root*. Media mogul Arianna Huffington asked her to write an inaugural post for the *Huffington Post*'s new site targeting black Americans.[7] When Rae started a $30,000 crowdfunding campaign to complete her first season, she raised $56,000. After pitching the show to networks,

Awkward Black Girl landed on a premium YouTube channel, iamOTHER, headed by Pharrell Williams. Two years later, after the Shonda Rhimes–produced *I Hate L.A. Dudes* faltered in development at ABC, Rae secured an HBO development deal for a series about a young black woman, *Insecure*, premiering fall 2016, with Larry Wilmore attached as a producer. Rae's success hinged on her sincere use and innovation of black culture and sitcom genre conventions, all filtered through black female cultural politics. She created an original representation and then experimented with distribution in ways that deviated from and continued a tradition beginning with BET. *Awkward Black Girl* proposes to represent its community of fans—primarily but not exclusively black women—in a way unseen on legacy television and does so convincingly.

Awkward Black Girl's concept and story resonated with black women, who evangelized the show online and in their communities. Rae, reading user comments and emails, sensed the fervor she created and built campaigns to keep viewers engaged, most of it channeled through Rae herself. She was active on Facebook, with pages for the show and herself: Rae could count five thousand friends and three thousand subscribers by early 2012 on Facebook, while the show's Facebook group had nearly sixty thousand fans at the same time.[8] By 2016, *Awkward Black Girl*'s Facebook page had more than 180,000 fans. A similar dynamic—accounts for both Rae and the show—could be seen on Twitter.[9] Facebook and Twitter pages, by 2010, were common components of most web series' social media marketing campaigns. Rae went beyond that with a personal Tumblr blog, on which she directly promoted both her show and related projects. Rae's ability to use her identity as a member of the community she represents greatly enhanced the show's marketability.

Rae's blog provides an interesting glimpse into how she promoted *Awkward Black Girl* as a community- and market-oriented project. The blog highlighted the show's merchandise, including T-shirts stating "I'm Awkward . . . And Black" or "I'm Awkward . . . And Mixed." Rae also posted artistic and cultural recommendations and contributions from fans.[10] Much of the blog's space went to support projects that shared *Awkward Black Girl*'s mission of reforming Hollywood, including, for instance, the Black Girl Project celebrating classic black TV programs along with clips and media by and about Hollywood producers combating the system.[11] Outside her blog Rae positioned herself as a thought leader on race in Hollywood by penning a number of opinion pieces on black representational politics and embarking on a nationwide college screening tour. Consistent with the show's simultaneous commitment to humor, many of Rae's publications and blog posts had no obvious connection to race or gender politics.[12]

In the years following *Awkward Black Girl*'s finale in 2013, Rae escalated her distribution efforts by releasing series from other writers, mostly in Hollywood.

As she worked with HBO on her series, in 2014 she launched an initiative to allow fans to support programming through the Color Creative initiative, supported by Patreon, a start-up that manages regular contributions. Color Creative extends Rae's practice of releasing romantic comedies from other producers on her YouTube channel. Rae started Color Creative as a pilot incubator, starting with a slate of three half-hour comedies in 2014. "It came from my place of frustration having gone through the pilot process with ABC and then currently with HBO," Rae said. "The process just felt really, really outdated to me, and really inefficient for writers." Yet by releasing pilots in a format that only legacy television development can support, Rae and producing partner Deniese Davis find themselves reliant on the old system. Says Rae, "To legitimize the program, we have to sell something. . . . We're still depending on these old television networks who are still using this old pilot system to say 'we'll buy it from you' when that would be admitting that this pilot system is stupid, and that's kind of weird. We want to be able to have a relationship with internet networks or work within the system to be able to say this is a new model."[13] Rae expresses disenchantment with legacy television development and hope for new networks like Netflix and Hulu. Selling a pilot to a legacy TV network would "validate us as an incubator, as a program," Davis said. Indeed, HBO eventually signed a deal with Rae to bring two series to the network, which they purchased in 2017, and Color Creative received a grant from the Pop Culture Collaborative to sustain Rae's development initiatives.[14]

Indie TV series like *High Maintenance* and *Awkward Black Girl* changed the art of TV, not only the stories told but also their production and release. In their search of creative freedom from the industry's cold marketing calculus and uninspiring labor conditions, independent television producers like Blichfeld, Sinclair, Gregory, and Rae leveraged creative autonomy to seamlessly connect production with fan desires. Indie producers show how television can harness the affordances of a networked distribution to expand production and engagement: specific stories, greater responsiveness to fan demands, and greater openness to the politics of cultural representation.

FURTHER READING

Christian, Aymar Jean. *Open TV: Innovation beyond Hollywood and the Rise of Web Television*. New York: New York University Press, 2018.

Pierson, Eric, et al. *Watching while Black: Centering the Television of Black Audiences*. New Brunswick, NJ: Rutgers University Press, 2013.

Wanzo, Rebecca. "Precarious-Girl Comedy: Issa Rae, Lena Dunham, and Abjection Aesthetics." *Camera Obscura* 31, no. 2 (2010): 27–59.

NOTES

1. Drew Grant, "'High Maintenance' Creators: It's Not TV, It's Art!" *New York Observer*, November 13, 2014, http://observer.com.

2. Emily Nussbaum, "Taster's Choice: 'High Maintenance' and 'My Mad Fat Diary,'" *New Yorker*, June 6 and 16, 2014, www.newyorker.com.

3. Ann Marie Baldonado, "Friends And Favors: 'High Maintenance' Creators Share Their Secret to Success," *NPR: Fresh Air*, March 4, 2015.

4. Katja Blichfeld, personal interview with author, March 30, 2013.

5. Henry Jenkins, Sam Ford, and Joshua Green, *Spreadable Media: Creating Value and Meaning in a Networked Culture* (New York: New York University Press, 2013).

6. Rebecca Wanzo, "Precarious-Girl Comedy: Issa Rae, Lena Dunham, and Abjection Aesthetics," *Camera Obscura* 31, no. 2 (2010): 27–59.

7. Ariana Huffington, "Introducing HuffPost BlackVoices: Covering Black America's Split-Screen Reality," *Huffington Post*, August 4, 2011, www.huffingtonpost.com; Matthew Fleischer, "AP Profiles Awkward Black Girl Creator Issa Rae," Adweek, September 9, 2011, www.adweek.com.

8. See Issa Rae, Facebook, www.facebook.com; and Awkward Black Girl, Facebook, www.facebook.com.

9. See Issa Rae, Twitter, http://twitter.com; and Awkward Black Girl, Twitter, http://twitter.com.

10. Issa Rae, "Ridiculously Awesome Awkward Black Girl Fan Art," *Issa Rae* (blog), August 22, 2011, http://blog.issarae.com/post/9253469983/ridiculously-awesome-awkward-black-girl-fan-art.

11. Issa Rae, "What Better Way to Celebrate Black history Month," *Issa Rae* (blog), February 10, 2012, http://blog.issarae.com/post/17412340526/tbgptumbles-what-better-way-to-celebrate-black. Examples include a *Daily Show* interview with George Lucas on his big-budget black war movie, *Red Tails* (Issa Rae, "First Viola, Then Steve McQueen, Now George Lucas Blasts Hollywood: A Change Gon' Come? (Thanks, Rob)," *Issa Rae* (blog), January 15, 2012, http://blog.issarae.com/post/15891230169/first-viola-then-steve-mcqueen-now-george-lucas); an article on female comic writers (Issa Rae, "Ladies Making Comics: How Media Clearly Reflects the Sexism and the Racism We Cannot See in . . . ," *Issa Rae* (blog), August 24, 2011, http://blog.issarae.com/post/9355654519/ladies-making-comics-how-media-clearly-reflects-the); and an excerpt from Indian American writer and actress Mindy Kaling from *The Office* (Issa Rae, "Just Read: 'Is Everyone Hanging Out without Me (and Other Concerns)' by Mindy Kaling," *Issa Rae* (blog), January 2, 2012, http://blog.issarae.com/post/15193378046/just-read-is-everyone-hanging-out-without-me).

12. See Issa Rae, "ABG College Tour," *Issa Rae* (blog), http://blog.issarae.com/ABGCollegeTour; Issa Rae, "Nothing Made You Happier than Seeing This When Walking into a Classroom as a Kid," *Issa Rae* (blog), January 22, 2012, http://blog.issarae.com/post/16296550787/calinative-lol-yuuuup.

13. Aymar Jean Christian, *Open TV: Innovation Beyond Hollywood and the Rise of Web Television* (New York: New York University Press, 2018), 130.

14. Jada Yuan, "'Awkward Black Girl' Goes to Hollywood," Vulture, October 2016, www.vulture.com.

37

Monty Python's Flying Circus
Layered Comedy

PHILIP SCEPANSKI

Abstract: While television episodes remain the same in reruns and on streaming services, audiences grow older as they repeatedly come back to favorites. Philip Scepanski examines *Monty Python's Flying Circus*'s "Spanish Inquisition" episode to explain how audiences unlock new and different pleasures as they approach familiar texts with new knowledge.

When I was nine or ten years old, I became a fan of *Monty Python's Flying Circus* for the overall silliness and dirty jokes. As I grew older, I started to get more out of the show. Exposure to a wider variety of film and television allowed me to make greater sense of its parodies—its imitations of other media—as well as the series' ability to play with my expectations about how television worked. I got a little older still, went to college, went to more college, and went to even more college, and began to understand jokes about European history, philosophy, and high art; the program remained the same, but my experience of it transformed over time.

For most of its relatively short history, television studies offered useful ways to think about different audiences' approaches to the medium, breaking viewers into groups by class, gender, political ideology, or some other combination of identity categories that distinguishes how they understand television.[1] Although there has been some work in related fields like mass communication studies about how audiences react to media over their lifespan, this issue has yet to significantly affect the way television studies thinks about audiences.[2] As my experience suggests, television and other media texts contain many overlapping appeals that reward divergent approaches and knowledges. Audience members unlock new pleasures based on what they bring to the text. In my case, new knowledge gathered from different sources made additional readings of *Flying Circus* possible at various moments in my life. This essay examines "The Spanish Inquisition" episode of *Monty Python's Flying Circus* from 1970, noting the ways it appeals to different types of knowledge and considering how audiences with varying levels and types of media literacy and education make sense of and enjoy the show. In doing so, the essay demonstrates how television shows can reward repeat viewings and build cult audiences, as well as how fans make sense of shows across their lifespan.

After the opening credits, the episode cuts to a sketch that begins with text reading "Jarrow—New Year's Eve 1911" over a black-and-white photo of billowing smokestacks. This opening and the scene that follows place the viewer in a period piece. Cutting to a wealthy sitting room, a woman in early twentieth-century period costume quietly crochets as someone knocks on the door. "Come in," she says, prompting a working-class man to enter. "Trouble at the mill," he explains, "One on't cross beams gone out askew on the treddle." Confused by his jargon, the woman asks the man to repeat himself and he obliges. Still struggling, she asks him to try again. "Mister Wentworth just told me to come in here and say that there was trouble at the mill, that's all. I didn't expect a kind of Spanish Inquisition."

A jarring musical chord punctures the scene as three men enter wearing bright red robes indicating that they are Roman Catholic cardinals. Although two sport fully coherent costumes, one inexplicably wears a leather aviator cap and goggles pushed up to his forehead. "Nobody expects the Spanish Inquisition!" announces the leader. "Our chief weapon is surprise. Surprise and fear. Fear and surprise . . . Our two weapons are fear and surprise, and ruthless efficiency. Our *three* weapons are fear, surprise, and ruthless efficiency, and an almost fanatical devotion to the pope. Our *four* . . . no . . . *amongst* our weapons . . . amongst our weaponry . . . are such elements as fear, surprise. I'll come in again." The mill worker sets them up again by announcing that he didn't expect a Spanish Inquisition, and the men reenter. The head cardinal attempts to deliver his speech from the top but adds "nice red uniforms" as an afterthought to the list of weapons. Frustrated, he begins again and tries a few more times before allowing his henchmen an attempt. The man in the leather hat then tries to deliver the lines but is even worse at it than his superior. Moving on, the third man reads the charges before briefly singing and dancing before the leader cuts him off.

We always make sense of media texts in relation to other media texts. Cultural theorist Mikhail Bakhtin argues that such intertextual comprehension is especially true of media forms like parodies that borrow liberally from other texts.[3] Still, audiences are likelier to make sense of some aspects of this sketch than others. At its most basic level, the cardinals are trying to appear threatening and deliver an officious speech but repeatedly fail in doing so. That they fail repeatedly and deliver their lines at urgent pace and in funny voices only increases the appeal. The cardinals' failure at more or less everything they attempt to accomplish is this routine's core gag, but repetition builds on that central idea. Henri Bergson understood laughter as a response to people who mechanically continue bad habits or plans rather than adapting or changing to fit circumstances at hand.[4] The cardinal attempts to correct himself on the fly but proves to be a poor improviser. Each time he notices a mistake, the leader begins again, repeating himself. Eventually, it becomes clear that he cannot complete the speech, meaning that the cardinal should adapt his plan. The more appropriate solution seems to be that he ought to slow down and plan out his speech before delivering it—a strategy that should be fairly obvious to just about anyone. Instead, he keeps slipping up, making this comparable, in Bergson's understanding, to someone who insistently takes the same icy sidewalk to work every morning and slips each day when they should change their plans and take a different path.

These are among the simplest reasons an audience might laugh at this routine—just about anyone can get the gag. These aspects require little to no cultural or historical knowledge, relying instead on the mostly self-evident humor of failure. This is not to say that these jokes would make sense to a newborn or someone who cannot speak English, but they are more or less available to anyone with basic cultural competency.

With slightly more knowledge, other aspects of this sketch come into focus. A little familiarity with costume and setting, for example, make the cardinals seem out of place in 1911 Jarrow. And the presence of the leather aviator's cap on one cardinal seems contradictory within the logic of his costume. Even if the audience has never heard of Jarrow—a town in Northeast England—or the Spanish Inquisition—which the show will later inform us belongs to the early sixteenth century—an audience member with only slight knowledge of costuming and time periods would be suspicious of the logic that places these medieval religious figures in the early twentieth century. Genre is also a point of contradiction here. The opening location and initial concern over the disaster at the mill bring to mind social realist drama whereas the dramatic music and attempts at grandiose speechmaking indicate a historical epic. Moreover, the charges being brought against the industrial worker and well-to-do woman seem odd and out of place, at least within traditional narrative construction that would have established characters' wrongdoing before moving to these accusations. Their confusion and protests of innocence help develop a sense that something here isn't quite right.

Understanding the humor of repetition and superiority described above requires little knowledge. Characters from the wrong period of history leveling nonsensical charges—which leans a bit more on an audience member's awareness of history and media literacy—speaks to theories of laughter as a response to surprise. As a hallmark of the Pythons' absurdist comedy style, one of the program's chief weapons is surprise: This sketch makes the audience laugh by upsetting expectations about time periods, film and television genres, and narrative causality. But in order to upset these expectations, the audience must have certain understandings of the situation to determine what does and does not fit. In this case, a slight understanding of period-appropriate costume, genre, and traditional narrative construction suffice to get these gags. But unlike certain other more obscure aspects of this sketch, these elements are relatively common knowledge that could probably be developed mostly by watching a modest amount of television and film.

Besides absurd juxtaposition, callbacks and interconnected sketches are another hallmark of the Monty Python style. In the middle of this sketch, the doorbell rings. A representative from the television network invites the mill worker to participate in a different sketch, effectively ending the Spanish Inquisition sketch and segueing into a new one. Unprepared for his role, this refugee from the Spanish Inquisition cannot complete the sketch because, although he patiently waits as a salesmen character delivers a long setup, the mill worker doesn't know the punchline he is expected to deliver. This joke relies on the audience's knowledge of the comedy genre. Jeffrey Sconce refers to this strategy of breaking the rules of comedy to get laughs as "metacomedy."[5] In this case, the sketch builds on expectations about how comedy should work, using a strategy similar to the kind employed when mixing industrial Jarrow and medieval Spain. The difference here is that it is not a mixing of incompatible historical periods but a flat denial of how a typical comedy sketch is supposed to work. There is a setup, but the sketch denies the satisfaction of a punchline, evoking Immanuel Kant's description of the comic as the shifting from "strained expectation" to "nothing."[6] Of course, it is never truly nothing that replaces expectation. In this case, the denial of what is expected leads to a mixture of frustration and delight as we watch the planned sketch go awry. Earlier, it was the cardinal's failure at which the audience laughed. Here, it is in part the mill worker and the network representative who failed, but more importantly, the television show itself failed to deliver a coherent sketch.

The mill worker asks his contact at the network about the punchline, prompting the network representative to check the script. While we never learn the punchline, we do learn that the network representative finds it quite funny—building on metacomedy's tendency to build the hope for but ultimately deny the satisfaction of a clear payoff. The error seems to have arisen out of bureaucracy, which makes this a slight at the expense of large organizations in general and the BBC in particular. In denying the viewer's ability to enjoy the joke, we get a sense that bureaucracies not only are inefficient but also can be cruel in the ways their machinery gets in the way of humanity. This reading becomes even more pronounced when the network representative not only refuses to return the man to his home but also asks if they can borrow the mill worker's head for a piece of animation. Confused, the mill worker only asks, "What?" before the network representative says "Jolly good." The man is dragged to the ground and his head is sawn off. The bizarre violence contrasts sharply with the respectability of the august BBC. This scene also echoes criticism of the Roman Catholic Church in "The Spanish Inquisition" sketches as a large bureaucracy with a history of un-prompted and bizarre cruelty. After some of Terry Gilliam's free-association-style animation, the episode again touches on this strategy as a roomful of button-down bureaucrats debate placing a tax on sex, with some confusion over whether they should perhaps tax "poo-poos" instead.

Bakhtin is useful here as well, as he noted how medieval humor would jux-tapose disreputable material aspects of the body with serious governmental and religious institutions and individuals.[7] Bakhtin also noted how that comic strat-egy continued into later art forms like Renaissance literature. Bakhtin died in the Soviet Union in 1975, so he probably never saw this episode of *Flying Circus*. If he had, the theorist would have likely appreciated the way the sketch had an official representative from the BBC decapitate their unsuspecting donor and govern-ment workers debate the merits of taxing sex and defecation.

After a sketch featuring "man-in-the-street" interviews about taxation, the show returns to the familiar setting of a middle-class living room. Unlike in the earlier sketch, which took place in 1911, this one appears to take place in a con-temporary 1970s setting. A young woman wears a short skirt and a blouse, her hair tied into a ponytail, suggesting fashion appropriate to the moment of this show's production. She sits next to an elderly woman, who shows vacation pho-tos to the younger one, narrating each photo one at a time. "This is Uncle Ted at the front of the house. This is Uncle Ted at the back of the house." Bored out of her mind, the young woman rolls her eyes as she rips up and throws away each photo. Finally, the elderly woman piques the younger woman's interest, "And this is the Spanish Inquisition, hiding behind the coal shed." "Oh!" the young woman exclaims, "I didn't expect the Spanish Inquisition!"

This callback is another typical strategy for the *Flying Circus*. In itself, the re-peated intrusion into seemingly unrelated sketches subverts expectations about how traditional narrative works in television or even sketch comedy. In case the historical illogic of the first Spanish Inquisition sequence was not clear, this itera-tion appears to take place in 1970, judging by the young woman's costume. The cardinals who initially appeared in 1911 have now leapt forward over fifty years. To add further absurdity to this timeline and drive home the point that these characters have strayed from an epic film, a text scroll and voiceover explain, "In

FIGURE 37.1.
An elderly woman,
transported from the
1970s to a sixteenth-
century dungeon,
is subjected to the
dreaded "comfy
chair" torture.

the early years of the 16th century, to combat the rising tide of religious unortho-doxy, the Pope gave Cardinal Ximinez of Spain leave to move without let or hin-drance throughout the land in a reign of violence, terror and torture that makes a smashing film. This was the Spanish Inquisition. . . ." Cardinal Ximinez and his lackeys take the elder woman from the 1970s to a dungeon appropriate for the sixteenth century. To the elderly woman's apparent delight, they proceed to "tor-ture" her with implements like soft cushions and a comfy chair. Needless to say, this is another example of the cardinals' incompetence.

Unlike the earlier sketch, the scrolling text explains the historical background of the Spanish Inquisition. While history teachers would surely like it to be common knowledge, the Spanish Inquisition as a historical event is not likely to be deeply understood by many audiences. For those who may be unfamiliar or only slightly knowledgeable, the show broadly explains the idea. But even then, it leaves out or obscures details: While the sketch refers to "a reign of violence, torture and ter-ror," it leaves to the imagination the incredible severity of torture by contemporary standards. For those even somewhat familiar with the horrific nature of medieval torture, the dissonance and surprise brought about by the cardinals' rather pleas-ant version of torture would make it even funnier. Furthermore, the sketch does not discuss how the Spanish Inquisition was often used as a pretense to persecute innocent Jews and Muslims. With that knowledge, the sketch takes on a darker humorous tone as we watch Ximinez and his men accuse people for no other rea-son than they haplessly uttered the setup to their favorite catchphrase.

Besides adding a more macabre hue, such knowledge reveals a more criti-cal tone to this sketch. The victims' clear innocence suggests that religious persecution is arbitrary. And while it blunts the emotional impact to see the old woman enjoying her comfy chair torture, it also shows that such persecution does little to effect change. Finally, the presence of the cardinals some five hundred years after their time shows that religious persecution is not only terribly outdated but also remains part of the world long past its expiration date. Although there are many ways to enjoy and make sense of this sketch, not all of them are available to all audiences. For a viewer unfamiliar with the history of the actual Spanish Inquisition and with more contemporary examples of persecution, this particularly critical understanding would not be possible.

In writing this essay, I wanted to make sure that what I thought I knew about the Spanish Inquisition was correct, which drove me to perform light research on the topic. I refreshed some education and learned a few new things about the topic. In looking deeper at the episode, I consulted some other points for doing general research as well as more focused resources like fan websites devoted to Monty Python.[8] Driven to learn more about this particular episode, a few elements of the sketch that had escaped me previously came into focus. For example, the cardinal in the leather aviator's helmet, whom the others call Biggles, references James Bigglesworth, a fictional hero from a series of UK young adult literature dating back to the 1930s.

In this case, my research was pointedly academic, but at earlier moments of my life, my membership in the Python cult drove me to research the show simply for the knowledge that would help me unlock more jokes. Since *Flying Circus* is a cult show with highly devoted fans, there were many others willing to indulge my interest at mid-1990s British comedy-focused Internet destinations like cathouse.org and alt.fan.monty-python. Such cultish fan work suggests that viewers can dig into new layers of meaning through research and conversations. New knowledge can unlock new humor, so television fandom drives those in search of deeper meanings to seek new knowledge. This effect extends beyond just the consumption of television—I'm sure that when it came time to learn about the actual Spanish Inquisition in high school history class, I paid closer attention than usual.

What these examples show more generally is that knowledge is relative. Biggles was a subject of pointed research for me but was likely an easily decoded pop-culture reference to many 1970s British audiences; however, the global fanbase of Monty Python would be unlikely to catch the meaning of this character. Acknowledging the variability in comprehension should give us pause before distinguishing between, for example, knowledge that comes from general cultural literacy and that which comes from serious academic study—especially when we study popular culture from an academic perspective. Nevertheless, the idea that television contains layered meanings waiting to be unlocked by audiences with different backgrounds, cultural contexts, knowledge bases, histories, and so forth is both a challenge and promise. It presents a challenge to critical and savvy viewers to consider the layered meanings inherent to different programs and how their viewing might (or should) change based on additional information that might be available to them. At the same time, it offers the promise that even if they can't make sense of something at the moment, there are meanings and perspectives lying beneath the accessible surface, waiting to reward them with additional depth with a little cultural digging.

FURTHER READING

Dobrogoszcz, Tomasz. *Nobody Expects the Spanish Inquisition: Cultural Contexts in Monty Python*. Lanham, MD: Rowman & Littlefield, 2014.

Landy, Marcia. *Monty Python's Flying Circus*. Detroit: Wayne State University Press, 2005.

Miller, Jeffrey S. *Something Completely Different: British Television and American Culture*. Minneapolis: University of Minnesota Press, 2000.

NOTES

1. Stuart Hall, "Encoding/Decoding," in *Media and Cultural Studies: Keyworks*, ed. Meenakshi Gigi Durham and Douglas M. Kellner (Malden, MA: Blackwell, 2001), 163–73; David Morley and Charlotte Brunsdon, *The Nationwide Television Studies* (London: Routledge, 1999); John Fiske, "Television: Polysemy and Popularity," *Critical Studies in Mass Communication* 3, no. 4 (December 1986): 391–408.
2. See Gayle R. Bessenoff and Regan E. Del Priore, "Women, Weight, and Age: Social Comparison to Magazine Images across the Lifespan," *Sex Roles* 56, nos. 3–4 (2007): 215–22; Jake Harwood, "Viewing Age: Lifespan Identity and Television Viewing Choices," *Journal of Broadcasting and Electronic Media* 41, no. 2 (1997): 203–12; Margot Van Der Goot, Johannes W. J. Beentjes, and Martine Van Selm, "Older Adults' Television Viewing from a Life-Span Perspective: Past Research and Future Challenges," *Annals of the International Communication Association* 30, no. 1 (2006): 431–69.
3. Mikhail Bakhtin, "Discourse in the Novel," in *The Dialogic Imagination*, ed. Michael Holquist, trans. Caryl Emerson and Michael Holquist (Austin: University of Texas Press, 1981), 259–422; Mikhail Bakhtin, *Rabelais and His World*, trans. Hélène Iswolsky, First Midland Book Edition (Bloomington: Indiana University Press, 1984).
4. Henri Bergson, "Laughter," in *Comedy: "An Essay on Comedy" by George Meredith; "Laughter" by Henri Bergson*, ed. Wylie Sypher (Garden City, NY: Doubleday, 1956), 61–190.
5. Jeffrey Sconce, "Tim and Eric's Awesome Show, Great Job! Metacomedy," in *How to Watch Television*, ed. Jason Mittell and Ethan Thompson (New York: New York University Press, 2013), 74–82.
6. Immanuel Kant, *Kant's Critique of Teleological Judgment*, trans. James Creed Meredeth (Oxford, UK: Clarendon Press, 1928), 199.
7. Bakhtin, *Rabelais and His World*.
8. Adam Fogg, "Monty Python's Completely Useless Website," www.intriguing.com/mp; "Montypython.net," www.montypython.net.

38

NFL Broadcasts

Interpretive Communities

MELISSA A. CLICK, HOLLY WILLSON HOLLADAY, AND
AMANDA NELL EDGAR

Abstract: This essay explores feelings about Colin Kaepernick and NFL player protests through interviews with current and former NFL fans, examining how these
fans maintained, changed, or fractured their lifelong relationships with televised
NFL games due to player protests during the national anthem. These interviews
are used to explore the concept of interpretive communities, which suggests that
the various meanings viewers make from television are enmeshed with their identities and experiences, group affiliations, and cultural contexts. In a cultural climate
politically charged—and divided—over issues like Black Lives Matter, immigration,
and sexual harassment, fans' positions on NFL programming provide a snapshot of
the ways sports fandom and politics intersect in contemporary American culture.

The first time San Francisco 49ers quarterback Colin Kaepernick refused to stand
during the U.S. national anthem at the opening of an August 2016 NFL game,
very few people noticed. Responding to questions, Kaepernick stated that he
was "not going to stand up to show pride in a flag for a country that oppresses
black people and people of color."[1] When Kaepernick switched to kneeling and
was joined by teammate Eric Reid the next month, more fans took notice, but
it was not until President Donald Trump tweeted his opposition to Kaepernick's
kneeling in September 2017 that the protests grew to a widespread cultural controversy. At that point, Twitter hosted more than four million posts with the
hashtags #TakeAKnee and #BoycottNFL.[2]

These posts not only supported or opposed Kaepernick's and others' protests;
they also engaged the political issues that sparked the protests, the meanings
of fandom for lifelong NFL supporters, and the television-viewing practices of

regular NFL audiences. When we watch television, we do so in particular personal, social, and political contexts, and these contexts influence the ways we understand programming. These contexts are all components of our *interpretive communities*, groups of people who share similar strategies and approaches to making sense of particular media, including televised sports programming and the televised commentary on sports broadcasting. The foundation for this concept is the idea of polysemy, a term that indicates that symbols like images and language have "many meanings," and thus the intended or apparent meanings of a complex set of symbols in a television program can vary widely for different audiences.[3] These various meanings are influenced by (at least) three interrelated factors: viewers' personal identities and experiences, relationships with family and friends, and beliefs about culture in general.

First, interpretive communities are influenced by viewers' personal identities. Demographics like race, gender, sexuality, and class as well as vocation, political affiliation, or even levels of fandom can influence how we experience the world and, consequently, how we bring that experience to the media we consume. For example, in the United States, black drivers are more likely than their white peers to be stopped by police while driving, and after they are pulled over, they are 20 percent more likely to receive a ticket and twice as likely to be searched.[4] Black audiences may be more likely, then, to empathize with Colin Kaepernick's messages about over-policing, since they are more likely to have experienced unfair treatment by police themselves. On the other hand, a fan who is a white police officer may interpret these messages differently, based on the way they move through the world as a white person, as well as their feelings of connection to their vocation. This is not to imply that our demographics predetermine our interpretation of messages. Instead, our identities influence the ways we experience the world, and these experiences shape our understandings of media messages.

Second, interpretive communities are influenced by friends and family with whom we watch and discuss media. Many viewers seek out others with similar viewpoints to discuss and collectively interpret the meanings in popular cultural messages.[5] NFL fans often watch televised broadcasts of football games in groups, and these groups bond around a sense of shared identity that informs not only the ways they interpret messages like Kaepernick's protests but also the ways they discuss those messages. A group of fans of Kaepernick's former team, the San Francisco 49ers, is more likely to have discussed Kaepernick prior to his protests, since he quarterbacked the team in three consecutive NFC Championship Games and led them to Super Bowl XLVII. Fans of the 49ers who were pleased with Kaepernick's performance and felt an allegiance to him as their quarterback may have felt more sympathetic and connected to his protest messages, simply by virtue of their shared identity as fans of the team. In tandem with personal identities and experiences, these communal interpretations can shape the ways groups of fans approach messages like those of Kaepernick's protests. Further, many groups of friends and family members also share demographic characteristics, vocation, or political affiliation. Building on our previous example, black 49ers fans may have developed more favorable feelings about Kaepernick's decision to "take a knee" than a multiracial group of police officers who are fans of the Green Bay Packers.

Third and finally, interpretive communities always are formed and exist within broader cultural contexts. The social and political messages that circulate alongside the television we watch influence the ways we interpret events like Kaepernick's protests. The NFL player protests took place within a preexisting political context that included conflicts about police violence against people of color, Trump's presidential campaign, and tensions in the cultural conversations surrounding racism, sexism, and reactionary populist politics. Many NFL fans had likely already heard of and formed opinions about some of these controversies separately from their NFL fandom, so their interpretations of Kaepernick's protests were informed not only by their personal identities and their communal fan groups but also by the cultural and political messages that shaped public opinion of the protests. This final factor of interpretive communities unites the other two. Our personal identities and experiences lead us to identify with particular political positions. We often discuss those topics with others who share our views. Then, finally, we use these individually and communally formed positions on broader cultural conversations to interpret specific events. In this way, audiences worked from the position of their interpretive communities to make sense of Kaepernick's protests, as well as the NFL's reactions to those protests and their choice of whether and how to #BoycottTheNFL.

To learn more about how NFL fans' interpretations of and responses to Kaepernick's protests were shaped by their interpretive communities, we interviewed both current and former NFL fans.[6] Between November 2017 and February 2018, we spoke to thirty-eight participants in audio-based interviews. Our sample was predominantly white and male, with twenty-nine white participants and twenty-nine male participants; twenty-four of the thirty-eight participants supported Kaepernick. In what follows, we highlight four fans' stories that represent some of the common themes we found in the interviews. Two of these fans had recently refused to watch the NFL, but for very different reasons; the two fans who continued to watch the NFL also differed in their motivations. These fans' stories demonstrate how their interpretive communities shape their fandom, and illustrate how fans communicate their support of (or opposition to) the NFL through their viewing practices. We begin with the two cases that support Kaepernick's actions.

Brian, a forty-one-year-old biracial consultant, described being a fan of professional football since childhood. He pointed out that his "father was a big football fan, so [in] early childhood I kinda started paying attention." In college, that attention grew: "When I watched more television . . . [I] pretty much watched at least some degree of NFL football every year. I guess that would be almost twenty years now." Brian mentioned that technological advancements in time-shifting have affected his viewing practices, observing that the games he watches are often prerecorded on his DVR so that he can "sit down and watch the broadcast in its full length if you really think that's going to be an enjoyable game, or you watch the abbreviated version which is already cut down to thirty or forty minutes for you." While Brian noted his Kansas City Chiefs fandom, he was reluctant to call himself a "die-hard" fan because he does not make an effort to go to games in person and is not bothered by missing games on television.

When asked about the role politics should play in sports, Brian asserted that "sports are for entertainment" and should therefore be free of political topics and investments. Brian's opinion was influenced by his belief that the NFL is a business, and political issues "should stay out of people's privately owned businesses." Despite his position on the intersection of politics and sports, Brian supported Kaepernick's right to protest because "it's for the cause [of racial justice] and the thing that the military fought for . . . they have that very right if they want to kneel as long as their employer allows them to since they're on the clock at that time." Brian offered that his viewership has continued unabated by the kneeling protests; even though he believed that sports and politics should be separate, the players' actions did not affect his perception that football viewership is entertaining, regardless of the overt political bent of the protests. Brian's responses indicate his membership in a variety of interpretive communities, from his family-initiated practices of viewing to his identity as a biracial Chiefs fan and his belief that politics should be separate from football.

Jada, a forty-one-year-old black educational consultant, has been an NFL fan since the mid-1980s, when she was six or seven. Growing up in San Diego, the Chargers were her favorite team; however, "in 1988, the 88–89 season, the Redskins beat the Broncos, and I became a fan of the Redskins." Although Jada explained that she typically watches the NFL at home, she worked for three years in a sports bar where she would watch the games every Sunday. She described that "my husband and I would sometimes go out even for Monday night or the Sunday games." Until recently, Jada and her husband have been longtime subscribers to the NFL's "Sunday Ticket" that gives satellite TV viewers access to NFL games broadcast on all networks.

Unlike Brian, Jada does believe politics should play a role in sports; she insisted, "I am a big proponent of people that have the spotlight on them, that have that platform, that they should use it. Not everybody has that voice." When we spoke with Jada in early December 2017, she had not been watching NFL games. Asserting that this is the first year since she became a fan that she did not watch, she said, "I'm 100 percent done . . . I'm definitely over it. These owners are not treating folks the way they should, so I'm not going to continue to give them my money." Jada's belief that the NFL profits from her viewership led her to cancel her family's subscription to NFL Sunday Ticket. This decision affects her family, particularly her husband who Jada believes is watching the games when she is not around. She also put away her Washington Redskins gear, insisting that "I'm not wearing anything other than my . . . Kap shirt to wear on Sundays."

Jada had been filling her newly available time with traveling and errands, and reported that not watching the NFL gave her "a lot of free time." She said the adjustment "was tough the first couple of weeks and it was harder than I thought it would be. And now it's like, 'oh, well.' I don't even know who's playing what, or when, and it's kind of a relief in a way." When we asked her how long she would boycott, Jada replied that the NFL "may have lost me forever." When we asked what might bring her back to watching NFL games, she said, "I said at the beginning of the season I will not watch football until Colin [Kaepernick] has a job, and I don't think that's going to happen. . . . I recognize that I can move along in my life without watching football, which at one point I didn't think was possible. So, yeah, until Kap has a job, I'm done."

Because both Brian and Jada experienced the player protests in the same American cultural context, developed a love for the NFL through their families, and support the players' protests, their interpretive communities overlap. Yet the differences in their personal identities and beliefs about the role politics should play in NFL programming ultimately led them to support the player protests in different ways. It may be that Jada's political investment and support of groups like Black Lives Matter, and her identification as black, overwhelms her investment in watching NFL games with friends and family. Brian, who believes that politics causes "nothing but stress and worry," finds it easier to focus on NFL football games as entertainment, not political, and thus maintains his relationship with televised NFL games. Brian's agreement with the players' stance on U.S. racial politics and his support of the players' rights to protest likely shape Brian's ability to overlook the ways that the protests shape NFL politics.

The following two fans' stories, which are framed by disdain for Kaepernick's actions, similarly demonstrate the complexities of interpretive communities. Like Brian and Jada, Mark, a thirty-four-year-old white male who works as a multifunctional information analyst, is a lifelong fan of professional football, which he credits to his father who "was always watching." Although he grew up in San Diego as a Chargers fan, his move to Philadelphia for college resulted in a shift in

FIGURE 38.1. This meme, shared widely online, demonstrates some NFL fans' interest in expressing their dislike of the player protests by boycotting television broadcasts of NFL games.

allegiance. He recalled, "About ten years ago [I] fell in love with the city and the [Eagles]." Mark shared that "when I was active army I would watch with friends or my soldiers." While he primarily now watches at home, the social appeal of NFL fandom continues for Mark through his participation in online fantasy football leagues.

Mark pointed out that he does not support the recent protests by Colin Kaepernick and other NFL players, due in large part to his perception that sports should function solely as entertainment. He commented that "sports is where I go to get away from politics and I don't want to be barraged with it 24/7 . . . I want to watch sports. I don't want people advocating for this or that." However, he conceded that he "is fine with athletes doing their own thing on their own time," but "anytime there's divided lines and people get in a pissing contest, sports is the wrong place for that." Mark's attitude toward the in-game protests left him "absolutely disgusted," and he "stopped watching any and all football games that were not the Eagles."

Mark's stance toward Kaepernick and other players' actions did not result in a full boycott of football viewership, as his commitment to his favored team overrides his dislike of the players' actions. Mark provided a rationale for the ways his altered viewership allowed him to continue watching football while simultaneously letting his feelings about the protests be known to television programmers: "I stopped streaming games. I mean, as my form of protest, I stopped streaming games so that they can't get stats on which games I'm watching. So, over-the-air broadcast. That's it." Mark's response to the NFL player protests reveals his membership in several interpretive communities. Despite his strong political beliefs about the player protests, which are likely intertwined with his identity as a veteran, Mark chooses to prioritize his lifelong NFL fandom, his identification as a resident of Philadelphia, and his affiliation to the Eagles all the while minimizing the NFL's ability to benefit from his viewership.

Like many fans we interviewed, David's interest in the NFL is tied to his home state. David, who is forty-six, white, and works in law enforcement, played college football and has served as an official at the college and high school levels. He suggested that in Kentucky most people support the Cincinnati Bengals, but he is "one of these odd birds that's a Cincinnati Reds fan and a Pittsburgh Steelers fan." He described himself as "a diehard football fan." Although David also identifies as a Republican, he complained about what he believes is a change in the visibility and role of the U.S. president, with President Trump voicing his opinion on sports generally and the NFL player protests specifically. He insisted that the U.S. president should "run the country . . . leave the NFL, you know, if you wanna go throw out the first pitch in the World Series, . . . I think it's a great, it's an historical thing that we've done as presidents, but to just jump in the middle, . . . just run the country, get our jobs . . . back, bring the people together, do that, don't get mixed into the sports thing. I don't agree with that."

As his feelings about Trump's involvement in sports convey, David believes sports should be entertaining, not political. When we talked with David in November 2017, he reported that while his Thanksgiving had been "great," he had also been sad "because this was the very first Thanksgiving I had never watched an NFL football game, ever. And it bothered me, it did." David insisted he would never watch the NFL on television again because of the player protests but shared that he missed watching it: "It bothers me every Sunday, every Monday, every Thursday that I'm not watching a ball game. But I'm okay with it because I'm an American first." In lieu of watching the NFL, David had been spending more time with his family. His resistance to the NFL was ultimately economic, as he maintained that he did not want players or the NFL to profit from his interest. "I think viewers like me, fans like me, are saying, 'Hey, I'm done with these rich punks, these thugs that go out and make money off of me, off of our hard earned money that we're spending for jerseys or for football cards or for whatever kind of stuff that they do, buy game tickets or whatever, they're not doing that to me.'"

Mark and David share strong negative feelings about the NFL player protests, which places them in intersecting interpretive communities even though only one of them is boycotting televised NFL games. Yet their differences from Brian and Jada cannot be fully understood with reference to their political involvement or their race. Both men are white, and Mark, who described himself as "extremely" involved in politics, still watches Eagles games on television. David, who is boycotting all NFL programming, is interested in politics, but he described the importance of engaging those who have different opinions from him, "We still gotta get along, we still gotta live and we still gotta survive and we still gotta love each other in this country to make it successful." It may be that these fans' disdain of the player protests is more connected to Mark's identity as a veteran and David's investment in conservative American patriotism. Like Jada, both Mark and David expressed their concerns about the NFL profiting from their fandom. These examples demonstrate that people typically belong to many interpretive communities, and that people in the same interpretive communities are differently invested in those communities even when in the same situations, making it a challenge to assume or predict how interpretive communities shape the meanings people make of television content.

Together, these four cases demonstrate that NFL broadcasts generally, and the player protests specifically, are polysemic. Exploring the "many meanings" these fans see in NFL broadcasts—meanings derived from their connections to family viewing habits and regional affiliations, and embedded in their beliefs about the role of politics in sports—helps us better understand the different responses NFL fans have had to Kaepernick's decision to "take a knee" during the national anthem. While commentators from journalism to social media have presumed to understand the NFL fan groups that both support and reject Colin Kaepernick's actions, these four fans' positions illustrate how audience members' interpretations of and connections to television programming are influenced by a complex mix of their identities, group affiliations, and beliefs about culture. All four are lifelong fans of NFL programming whose viewing patterns originated from family habits and whose regional identities shaped their team preferences. All have an acute awareness of their consumption of NFL programming as economic and symbolic. Set in a contemporary American cultural context, their similar, ritualistic viewing behaviors thus indicate that they share affiliation in the same interpretive community, interpreting and experiencing NFL programming in similar ways.

Yet their responses to Colin Kaepernick's decision to "take a knee" illuminate how their identities, group affiliations, and cultural beliefs affect their fandom, and thus their viewership. While Brian and Jada shared support of Kaepernick's actions, their responses to NFL programming are contradictory. Likewise, Mark and David shared disdain of Kaepernick's actions, but they expressed that disdain differently. Jada and David are boycotting NFL programming, but for very different reasons. As these cases show, the concept of interpretive communities, grounded with audience interviews, gives us a clearer sense of how identities, group affiliation, and cultural values influence fans' viewing habits and frame their beliefs about the NFL player protests, sports, and politics. Beyond analyses that explore individual episodes or programs solely via textual analysis, research that foregrounds audiences' interpretations allows us to consider how identities and contexts shape the ways television's multiple meanings are received.

FURTHER READING

Bobo, Jacqueline. *Black Women as Cultural Readers*. New York: Columbia University Press, 1995.

Click, Melissa A., and Suzanne Scott, eds. *The Routledge Companion to Media Fandom*. New York: Routledge, 2017.

Gray, Jonathan, Cornel Sandvoss, and C. Lee Harrington, eds. *Fandom: Identities and Communities in a Mediated World*. 2nd ed. New York: New York University Press, 2017.

Radway, Janice. "Identifying Ideological Seams: Mass Culture, Analytical Method, and Political Practice." *Communication* 9 (1986): 93–124.

NOTES

1. Steve Wyche, "Colin Kaepernick Explains Why He Sat during National Anthem," NFL. com, August 27, 2016, www.nfl.com.
2. Kristina Monllos, "This Social Analytics Firm Says the 4 Million #TakeAKnee Tweets Are Just the Beginning," Adweek, September 25, 2017, www.adweek.com.
3. Stuart Hall, , "Encoding/Decoding," in *Culture, Media, Language: Working Papers in Cultural Studies, 1972–79*, ed. Stuart Hall, Dorothy Hobson, Andrew Lowe, and Paul Willis (London: Hutchinson, 1980), 128–38.
4. Emma Pierson et al., "A Large-Scale Analysis of Racial Disparities in Police Stops across the United States," Stanford Computational Policy Lab, March 13, 2019, https://5harad. com.
5. Jacqueline Bobo, *Black Women as Cultural Readers* (New York: Columbia University Press, 1995).
6. After receiving approval from our university institutional review boards (administrative boards that oversee research conducted at universities to ensure that research subjects are treated ethically), we used social media (Facebook, Twitter, and Instagram) and NFL fan sites to recruit current NFL fans and those who had given up their fandom to support or oppose Kaepernick's protest. All interview subjects consented to us quoting their responses using pseudonyms.

39

Pardon the Interruption
Sports Debate

ETHAN TUSSEY

Abstract: ESPN's *Pardon the Interruption* represents a turning point in sports programming, the beginning of a shift away from game recaps and highlights and toward the sports debate format. The success of *PTI* inspired twenty-four-hour sports networks to embrace debate as a strategy for maintaining relevance in a digital age. Ethan Tussey argues that the ubiquity of the sports debate format has effectively pushed the politics of sports out from the margins and into mainstream conversation.

One of the most iconic moments in television sports history occurred at the 1968 Olympic Games when John Carlos and Tommie Smith, standing on the medal podium, raised their black-gloved fists in protest during the playing of the U.S. national anthem. As famous as the moment is today, the initial reaction from the sports media at the time was to condemn or downplay the significance of the protest.[1] Sports television quickly moved on from coverage of the political protest, returning to reports on game results and strategy. A decade later, ESPN built an entire network around sports, but its flagship program, *SportsCenter*, replicated the apolitical view of its forebears, choosing to dedicate the majority of its coverage to reporting sports news, game stories, and spectacular highlights.[2] Though sports have always been political, sports television has traditionally eschewed politics because television producers saw sports as a safe space where people from different points of view could come together. Since the turn of the twenty-first century, though, sports programming has become much more overtly political thanks largely to the success of the ESPN show *Pardon the Interruption* (*PTI*), which introduced a unique debate format to excavate the subtext of sports and make audiences aware of the deeper implications of athletics.

ESPN's decision to embrace debate was due to not a sudden interest in politics but rather the side effect of sports television's response to changes in the television industry. *PTI* was launched in 2001, in the era that Amanda Lotz has called the post-network era, in which production practices, "including the making, distribution, and financing of television," changed in relation to upheaval caused by digital technologies.[3] Anticipating this upheaval, ESPN executive Jim Cohen went in search of a show that could be like Comedy Central's *The Daily Show* for sports, offering "daily takes on the news."[4] While traditional sports programming has struggled to compete with the immediacy of online sports news, sports debate shows entice viewers to check in daily. Through debate games and aesthetic innovations, *PTI* acknowledges the demands on audience attention and promises to deliver commentary that is worth a viewer's time, while simultaneously presenting a wider spectrum of opinions on sports than at any other time in sports media history. These opinions are amplified across the ESPN media platforms, extending debate and adding political heft to sports events.

Key to *PTI*'s success are the talents of its hosts, former *Washington Post* sports columnists Tony Kornheiser and Michael Wilbon. Newspaper columnists, as opposed to television anchors, earn their positions through their ability to provide opinion and commentary. Kornheiser and Wilbon had developed critical distance and cynicism over the course of their careers covering sports, so they were prepared to provide political perspective to a daily sports debate program. While ESPN had employed newspaper columnists since the earliest days of the network, they had largely been relegated to a Sunday morning talk show called *The Sports Reporters*.[5] The early faces of ESPN were the television anchors of *SportsCenter*—Chris Berman, Dan Patrick, Stuart Scott, Linda Cohn, and others, most of whom began their careers in front of the camera. *SportsCenter*'s anchors garnered a national following by bringing style, knowledge, and humor to sports highlights, making ESPN the most-watched cable network within five years of its founding.[6]

According to Grant Farred, *SportsCenter* distinguished itself from sports television shows that preceded it because it "did not oscillate between the pointlessly quantitative (TV sports news) and the endlessly unquantifiable (radio and watercooler talk, where debates are open-ended)."[7] Instead, it used acerbic humor and popular culture vernacular to poke fun at the seriousness of sports.[8] Keith Olbermann and Dan Patrick (1992–1997) represented the apex of this style; as Bob Keisser once described them, "Olbermann will make a reference to Shakespeare while talking about the AL West or cast about a remark on D-Day or the moon landing when talking about a baseball strike or a Ken Griffey home run. Patrick will let these highbrow shots ruminate, then take the tone to a more base level

FIGURE 39.1.
Keith
Olbermann and
Dan Patrick on
SportsCenter,
July 8, 1992
(Credit: Rick
LaBranche/
ESPN Images).

with an interesting stat or casual aside about Olbermann's ever-changing hairdo."[9] The anchors' humor and cleverness made catching up on the day's events fun, but not political.

Take, for example, *SportsCenter*'s coverage of the national anthem protest by Mahmoud Abdul-Rauf in the 1995–1996 NBA basketball season. Abdul-Rauf, the starting point guard for the Denver Nuggets, had been sitting during the national anthem for sixty games before a radio caller informed the Denver media of the protest. When the NBA suspended Abdul-Rauf for violating league policy, ESPN dispatched a reporter to interview him.[10] *SportsCenter* segments in this era reflected the reportage style traditional in sports media: thirty-second informative segments with very little political contextualization.[11] *SportsCenter* anchor Bob Ley simply preceded the interview with the report that ESPN had learned Abdul-Rauf would rejoin the Nuggets in their next game against the Chicago Bulls.[12] In the interview, Abdul-Rauf explained that he felt the flag was a symbol of "oppression and tyranny" but said he would find a "better approach" to expressing his beliefs.[13] The producers agreed to present the interview as completely as "time would allow," a promise indicative of *SportsCenter*'s brisk pace and lack of commentary. In the days following Abdul-Rauf's interview, *SportsCenter* NBA beat reporter David Aldridge broke a story that Charlotte Hornets owner George Shinn required his players to pray together on the court prior to home games. While the story showed that tolerance of religious expression was inconsistent across the league, these findings were presented as investigative reporting and not commentary that could make the league's hypocrisy explicit.[14] *SportsCenter* did not ignore political stories, but they reported and quipped more than they debated and commented.[15]

In contrast, *PTI*'s coverage of a national anthem protest, this time by San Francisco 49ers quarterback Colin Kaepernick during the 2016 NFL preseason, dedicated exponentially more time to debate from multiple perspectives over the course of days. From September 6 to September 19, Kornheiser and Wilbon dedicated daily two- to four-minute segments discussing the legacy of protest in sports, American traditions of social protest, and the significance of Kaepernick's race and position in the NFL.[16] Their arguing is more performance than passionate disagreement. They shout at each other and talk over one another, but they also make reference to the structure of the show that requires them to be on the opposite sides of a debate. *PTI* Producer Erik Rydholm explains that the performance works because of the unique relationship between the hosts, the "only relationship I'd ever seen in which two people who clearly loved each other could scream at each other but neither took it personally."[17] The familiarity, irony, and faux-bombast style became a signature of the sports debate genre. The style of these debates is important because ESPN prohibits employees from making more overt political commentary, particularly comments made outside of their debate formats. For example, *SportsCenter* anchor Jemele Hill was suspended by the network for suggesting on her Twitter account that fans boycott advertisers to send a message to NFL owners that oppose the anthem protests.[18]

While the debates on *PTI* do not rise to the level of calling for boycotts, they do provide a space for a thorough conversation that includes a variety of perspectives. When a story is new it receives a place of prominence in *PTI*'s "A block," or the group of stories that precede the first commercial break. On the second and third day of a story, the debate will move down the A block behind more recent news. As the story winds down, it will be moved into the "B block," structured around several "games" designed to force the hosts to take positions that they may not actually hold. In one such game, "Role Play," the hosts embody the persona of a sports figure in the news that week. With their faces covered by holding a picture printout of the figure, Kornheiser and Wilbon spout opinions as if they were that figure. The game offers an opportunity to imagine the private persona that sports personalities hide from the public. A segment of "Role Play" from November 28, 2012, featured Kornheiser playing Pittsburgh Steelers quarterback Ben Roethlisberger as Wilbon interviewed him about his injury and asked whether he would play in an upcoming game. Kornheiser is not actually interested in reporting on Roethlisberger's fitness, and instead takes the opportunity to discuss the quarterback's brand of toughness and masculinity. He says (as Roethlisberger), "My move is to completely exaggerate all my illnesses and then walk out there and play great."[19] Whereas journalists on *SportsCenter* provide the latest information from medical staff to answer whether a player will likely take the field,

Kornheiser uses "Role Play" as an opportunity to reveal how athletes use media narratives to enhance their brands and cultivate mythologies around masculinity.

When the Kaepernick story reached the "B block" on day 5 of coverage, it was framed by the game "Mailbag," which provided the hosts a fresh angle for discussing the meaning of protests. While "Role Play" offers the hosts the opportunity to put words in the mouth of sports figures, "Mailbag" represents the audience's chance to put words in the mouths of the hosts. In this game, Kornheiser and Wilbon answer viewer email in the style of a radio call-in show. As with most of the performative elements in the show, the hosts acknowledge the contrivance of the game, thus drawing attention to the artifice of their argument. During the NFL anthem protests, the question from the Mailbag was about which of the anthem protests from that Sunday's games stood out from the others.[20] Wilbon refused to answer the question because for him the Sunday protests were all copycats of Kaepernick, and were thus less meaningful than the political project he originated. Kornheiser considered the question historically, stating that "social protest is the backbone of American democracy" and that these protests carried additional weight because they occurred on the anniversary of 9/11. In this instance, the hosts redirect the Mailbag question to revisit their previous arguments and consider them in light of the latest developments.

While Kornheiser and Wilbon often sarcastically ridicule their audience, the aesthetics of the show do cater to audience expectations in the digital era. "Mailbag" can be seen as just one response to the audience's desire for a level of interactivity and control. In the development of *PTI*, ESPN deliberately looked for talent that could bring a different visual approach to sports programming, and their aesthetic innovations have become industry standards.[21] The network hired Erik Rydholm, a veteran of Chicago television and founder of the successful online financial service the Motley Fool, and paired him with Matthew Kelliher, an assistant producer of *SportsCenter*.[22] The partnership bore innovation in the form of the "rundown," a chronological list of the show's topics aligned on the right side of the screen. Rydholm attributes the inspiration for the "rundown" to his previous work experience: "Coming out of the Internet, I felt like we had a higher responsibility toward the viewer's investment of time. To convince the customer to come into our conversation, we put a rundown on the screen of what we were talking about—in case people weren't interested in that subject, they might be interested in what was coming next."[23] The "rundown," then, is a tool that helps the audience manage their time.

The addition of a countdown clock for each segment reinforced not only the interactive aesthetic typical of online platforms but also the post-network television audience's expectation of control and customizability. The clock was originally conceived as a way to indicate how long viewers had to wait until *SportsCenter*

FIGURE 39.2.
Tony
Kornheiser
and Michael
Wilbon on
*Pardon the
Interruption*,
March 6,
2017.

aired. According to Rydholm, Kelliher had the idea to make the clock a part of each segment so that viewers knew how long Kornheiser and Wilbon would be spending on a given topic. Rydholm believes that the clock "appeal[s] to the rational part of your brain over the emotional part—that is, if you've checked out on this conversation and it doesn't interest you at all, you know it's going to be over in 1:15, 1:14, 1:13, so you can make the decision, 'I will hang out for 1:13 until they change topics.'"[24] In addition to enticing the viewer to stay with the program, the timed conversations on each topic limit the depth of conversation between the hosts. The short conversations are strategic, providing enough time to present a perspective, while also giving the producers the opportunity to return to the story throughout the week to cover another angle.[25] If viewers are interested in the subject, they are encouraged to return each day to see how the conversation evolves. *PTI*'s aesthetic provides viewers with a sense of control, while also enticing them to rejoin linear television flow.

Media scholar Karen Vered argues that the adoption of computer interface aesthetics, like *PTI*'s "rundown" and countdown clock, effectively transform television from something that is watched to something that is "interfaced with."[26] For example, the rundown and the clock may have offered viewers a sense of control over the national anthem protest story. Those interested in Kornheiser and Wilbon's evolving perspectives could check the rundown at the beginning of the show and see if the protests would be discussed. As the producers moved the story from early in the A block to late in the B block, they could entice viewers interested in that story to watch the preceding content. In the process, the audience would be introduced to other stories that would similarly make their way through the show's segments and games in the coming weeks. Given Kornheiser and Wilbon's politically charged debates, a viewer's decision to allocate attention to the protest story is a kind of political decision. The audience uses the clock and rundown to manage their attention, often between television screen and mobile device. Choosing segments on the rundown is a deliberate decision to engage in the ongoing conversation in the public sphere and an endorsement of the value of the debate. Even those that choose to ignore the story may not change the channel as they are encouraged by the clock to wait out the discussion.

Criticism of sports debate programs claim that this genre often devolves into shouting matches where combatants "scream declarative statements at each other over straw man arguments."[27] Such arguments are often referred to as "hot takes," which *Salon*'s Simon Maloy describes as "provocative commentary that is based almost entirely on shallow moralizing."[28] This form of writing is largely associated with online "click bait," even though the term "hot takes" actually emerged in relation to the socially conscious sports columnists of the 1960s and 1970s.[29] Like their sports writer forefathers, Kornheiser and Wilbon are undoubtedly in the business of "hot takes," but it would be a mistake to dismiss their conversations as "shallow moralizing." Indeed, sports debate shows must be seen as television's contribution to a broader conversation that takes place across a multimedia landscape.

Media scholars Brett Hutchins and David Rowe point out that sports programming has entered an age of "digital plentitude" that "challenges the hegemony of television sports networks and major sports organizations."[30] Digital platforms allow greater participation in the "media sports cultural complex" by offering a variety of distribution channels to television producers, athletes, fans, and cultural commentators.[31] Sports debate shows may offer the opinions of a couple of sports columnists, but those debates extend to everyday sports fandom on sports radio and podcast networks like The Ringer and on websites like Reddit, Barstool, SBNation, and Bleacher Report. Matt Hills argues that fandom in the digital age is partially defined by "infra-ordinary waiting" in which fan communities strengthen each other through shared anticipation and speculation in the downtime between releases of their favorite media content.[32] Fans can be protective, aggressive, or reassuring, but they thrive on the daily dispatches of Internet conversation and speculation. For sports, the anticipated events are the games, and sports debate shows provide fodder for these downtimes. Research on the media habits of sports fans indicates that they are more likely than fans of other genres to use multiple media platforms to gather information.[33] It is therefore likely that sports fans do not stop at the "hot takes," and instead look for additional commentary, such as newspapers, websites, and podcasts, to develop their understanding of a topic. In the case of the anthem protests, sports fans that use *PTI* as a starting point will find a plethora of thoughtful content on the history and status of protest in sports.[34] In this "digital plentitude," sports debates transcend "hot takes" because sports fans are aware of not only the outcomes of the games but also the social and political implications of their fandom.

PTI inspired an industrial reprioritization of the skills sets needed for on-air talent and the transformation of sports program aesthetics. These formal changes correspond with a growing awareness of the intersection of sports and politics. The embrace of controversy, debate, and diverse perspectives has led ESPN to invest in other commentary-based cultural forms such as documentary filmmaking, long-form journalism, and podcasting.[35] In 2017, ESPN's brand shifted toward politically themed prestige projects, earning the network an Academy Award for Best Documentary for the film *O.J.: Made in America*.[36] It has also earned them criticism from right-wing media outlets that claim ESPN is promoting a "liberal agenda."[37] Media critic Bryan Curtis claims that sportswriters no longer feel they have to hide their political perspective as did so many of their newspaper predecessors.[38] Contemporary sportswriters, many of whom appear on sports debate programs, wean themselves on "hot takes" as they make their name and take jobs in corporations that see sports as a part of a broader cultural conversation. *PTI* led the charge in establishing this new politically engaged sports landscape by successfully developing a sports debate format and user-centric aesthetics ideal for the digital age. In addition to grabbing ratings and rivaling *SportsCenter* as the voice of ESPN, *PTI* pushed sports debate into the broader cultural conversation.

FURTHER READING

Hutchins, Brett, and David Rowe. *Sport beyond Television: The Internet, Digital Media and the Rise of Networked Media Sport*. New York: Routledge, 2012.

Johnson, Victoria. *Sports Television*. New York: Routledge, 2019.

Vogan, Travis. *ESPN: The Making of a Sports Media Empire*. Champagne: University of Illinois Press, 2015.

NOTES

1. Jason Peterson, "A 'Race' for Equality: Print Media Coverage of the 1968 Olympic Protest by Tommie Smith and John Carlos," *American Journalism* 26, no. 2 (June 2013): 99–121.

2. I do not mean to suggest that ESPN only had *SportsCenter*-style programming. The network has tried many styles of programs through the years and has devoted considerable time to longer investigative journalism through programs like *Outside the Lines* and a once a week sports debate show called *The Sports Reporters*.

3. Amanda Lotz, "Introduction," in *Beyond Prime Time: Television Programming in the Post-Network Era* (New York: Routledge, 2009), 7.

4. James Andrew Miller and Tom Shales, *Those Guys Have All the Fun* (New York: Little, Brown, 2011), 472.

5. Richard Deitsch, "ESPN Canceling The Sports Reporters after Nearly 30 Years on the Air," *Sports Illustrated*, January 23, 2017.

6. Leonard Shapiro, "With World Watching, ESPN Is Programmed for Success," *Washington Post*, December 27, 1995.

7. Grant Farred, "Cool as the Other Side of the Pillow: How ESPN's SportsCenter Has Changed Television Sports Talk," *Journal of Sport and Social Issues* 24 (May 2000): 99–100.

8. Ibid.

9. Bob Keisser, "Dan and Keith: That's my 'SportsCenter' highlight," *Knight-Ridder News Service*, July 23, 1994.

10. Steve Zipay, "ESPN's Rauf Scoop," *Newsday* March 15, 1996.

11. Jacob S. Turner, "This Is SportsCenter: A Longitudinal Content Analysis of ESPN's Signature Television Sports-News Program from 1999 and 2009," *Journal of Sports Media* 9, no. 1 (Spring 2014): 45–70; Jeffrey Allan Welch, "Television Sports Reporting of Negative News: A Content Analysis of ESPN News and CNN Sports Tonight" (master's thesis, Wichita State University, 1996).

12. Prentis Rogers, "March Madness Puts Tyson-Bruno in Background," *Atlanta Journal Constitution*, March 15, 1996.

13. "Abdul-Rauf Says He'll Stand for Anthem," *United Press International*, March 14, 1996.

14. Milton Kent, "In My Opinion ABC Skates Circles around UMass-Georgetown," *Charleston Daily Mail*, March 26, 1996.

15. "NBA Report/Abdul-Rauf: I've Had Death Threats," *Newsday*, March 22, 1996.

16. These debates occurred on the following episodes of PTI: September 6, 2016, "CFB Week 1 in the Books"; September 7, 2016, "Unpatriotic?"; September 8, 2016, "Are You Ready for Some Football?"; September 9, 2016, "Taking Hits"; September 12, 2016, "NFL Week 1 Recap"; September 13, 2016, "Steelers Win Big."

17. Miller and Shales, *Those Guys*, 472.

18. Kevin Draper and Ken Belson, "Jemele Hill Suspended by ESPN after Response to Jerry Jones," *New York Times*, October 9, 2017.

19. *Pardon the Interruption* (*PIT*), November 28, 2012, YouTube, www.youtube.com.

20. *PTI*, episode NFL week 1 recap, September 12, 2016.

21. Miller and Shales, *Those Guys*, 473.

22. Noah Frank, "Behind the Scenes at 'Pardon the Interruption,'" WTOP, January 23, 2015, https://wtop.com.

23. Miller and Shales, *Those Guys*, 473–74.

24. Ibid.

25. Frank, "Behind the Scenes."

26. Karen Vered, "Televisual Aesthetics in Y2K: From Windows on the World to a Windows Interface," *Convergence* 8, no. 3 (2002): 51.

27. Chris Conrad, "Chris Conrad Column," *McClatchy-Tribune Regional News*, January 13, 2012.

28. Elspeth Reeve, "A History of the Hot Take," *New Republic*, April 12, 2015.

29. Tomas Rios, "A Brief History of Bad Sports Writing," Pacific Standard. August 15, 2013.

30. Brett Hutchins and David Rowe, "From Broadcast Scarcity to Digital Plentitude: The Changing Dynamics of the Media Sport Content Economy," *Television and New Media* 10, no. 4 (July 2009): 356.

31. Ibid.

32. Matt Hills, "Always-On Fandom, Waiting and Bingeing: Psychoanalysis as an Engagement with Fans' 'Infra-Ordinary' Experiences," in *The Routledge Companion to Media Fandom*, ed. Melissa A. Click and Suzanne Scott (Basingstoke, UK: Taylor & Francis, 2017), 22.

33. Walter Gantz, Zheng Wang, Bryant Paul, and Robert F. Potter, "Sports versus All Comers: Comparing TV Sports Fans with Fans of Other Programming Genres," *Journal of Broadcasting and Electronic Media* 50, no. 1 (March 2006): 95–118.

34. For a good example of the variety of commentary, see Rhiannon Walker, "A Comprehensive Aggregation of Colin Kaepernick Supporters, Haters and Everyone in Between," *The Undefeated*, August 30, 2016.

35. As financial circumstances have changed, ESPN has recently been downsizing. See Matt Bonesteel and Cindy Boren, "ESPN's Massive Round of Layoffs Hit Familiar Faces, Including Marc Stein, Andrew Brandt and Adam Caplan," *Washington Post*, May 1, 2017.

36. For more on ESPN's prestige programming, see Travis Vogan and David Dowling, "Bill Simmons, Grantland.com, and ESPN's Corporate Reinvention of Literary Sports Writing Online," *Convergence: The International Journal of Research into New Media Technologies* 22, no. 1 (2016): 18–34.

37. Ian Crouch, "ESPN Can't Win in Trump's Rowdy America," *New Yorker*, September 12, 2017.

38. Bryan Curtis, "The End of 'Stick to Sports,'" *The Ringer*, January 30, 2017.

40

The Walking Dead
Adapting Comics

HENRY JENKINS

Abstract: One of the key ways that television connects to other media is by adapting preexisting properties from films, comics, and other formats. Henry Jenkins uses one of the most popular of such recent adaptations, *The Walking Dead*, to highlight the perils and possibilities of adaptations, and how tapping into preexisting fan bases can pose challenges to television producers.

The comic book industry now functions as Hollywood's research and development department, with a growing number of media properties inspired by graphic novels, including not only superhero films (*Green Lantern, X-Men: First Class, Thor*) and both live-action and animated television series (*Smallville, The Bold and the Brave*), but also films from many other genres (*A History of Violence, American Splendor, 20 Days of Night, Scott Pilgrim vs. the World*). There are many possible explanations for Hollywood's comic book fixation:

1. DC and Marvel are owned by Warner Brothers and Disney, respectively, who cherry pick what they think will satisfy mass audience interests.
2. Comics-based stories are to contemporary cinema what magazine short stories were to classical Hollywood—more or less presold material.
3. Hardcore comics readers fall into a highly desired demographic—teen and twentysomething males—who have abandoned television in recent years for other media.
4. Comic books are a visual medium, offering something like a storyboard establishing basic iconography and visual practices for moving image media.
5. Digital special effects have caught up to comics' most cosmic storytelling, allowing special-effects houses to expand their technical capacities.

6. Contemporary television and comics involve a complex mix of the episodic and the serial, deploying long-form storytelling differently from most films or novels.

7. The streamlined structure of comics offers emotional intensification closely aligned with contemporary screen practices.

Despite such claims, comics adaptations often radically depart from elements popular with their original reading audiences. Mainstream comics readership has been in sharp decline for several decades: today's top-selling title reaches fewer than a hundred thousand readers per month—a drop in the bucket compared with the audiences required for cable success, let alone broadcast networks. Some graphic novels have moved from specialty shops to chain bookstores, attracting a "crossover" readership, including more women and more "casual" fans. Adapting a comic for film or television often involves building on that crossover potential rather than addressing hardcore fans, stripping away encrusted mythology about the nature of comics' popularity.

AMC's *The Walking Dead* is a notable exception, establishing its reputation as "faithful" to the spirit if not the letter of the original, even while introducing its original characters, themes, and storyworld to a new audience. Robert Kirkman's comic series was a key example of the crossover readership that graphic novels can find at mainstream bookstores. Kirkman has freely acknowledged his debts to George Romero's *Living Dead* film series, while others note strong parallels with *28 Days Later*. *The Walking Dead's* success with crossover readers and Kirkman's reliance on formulas from other commercially successful franchises in the genre explain why producers felt they could remain "true" to the comics while reaching a more expansive viewership. Using "Wildfire," the fifth episode from *The Walking Dead's* first season, I will explore what aspects of the comic reached television, what changes occurred, and why hardcore fans accepted some changes and not others. As a longtime *Walking Dead* reader, I am well situated to explore fan response to shifts from the original.

To understand what *The Walking Dead* meant to comics readers, one might well start with its extensive letter column. Here, dedicated fans ask questions and offer opinions about every major plot development. Kirkman established a deeply personal relationship with his fans, sharing behind-the-scenes information about his efforts to get the series optioned and then developed for television, responding to reader controversies, and discussing the comic's core premises and genre conventions ("the rules"). Kirkman summarized his goals in the first *Walking Dead* graphic novel:

With *The Walking Dead*, I want to explore how people deal with extreme situations and how these events CHANGE them. . . . You guys are going to get to see Rick change and mature to the point that when you look back on this book you won't even recognize him. . . . I hope to show you reflections of your friends, your neighbors, your families, and yourselves, and what their reactions are to the extreme situations in this book. . . . This is more about watching Rick survive than it is about watching Zombies pop around the corner and scare you. . . . The idea behind *The Walking Dead* is to stay with the character, in this case, Rick Grimes for as long as is humanly possible. . . . *The Walking Dead* will be the zombie movie that never ends.[1]

If, as Robin Wood formulated, the horror genre examines how normality is threatened by the monstrous, Kirkman's focus is less on the monstrous and more on human costs.[2] The comic's artwork (originally by Tony Moore but mostly by Charlie Adlard) offers gore-hounds detailed renderings of rotting faces (lovingly recreated for the television series by makeup artist Greg Nicotero) and blood splattering as humans and zombies battle, but it is also focused on melodramatic moments, as human characters struggle to maintain normality in the face of the monstrous. This merger of horror and melodrama may explain why, despite its gore, *The Walking Dead* comics appeal almost as much to female readers as they do to the men who constitute the core comics market. Early on, some fans criticized the comic's shambling "pace," going several issues without zombie encounters. However, once they got a taste of Kirkman's storytelling, many realized how these scenes contributed to the reader's deeper investment in the characters' plights.

Given his intimate and ongoing relationship with readers, Kirkman's participation as an executive producer on the television adaptation was key for establishing credibility with his long-term readers. Series publicity tapped Kirkman's street cred alongside AMC's own reputation for groundbreaking, character-focused television dramas (*Mad Men, Breaking Bad*) and the reputations of executive producers Frank Darabont (*The Green Mile, The Shawshank Redemption*) and Gale Anne Hurd (*Aliens, The Abyss, The Terminator* franchise) with filmgoers, establishing an aura of exceptionality.

The Walking Dead was a key discussion topic at the 2010 San Diego Comic-Con, a gathering of more than 200,000 influential fans. Posters, specifically produced for the convention, compared the television characters with their comic-book counterparts. The trade room display reconstructed an iconic comic location, a farmhouse where a family had killed themselves rather than change into zombies. Both tactics reaffirmed that the series was closely based on the comics. And Kirkman was front and center, promising fans that the series would capture the essence of his long-articulated vision. If the producers won the hearts of the hardcore fans, they might count on them to actively rally viewers for the series premiere. Thanks, in part, to the fan support in spreading the word and building enthusiasm, *The Walking Dead* broke all ratings records for basic cable for its debut episode and broke them again with the launch of season 2.

By the time *The Walking Dead* reached the air, Kirkman had produced and published twelve full-length graphic novels, representing more than seventy issues. Yet the first season of the television series covered only the first six issues. On the one hand, this expansive narrative offered a rich roadmap. On the other, it threatened to lock the producers down too much, making it hard for the series to grow on its own terms. Speaking at the Paleyfest in Los Angeles after season 1, Kirkman acknowledged that exploring different paths through the material allowed him to explore roads not taken in his own creative process.

The challenge was to give veteran fans recognizable versions of the established characters and iconic moments. Fans had to be able to follow the story structure in broad outlines, even as the producers were changing major and minor plot points, adding new themes and character moments. The audience anticipated that any changes would be consistent with Kirkman's oft-articulated "ground rules" and yet the producers wanted the freedom to take the story in some new directions. *The Walking Dead* had built its reputation for surprising its readers in every issue—any character could die at any moment, and taboos could be shattered without blinking an eye. How could the television series have that same impact if the most dedicated fans already knew what was going to happen next?

"Wildfire" was perhaps season 1's most emotionally powerful episode, where many core themes came into sharpest focus. It was based upon the final chapter of the first graphic novel, which set the tone for the rest of the comics series. The episode includes several memorable moments from the comics, specifically the death of two major characters (Amy and Jim), yet also several shifts that hint at how dramatically the producers had revised things. Fans embraced some of these changes, while others saw them as violating their collective sense of the franchise.

As "Wildfire" opens, the protagonists are recovering from a traumatic and abrupt zombie attack that killed several recurring characters and forced the survivors to confront the vulnerability of their encampment, thereby preparing them to seek a new "home" elsewhere in what is a recurring quest in the comics. The attack's basic outline remains consistent with the graphic novel. For example, Amy gets caught by surprise when she separates from the others, while Jim gets chomped in the ensuing battle. The brutal attack disrupts a much more peaceful "fish fry" scene, which provides an excuse for characters to reveal bits of their backstory. The ruthless battle shows how each character has begun to acquire self-defense and survival skills.

Yet a central emotional incident, Andrea's prolonged watch over her dead sister Amy's body, occupied only two panels of Kirkman's original comic. There, Andrea tells Dale, "I can't let her come back like that," capturing the dread of a

FIGURE 40.1. This AMC promo suggested that the TV adaptation of *The Walking Dead* would be a mirror image of the comic.

loved one transforming into the undead. The television series used this line as a starting point for a much more elaborated character study, built across several episodes as the two sisters, a decade-plus apart in age in this version (though not in the original), offer each other physical and emotional support. The two sisters talk in a boat about the family tradition of fishing and how their father responded to their different needs. Andrea plans to give Amy a birthday present, telling Dale that she was never there for her sister's birthdays growing up. The image of Andrea unwrapping the present and hanging the fishing lure around her dead sister's neck represents the melodramatic payoff fans expect from *The Walking Dead* in whatever medium. The expansion of this incident into a prolonged melodramatic sequence has to do both with issues of modality (the range of subtle facial expressions available to a performer working in live action as opposed to the compression required to convey the same emotional effect through static images) and AMC's branding as a network known for "complex narratives," "mature themes," and "quality acting."

"Wildfire" shows Andrea protecting Amy's body as the others seek to convince her to allow her sister to be buried, we hear the sounds of picks thrashing through the skulls of other zombies in the background and watch bodies being prepared to be burned. And, finally, Amy returns to life for a few seconds. Andrea looks intently into Amy's eyes, seeking any signs of human memory and consciousness, stroking her sister's face as Amy's gasps turn into animalistic grunts. The producers play with these ambiguities through their use of makeup: Amy is more human-looking compared to the other zombies, where the focus is on their bones, teeth, and muscle rather than their eyes, flesh, and hair. In the end, Andrea shoots her sister with the pistol she's been clutching—an act of mercy rather than violence.

Much of the sequence is shot in tight close-ups, focusing attention all the more directly on the characters' reactions. This is the first time the television series shows humans transition into zombies. Several issues after this point in the story

FIGURE 40.2.
Andrea watches
over Amy's death
in a melodramatic
sequence suited to
both live-action
TV and AMC's
"quality" branding.

(issue 11), the comic revisits this theme with a troubling story of Hershel, a father who has kept his zombie daughter chained and locked in a barn, unable to accept the irreversibility of her fate (an incident which was enacted on screen near the climax of the series' second season). Here, Andrea's willingness to dispatch Amy is a sign of her determination to live.

By contrast, the comic explores Jim's death in more depth. While Jim's family had been lost in a previous zombie attack, Jim was able to escape because the zombies were so distracted eating his other family members. The book's Jim is a loner who has not forged intimate bonds with the others, but who aggressively defends the camp during the zombie attack. In the comic, Jim is so overwrought with guilt and anger that he smashes one zombie's skull to a pulp. In the television series, this action is shifted onto an abused wife who undergoes a cathartic breakdown while preparing her dead husband for burial. On the one hand, this shift gave a powerful payoff for a new subplot built on the comic's discussion of how the zombie attacks had shifted traditional gender politics, and on the other, it allowed a tighter focus on Jim's slow acceptance of the prospect of becoming a zombie.

In both media, Jim initially hides the reality of being bitten from the other campers. Finally, he breaks down when someone notices his wounds. While the producers used the comic as a visual reference for this iconic moment, there are also substantial differences in the staging, including the shift of the bite from Jim's arm to his stomach and the ways the other campers manhandle him to reveal the bite.

Jim's story conveys the dread with which a bitten human begins preparing for a transformation into a zombie. In both the comic and the television series, Jim asks to be left, propped up against a tree so that he might rejoin his family when the inevitable change comes. Here, again, the television series elaborates on these basic plot details, prolonging his transformation to show the conflicting attitudes of the other campers to his choice. The television series is far more explicit than the comic about parallels with contemporary debates about the right of the terminally ill to control the terms of their own death.

In both sets of changes highlighted here, the television series remains true to the spirit of the original comic if not to the letter—especially in its focus on the processes of mourning and loss and the consequences of violence, both of which are often overlooked in traditional horror narratives. Both represent elaborations and extensions of elements from the original book. And both link these personal narratives with the community's collective experience, as in the scene where many from the camp say goodbye to Jim as he lies against a tree awaiting his fate. Some offer him comfort, others walk past unable to speak.

At the same time, two other "Wildfire" plotlines represent more decisive breaks with the comics: the confrontation between Shane and Rick and the introduction of the Center for Disease Control. Rick had been cut off from his wife and son when Shane, his best friend, helped them escape, while Rick was lying comatose in the hospital. Believing Rick to be dead, Lori and Shane couple until Rick finds his way back to his family. In Kirkman's original, Dale warns Rick that Shane made advances on Lori. In the television series, Rick has no idea of the potential infidelity, but the audience knows that Shane and Lori have made love. In the graphic novel, the two men go out to the woods to have it out. In the final panels of the first graphic novel, Shane attempts to kill Rick and is shot in the head by Rick's eight-year-old son, Carl. The boy collapses in his father's arms and says, "It's not the same as killing the dead ones, Daddy." Rick responds, "It never should be, Son. It never should be."

In "Wildfire," tension mounts throughout the episode as the two men clash over what the group should do next. Both turn to Lori for moral support, which she is unable to offer, saying instead that "Neither one of you were entirely wrong." In the television version, Shane initially mistakes Rick for a deer in the woods until he has his friend in his gun sights and then finds himself unable to draw down. Dale, rather than Carl, comes upon the two men, ending Shane's moral dilemma. When he returns from the woods, Shane seems ready to accept Rick's leadership. Shane's survival represents a decisive shift from the original, though by the season's end, its ramifications were not clear. Perhaps this is a case where Kirkman saw unrealized potentials that, given a chance, he wanted to mine more deeply.

But, in removing Carl from the scene, the television producers could be accused of pulling punches, given how central the sequence of the young boy shooting the adult male had been in the comic's original version (and its refusal to engage in sentimental constructions of childhood innocence). Carl's repeated brushes with violence, and his willingness to take action when adults hesitate, are recurring motifs throughout the books. If the comics often shocked readers by abruptly killing off long-established characters, here the producers surprised some viewers by refusing to kill a character whose death represented an early turning point in the comics.

The visit to the Center for Disease Control, which is introduced in the closing scenes of "Wildfire" and becomes the focus for the season's final episode, "TS-19," has no direct counterpart in the comic book series. One of the hard and fast rules Kirkman established in the comics was that he was never going to provide a rational explanation for how the zombie outbreak occurred. As Kirkman argues in an early letter column:

> As far as the explanation for the zombies go, I think that aside from the zombies being in the book, this is a fairly realistic story, and that's what makes it work. The people do real things, and it's all very down to Earth . . . almost normal. ANY explanation would be borderline science fiction . . . and it would disrupt the normalness. In my mind, the story has moved on. I'm more interested in what happens next then what happened before that caused it all.[3]

One reason Kirkman has Rick in a coma at the start of the comic series is so that the audience is not exposed to the inevitable theorizing which would surround a society coping with such a catastrophe. (A web series, produced for the launch of the second season, further explored what had happened when Rick was in his coma, offering a range of contradictory possible explanations for the zombie epidemic.)

Many fans were anxious about the introduction of the CDC subplot, which implied a medical explanation. At the same time, the closing scenes at the CDC also represent the first time we've cut away from Rick or the other members of his party to see another perspective on the unfolding events (in this case, that of an exhausted and suicidal scientist). For both reasons, many fans saw this subplot as another dramatic break with the spirit of the comic.

And it came at an unfortunate moment—at the end of the abbreviated first season, as the last taste before an almost year-long hiatus. If the series' publicity and presentation had largely reassured long time readers that the series would follow the established "rules," these final developments cost the producers some hard-won credibility, especially when coupled with news that the production company had fired most of the staff writers who worked on the first season, that AMC was reducing the budget per episode for the series, and that producer Frank Darabont was also leaving under duress.

By this point, *The Walking Dead* was the biggest ratings success in AMC's history, leaving many comics fans to worry whether their support was still necessary for the series' success. It would not be the first time that a series acknowledged a cult audience's support only long enough to expand its following, and then pivoted to focus on the new viewers who constituted the bulk of its rating points.

As this *Walking Dead* example suggests, there is no easy path for adapting comics for the small screen. There are strong connections between the ways seriality works in comics and television, but also significant differences that make a one-to-one mapping less desirable than it might seem. Television producers want to leave their own marks on the material by exploring new paths and occasionally surprising their loyal fans. The challenge is how to make these adjustments consistent not with the details of the original stories, but with their "ground rules," their underlying logic, and one good place to watch this informal "contract" between reader and creators take shape is through the letter columns published in the back of the comics. It is through this process that the producers can help figure out what they owe to the comics and to their readers.

FURTHER READING

Gardner, Jared. *Projections: Comics and the History of Twenty-First-Century Storytelling*. Palo Alto, CA: Stanford University Press, 2012.

Gordon, Ian, Mark Jancovich, and Matthew P. McAllister, eds. *Film and Comic Books*. Jackson: University Press of Mississippi, 2007.

McRobbie, Angela. *The Horror Sensorium: Media and the Senses*. Jefferson, NC: McFarland, 2013.

Pustz, Matthew. *Comic Book Culture: Fan Boys and True Believers*. Jackson, MI: University Press of Mississippi, 2000.

Smith, Matthew J., and Randy Duncan, eds. *Critical Approaches to Comics: Theories and Methods*. New York: Routledge, 2011.

NOTES

1. Robert Kirkman, *The Walking Dead*, vol. 1, *Days Gone Bye* (New York: Image, 2006).
2. Robin Wood, "An Introduction to the American Horror Film," in *Movies and Methods*, vol. 2, ed. Bill Nichols (Berkeley: University of California Press, 1985).
3. Robert Kirkman, "Letter Hacks," *The Walking Dead* 8 (July 2004).

Acknowledgments

When we wrote the acknowledgments for the first edition of *How to Watch Television*, we began by thanking the forty busy academics who eagerly jumped onboard for their commitment to improving media studies pedagogy, and their willingness to commit to a shared approach to writing and a tight deadline. Let us again thank those original contributors, even as we welcome and thank the twenty-two new contributors to this second edition. We again extend our utmost gratitude for delivering such excellent work with minimal pestering.

Thank you to Eric Zinner, Dolma Ombadykow, and the rest of New York University Press's staff for their continued commitment to this project. This is a second edition we can all be very proud of.

ETHAN

As I wrote in the first edition, I've wanted to make a book like *How to Watch Television* since working as a teaching assistant at USC, and it was gratifying when so many scholars joined the project. It has been even better to see the first edition embraced by so many in the field. Thank you to everyone who uses this book to support their teaching! Again, many thanks to Jason for all his hard work. We have relied upon one another to bring this second edition to life possibly even more than we did the first go-round.

Biggest thanks to my wife and primary TV-watching partner, Maria, and our three kids (who are now making steady progress toward adulthood) Jenna, Dax, and Mia. You all make me feel lucky and proud every day.

JASON

I owe many thanks to Ethan for first devising the idea for this book and approaching me to contribute an essay—and then welcoming me as a co-editor in what has turned out to be a greatly rewarding collaborative process, now over many years and two editions! It's rare to work so closely with someone where we agree on almost every decision throughout, and thus I have been spoiled for future collaborations.

As always, I could not have accomplished my work without the love and support of my partner Ruth, and my children, Greta, Anya, and Walter, for everything they have taught me.

About the Contributors

Evelyn Alsultany is Associate Professor in the Department of American Studies and Ethnicity at the University of Southern California. She is the author of *Arabs and Muslims in the Media: Race and Representation after 9/11*. She is co-editor with Rabab Abdulhadi and Nadine Naber of *Arab and Arab American Feminisms: Gender, Violence, and Belonging* and with Ella Shohat of *Between the Middle East and the Americas: The Cultural Politics of Diaspora*. She is also guest curator of the Arab American National Museum's online exhibit, "Reclaiming Identity: Dismantling Arab Stereotypes" (www.arabstereotypes.org).

Ben Aslinger is Associate Professor and Chair of the Department of Media Studies at Bentley University. He is the co-editor with Nina B. Huntemann of *Gaming Globally: Production, Play, and Place*, and with Germaine R. Halegoua of *Locating Emerging Media*. He is currently working on an edited collection on queer media industries with Julia Himberg.

Miranda J. Banks is Associate Professor of Film, TV, and Media Studies at Loyola Marymount University and currently serves on the board of directors of the Society of Cinema and Media Studies. She is the author of *The Writers: A History of American Screenwriters and Their Guild* and co-editor with Vicki Mayer and John Thornton Caldwell of *Production Studies: Cultural Studies of Media Industries* and with Bridget Conor and Vicki Mayer of *Production Studies: The Sequel!*.

Ron Becker is Professor of Media and Culture at Miami University of Ohio. He is the author of *Gay TV and Straight America*. His work has also appeared in *The Television Studies Reader*; *Queer TV: Theories, Histories, Politics*; *The Great American Makeover: Television, History and Nation*; *The Historical Journal of Radio, Film, and Television*; and *Television and New Media*.

Mary Beltrán is Associate Professor and Associate Chair in the Department of Radio-Television-Film and an affiliate of Mexican American and Latina/o Studies and Women's and Gender Studies at the University of Texas at Austin. She is the author of *Latina/o Stars in U.S. Eyes* and co-editor with Camilla Fojas of *Mixed Race*

Hollywood. She is currently working on a new book, *Latino, Latina, and Latinx Television: Navigations of U.S. Storytelling.*

Jeremy G. Butler is Professor of Creative Media at the University of Alabama. He wrote the textbook *Television: Visual Storytelling and Screen Cultures.* His other book projects include *Television Style* and *The Sitcom.* He has published articles on *Mad Men, ER, Roseanne, Miami Vice, Imitation of Life*, soap opera, the sitcom, and other topics in journals such as *Cinema Journal, Journal of Film and Video*, and *Screen.*

Aymar Jean Christian is Associate Professor of Communication Studies at Northwestern University. His first book, *Open TV: Innovation Beyond Hollywood and the Rise of Web Television* argues the web brought innovation to television by opening development to independent producers. His work has been published in numerous academic journals, including *The International Journal of Communication, Television and New Media, Cinema Journal, Continuum*, and *Transformative Works and Cultures.*

Melissa A. Click is Assistant Professor of Communication Studies at Gonzaga University. Her work on fans, audiences, and popular culture has been published in *Television and New Media*, the *International Journal of Communication Studies, Popular Communication*, and *Popular Music and Society.* She is editor of *Anti-Fandom: Dislike and Hate in the Digital Age* and the co-editor of *The Routledge Companion to Media Fandom* and *Bitten by Twilight.*

Amber Day is Professor of Media and Performance Studies in the English and Cultural Studies Department at Bryant University. She is the author of *Satire and Dissent: Interventions in Contemporary Political Debate* and the editor of *DIY Utopia: Cultural Imagination and the Remaking of the Possible.* Her research focuses broadly on the intersections of art and political speech, including satire and irony, political performance and activism, and public debate.

Abigail De Kosnik is Associate Professor at the University of California, Berkeley, in the Berkeley Center for New Media (BCNM) and the Department of Theater, Dance and Performance Studies, and is the Director of BCNM. She is the author of *Rogue Archives: Digital Cultural Memory and Media Fandom* and co-editor with Keith Feldman of *#identity: Hashtagging Race, Gender, Sexuality, and Nation.* She has published articles on media fandom, popular digital culture, and performance studies in *Cinema Journal, The International Journal of Communication, Modern Drama, Transformative Works and Cultures, Verge: Studies in Global Asias, Performance Research*, and elsewhere. De Kosnik is Filipina American.

Amanda Nell Edgar is Assistant Professor in the Department of Communication and Film at the University of Memphis. She studies the politics of sound in popular culture. She is the author of *Culturally Speaking: The Rhetoric of Voice and Identity in a Mediated Culture* and co-author with Andre E. Johnson of *The Struggle Over Black Lives Matter and All Lives Matter*.

Racquel Gates is Associate Professor at the College of Staten Island, CUNY. Her research focuses on blackness and popular culture, with special attention to discourses of taste and quality. She is the author of *Double Negative: The Black Image and Popular Culture* and has written numerous essays on film and media, some of which appear in *Film Quarterly*, *Television and New Media*, the *New York Times*, and the *Los Angeles Review of Books*.

Jonathan Gray is the Hamel Family Distinguished Chair of Communication Arts and Professor of Media and Cultural Studies at University of Wisconsin–Madison. He is author or co-editor of numerous books, including *Television Entertainment*, *Television Studies* (with Amanda D. Lotz), and *Keywords for Media Studies*. He is also Chief Editor of *International Journal of Cultural Studies*.

Hunter Hargraves is Assistant Professor in the Department of Cinema and Television Arts at California State University, Fullerton. He is the author of the forthcoming book *Uncomfortable Television*, and his research on contemporary American television has appeared in *Cinema Journal*, *Television and New Media*, *Celebrity Studies*, *Camera Obscura*, and *A Companion to Reality Television*.

Heather Hendershot is Professor of Film and Media at MIT. She is the editor of *Nickelodeon Nation: The History, Politics, and Economics of America's Only TV Channel for Kids* and the author of *Saturday Morning Censors: Television Regulation before the V-Chip*, *Shaking the World for Jesus: Media and Conservative Evangelical Culture*, *What's Fair on the Air? Cold War Right-Wing Broadcasting and the Public Interest*, and *Open to Debate: How William F. Buckley Put Liberal America on the Firing Line*.

Holly Willson Holladay is Assistant Professor in the Department of Media, Journalism and Film at Missouri State University. Her research focuses on the relationship between media texts, media audiences, and negotiations of identity (e.g., gender, class, race, and sexuality). Her work has been published in *Television and New Media*, *Southern Communication Journal*, *The Journal of Popular Culture*, and *Participations: International Journal of Audience Research*, and a number of edited collections.

Anikó Imre is Professor of Cinema and Media Studies at the University of Southern California. She works in comparative media studies with a special focus on European television and film, (post-)socialism, gender, sexuality, and race. Her most recent book is *TV Socialism*.

Henry Jenkins is the Provost's Professor of Communication, Journalism, Cinematic Arts and Education at the University of Southern California. His most recent books include *By Any Media Necessary: The New Youth Activism*, *Popular Culture and the Civic Imagination: Case Studies of Creative Social Change*, and *Comics and Stuff*. He blogs at henryjenkins.org and hosts the *How Do You Like It So Far?* podcast.

Derek Johnson is Professor of Media and Cultural Studies in the Department of Communication Arts at the University of Wisconsin–Madison. He is the author of *Transgenerational Media Industries: Adults, Children, and the Reproduction of Culture* and *Media Franchising: Creative License and Collaboration in the Culture Industries*, the editor of *From Networks to Netflix: A Guide to Changing Channels*, and co-editor of *Point of Sale: Analyzing Media Retail*, *A Companion to Media Authorship*, and *Making Media Work: Cultures of Management in the Entertainment Industries*.

Jeffrey P. Jones is Executive Director of the George Foster Peabody Awards, Director of the Peabody Media Center, and Lambdin Kay Chair for the Peabodys at the University of Georgia. He is the author and editor of six books, including *Entertaining Politics: Satiric Television and Civic Engagement*; *Satire TV: Politics and Comedy in the Post-Network Era*; and *Television, the Peabody Archives, and Cultural Memory*. His research focuses on popular politics, or the ways in which politics are presented and engaged through popular culture.

Mary Celeste Kearney is Director of Gender Studies and Associate Professor of Film, Television, and Theatre at the University of Notre Dame. She is author of *Girls Make Media* and *Gender and Rock*, editor of *The Gender and Media Reader* and *Mediated Girlhoods: New Explorations of Girls' Media Culture*, and co-editor with Morgan Blue of *Mediated Girlhoods'* second volume and with Michael Kackman of *The Craft of Criticism: Critical Media Studies in Practice*.

Amanda Keeler is Assistant Professor of Digital Media in the Diederich College of Communication at Marquette University, where she teaches courses in media aesthetics, radio and television history, and scriptwriting. She has published several essays on television and radio, including work on *Gilmore Girls*, the ABC *Afterschool Specials*, *The Walking Dead*, and *Dimension X*. She is the Network Co-Director for the Library of Congress Radio Preservation Task Force.

Amanda Ann Klein is Associate Professor of Film Studies in the English Department at East Carolina University. She is the author of *American Film Cycles: Reframing Genres, Screening Social Problems, and Defining Subcultures* and co-editor with R. Barton Palmer of *Multiplicities: Cycles, Sequels, Remakes and Reboots in Film and Television*. She is currently working on a new book: *Millennials Killed the Video Star*, a study of MTV's reality programming.

Suzanne Leonard is Professor of English and Director of the Graduate Program in Gender/Cultural Studies at Simmons University in Boston. She is the author of *Wife, Inc.: The Business of Marriage in the Twenty-First Century*, *Fatal Attraction*, and co-editor with Yvonne Tasker of *Fifty Hollywood Directors*.

Elana Levine is Professor of Media, Cinema, and Digital Studies in the Department of English at the University of Wisconsin–Milwaukee. She is the author of *Her Stories: Daytime Soap Opera and US Television History*, co-author with Michael Z. Newman of *Legitimating Television: Media Convergence and Cultural Status*, author of *Wallowing in Sex: The New Sexual Culture of 1970s American Television*, editor of *Cupcakes, Pinterest, and Ladyporn: Feminized Popular Culture in the Early 21st Century*, and co-editor with Lisa Parks of *Undead TV: Essays on Buffy the Vampire Slayer*.

Amanda D. Lotz is Professor of Media Studies at the Digital Media Research Centre at Queensland University of Technology. She is the author, co-author, or editor of nine books that explore television and media industries including *We Now Disrupt This Broadcast: How Cable Transformed Television and the Internet Revolutionized It All*, *The Television Will Be Revolutionized*, and *Television Studies*, with Jonathan Gray.

Myles McNutt is Assistant Professor of Communication and Theatre Arts at Old Dominion University in Norfolk, Virginia, where he researches and teaches on the media industries. In addition to published work in *Television and New Media*, *Media Industries Journal*, and *The Velvet Light Trap*, he also serves as a contributor for *The A.V. Club*—where he reviewed *Gilmore Girls: A Day in the Life* in 2016—and writes media analysis on his personal blog, *Cultural Learnings*.

Ritesh Mehta works in film and TV development in Los Angeles. He has extensive experience programming for film festivals such as AFI Fest, Outfest, and the Indian Film Festival of Los Angeles, and as a Reader for the Sundance, Fox and Disney television writers labs focusing on diversity and inclusion. His research has been published in *Poetics*, *Cognition*, and *Transformative Works and Cultures*; he has co-authored the digital book *Flows of Reading: Engaging with Texts*; and he is a regular contributor to *MovieMaker Magazine*. Mehta received his PhD in communication from the Annenberg School at the University of Southern California.

Taylor Cole Miller is Academic Director of the Peabody Media Center and Assistant Professor of Entertainment and Media Studies at the University of Georgia. In addition to published pieces in several anthologies, journals, and popular press, he is currently working on two book projects: one on the history and queer potential of television syndication and the other a co-authored book on *The Golden Girls* and fandom.

David Miranda Hardy is Assistant Professor of Film and Media Culture at Middlebury College, where he teaches film production and screenwriting. He is the sound designer for more than sixty feature films, most recently Pablo Larrain's Oscar-nominated *Jackie*, and has written and directed numerous short films. He is Head of Content Development for Filmo Estudios/Filmosonido, his production company in Chile. His first television series, *Bala Loca*, is distributed internationally on Netflix and was nominated for a Peabody and a Platino Award.

Jason Mittell is Professor of Film and Media Culture and American Studies at Middlebury College. He is the author of *Genre and Television: From Cop Shows to Cartoons in American Culture*, *Television and American Culture*, *Complex Television: The Poetics of Contemporary Television Storytelling*, *The Videographic Essay: Criticism in Sound and Image* (with Christian Keathley and Catherine Grant), and *Narrative Theory and Adaptation*. He is project manager for *[in]Transition: Journal of Videographic Film and Moving Image Studies*, co-director of the NEH-supported workshop series Scholarship in Sound and Image, and author of numerous video essays.

Michael Z. Newman is Professor of Media, Cinema, and Digital Studies at the University of Wisconsin–Milwaukee in the Department of English. He is the author of *Indie: An American Film Culture*, *Video Revolutions: On the History of a Medium*, *Atari Age: The Emergence of Video Games in America*, and the co-author with Elana Levine of *Legitimating Television: Media Convergence and Cultural Status*.

Sean O'Sullivan is Associate Professor of English at The Ohio State University. He is the author of the book *Mike Leigh* and has written numerous articles on television storytelling, including such topics as *Deadwood* and Charles Dickens; Krzysztof Kieslowski's *The Decalogue*; Dennis Potter's *The Singing Detective*; third seasons; fifth episodes; and the six central elements of serial narrative.

Laurie Ouellette is Professor of Cultural Studies and Comparative Literature and Communication Studies at the University of Minnesota. She has written about television and other topics for *Cultural Studies, Television and New Media, Cinema Journal, European Journal of Cultural Studies,* and other journals. Her most recent books include *Lifestyle TV* and the co-edited volume with Jonathan Gray *Keywords for Media Studies.*

Kevin Sandler is Associate Professor in the Film and Media Studies Program at Arizona State University, where he specializes in the contemporary U.S. media business, with a particular focus on censorship and animation. He is the author of *The Naked Truth: Why Hollywood Doesn't Make X-Rated Movies,* the co-editor with Gaylyn Studlar of *Titanic: Anatomy of a Blockbuster,* and editor of *Reading the Rabbit: Explorations in Warner Bros. Animation.* His upcoming book is *Scooby-Doo.*

Philip Scepanski is Assistant Professor of Film and Television at Marist College whose research focuses on television history, cultural theory, comedy, and trauma. His book project, "Tragedy Plus Time: National Trauma and Television Comedy," explores the ways in which American television comedy responds to events like the assassination of John F. Kennedy, the 1992 Los Angeles riots, and 9/11. His work has also appeared in numerous journals and collections, most recently *Television and New Media* and *The Comedy Studies Reader.*

Suzanne Scott is Assistant Professor in the Department of Radio-Television-Film at the University of Texas at Austin. She is the author of *Fake Geek Girls: Fandom, Gender, and the Convergence Culture Industry* and co-editor with Melissa A. Click of *The Routledge Companion to Media Fandom.*

Luke Stadel is an entertainment industry researcher and consultant based in Los Angeles. He received his PhD in screen cultures from Northwestern University and has published in numerous peer-reviewed journals on the history of film, television, and media technologies.

Louisa Stein is Associate Professor of Film and Media Culture at Middlebury College. Louisa is author of *Millennial Fandom: Television Audiences in the Transmedia Age* and co-editor with Allison McCracken, Alexander Cho, and Indira Neill Hoch, of *A Tumblr Book,* with Kristina Busse of *Sherlock and Transmedia Fandom,* and with Sharon Marie Ross of *Teen Television: Programming and Fandom.* Her work explores audience engagement in transmedia culture, with emphasis on questions of cultural and digital contexts, gender, and generation.

Ethan Thompson is Professor of Media Arts at Texas A&M University–Corpus Christi. He is the author of *Parody and Taste in Postwar American Television Culture* and co-editor with Jeffrey P. Jones and Lucas Hatlen of *Television History, The Peabody Archive, and Cultural Memory* and with Jonathan Gray and Jeffrey P. Jones of *Satire TV: Politics and Comedy in the Post-Network Era.* He directed the documentary *TV Family* about a forgotten forerunner to reality television.

Ethan Tussey is Associate Professor of Moving Image Studies in the School of Film, Media and Theatre at Georgia State University. His work explores the relationship between the entertainment industry and the digitally empowered public. His book *The Procrastination Economy: The Big Business of Downtime* details the economic and social value of mobile device use in the contexts of the workplace, the commute, the waiting room, and the living room.

Kristen J. Warner is Associate Professor in the Department of Journalism and Creative Media at the University of Alabama. She is the author of *The Cultural Politics of Colorblind TV Casting.* Warner's research interests are centered on the media industries, race, representation, and creative labor. Warner's work can be found in academic journals, a host of anthologies, websites such as the *Los Angeles Review of Books* and *Film Quarterly,* and of course Twitter.

Index

Lightning Source UK Ltd.
Milton Keynes UK
UKHW031004200320
360651UK00021B/1088